Rugby League
A Critical History
1980-2013

LEAGUE PUBLICATIONS LTD

League Publications Ltd
Wellington House
Briggate
Brighouse HD6 1DN
England

First published in Great Britain in 2013
by League Publications Ltd

www.totalrl.com

A CIP catalogue record for this book is available
from the British Library

ISBN: 978-1-901347-27-2

Designed and Typeset by League Publications Limited
Printed by Charlesworth Press, Wakefield

I would like to dedicate this book to Terry Newton, a brilliant player and a great bloke who took his own life on 26 September 2010. To this day, I have never seen a more committed rugby player. Terry was the cover star of the first issue of Thirteen, a magazine I published in 2005, and it was always a pleasure to deal with him. I watched him play most weeks for Leeds Rhinos between 1996 and 1999 when I studied in the city and saw him progress from a fringe second-rower into one of the best hookers in the game. Terry also played for Wigan, Bradford, Wakefield and Great Britain. After his death, a campaign called State of Mind was set up, and with the help of NHS experts, volunteers, players, the RFL and the Rugby League Cares charity, they raise awareness of mental fitness in order to help maintain mental well-being among rugby league players. They can be found at www.stateofmindrugby.com.

ACKNOWLEDGEMENTS

I am indebted to League Publications Ltd, the publishers of League Express and Rugby League World, for the proof-reading, design and publishing of this book and to a variety of rugby league writers, past and present, including Gareth Hodgson, Lewis Mills, Jason Emery, Bryce Eulenstein, David Gilbank and Mike Rylance for their assistance along the way. I am honoured that one of rugby's all-time greats, and good friend of mine, Garry Schofield, has been kind enough to write the foreword - it should be acknowledged, though, that he had no knowledge of where he featured in the top 100 players list until the book went to print. Thanks also to other friends and family for their support, and most of all, thank you to Katy for the anti-procrastination kit, without which this book may never have seen the light of day!

ABOUT THE AUTHOR

In 2005 Richard de la Rivière published and edited a monthly magazine, Thirteen, before editing Rugby League World between 2007 and 2010. He has worked as a journalist for League Express newspaper from 2006 in which his historical column, On This Day, is published. He has interviewed most of the game's great players and coaches from the period that this book examines and has reported on rugby league from such exotic locations as Sydney, Brisbane, Florida, Johannesburg, Belgrade, Perpignan, London, Edinburgh and Workington. Not bad for a supposed M62-corridor sport!

His rugby league highlights include interviewing Russell Crowe, presenting the Golden Boot to Billy Slater, running Lancaster RLFC and playing for the Great Britian All Stars in a charity match at Knowsley Road. On the flip side, he had to share a room for sixteen days with Garry Schofield in South Africa on the BARLA Young Lions tour in 2010, an experience from which he is still recovering.

He can be found on Twitter - @richdelariviere. This is his first book.

CONTENTS LIST

Introduction

Foreword by Garry Schofield OBE

1	The International Game 1980 - 1995	15
2	The International Game 1996 - 2012	43
3	The British Domestic Game 1980 - 1995	71
4	The Super League War	91
5	Super League	103
6	Summer Rugby - Has it worked?	129
7	Australian Rugby League	149
8	The History of State of Origin	169
9	The History of the Golden Boot Award	183
10	The Top 100 Players from 1980 to 2012	199
11	Statistical Wrap-Up	227

Bibliography

INTRODUCTION

The question I was most asked in putting this book together was 'why 1980?'

Well, for a start, 1980 was a landmark year for the sport with the two Hull clubs meeting at Wembley, Wigan relegated and professional rugby league back in the capital for the first time since 1937. The birth of State of Origin, meanwhile, signalled a new era for rugby league in Australia.

Two years later, the 1982 Australian tourists swept all before them leaving the British game on the bones of its backside. No study of the modern game can be complete without an in-depth analysis of that tour and the ripples it caused. How Great Britain re-built while Australia continued to strengthen led to one of the most exciting periods in the game's history when Malcolm Reilly's Lions, with Ellery Hanley, Garry Schofield and Martin Offiah at their peaks, came so close to knocking them off their perch.

I didn't want to produce the sort of historical account which recorded only the tries, the games and the personalities. There's still an abundance of that, of course, including a list of my top 100 players from the last 33 years, but examining the multitude of policy changes that the game's governing bodies have implemented in the modern era is just as important. Going back to 1980 gave me the chance to compare the two sixteen-year periods before and after Super League came along in the UK. Has Super League improved things? Has it even failed the game in some areas? And why have Great Britain and England been so uncompetitive for so long?

Some fans deserted the game for good in the mid-1990s, but those who stuck with it, and those who were attracted to it via Super League's innovative marketing campaigns in its early years, were lucky enough to witness a vibrant competition which rarely fell short in the entertainment stakes. But in the background has always lurked Australia, and their presence continues to shape the British game, for better or worse. Like a dog chasing its tail, the RFL has tried so many things to close the gap. Some have worked, but many haven't and things which remain absolutely stable in other sports are regularly tinkered with in rugby league. Nothing is sacred - the rules of the game, the formats of the competitions, not even the name of the international team.

Rugby league has almost been as interesting off the field in the last 33 years as it has been gloriously entertaining on it and I hope this book has encapsulated as much of that as possible.

Foreword by Garry Schofield OBE

I remember 1980 very well.

I was playing in the Hunslet Parkside under-15 and 16 teams, very much with an eye on a professional career one day. I also remember the Hull Kingston Rovers v Hull FC Wembley Cup Final, hoping one day that I would be able to experience an occasion like that.

The next four years flew by and before I knew it I had become the youngest-ever British Lion, chosen to tour Australia, New Zealand and Papua New Guinea at the age of 18. I thoroughly enjoyed my playing career and despite a few lows which went hand-in-hand with many highs, I wouldn't change a thing. I wish my time as a coach had been different, of course, but looking at the whole picture, rugby league has been wonderfully kind to me and I owe the game a lot.

Some players switch off from the game when they stop playing and never watch it because they regarded it as just a job. Others are different though, and I watch as much Super League, Championship rugby and NRL as I can. I love seeing new players come through and predicting which will go on to enjoy great careers. Like all supporters, I have strong opinions on rugby league's performance, on and off the field.

In expressing a lot of those I have sometimes been derided as negative, but nothing could be further from the truth. The tone of my opinions when I discuss something I'm not happy about is no different to that of supporters whose team is struggling. In the main, I object to the lack of serious debate that goes on in the game. Sky Sports spent years telling us that everything is wonderful and, understandably I suppose, the Rugby Football League puts a positive spin on whatever they can. But it is wrong for the media, of which I consider myself a member, to accept this at face value, especially at a time when the game is struggling on so many levels.

Therefore a book like this which critiques much that has happened in modern times is to be welcomed. Naturally I've really enjoyed reminiscing over the good old days but in particular I think that chapter six makes for great reading, as does the ten reasons for our international team's failure since 1996 in chapter two.

Writing this in April 2013, I believe that progress has been made since the disastrous World Cup of 2008 in terms of our production of world-class rugby league players. I have long called for our young players to go to Australia and it is great to see so many Englishmen not just playing in the NRL, but playing so well. Some problems remain, though, and it is noticeable that while we are producing excellent forwards and outside backs, we look to be nowhere nearer solving the playmaking problem that has blighted the Great Britain and England team in the summer era.

Off the field I don't think good enough progress has been made. Super League appeared to promise so much and when I look back to many of the things that Maurice Lindsay said to promote it in 1995, I despair. Those, like me, who asked questions about the Super League and summer ideas back then were castigated as dinosaurs. With hindsight, I think that even Lindsay might wish that he had taken some more ideas on board and not rushed into things as he did. He is now long gone, but it is us who are left with a Challenge Cup and an international game that have been a pale shadow of their former selves for most of the Super League era.

Unlike other major sports, rugby league has never been sure of its direction but it still manages to produce an endless stream of magnificent entertainment. This book has brought back the most fantastic memories, some of which I was involved in and some of which I was not. I hope you enjoy it as much as I have.

Garry Schofield, April 2013

CHAPTER ONE
INTERNATIONAL RUGBY LEAGUE (1980-1995)

"Look at this. Henderson Gill! ... That's a great try. And he does a bit of a boogie! The Union Jacks flags here have gone absolutely crazy."
- *Australian Channel Nine commentator Darrell Eastlake, 1988*

They came, they saw and they absolutely battered us.

The 1982 Kangaroos changed so much. A wonderful collection of talents combined to produce a level of performance which ushered in an era of Southern Hemisphere domination that has never been closed. They were already better, but this tour put Australia into virtually uncatchable territory. Their performances signalled a welcome end to the thuggery which had blighted the sport in the 1970s, and they helped give rugby league over the next decade as high a profile as it had had for years.

The time period which this chapter examines isn't just about the exploits of Wally Lewis, Mal Meninga and the many other fabulous players who were all too often the scourge of Great Britain. Happily, the rocketing of standards in Australia brought about a wonderful resurgence in the British game in the last ten years of its winter existence. The emergence of a clutch of young players between 1982 and 1984, who would carry British Rugby League for a decade and more, was the silver lining on the dark cloud that was the 1982 Ashes. Further Anglo-Australian series may have been lost in 1984, 1986 and 1988, but Great Britain's response to Australia's scorched-earth brand of rugby league provided a truly fascinating period in the game's international history, and despite the multiple defeats in subsequent years, there were numerous highs for Britain - not least Garry Schofield's 'try of the decade' in Australia in 1984, his quartet of tries at Central Park against the Kiwis in 1985, Joe Lydon's scintillating finish at Old Trafford in 1986 which bamboozled Garry Jack, the game's finest fullback and, of course, that amazing moment when Mike Gregory ran 70 metres to seal an incredible 26-12 win for the 1988 Lions in Sydney. There was plenty more, too, as Malcolm Reilly led a confident Great Britain side into the 1990s - Wembley, Melbourne and twice more under the twin towers, while series wins over New Zealand became routine.

As the new decade began, the shadow of the disastrous 1979 British Lions tour of Australia and New Zealand loomed large. Having lost the 1978 Ashes by two games to one on home soil, a new-look British squad, captained by Doug Laughton, had travelled south confident of returning with the Ashes which they had last held in 1970, but they were whitewashed by Australia and mocked by their media. The tour was the first in history to lose money, recording a deficit of £31,590 and the first-Test attendance - a game in which Australia cantered to an easy 35-0 win - was the lowest such crowd in Australia since 1910. A series win in New Zealand did raise spirits but failed to disguise the fact that the tour had been a shambles, on and off the field.

Test rugby in the 1980s got off to a low-key start, as Britain hosted the tenth New Zealand tourists. It was the first Kiwi tour since 1971, compared to which it was a success, with aggregate Test crowds almost doubling from 13,351 to 26,187. This fascinating series finished tied at one game apiece, with another drawn. The Kiwis, who had lost twice to Australia in June, had brought over a young squad, but the tour would launch the careers of James Leuluai, Dane O'Hara, Mark Graham and Fred Ah Kuoi, to name but a few.

Going into the first Test at Wigan, the Kiwis had beaten Blackpool and Hull, but then lost games against Cumbria, St Helens and Bradford. Great Britain, under Johnny Whiteley's coaching for the first time, and fielding seven debutants, were hot favourites to win, but it was the tourists who caught the eye with a hugely impressive display of strong running, skilful ballplaying and support play, in contrast to the duller style of football exhibited by the home team. "Our club game has become too stereotyped becoming related to one-man rugby," said Whiteley. The Test was still entertaining, although a crowd figure of 7,031 at Wigan's Central Park was symptomatic of the game's current malaise. Fred Ah Kuoi and Tony Coll scored the Kiwi tries, before tries from Barrow's Chris Camilleri and Hull KR's Mike Smith forced a 14-all draw.

The Kiwis went on to win at Hull Kingston Rovers and Leeds, before losing 11-7 at Warrington four days before the second Test at Bradford. Whereas Warrington could beat the Kiwis, Whiteley's men couldn't as they went down 12-8 and gave up any hope of winning the series. Michael O'Donnell and Dane O'Hara posted three-pointers, with Britain failing to cross their opponent's line. At least the crowd was better, with 10,946 passing through the Odsal turnstiles.

Des Drummond, a 22-year-old Jamaican, who would go on to become one of the most iconic rugby league players of the modern era, restored some credibility in game three, scoring the only two tries of the match - the second of which while the British management were deciding whether or not to leave him on the field after he had picked up an ankle injury. He also saved a certain try with a great tackle on Bruce Dickison and was named man of the match. With a tied series, Great Britain had escaped with a little credibility - something they would spend much of the subsequent years yearning for.

It is hard to think of a team in any sport that has received a wake-up call like Great Britain's Rugby League side did courtesy of the 1982 Kangaroos. Since their 1978 tour, which had ended with defeat in France, Australian standards had surged ahead. Two years earlier, State of Origin had erupted onto the scene; a concept which would go on to become the centrepiece in the Australian calendar for three decades and more. By 1982, young superstars like Wally Lewis and Mal Meninga had helped Queensland to three successive Origin successes. Domestically, Steve Gearin's phenomenal Grand Final try for Canterbury against Eastern Suburbs in 1980 helped the game's profile surge to a new level, and the emergence of brilliant young footballers like Peter Sterling and Brett Kenny saw the unfashionable Parramatta club scale the heights that had always eluded them.

In contrast, British progress since the disastrous 1979 Lions tour of Australia was barely tangible, if indeed it existed at all. Brute strength may have been there, but fitness and skill levels had been left floundering compared to what was happening down under, as the dual-code-international-turned-commentator, Ray French, recalled. "I went over to watch the Australians [train], and I was amazed at the difference in the training ... the difference in the training to what I'd done, the difference in the training to what I'd watched in England at that time. I came away from Leeds thinking 'How can we beat these?' I [then] went off to Hull where Great Britain were training in the afternoon. Johnny Whiteley [was the] coach. He said: 'Before you start, do a couple of laps'. And I've never seen an outfit as unfit in all my life. In fact, Johnny, who must have been in his 50s, ran with them and must have beat the lot! He looked at me and I thought 'Good God, we have no chance.'

French's fears were further exacerbated by the fact that Great Britain's last outing had produced a 19-2 defeat against France in December 1981, but for once, some of the Australian media were pessimistic about their own side's chances. The squad announcement on 26 September was met with fierce criticism. There was, said the critics, a swaying towards older players over youth. Rod Reddy, for instance, had only played nine games for St George in the 1982 Winfield Cup, spending time in the reserve grade. By comparison, players like Paul Vautin, John Ferguson, Kevin Hastings, Colin Scott, Phil Blake and Phil Sigsworth were overlooked to the bemusement of some. As well as that, Mick Cronin, Terry Lamb, Graham Eadie, Alan Thompson and Terry Fahey were unavailable to tour. Ian Walsh, the 1960's St George and Australia hooker, in Sydney's Daily Telegraph, was scathing: "To me it is a mediocre Kangaroo team. The demands of youth have been ignored and the team looks like a squad from an old men's home."

Walsh was proved hopelessly wrong as the tourists became the first Australians to visit the Northern Hemisphere and return home undefeated, playing a brand of rugby league that left everybody totally bewildered with shock and admiration. If the Rugby Football League didn't know it at the time, they couldn't hide from the inescapable truth that Great Britain were miles away from that standard. Coached by Frank Stanton, Australia conceded double figures in only one game, and that was in their first outing - against Hull Kingston Rovers, who scored exactly ten. They saw off most of their opponents with consummate ease, playing high-octane, intense football that the British players could only dream of. Second-rower Wayne Pearce ran the ball like a man 20 years ahead of his time. Brett Kenny was so good that he even kept the vice-captain, the great Wally Lewis, almost a footballing god in his native Queensland, out of the side. A three-quarter called Mal Meninga introduced himself to British crowds in the style they would become all too painfully accustomed to, while the third-choice scrum-half when the squad jetted out, Peter Sterling, a genius to his bootstraps, ran the show with ball in hand.

"In truth I was probably number three behind Steve Mortimer and Mark Murray," he said. "I'd have been quite happy to play on the wing in a midweek game in the snow at Blackpool! I was just happy to be there. As it turned out I got a chance in the first game and never looked back. All the lads got on and we had a lot of success. I remember the game at the Boulevard where we won narrowly in 1982 and that was a big factor in me going back to Hull the following year. [Eric] Grothe got the winning try and the crowd was great."

Australia only found themselves in trouble a couple of times throughout the tour. At Craven Park, in their first tour match, they trailed Hull KR 8-5 at half-time and were a man down but Sterling rescued them with a superb man-of-the-match performance as they laid on five second-half tries, including a magnificent 70-metre try from Meninga. In game two, Wigan performed credibly, going down 13-9, the Kangaroos' narrowest win on tour, although it was the tourists' midweek side - nicknamed the Emus - that Wigan faced. Lowly Bradford, in big financial strife at the time, also did well, only behind 7-6 late on to a much stronger Australian side, before going down 13-6. In fact, their coach, Peter Fox, clearly frustrated by gloating Australians, was so buoyed by Northern's display that he shouted to the Australian media in the Odsal tunnel: "Is that good enough for you? What about your so-called super fitness?"

Champions-elect Hull led 7-0 at half-time against the Kangaroos' strongest side before two tries by Grothe and one from fellow winger, Kerry Boustead, turned the tide, but while a handful of club sides made life difficult for the Australians, Great Britain could do no such thing. They were absolutely annihilated in the first Test 40-4 - and don't forget that a try was worth only three points in 1982. They had been just 10-4 in arrears at the break but were

torn to pieces courtesy of a blistering six-try Kangaroo performance in the second 40. For years, that Australian performance remained the benchmark for rugby league perfection. Few had seen anything like it before.

The margin was a bit lower in game two, only 27-6, although Les Boyd was sent off for kicking Fulham's John Dalgreen - an action later described by Sterling as "a pretty selfish and stupid thing to do." That game, played at Central Park, saw probably the highlight of the series, when substitute Lewis, on for Grothe, sent Meninga in for a try at the corner with a sensational 25-yard spiralling pass which took four defenders out of play. "I remember walking past Frank Stanton on the bench and letting him know what I thought of him," said Lewis.

Britain competed reasonably well in a fiery game three at Headingley, even with Lee Crooks sent off. With a younger team which included Andy Gregory at scrum-half, they were competitive for much of the contest with the score 14-8 after 70 minutes, before tries by Kerry Boustead, Steve Rogers, Wayne Pearce and Brett Kenny cruelly saw the score finish up 32-8. Worryingly for Great Britain, France provided a sterner challenge for the green and golds, losing their Test matches with Australia by the much smaller margins of 15-4 and 23-9.

The Kangaroos' tour statistics were incredible. They had played 22 matches, winning all of them, scoring 714 points and conceding just 100. Australia scored a record 99 points in the three Ashes Tests, compared to just 18 from Great Britain which included only one try - scored by Steve Evans, the Hull winger. In the twelve other matches played on British soil, the Kangaroos conceded just six further tries (scored by Steve Hartley, Gary Prohm, Henderson Gill,

Brynmor Williams, Hussein M'Barki and David Topliss), and they shipped in a mere two in seven games in France, where they scored 69 themselves.

As for the British, Ray French concluded: "It was this arrogance that you can't tell us anything. 'We invented the game. You can't play rugby. It's just a blip'. It wasn't." Harry Edgar, the editor of Open Rugby magazine, was determined to look to the future. "Let us hope some short-term lessons have been learned. The basic one [is] that some players' Test careers should be over. New blood has to be tried. The British side that lined up for the Boothferry Park Test contained so many players that had been tried and failed before against the Australians, it was incredible. The first 40 minutes of the third Test gave some people hope for the future, in that Great Britain held the Aussies to just a 6-4 margin, played with bags more spirit and fire, and some players revealed an ability to open up gaps in the defence by moving the ball wide and supporting. The most positive aspects had to be the performances by Andrew Gregory, Peter Smith and Mick Crane. Gregory showed he should have been there from the start rather than the two 30-plus scrum halves who went before."

The 1982 Kangaroos had revolutionised the game. Great Britain's subsequent efforts to catch them would result in a magnificent era for the game.

Great Britain had 18 months to start to put things right before they toured the Southern Hemisphere in 1984 - a tour that was the first step in their rebuilding. A year prior to that, New Zealand had demonstrated that the Australians weren't invincible by producing a stunning performance to win the second of their Tests at Lang Park to force a draw in their mini-series and to end Australia's remarkable run of sixteen straight Test wins. But it also showed that Great Britain were a considerable way behind their Southern Hemisphere counterparts, although 1983 also saw the emergence of Ellery Hanley and Garry Schofield - two future Great Britain captains, who would have a significant bearing on Test football for more than a decade - as major forces in the English game. Hanley's incredible try in the 1983 Challenge Cup semi-final, when he raced up the Headingley touchline, beating defender after defender, to score for Bradford Northern against Featherstone Rovers, marked the coming of age of one of the game's bona-fide legends. A few months later, Schofield, once the amateur game's brightest star, burst onto the scene at Hull FC and could not stop scoring tries. Up to the 1992 World Cup Final, both men were at the forefront of Great Britain's attempts to close the gap that Australia had opened up in such spectacular fashion.

Although the 1984 British Lions, which included Hanley, Schofield and a host of other young players, hit upon a definite improvement from their 1982 horror show, they were still whitewashed by both Australia and New Zealand.

"I remember the headline in Rugby League Week after the first Ashes Test," the Lions captain, Brian Noble, recalled. "It said something like, 'Bruising Battle – Test Matches are Back!', because it was on the back of the 1982 Ashes when they'd flogged us all over the place. We competed in 1984 although we didn't come away with a win. [Coach] Frank [Myler] picked a team, the nucleus of which would be around for a long time. There was Joe Lydon, Ellery Hanley, Kevin Beardmore, David Hobbs, Andy Gregory, Tony Myler, Lee Crooks, Andy Goodway, Garry Schofield etc. They all went on to become iconic players and form the nucleus of the Great Britain side for a long time. Those blokes were all in their early 20s."

The 1984 tour is remembered in Australia for Wally Lewis, by now their captain, being jeered by the Sydney crowd in the first Test - he was hated in New South Wales as a result of his State of Origin success for Queensland. "It was the most disappointing day in my representative career," he said. "The fans in Sydney provided a more generous welcome for the British team than they did for their own captain."

Johnny Raper, the great Australian loose forward of the 1960s, had noticed a significant improvement in the Lions in the early tour matches. "They are no longer soft in the belly and will stretch Australia," he said. Great Britain may have lost the three Tests but the scores were much closer than in 1982, and in Schofield, at 18 the youngest-ever Lion, beating Alex Murphy's record set in 1958, they scored two of the best tries of the series. Schofield had his winger Des Drummond to thank for both. For the first, Drummond beat several defenders on a superb run from the touchline to the posts before producing a wonderful offload over the back of his head to the supporting Schofield. At Lang Park, the Hull centre scored what was later described as the try of the decade, finishing off an incredible move involving Drummond again and Andy Goodway. The 80-metre move was executed at full pace, with Schofield and Drummond inter-passing before the winger found Goodway who sent the Hull centre to the corner.

Great Britain may have only scored one try per game, but they provided a constant attacking threat with three or four line breaks in each of the first two games, posing much more of a challenge than they had in 1982. Nearly all of them involved Schofield, linking usually with Drummond or the stand-off, Tony Myler. Sadly, though, the tour statistics did not make for pretty reading. While performances were massively improved and hopes for the future were high, Great Britain were whitewashed in Australia and New Zealand, with a threadbare squad, decimated by injury, having to face the Kiwis. The third Test score of 32-16 was a New Zealand record score against Great Britain at the time.

"What I remember is that the Australians were way, way better than us," Hanley reflected. "Individually and collectively, they were way too good for us."

Now coached by Maurice Bamford, Great Britain gained a more solid foothold on their road to recovery in 1985 against New Zealand. They could only draw the series but were the better team over the three Tests, losing narrowly in game one before pulling off a resounding win in the next Test, with the third drawn.

Before they arrived in the UK, the Kiwis had lost a tight series against the Aussies, but recorded a superb 18-0 win in the last Test. The first two matches had been close with the second won by the Australians on the hooter, and New Zealand had outscored the Australians over the three matches. So when the Kiwis arrived in the UK, they were supremely confident of defeating a British side which had lost 24-16 in France seven months earlier.

Great Britain were beaten 24-22 in the first game at Headingley, despite scoring a truly wonderful, flowing, length-of-the-field try which saw the ball transferred through several pairs of hands. The final pass from Hanley to Joe Lydon was forward, but James Leuluai's late winner should have been disallowed for the same reason. In game two, at Wigan, the hosts needed a matchwinner and Garry Schofield was just the man. With the ever-classy Tony Myler and Harry Pinner pulling the strings, the master poacher scored all four of Great Britain's tries as they emphatically levelled the series.

Shaun Edwards was another young player who emerged in the mid-1980s and he figured in a brutal third Test - a 6-6 draw, which required on-field police intervention at one point. "I think it was the dawn of good times for Great Britain," he said. "We got a drawn series against probably the best team in the world at the time as they'd just beaten the Australians 18-0. It was probably the dirtiest game of rugby I've ever played in. It was very tight and it was down to Lee Crooks to kick a last-minute goal to level the game and the series. The year before New Zealand had beaten Great Britain 3-0 so the improvement was there to be seen."

Pleasingly for the Rugby Football League, interest in the British game was on the up. The impact of the 1982 Australians and the emergence of so many high-quality players were the main reasons, along with a stunning Challenge Cup Final in the early summer of 1985. Crowds for the home series against the Kiwis in 1980 had averaged 8,729 but had nearly doubled to 16,768 in 1985. Playing standards were also heading in the right direction with considerable help from short-term imports like Mal Meninga at St Helens, Brett Kenny at Wigan and Peter Sterling at Hull.

With those performances against New Zealand in mind, Britain welcomed the 1986 Kangaroos, a squad that contained the most stupendous talents. At fullback was Garry Jack who went on to win the Golden Boot, awarded to the world's best player, for his performances that year. The three-quarters boasted Brett Kenny and Gene Miles. In the halves were Peter Sterling and Wally Lewis, both widely regarded as the game's greatest-ever in their respective positions by then. This time Lewis was the captain and there was no doubting his selection. Being benched for the 1982 series was just a blip in an otherwise sensational career. He was the golden boy of Australian rugby league, and the man who had almost single-handedly made the State of Origin concept work with a series of breathtaking displays that had seen perennial underdogs Queensland lift the shield in each of its first five years.

Comparing the Great Britain team to its 1982 version, it had certainly improved. This one was fitter, younger and more skilful with more players in it that the Australians would have regarded as good enough to play in their Winfield Cup competition, whereas in 1982 it was reported that they had only rated Des Drummond. In fact half a dozen Great Britain players from the 1986 series had acquired Australian club experience, but any optimism was cruelly wiped away after a clinical Australian performance at Old Trafford in the first Test in front of 50,583 supporters, a British Test record. The tourists won 38-16 with Michael O'Connor and Gene Miles scoring hat-tricks, although the try of the match went to Joe Lydon in the 54th minute, as Lewis recalled. "Our fullback was Garry Jack, one of the greatest fullbacks I ever saw. He showed Joe the sideline but Joe did an in-and-away and scored an amazing try."

For the fourth time in just over two years, Great Britain had lost a Test but had scored a try that brought the house down. The fullback's try, coming just minutes after Garry Schofield had scored, brought the score back to 16-10, but Henderson Gill botched the kick off and Australia pulled away again with Miles's second. After the game the Great Britain coach, Maurice Bamford, pledged to pick the same side for the second Test a fortnight later, but his gesture of loyalty backfired as Australia powered on and sewed up the Ashes with a devastating performance at Elland Road to win 34-4, with Jack scoring twice. Britain restored some credibility in game three at Wigan after Bamford made the sort of changes he might have done 14 days earlier. Schofield's 46th-minute try, goaled by Lydon, levelled the scores at 12-all, and gave the hosts a genuine chance of winning their first Test against the Kangaroos for eight years, but Australia pulled away to win 24-15, with Lewis scoring a beautiful solo match-clinching try.

Whereas the Kangaroos usually bemoaned refereeing decisions, especially on previous trips to France, even they were happy to admit they enjoyed good fortune at Central Park. Two of their tries, both converted, were more than dubious. They were Miles's second-minute try off a forward pass from fellow Queenslander Greg Dowling, and a penalty try which referee Julien Rascagneres awarded to winger Dale Shearer who was taken out by Lydon after kicking ahead. "There was no way it should have been a penalty try," said Sterling later, with doubts over whether Shearer could have reached the ball before it went dead.

The tour was another magnificent success. The Ashes series crowd aggregate of 101,560 was only bettered by the 1948 tour figure of 114,883. The average gate of their 13 matches in England was 16,313, second only to the figure of 16,732 in 1948, and a third higher than 1982 results. The first Test crowd of 50,583 delivered the biggest gate receipts away from Wembley of £251,061, and the 30,622 crowd who witnessed the opening tour match against Wigan was the biggest crowd for any tour match in Kangaroo history. Both countries pocketed a handsome six-figure profit.

In the tour matches, Oldham came closest, up against the Emus, the name for the tourists' second-stringers, losing just 16-22 with Stuart Raper, son of Johnny, enjoying a fine match at loose forward for the Roughyeds. Wigan pushed them close, losing 18-26, but they were 18 points down after 47 minutes. Otherwise, Australia were dominant, scoring 30 points or more in nine games and scoring 85 tries in both tour matches and Tests.

France offered little resistance either; their 1968 and 1978 heroics now merely a distant memory. Australia breezed through the seven matches, scoring a half-century of points in each of the last three games. They won the Tests 44-2 and 52-0 and Terry Lamb made history by becoming the first-ever tourist to play in every match of the tour.

Many claimed the 1986 Kangaroos were better than their 1982 counterparts. "This is the hottest side I've ever seen," said the ARL president, Ken Arthurson. "The 1982 Roos were a wonderful team but many of them were near the end of careers and took little rests in games." They were still too good for Great Britain, but in Schofield, Lydon, Hanley, Tony Myler and Lee Crooks, Britain had players who didn't look out of place on the same field as them.

Great Britain's third-Test performance gave them something to build on and, when Bamford stepped down, in came a coach who would take the side to the next level. Malcolm Reilly might not have tasted Ashes success as a coach, as he had as a player in 1970, but he produced four series wins over the Kiwis (this includes the 1992 series, when the trophy was awarded to Great Britain on aggregate over the two games), masterminded three never-to-be-forgotten wins over Australia and was less than ten minutes away from winning the

1992 World Cup at Wembley, all in six excellent years. "Malcolm was a truly wonderful coach," said Schofield. "He was a brilliant man-manager."

Reilly was one of the toughest players of his generation, and after helping Castleford to Challenge Cup success in 1969 and 1970 and Great Britain to an Ashes triumph down under in 1970, he moved to Australia to play for Manly. There, he won Grand Finals in 1972 and 1973 and carved out a reputation as one of the most fearsome players in the game. He returned home as player-coach of Castleford who won the Challenge Cup under his guidance in 1986. He appeared to have the coaching ability, the mental toughness and the stature to take Great Britain to the next level.

After a quiet year in 1987 in which Great Britain beat France twice and Papua New Guinea, they geared up for another tour of Australia the following year by beating France 30-12 at Headingley in March. Australia lost their only Test of the year 13-6 to New Zealand, with Hugh McGahan in the sort of form that would see him share that year's Golden Boot, to give Britain hope that they could inflict similar pain on the green and golds.

Preparations for the Lions tour soon descended into chaos with a series of withdrawals - not least those of Des Drummond and Joe Lydon who were excluded after being involved in separate incidents involving spectators. As well as that, Steve Hampson withdrew with a broken arm, Andy Goodway chose to remain at home to open a restaurant and a number of players, including Garry Schofield, Shaun Edwards and Lee Crooks, had to return home after the tour began due to injury, as the Wigan stand-off remembered all too painfully. "It was one of, if not, the biggest disappointments of my career," said Edwards. "Me and Andy Gregory were all set to go to Australia and take on Lewis and Sterling but after five minutes it was all over for me. It was probably the worst time of my career. I ended up in the television studio back home."

The tour was a test of everybody's character, not least Reilly's. Statistically, again, it would go down as one of the worst, as not only were the Ashes lost, but the side lost several tour matches, and some by embarrassing margins such as the 30-0 reversal to Manly, but, given what his side were up against, and given the challenges they faced, the 26-12 third Test triumph deservedly goes down as one of the finest and most unlikely wins in Test football history. According to Reilly: "The first game was fairly close and we were winning at half-time but then Sam Backo scored and Sterling and Lewis picked up their games and they won it 17-6. In the second Test in Brisbane, the tactics were all wrong. I probably went over the top with the motivational side of things and our hearts ruled our heads. We gave away too many penalties. You'd have thought the morale of the side would have been down especially given the injuries but it wasn't. We knew that as a unit we could play better and we knew we could beat them."

With the Ashes gone again after a 34-14 defeat in Brisbane, Reilly struggled to scrape a team together for the dead-rubber Test at Sydney on 9 July. Not only had Edwards been ruled out of the tour with injury, but he was followed by Schofield, Crooks, Paul Medley and Paul Dixon, while Kevin Beardmore, Paul Groves and Richie Eyres were also ruled out on fitness grounds. Paul Hulme was called up as fourth-choice hooker, joining his brother, David, in the side, the duo becoming only the fourth pair of brothers to play for the Lions.

Great Britain got off to a superb start, leading 10-0 after 21 minutes and after thwarting an Australian comeback, finished the match with two of the most Test memorable tries to record an unbelievable 26-12 win. "It was a great result," said Reilly. "We couldn't train with a full team until two days before the games and players had to play with injuries. The Hulme brothers filled in at hooker and stand-off and Phil Ford was outstanding. Then of course there was the Henderson Gill try and that huge grin."

As good as Gill's try was, the moment of the match and perhaps of the whole decade, came as Mike Gregory scored the game's clinching try from 70 metres as he recalled in his 2006 autobiography, Biting Back: "It started when [Andy] Greg drove the ball up from dummy half and evaded four Aussies with his nuggety strength. He ducked under a few swinging arms, drew fullback Garry Jack, and gave me the ball. I was still on our 25-yard line, but I knew I still had the fitness and strength, and I just went for it. Wally Lewis and Wayne Pearce, two of the greatest players ever to wear the green and gold, were chasing me down but I did have the step on them and I knew Martin Offiah was supporting me. I could hear him at the side of me, shouting 'Just give me the ball!' But I could see Lewis giving up as I glanced behind, after trying to pull Martin back, and then out of the corner of my right eye I could see that I could hold off Pearce as well. Thinking 'if I'm going to run all this way, I may as well score' I just pinned my ears back and made it to the sticks - a special moment." His namesake, Andy, remembered: "Being named man of the match in Sydney and being part of a winning side against Australia was one of the highlights of my career. You can't get much better than that."

It was a momentous victory - Great Britain's first over Australia in 16 games with the last coming in 1978, but they couldn't build on their good work in Sydney when they crossed the Tasman to play New Zealand, in a game that was effectively a World Cup semi-final. The 1988 World Cup Final was to be contested by the top two sides from a series of 'pool' games from 1985, with one Test from each series counting as a World Cup-rated game. Britain's win against Australia was one such game, but they needed to repeat the trick against the Kiwis in Christchurch just eight days after their Sydney miracle to reach the World Cup Final. They couldn't - New Zealand beat them 12-10

thanks to two Gary Freeman tries. Paul Loughlin and David Hulme scored the Lions tries, but Loughlin could only convert one.

With the Lions tour over, international rugby league had a World Cup Final to look forward to, its first since 1977 when Australia, captained by Arthur Beetson, had beaten Great Britain 13-12 at the Sydney Cricket Ground. The match was played at Auckland's Eden Park, home of the All Blacks, on 9 October, and remains one of the sport's biggest if-onlys. New Zealand, regarded by some as favourites, went into overdrive in promoting the game. Having beaten the Australians in their only match in 1987, and having seen a weakened Great Britain beat Australia by 14 points in their last outing, the Kiwis could smell blood and with Brett Kenny and Mal Meninga missing, hope was heightened. An expectant crowd of 47,363 turned up - all tickets sold weeks in advance - and had New Zealand won, rugby league might have made massive strides in the union-dominated country. Unfortunately, the game was an anti-climax, with the visitors 21-0 up at half-time, and even though the Australian captain, Wally Lewis, broke an arm in the first half, his side were still far too good. Lewis sustained the injury in the fifth minute, but bravely played on until four minutes from half-time. With one great playmaker injured, the green and golds turned to another - Allan Langer - to get them home, and he did, scoring twice in a man-of-the-match performance.

In 1989 Great Britain won their only series of the decade against Southern Hemisphere opposition when they came from a match down, and a man down in the second Test, to beat New Zealand. The Kiwis picked up the first game 24-16 at Old Trafford, before Great Britain produced a fantastic display to cope with the second-minute dismissal of fullback Steve Hampson and win the second Test 26-6 at Elland Road. And they wrapped up the series with a 10-6 win at Central Park. Reilly was up and running. Hampson, was also sent off for Wigan the next day against Castleford. "The first one," he said, "I still blame Malcolm Reilly for, because he was winding us up all week about Gary Freeman and how we should go for him if we could. So in the first minute he grabbed hold of me. I wouldn't have kicked him so I turned and headbutted him. I'd never even been spoken to by a referee in my career and I got sent off, although I still think I should only have been sin binned. Anyway, I played for Wigan against Castleford the next day and I tripped Steve Larder and got sent off again. Two red cards in one weekend!"

"We didn't get the selection right in the first game," Reilly admitted. "Unless you coach someone week-in week-out in club football, you don't always know how mentally tough they are and how prepared they are to give that extra yard. I selected one or two who weren't up to it and we got touched up. In the second Test at Elland Road, we kicked down after the first set and Gary Freeman had the ball in his own in-goal area. Steve Hampson headbutted him and got sent off. Gary was a bit of a nark and he was probably verballing Steve, but you don't lose it like that. So the guys really had to stand up. I remember having a fall out with Andy Goodway in a pre-match team meeting because he'd turned up late. I didn't think his attitude was as it should have been, but he moved into the centres from the back-row after the sending-off and had a great game, winning man of the match and scoring two tries. Then we went on to win the series."

A decade that had started so badly at least drew to a close with silverware.

Great Britain entered the 1990s boasting a far superior set of players than ten years earlier, with the standards set by Wigan and Widnes beginning to bear fruit. Wigan were a few years into a stunning decade-long dynasty of the game, which saw them collect most of the trophies on offer. The Chemics didn't stay at the top for long, but in the late 'eighties had assembled a magnificent side which won back-to-back championships. The other sides' pursuit of these north-west giants resulted in domestic standards improving.

Great Britain had responded well to what had happened in 1982, and in 1990 they produced their best year in modern times, although their first two games resulted in embarrassing defeats to France and Papua New Guinea. In July they toured New Zealand and turned things around in the most spectacular fashion, winning twice and only losing the third because Martin Offiah dropped the ball over the line showboating.

"We were very strong then," said Malcolm Reilly, "and the confidence was flowing. We'd taken a young side over there in 1990. I took Bobbie Goulding out of the Wigan second string and he forged a good relationship with Garry Schofield, who had been moved to six from centre. We weren't expected to do well but we won the first two Tests and should have won the third. We won the first 11-10 then Martin Offiah had a big say in the second with an important try."

Schofield had missed the 1989 Kiwi series with injury and, having moved from the centres to stand-off, he made a poor start to what would turn out to be his Golden Boot year but the positional switch would prove to be a key factor in Great Britain overtaking the Kiwis and coming so close to Australia over the next few years. "I had an awful game [against Papua New Guinea], absolutely shocking," he said. "Nothing went right for me at all and when we were back at the hotel, Malcolm Reilly came up to me and actually asked me if I knew how to play stand-off! 'You're the main man on the field and you take charge!' he told me, but he hadn't said that before the game. I got murdered for it and everyone was asking why, when I was usually a centre, I was playing at stand-off for my country. He said he wanted me to take control, it was like music to my ears. That's not coaching, it's man-management and Malcolm was brilliant at it."

Under Mike Gregory's captaincy, vice-captain Schofield went on to dominate the Kiwi Test series - one which Great Britain managed to win with a number of their best players in Ellery Hanley, Andy Platt, Andy Gregory and Shaun Edwards missing. Great Britain edged the first two Tests by the narrowest of margins with Schofield seemingly at the heart of all the scoring plays. He was the best player on the field in all three games in the series.

"I loved it when Phil Clarke told me that Shaun Edwards's dad put pictures of me wearing the Great Britain number-six jersey up in his kitchen to motivate him into getting the jersey back!" he said. "But from then on, Shaun wasn't getting that jersey back, it was mine."

Buoyed by such a magnificent series win in New Zealand, thoughts turned immediately to the autumn Kangaroo tour. Unlike 1986 when victory wasn't expected, in 1990 it was a very realistic possibility. Great Britain had gone 20 years without winning the Ashes, but with Ellery Hanley and Andy Gregory to be added to the team who triumphed against the odds in New Zealand, it was at the front of everybody's minds.

The Australian build-up centred around one man, and that was a player who didn't even get on the plane. The exclusion of Wally Lewis, the 1986 captain, on grounds of fitness, still rankles bitterly with him today. He recovered from a broken arm to play for Brisbane Broncos in a play-off match against Canberra Raiders, but he was deemed unfit to tour. It is still regarded as one of the biggest controversies in Australian Rugby League history, up there with the Len Smith exclusion in 1948, another captain who missed out on touring Europe.

Peter Sterling, Brett Kenny, Garry Jack and Gene Miles were also missing, heightening British hopes further. In Lewis's absence, Mal Meninga took the captaincy, and Australia were barely threatened in their first five games, beating St Helens, Wakefield, Wigan, Cumbria and Leeds, although the latter only lost 22-10 with Laurie Daley and Garry Schofield involved in a thoroughly absorbing battle at stand-off just six days before the first Test.

The hiring of Wembley for that first Test paid handsome dividends, but it was nevertheless a brave move by the Rugby Football League as, on the two occasions it had hosted internationals before, in 1963 and 1973, only meagre crowds of 13,946 and 9,874 had attended. This time 54,569 clicked through the turnstiles to prove that British rugby league was becoming ever more popular with the public - perhaps as a result of the Lions' 1988 win in Sydney, or the high profile that Wigan's growing domination was bringing. Either way, tickets to big rugby league events were finally fast becoming much sought after.

The British record Test crowd had the time of their lives as their team stunned the Kangaroos at Wembley with a quite brilliant 19-12 win. Wingers Paul Eastwood (two) and Martin Offiah scored the tries with Schofield adding a drop goal. Britain had finally beaten Australia on home soil again, for the first time since Odsal 1978. "Wembley was a massive experience – it was incredible," said Schofield. "We played the game at our pace, kicking early in the tackle count, walking to scrums and frustrating the Aussies. The first 40 minutes were great and we knew we had the Aussies where we wanted them. Malcolm told us to stick to what we were doing and we'd win. Not one player went from the gameplan and we delivered a really professional performance in the second half. Ellery had a great game and we typified what British Rugby League was all about by producing some great off-the-cuff play."

Australia, stunned, went back to the drawing board. Comfortable wins over Warrington, Castleford and Halifax led them into the second Test, where Allan Langer was dropped and Ricky Stuart shifted from the unfamiliar number-six jersey to his favoured seven. Cliff Lyons, the imperious Manly five-eighth, partnered him. In other changes, Daley and Dale Shearer came into the three-quarters, Benny Elias and Glenn Lazarus were picked in the front row and Brad Mackay, the St George loose forward, came into the starting line-up.

With so much on the line, what followed was 80 minutes of gripping theatre, still sometimes referred to as the greatest international ever played. Schofield and Paul Dixon engineered a great try for the hosts before Lyons scored a dazzling try early in the second half. Going into the last ten minutes, with Australia ahead by four, Paul Loughlin's left arm stretched out to snaffle a half-way line pass thrown by Stuart. He brought the ball in and raced away to score, roared on by a disbelieving Old Trafford crowd who sensed the Ashes were coming home. Crucially, though, Eastwood missed the kick, and even a draw was snatched away when Lee Jackson bought Stuart's dummy, and Meninga finished off a length-of-the-field move after taking out Carl Gibson. Great Britain were left to rue the 45th-minute departure of Martin Offiah, who would have had the speed to get back in cover.

Coach Reilly believed that if Loughlin's try had been converted, the Ashes would have been won. "Had we gone 12-10 up, we'd have grown an extra leg and won the Ashes in my opinion. Ellery that day had an outstanding game. He put himself all over the park and there wasn't the energy to stop the break after Stuart threw that outrageous dummy and made that break for Meninga to score, but even so, Meninga stopped Carl Gibson getting across to cover Stuart. With today's technology, they'd have pulled that back for the infringement. That loss deflated us after we'd got so close."

Martin Offiah was in the dressing room, injured, when the winning try was scored. "I watched the try unfold on a monitor in the Old Trafford dressing room as I was lying on the treatment table. Carl Gibson went on to the wing and there was no way they'd have gone the length of the field if I'd been out there."

Meninga's try didn't just win the second Test, it swung the momentum back in the favour of the tourists, who went on to win the decider 14-0. Andy Gregory was inconsolable. "That was the nearest we got to winning the Ashes," he said. "I sat in the changing rooms afterwards and just thought that sport was supposed to be enjoyable. It was the lowest I'd ever been in my life."

The Kangaroo tour had made a huge impression on the British public. The aggregate crowd of 133,684 for the three Tests easily beat the previous best of 114,883 set in 1948. Likewise the average crowd over the whole tour set a new record with the 19,995 figure beating 1948's 16,732, but if one thing showed how high profile league was back then, it was that Mal Meninga won the BBC's Overseas Sports Personality of the Year award, a wonderful achievement especially given there had been a football World Cup that year.

"The perfect half of football."

That was Garry Schofield's summary of Great Britain's first-half performance in Melbourne in 1992, as his men levelled the Ashes series with a performance that deserves to be ranked up there with Rorke's Drift, Brisbane '58 and Sydney four years earlier as one of Great Britain's best on Australian soil. Schofield regards the game as his greatest Rugby League experience, and many of his teammates would surely say the same. At half-time, having lost the first Test, and up against some of the greatest players ever to lace on a boot like Mal Meninga, Laurie Daley, Allan Langer, Paul Sironen, Bradley Clyde, Steve Walters and Glenn Lazarus, Great Britain led 22-0, following tries from Phil

Clarke, Paul Newlove and Schofield, who had taken over the tour captaincy from Ellery Hanley. Australia managed a couple of second-half tries but they never looked like winning and when Graham Steadman and Martin Offiah both scored fantastic tries, Great Britain sewed up a convincing 33-10 win.

The 1992 tour, though, started inauspiciously as Castleford fullback Graham Steadman remembered. "We didn't hit our straps for a number of reasons. The first few weeks were difficult and we lost the first Test, although we were unlucky not to score a couple of tries in the first half. But we stuck together and Malcolm didn't panic. He instilled the belief into the squad. Malcolm brought the squad together and it was like a club environment. There were no cliques and we all knew we'd have to contribute."

A week before the second Test, Great Britain's first-choice side lost to Parramatta with Brett Kenny rolling back the years with a vintage display, this time at loose forward. There was also the seemingly never-ending circus involving Britain's most famous player - their captain, Ellery Hanley. After an inconsistent season, Hanley's selection was something of a surprise as he was suffering from hamstring and foot injuries. He was unable to take part in the early matches, including the first Test - a disappointing 6-22 loss in Sydney. The will-he-be-fit-won't-he-be-fit soap opera was further exacerbated by the fact that, as he did for most of his playing career, he refused to talk to the press. In the end, his tour started and ended on the same night, as he re-injured his hamstring just seven minutes into the tour match at Newcastle, three days before the Melbourne Test. Schofield, ever willing with the media by contrast, officially took over the tour captaincy. As journalist Dave Hadfield, covering the tour for Open Rugby, wrote: "The presence of an injured passenger - and one carrying the personal baggage of attitudes that he does - in such a key position was a distraction from the business in hand that the party did not need. The difference in atmosphere when the whole charade was finally exposed for what it was, was startling."

Up stepped the Wigan loose forward, Phil Clarke. "The loss of Ellery, a pivotal player in our plans to beat the Aussies, would have hurt any team," said Steadman. "To lose Ellery was a big loss. He wasn't only one of the world's best players, he was our captain, but Phil Clarke replaced him at loose forward and had a commendable tour."

Joining Clarke in that pack were five of his Wigan teammates - Kelvin Skerrett, Martin Dermott, Andy Platt, Denis Betts and the wildcard Billy McGinty, a surprise selection, but a player who had a storming game, with his small stature and mobility providing a sharp contrast to the Australian giants who endured a forgettable night.

"Heading to the ground - I'll never forget it," said Steadman. "Big Roy

Dickinson, the former Leeds player, had a full marching band of about 200 people going towards the stadium. It was comical I suppose, but it also really inspired us. We couldn't believe the amount of people who had gone out there to support us. When we got into the stadium, the feeling was incredible. Everything felt right. We also heard that the Aussies had a post-match celebration planned, assuming they'd wrap up the Ashes that night, so that gave us even more motivation. On the evening we played the elements, and were smarter than the Aussies were. Paul Eastwood had a great kicking game and slotted a couple of early penalties. Everyone hit top form and I don't remember having to make a tackle in the first 20 minutes. It oozes confidence because you know if a ball is dropped, your front-line defence will front up. Paul Newlove had a great game and he scored one of those first-half tries, with Phil and Garry Schofield getting the others. The Aussies are always dangerous and came back with a couple of tries in the second half, so we knew we had to keep playing the territory game and not stop playing. I got a pass, and had Mal Meninga in front of me. I normally stepped off my left foot, but for some reason stepped off my right and was too quick for Andrew Ettingshausen and squeezed into the corner. We knew we had it then."

The match was Shaun Edwards' first start against Australia. "It was a wet-weather night which suited us fine," he said. "They were trying to throw the ball around and we really pressured them. The rest is history. 33-10 in Australia is fantastic."

Great Britain had just a week to prepare for the third Test. After their second string had disposed of Gold Coast 28-10, the two nations squared up to each other at Brisbane's Lang Park. Australia welcomed back Brad Fittler, who had missed the match in Melbourne to mourn the death of his Penrith teammate Ben Alexander. Great Britain were unchanged. Australia led 8-4 at the break, with all points kicked by Mal Meninga and Paul Eastwood. The crucial moments arrived in the 47th and 55th minutes as Laurie Daley and Meninga scored the tries that kept the Ashes in Australia. Martin Offiah pulled one back with four minutes left.

"We trained very well again and only lost 16-10," said Edwards. "It was a very hot night and the locals were surprised saying that it was normally cool at that time of the year, so it suited them as they were used to the heat. It was wet the next night though! I felt that if it had rained like that when we'd played then we'd have won. But on the night we gave away too many penalties and they got a mountain of field position. Their forwards were bigger and we got a battering. I made 37 tackles that night, which is a lot for a halfback, but that had a knock on effect when I had the ball."

Great Britain had to wait a little over three-and-a-half months to have another crack at their formidable opponents and this time it was at Wembley in the 1992 World Cup Final. The Rugby Football League did a wonderful job of marketing the game, in particular with a memorable poster campaign in the London Underground featuring Martin Offiah and the caption "Will the Aussies catch Offiah at Wembley?" It worked, and they were rewarded with a world-record Test crowd of 73,361 and with Ellery Hanley back in the team they were confident of victory. A late Steve Renouf try, however, robbed them of that, and Australia won the big prize with a 10-6 scoreline.

Crucially Garry Schofield, who retained the captaincy despite Hanley's re-introduction to the side, was shifted back out to the centres in order to accommodate Deryck Fox partnering Shaun Edwards in the halves. Fox kicked well, but as Edwards admits, Malcolm Reilly's decision to field all three didn't work. "I think the problem was the team selection," he said. "Malcolm picked Deryck Fox and myself with Schoey in the centres which I felt was a mistake. He should have just picked two out of the three of us. But having said that we were winning the game with eight minutes left. Unfortunately for us, Gary Connolly, a great defensive centre, had to go off injured, which was rare for him. Steve Renouf got on the outside of his replacement John Devereux and we lost the World Cup."

Great Britain had to wait two years for another crack at the Aussies but responded superbly to their Wembley disappointment by whitewashing New Zealand in an autumn Test series held on home soil a year later. While the 1993 Kiwis are often regarded as a poor side, they had performed well against Australia shortly before their departure, drawing one game and losing two narrowly. They also picked up a number of good wins on tour, not least beating Wigan 25-18 at Central Park, but in the Tests they were outclassed by a superb British side.

"That was the best Great Britain team I played in," said Shaun Edwards. "We beat a strong New Zealand team and to win a series 3-0 against any Southern Hemisphere team is no mean feat. Malcolm had us trained to perfection and Schoey did a good job as captain. The understanding between the team was fantastic and I remember John Devereux's incredible try at Wigan which was one of the best Test tries."

The first game was played at Wembley, a brave step for a Kiwi Test. The 36,131-strong crowd saw the home side win 17-0 with debutant winger Jason Robinson scoring two tries. Devereux added the other. At Wigan in the second Test, Great Britain produced an excellent display of free-flowing football to prevail 29-12 with Devereux scoring twice. There were five different tryscorers in the third Test at Headingley, as Great Britain won 29-10, including the 18-year-old debutant forward Andrew Farrell, who had played for the Great Britain Academy, Great Britain under-21s and the full Test side within the space of just three weeks.

A 3-0 series win over the Kiwis was a great achievement but Reilly's team was starting to break up. The series was to be his last as coach and Schofield's last as captain and Ellery Hanley, Joe Lydon, Andy Platt and Andy Gregory had also played their last Great Britain games by then. "We had a good squad back then and they gelled," said Reilly of his reign. "We put the belief into them and the 1988 win in Sydney provided a lot of confidence. I'm very proud to be associated with that period and I was sad to resign, but I got the chance to coach in Australia. If I hadn't taken it might not have happened again and I've got some great memories of that too. It justified itself but I regret not being able to beat Australia in a series."

Reilly resigned shortly before the 1994 Ashes series in order to take up a coaching position with Newcastle Knights in Australia, and his replacement was a man who had never been a head coach. Ellery Hanley was still in great form as a player, and also held a coaching role at Leeds under Doug Laughton. He was a shock choice, although he wasn't tempted to pick himself to play. "Never," he said. "It didn't cross my mind at all. I thought that there were players who would fill the roles much better than I did and would give more to the team. My workload was enormous. I was working with the players, trying to get them to peak and to play consistently. I was managing the team and to then play would have been wrong. It wouldn't have worked."

British confidence was high, largely on the back of Wigan's superb win over Brisbane Broncos in Brisbane to win the World Club Challenge in the June, and, as everyone old enough remembers, Great Britain had their new captain, Shaun Edwards, sent off in the first half of the first Test yet recovered to win 8-4 thanks to a sublime try by their fullback, Jonathan Davies.

"Going into the game I was thinking of the recent Wigan v Australia game," said Edwards. "We'd played really badly, dropped lots of ball but still could have beaten them. We lost 20-30. So I really, really thought we would beat Australia on that day. We went into the game with a lot of confidence and were on top early on. Jonathan Davies missed a pretty easy penalty shot early on but then I got sent off. They got an overlap and I over-chased trying to cover. Bradley Clyde stepped inside and he was going to score. I aimed for his chest but mistimed it and hit him under his chin. I couldn't watch the game. I was sat outside Wembley smoking a cigarette and I don't even smoke! I'd got a cigarette off someone and I was a bag of nerves but I was absolutely delighted the lads won."

For Davies, it was an obvious career highlight. His try was one of the best of the modern era as he took Denis Betts's pass on the halfway line, broke through the defence, slipped through the gears and beat Brett Mullins, the Australian fullback, for pace and scored in the corner. "Being selected for Great Britain was the highlight of my career and to beat the Australians with only 12 men was a fantastic achievement," he said. "Great Britain had played Canberra Raiders in the World Sevens at the Sydney Football Stadium and I scored a try by beating Brett Mullins for pace on the outside and scoring in the corner. The try I scored at Wembley was virtually the same. Before the tournament, Mullins had boasted about his pace as well!"

Again, Great Britain couldn't make their first-Test win count as the series went on. Australia won with ease at Old Trafford 38-8 and, although the decider at Elland Road was a much closer game at 23-4, it never looked like being Great Britain's day. "I wasn't with the team that much but I sensed on the bus on the way to the ground that there wasn't the same intensity amongst the guys and we paid the price by getting humiliated in the end," said Edwards of the second Test, for which he was banned. He came back into the side the for third Test: "At Elland Road we were incredibly unlucky. We got on top early on but suffered injuries and were down to our last 13 players. We were winning 4-0 and just before half time they scored one of the most fortuitous tries you'll ever see, with the ball bouncing off Paul Newlove's head. We were right in the game until about eight minutes to go but I have to say that we came off the pitch having given absolutely everything. We had no subs left either."

It was Edwards's last Test, and also Garry Schofield's, who came off the bench in the second and third games to equal Mick Sullivan's record of 46 Test caps. It also spelt the end of Hanley's involvement in Anglo-Australian Tests, as he followed Reilly down under to take up a playing contract with Balmain Tigers at the height of the Super League war. "When I look back to that Ashes series," Hanley said, "Australia were the better side and, in terms of their competition, they were better prepared. Even at 1-0 down in a series, they had the knowledge, the discipline and the mental toughness to overcome the handicap. Their playing environment gives them that."

The Centenary World Cup, played in October 1995, remains the highlight of international rugby league's modern era. Apart from an England victory, it ticked every box and sent the British game into its new era in the highest of spirits.

Crowds were higher than expected and the decision to use Wembley twice was thoroughly vindicated. England packed out Central Park for their game with Fiji and the crowd of 26,263 was even higher than when they played Australia in the same town fourteen years later. Wales played in front of full houses at Cardiff and Swansea before taking 10,000 to Manchester for their semi-final against England.

On the field, some of the games deserve to be remembered as some of the finest international matches ever played, not least Tonga's incredible performance against New Zealand in the group stages at Warrington which culminated in late, heartbreaking defeat; Wales's stunning night against Samoa at Vetch Field in front of one of the most passionate and boisterous crowds in rugby league history and also New Zealand's stunning comeback in the semi-final at Huddersfield which had Australia on the ropes before the holders nicked the game in extra-time.

The action got underway at Wembley on 7 October as England beat Australia 20-16. The game was preceded by a memorable opening ceremony performed by Diana Ross, the American singer who had carried out the same duties at the 1994 soccer World Cup in America. At least she wasn't required to kick a goal this time. Andy Farrell scored England's first try, powering over from a scrum close to the Kangaroos' line and taking Steve Menzies, who had scored the only other first-half try, and Geoff Toovey over with him. After the interval, Chris Joynt scored a fortuitous try from his own grubber before Mark Coyne levelled the scores at 10-all. The game's defining moment came when John Hopoate lost the ball in a two-man tackle on his own twenty-metre line, allowing Jason Robinson to pick up and give England the lead. Paul Newlove then intercepted Jim Dymock's pass to give England an unassailable 20-10 lead before Menzies scored his second in the dying stages.

England's win - and subsequent group topping - gave them the easier semi-final, assuming other matches went to form - which they did, and it gave the competition a tremendous shot in the arm with the game played on a Saturday afternoon in front of a live Grandstand audience which meant that England's meeting with Fiji, the following Wednesday, became a far hotter ticket that anybody could have anticipated.

Australia, as a result of the Super League war, weren't at their strongest. Only Australian Rugby League (ARL) players, as opposed to Super League-aligned, were chosen, meaning that supreme talents like Laurie Daley, Bradley Clyde, Allan Langer, Ricky Stuart, Wendall Sailor, Glenn Lazarus and Steve Walters were left at home. But Australia regularly boast that they could field three or four international-standard sides, and here was their chance to prove it. Brad Fittler was regarded by some as the world's best player having performed superbly in a recent Test series against New Zealand, Menzies was enjoying a blistering 1995, breaking the mould for a wide-running, tryscoring forward, while a young scrum-half called Andrew Johns would go on to be named man of the tournament. Predictably, they swept aside Fiji and South Africa with ease, but so too did England.

Elsewhere in group one, Fiji's performance in beating South Africa at Cougar Park in Keighley on the opening weekend, was spellbinding. Coached by Graham Murray, and without their best player James Pickering, they demolished their opponents with a magnificent display of attacking football, with Waisale Sovatabua, a future Cup-winner with Sheffield, scoring twice.

In group two, Tonga stole the hearts of Warrington by coming within a whisker of providing the shock of not just the tournament, but of World Cup history too. Buoyed by a superb performance by hooker Duane Mann, a former Kiwi, they led 24-12 with just minutes left, but the Kiwis scored twice with Matthew Ridge converting both before his late field goal kickstarted their campaign. He revealed in his autobiography that there were problems within the camp with squad members who weren't selected to play, in particular their former captain, Gary Freeman. "I look over and see Gary sitting on the sideline smiling. It makes me want to scream. From then on I'm playing to win because I know Gary Freeman's going to be happy if we lose." The Tongans moved onto Hull where, 48 hours later, they had to face up to a fresh Papua New Guinea side which included Queensland's State of Origin winning captain Adrian Lam and a raw, unknown stand-off called Stanley Gene. Given their fatigue, a 28-28 draw was probably a moral victory for Tonga, who went on to secure second spot in the group when the Kiwis beat the Kumuls 22-6 with Lam, who ended up in the team of the tournament, outstanding for the beaten side.

Group three was all about Wales, who had to see of France and Western

Samoa in order to qualify for the semi-finals. The Welsh international team had been revived for the 1975 World Cup and they played regularly until 1984. There was then a seven-year hiatus before international matches resumed for the Welsh, leading nicely into this World Cup, for which their preparation was excellent as they won the 1995 European Championship against England and France and enjoyed a pre-World Cup tour of America.

France exited the competition in disappointing fashion, losing 28-10 to the hosts and 56-10 to the Samoans with Wigan's fearsome three-quarter Va'aiga Tuigamala scoring twice. Having won by nearly twice the margin against the French than the Welsh, Western Samoa went into the deciding group match at Swansea against Wales as favourites, but things don't always go to script and 15,385 fans crammed into Vetch Field to see Jonathan Davies's men. With other ex-union internationals in their side like Allan Bateman, John Devereux, Adrian Hadley, David Young, Paul Moriarty, Rowland Phillips as well as the recently transferred Scott Quinnell, interest in the Valleys was high, but the Samoans had also assembled a superb side with John Schuster, Sam Panapa, Willie Poching, Vila Matautia, Apollo Perelini, Mark Elia and Joe Vagana joining Tuigamala.

Amid a sensational atmosphere, Wales were too good for their opponents with teenage fullback Iestyn Harris outshining his illustrious elders, producing a blinding display that went a long way to him being named in the end-of-tournament World Cup XIII. He scored the game's opening try before Anthony Sullivan and Kevin Ellis added further scores. "I think we have really captured the imagination of the Welsh public," said Davies.

From there, they travelled to Manchester to face England in the semi-final followed by a reported 10,000 supporters. The key man for the English was the St Helens scrum-half Bobbie Goulding who had replaced the injured Shaun Edwards in the starting line-up. Opposing Goulding was Workington's Kevin Ellis who had masterminded England's downfall six eight months earlier in the European Championships, scoring twice in an 18-16 win, which led to them picking up the trophy, although Goulding confidently predicted that he would get the better of the former union player when it really mattered. Sure enough, Goulding's clever kicking game proved the difference, with two high kicks to Martin Offiah leading to tries, although whether they should have been awarded is another matter. Paul Newlove, Denis Betts and Phil Clarke scored England's other tries, with substitute Rowland Phillips scoring a late dummy-half try for the vanquished Dragons, who ended up on the wrong end of a 25-10 scoreline. Phillips, in magnificent club form at Workington, and who had been fantastic in that European Championship win, was left on the bench for far too long and his introductory impact was immediate as he scored Wales's only four-pointer.

A day later Australia and New Zealand played out one of rugby league's all-time great internationals, although prior to kick-off and, indeed, with twenty minutes to play, nobody could have predicted such a thriller. Australia had beaten the Kiwis by three games to nil in a June Test series, without looking in danger of losing any of them. In the World Cup, even though Australia had lost their opening match, it was the Kiwis who had disappointed the most, poor as they were against Tonga without being much better against Papua New Guinea. The first hour of the semi-final went as expected with a Menzies-inspired Australia leading 20-6. But Richie Barnett scored, and then Tony Iro did likewise to make things interesting. Trailing by four with three minutes left, Kevin Iro scored in the corner to bring the house down. Ridge's touchline conversion would, unthinkably, send Bob Fulton's Kangaroos packing. Ridge was the metronomic Manly goalkicker whose prolific points tally had led the Sea Eagles to the Minor Premiership and to the Grand Final, but he fluffed it badly and his kick barely got off the floor.

A minute later, though, he lined up a drop goal from over 40 metres on his weaker left foot which he described in his book. "As my boot connects I think 'Aw you beaut. It's there.' Fittler hits me half a second later. And we're both lying on the ground, but we're watching the flight of the ball as if it's in slow motion. The wind's gusting but I've compensated for that. The ball's sailing along, just a foot outside the left-hand upright and I'm thinking 'Aw look at that. It's just gonna swing in beautifully and go straight down the middle.' And I'm waiting for that wind to push it right. And I'm waiting. And I'm... It starts to bend. It's bending. It's bend... It's bloody missed! I've hit it that flippin' well that the wind's hardly had any effect on the ball. Fittler turns and says, 'Aw bad luck mate.' And he means it."

With ball in air, Fulton must have feared the reception which awaited him in Sydney, but his side survived and in an anti-climactic period of extra-time, Terry Hill, who had earlier been sin-binned, and Fittler scored tries to win the game for Australia. "I live with that drop goal for months," Ridge continued. "I wake up in the night thinking 'How could I miss it? I kicked it so perfectly. I also live with my pathetic sideline conversion attempt."

The final, on 28 October, provided England with a chance to win significant international silverware for the first time since the 1972 World Cup, won so memorably by Clive Sullivan's men in France, as Australia's near-collapse against the Kiwis demonstrated weaknesses that England could expose. Those looking for omens could point to the fact that Australia had lost in four of their five previous visits to Wembley (1973, 1990, 1994 and 1995), prevailing only in the 1992 World Cup Final thanks to Steve Renouf's late try.

In a selection surprise ahead of the final, Phil Larder gambled by picking

Gary Connolly in the centres. Connolly, unquestionably a world-class player, hadn't featured in the tournament due to a bout of pneumonia. Underweight and lacking in match fitness, he was still one of England's better players in the final and it allowed Larder to field a truly world-class three-quarter line of Robinson, Connolly, Newlove and Offiah.

Unfortunately, there was no-one other than Goulding capable of providing them with the tools they required to finish the job. In a stunningly bad decision, Great Britain's joint-record cap Garry Schofield had been omitted from the squad, not even included in a 40-man train-on group announced a few months before the competition. It backfired badly as, with Goulding below his best, England had no other ballplayers in the key positions, with Castleford's Tony Smith occupying the stand-off jersey. Smith was an accomplished support player, but he was found wanting in creating play for his star-studded three-quarters as England lost 16-8 courtesy of Rod Wishart and Tim Brasher tries. Six days after the final, Schofield showed England what they had missed by starring in Leeds's 23-11 win over Wigan in a classic at Headingley.

England's defeat cut badly, and nearly two months later on the BBC's Sports Personality of the Year programme, Martin Offiah was still upset about a decision to deny him a try when he was adjudged to have a foot in touch. The tournament, though, was an undisputed success, and it gave Super League a welcome boost ahead of its inception in 1996. The British game had taken great strides during the mid-'eighties to the mid-'nineties period. Would the £87 million invested by Rupert Murdoch help the British game capitalise on that progress and help them finally overhaul the Australians?

CHAPTER TWO
INTERNATIONAL RUGBY LEAGUE (1996-2012)

"It was embarrassing. I was sinking with every try.
We just have to learn from it. We have to be hungrier."
- *Great Britain captain, Andy Farrell, 2002.*

Played 51. Won 14. Drawn 2. Lost 35. For 851. Against 1308.

Great Britain and England's combined record in matches against Australia and New Zealand in rugby league's summer era is hardly impressive. Between them, they have won one series - against New Zealand in 2007 - and have lost a further fourteen. England have been horribly off the pace in both of the World Cups played in this period, losing 49-6 to New Zealand in the 2000 semi-final and 52-4 to Australia in 2008. For many reasons, which this chapter will explore, the summer rugby gods have failed to smile on the national team.

There have been some high points, with most of them coming between 2001 and 2006 when either David Waite or Brian Noble was coach, although both men still oversaw some atrocious defeats. Injuries and bad luck have played their part, but even so, the Southern Hemisphere players have improved at a faster rate and by 2010 and 2011 the gap had grown further still. Neither Great Britain nor England have been anywhere near good enough since the inception of Super League. Sure, there were great wins over Australia in 1997, 2001, 2004 and 2006, but they've been hugely outweighed by the bad. From the first half at Elland Road in 1997, to the second-half capitulation at Bolton in 1998, to the stunning late collapse in Brisbane a year later, to the woeful World Cup semi-final in 2000, to the nightmare Tri-Nations Final in 2004, that has happened far too often, and that's without knowing where to begin with the 2008 World Cup. Great players have come and gone, while imperious talents like Tommy Martyn and Lee Briers have surprisingly been deemed surplus to requirements, yet a series success against the bottle-green-and-wattle-gold shirts seems as far away as ever.

If November is associated with failure, then December is the month where everyone tries to figure out what on earth went wrong. Every possible reason has been aired many times over, some more valid than others; and the Rugby Football League, in between restructuring Super League, the Championships, the Challenge Cup and anything else they can find that needs tinkering with, have to come up with the right solutions. Whether they have done that or not can only be judged by England performances from 2013 onwards, but it can't be denied that the governing body throughout the Super League years has harmed the international game - unintentionally, of course - with a series of catastrophic decisions that have not paid dividends.

Prior to 1996, internationals were televised on BBC 1 on Saturday afternoons in front of huge audiences but since then most have been on Sky Sports early on Saturday evenings. Accordingly, international television audiences - which had hit nine million on the BBC for the deciding Test against the Kiwis in 1985 - the game's profile and Test crowds have declined alarmingly - home attendances against the Kangaroos dropped by 11,062 per game in the Super League years compared to the 1980-1995 period. With 19 such games played between 1996 and 2011, that is 210,178 potential paying customers lost to the game. Throughout the summer era, international players have complained that they play too many domestic games compared to NRL players and that, in recent years, an increase to fourteen teams has diluted Super League standards.

As well as that, in 1996, ten players were sent home from Great Britain's tour of New Zealand in order to save money - a public-relations disaster which portrayed the game in a poor light. Keith Senior later admitted he wanted to be one of the players who were sent home, such was the low morale. The 2000 World Cup was badly planned, badly executed, badly supported and lost a fortune. Then the RFL scrapped the popular Ashes while tour matches between the tourists and the leading club sides, which extended media interest in the tour and helped to build up the next Test, are long gone.

The Ashes, and the best-of-three series with New Zealand, were replaced with a Tri-Nations which worked well in 2004, 2005 and 2006, but then it was expanded it to a Four Nations, which meant introducing a team who were well off the pace. Predictably, the countries who have entered it so far as the fourth side - France, Papua New Guinea and Wales - have dragged down overall competition standards as their approach to games has largely been to avoid a thrashing. This tournament 'expansion' has also seen the matches between each side reduced from two to one, and has effectively nullified the importance of most of the group games. The tournament basically boils down to the winner of the solitary England-New Zealand fixture playing Australia in the final. At least with the Tri-Nations between 2004 and 2006, Great Britain played the Kiwis twice, so it took 160 minutes over three weekends for the better side to emerge, rather than just 80 minutes, while their games against Australia also became more of a factor. In none of the 2004, 2005 and 2006 competitions did Australia win all four group games, yet they've never lost a group game in the Four Nations. The longer pathway provided them with far more of a challenge.

In 2006, came the worst decision of them all. The Rugby Football League's decision to scrap the Great Britain concept, in favour of England, might have looked like a common-sense move on the face of it by someone who didn't scratch beneath the surface, but it has caused problems that the RFL clearly didn't foresee.

The structure of Test football between 1995 and 2006 worked well. Great Britain were in action in every year apart from World Cup years when there was no lack of incentive for the best British players to play for Wales, Ireland or Scotland if they qualified. This strengthened the competition, giving it more competitive teams. As a result, one of the few plus points of the disappointing 2000 World Cup was the performance of the Ireland team, which was boosted by the inclusions of Chris Joynt, Terry O'Connor, Barrie McDermott, Tommy Martyn, Steve Prescott and many others. With strong British-based players on board, they were then able to attract Luke Ricketson and Kevin Campion from the NRL - both of them wonderful coups - while British-based Australians like Michael Withers and David Barnhill joined up too. Ireland boasted a very strong side and were only deprived the services of Gary Connolly, James Lowes, Mick Cassidy and Shaun Edwards on fitness grounds. The crucial aspect under the old structure was that any of those British players could then play for Great Britain in 2001 against the touring Kangaroos.

In contrast to the aftermath of Great Britain being scrapped, if a top Super League player who qualifies for both England and Ireland decides to play for Ireland, he has to forego the opportunity of playing regularly against Australia and New Zealand. Asked if he would have played for Ireland if the current rules applied, Joynt fired back, "Of course not!" Keiron Cunningham, who played for Wales, answered likewise, while Iestyn Harris, the coach of Wales, upon being told in 2009 that Garreth Carvell had understandably decided to switch to England from Wales, told Rugby League World magazine that the futures of the Celtic nations were being compromised.

He was proved right. By 2011 and 2012, Scotland and Ireland were fielding sides with barely a regular Super League player in them and the Scots were hindered badly by the Danny Brough saga in 2009. Just a couple of months after captaining Scotland in the World Cup, Brough told Rugby League World that he had no option but to switch to England if he wanted to realise his international ambitions. He explained that when he decided to play for Scotland as a York City Knights player in 2004, he did it knowing that if he became a top player, he could still play in Ashes or Tri-Nations series as a Great Britain player, but that was taken away from him and other Celtic-nation internationals when Great Britain was scrapped. So along with Carvell and Chris Bridge, Ben Harrison, Dave Halley, Mike McIlorum, Michael Platt and others he switched his allegiances to England. An even bigger hammerblow to the RFL's credibility came when young Rhys Evans, Warrington's Welsh starlet, turned his back on Wales for England, citing the same reasons as Brough despite being a couple of years away from being a Warrington regular.

Lee Gilmour is another top player who represented Scotland early in his career. He said: "I find it a bit strange that they've scrapped Great Britain and have really weakened Scotland, Wales and Ireland in the process. We have [had] a Super League team in Wales and we've had Magic Weekends in Scotland and Wales to promote the game there yet they do this and all the players have withdrawn from the smaller nations as a result. It makes you wonder what they're trying to do, in weakening Scotland, Wales and Ireland so much."

It isn't just the Celtic nations who have suffered. Rugby league has lost a wonderful brand and established icon in Great Britain. In 2004, 39,120 people turned up to watch Great Britain in the Tri-Nations Final, yet in 2009 more than 8,000 was knocked off that figure when England played the same opponents at the same stadium. The players would largely be the same, but England is a weaker rugby league brand and, therefore, a tougher sell. On the field even England, in comparison to Great Britain, are weaker, despite the numerous Celtic players wanting to join them. A future Jonathan Davies or Brian Carney is now lost to the top international side, while one player who resisted the temptation to switch to England was Lee Briers. The Warrington player is a classic late-developer, playing his best football towards the end of his career. While England have fielded unconvincing halfback pairings like Kyle Eastmond and Sam Tomkins in 2009 - two excellent individual players but both inexperienced and lacking the ability to marshal a team - and Rangi Chase and Kevin Sinfield in 2011; Briers, with the best kicking game in Super League, and the most sublime creative skills, was nowhere to be seen. He was badly missed in the 2009 and 2011 Four Nations Finals when none of England's supposed playmakers looked like opening up a typically mean Kangaroo defence.

Looking at it from every angle, the scrapping of Great Britain has been a failure. It has a handful of supporters who point to the fact that more 'genuine' locals are playing for their countries, but that has only been achieved by vastly reducing the standards of the team, and, of course, a 'genuine' Welshman in Rhys Evans doesn't want to play for them under this system. One popular theory is that the decision was taken in order to maximise funding from Sport England, but that was emphatically denied by the RFL soon after. It is far more likely that the move was rubber-stamped by a group of people who simply failed to understand the dynamics of international rugby league.

After an enthralling first Super League season, the Great Britain players embarked on a tour that would signal a new era for the international game, but despite England's good performances in the 1995 World Cup, Phil Larder's Lions failed to capitalise when they toured Papua New Guinea, Fiji and New

Zealand. In fairness to them, there was a number of top players unavailable for selection. Ellery Hanley was still playing in Australia for Balmain, but had been long retired from the national side, while Garry Schofield had dropped down a division earlier in the year effectively ruling him out of a chance to gain his much-coveted, record-breaking 47th cap. Other international veterans like Shaun Edwards (knee operation) and the overlooked Martin Offiah were missing, while Phil Clarke had been forced to retire after breaking his neck playing for Sydney Roosters. Unfortunately, players still in their peak like Jason Robinson, Gary Connolly and Lee Jackson were ineligible to play as they had signed Australian Rugby League contracts at the height of the Super League War and Paul Newlove, who had enjoyed a sensational season for the newly crowned champions, St Helens, had a hamstring injury.

In came a plethora of fresh talent who would go on to enjoy wonderful Super League careers. It was abundantly clear during Super League One that Adrian Morley, Paul Sculthorpe, Keiron Cunningham, Kris Radlinski and Iestyn Harris were going to be outstanding players, if they already weren't; and they all got their first taste of Great Britain action on that tour, while Bobbie Goulding, fresh from leading Saints to the title, would be pulling the strings in the number-seven jersey. Super League's first Man of Steel, Andy Farrell, much to the disappointment of his former Wigan teammate Denis Betts, was made captain.

Sadly, the tour is generally bracketed in the 'disastrous' category. Three thousand potential touring supporters dwindled to just 300 when it was announced that there would be no games with Australia, because of the Super League War, and by the time Rugby Football League supremo Maurice Lindsay sent home ten players after the first Test, with no more midweek matches scheduled, in order to skimp on hotel bills, it was impossible to persuade anybody otherwise. On the other hand, Great Britain were unlucky to lose that first Test, only doing so after Adrian Morley's 70th-minute sin-binning and two subsequent tries by union-convert John Timu. They followed that up with an 18-15 defeat in the second, and, in the blink of an eye, the series was gone. The star-studded Kiwis went on to whitewash the deflated Lions with Daryl Powell sent off in the closing stages of game three in what would prove to be his final Test. It was a case of so near yet so far for Great Britain. It could, and should, have been so different.

Andy Goodway was appointed the new Great Britain coach ahead of the visit by the 1997 Australian side. Joining Goodway on the coaching staff was Shaun McRae, the St Helens coach who had previously been on the staff of both Australia and New Zealand, as well as Canberra Raiders. The Rugby Football League and Joe Lydon, whom they had charged with finding a new coach, were adamant that McRae's nationality should not be a problem, but they failed to explain why, in having decided to employ him at all, they didn't hand the top job to a man who had won a Super League and two Challenge Cups in two seasons at Saints, ahead of the vastly inexperienced Goodway, who ended up being sacked by Oldham towards the end of the domestic season.

Again the Super League War hung over the international game and this time it was the Australian Rugby League players who were left out of Australia's squad, whereas it had been they who formed their 1995 World Cup squad. By 1997 the ARL was perhaps the stronger competition and had just produced possibly the greatest Grand Final as Mal Reilly's Newcastle Knights had stunned Manly with a try seven seconds from time. Australia may have been without Brad Fittler, Steve Menzies and Andrew Johns from their World Cup side, but what did that matter when they could call upon Laurie Daley, Gorden Tallis and a young fullback by the name of Darren Lockyer?

Unfortunately Great Britain had a weaker side than England's World Cup team of two years earlier and were badly beaten in Tests one and three, although they provided some magnificent memories at Old Trafford with a 20-12 win to keep the series alive, with Andy Farrell and Jason Robinson scoring. Any hopes, however, of a best-of-three win were pretty much extinguished in the first minute of the decider at Elland Road when Canberra's Ken Nagas scored within a minute.

Adrian Morley and Paul Sculthorpe were now established as top international players, while Jason Robinson scored in each Test. Andy Farrell endured a mixed series - superb in game two when his beautifully taken first-half try set Great Britain on their way, but otherwise he came off second best to Daley, who was thoroughly dominant in Australia's two wins. What was disappointing, however, for British fans, was that Australia's tour consisted of only three games. The months-long tours, as recent as 1994, were gone; now a permanent casualty of the Super League War.

Goodway remained in the post for two more campaigns, and with Super League proving to be thoroughly entertaining for all, there was plenty of optimism ahead of the incoming 1998 New Zealand tour. One reason for that was that British game had tightened up since the ignominy of the horrendous 1997 World Club Championship competition which saw European teams hammered game after game. Between them, they had only won a paltry eight games out of 64.

Wigan and Leeds led the way in 1998 and with the exception of London Broncos and Salford, every team appeared to have improved from 1997, and, as good as they were, the Kiwis weren't the Kangaroos. They were beatable; but for whatever reason, Great Britain couldn't cut the mustard and the series was lost after a shambolic second-half performance in the second Test at Bolton. A genius Iestyn Harris try had given Great Britain an eight-point buffer on the stroke of half-time but they followed it up with as bad a second-half display as anybody could remember. The first Test had been close, but Goodway erred by leaving Leeds's Harris - one of the most obvious winners of the Man of Steel - on the bench. Great Britain played well, but were always behind, although had the referee, Bill Harrigan, awarded a penalty try on the hooter, when Keith Senior was tackled in the air by Robbie Paul in the Kiwis' in-goal area when all he had to do was land on the ground to score, they could have escaped with a draw. The third Test at Watford, though, was tied, when Tony Smith's last-gasp drop goal secured a 23-all draw.

Great Britain had competed well in five of the six halves of football over the series, but, whereas in 1996 and 1997 they had some excuses, this time they didn't. The tourists were clearly the better side and cut the at-times feeble British defence open at will. Changes needed to be made, but they weren't.

With Goodway still coach, and Farrell, whose performances against the Kiwis were poor, still captain, the Great Britain squad that flew down under for the 1999 Tri-Series had a familiar feel to it. On paper, the strongest side looked very good, although St Helens's Super League-winning captain Chris Joynt was a surprise omission for Britain's first match of the competition against Australia in Brisbane. Andy Hay, a prolific tryscorer for a forward, but far less fearsome a forward, was picked on the bench instead.

Needing to win to stay in the competition having been beaten by New Zealand on the opening weekend of the competition, Australia demolished the Lions 42-6. The last twenty minutes were a nightmare for the tourists as they shipped in try after try, including one by Wendall Sailor who took a twenty-metre tap to himself and strolled in from 80 metres. Great Britain had performed well until the hour mark and were very unlucky to be 10-6 down at the break. Denis Betts had been harshly sin-binned by David Pakieto, a referee from the comparatively substandard New Zealand competition, with the score at 0-0. In his absence, Australia scored twice although Harris scored a superb solo try to leave only a four-point gap between the sides. Even though Morley produced one of the performances of his career in being the best forward on the pitch, there were no excuses for Britain's late horror show.

Britain needed a twenty-point win over the Kiwis in Auckland to reach the final, but without playing anywhere near their best, and without their go-to man Stacey Jones who had broken an arm in a friendly with Tonga a week earlier, New Zealand sauntered past the Lions, winning 26-4, to send them packing. But before they flew home, they had to play New Zealand Maoris, rather humiliating, in a curtain-raiser to the final. Australia, for the record, won the final 22-20 in a wonderful match which demonstrated just how far off the mark the Lions were.

So why was such a good British team, on paper at least, so incapable of performing on the big stage? In Kris Radlinski, Jason Robinson, Gary Connolly, Keith Senior, Anthony Sullivan, Iestyn Harris and Sean Long, there was no shortage of matchwinners in the backs, while there was plenty of steel and craft up front with Paul Sculthorpe, Andy Farrell, Keiron Cunningham and the awesome Morley in the forwards. A hint of the problems came during the following year in the lead up to the 2000 World Cup.

With England and Wales joined in the World Cup for the first time by Ireland and Scotland, and with the grandparent qualification rule in full swing in most sports, it seemed that everybody who qualified for a Celtic nation deserted England ahead of the World Cup. Even Paul Newlove and Adrian Morley, who only qualified for England, tried to engineer a switch to Ireland or Wales - Morley admitted in his 2012 autobiography that his brother, Chris, didn't qualify for Wales despite playing for them. "I think it showed that there was a problem with the international game in that people were not enjoying it," said Ireland's Chris Joynt in his autobiography. "Why else would Terry O'Connor, Gary Connolly and I have opted not to play for England? That is no disrespect to Ireland and I believe I made the right choice."

With injuries also a factor, England were down to the bare bones by the time they walked out at Twickenham on the opening day of the World Cup, although coach John Kear did a commendable job in assembling a young side that posed the Kangaroos a few problems at rugby union headquarters. Kear launched the international careers of Kevin Sinfield, Jamie Peacock, Paul Wellens and Stuart Fielden, while Wendell Sailor, the great Kangaroo wing, was so impressed by England's widemen that he joked afterwards that he would be seeking proof that Leon Pryce and Chev Walker were indeed teenagers.

England were never going to win the World Cup. From Great Britain's strongest side, they lost Keiron Cunningham and Iestyn Harris to Wales, although that had been expected given they had donned the red in the previous World Cup, but what was unforeseen was the loss of a batch of players to the Irish, which included Joynt, Terry O'Connor and Barrie McDermott, while Gary Connolly and James Lowes, who would have played for Ireland, only missed out through injury. Ireland's star player was Tommy Martyn, the St Helens stand-off, although, for whatever reason, he never managed to impress Great Britain selectors. His exclusion from Andy Goodway's 1998 squad was particularly head-scratching as he had been in great form for an otherwise poor Saints in the 1998 play-offs. While searching for reasons why the national side rarely broke down the fearsome Southern Hemisphere defences in the early Super League days, the repeated, inexplicable omission of Martyn is up there.

In contrast to Kear's mountain of problems, Australia flew over the most impressive-looking squad side since their 1986 Ashes winners. At fullback was the brilliant Darren Lockyer. Sailor and Mat Rogers occupied the wing spots. Adam MacDougall and Matt Gidley played inside them with captain Brad Fittler and Brett Kimmorley a wonderful halfback pair. For a second World Cup, Andrew Johns could only find a place at hooker, and what a magnificent dummy-half he made. He was bookended by the fearsome Shane Webcke and Robbie Kearns, while Gorden Tallis, Bryan Fletcher and Scott Hill formed a quite incredible back row - Nathan Hindmarsh could only find a spot on the bench. There were no Kangaroo cry-offs in 2000; they all wanted to be at the World Cup and that was bad news for England.

It wasn't great for New Zealand either, who had assembled a superb side since coming so close to toppling the Kangaroos in 1995. They even landed Tonie Carroll, a Queensland State of Origin player, who wasn't wanted by the green and golds. He enjoyed a magnificent tournament and players like Richie Barnett, Stacey Jones, Henry Paul, Stephen Kearney, Lesley Vainikolo, Richard Swain and Ruben Wiki were too good for their English counterparts.

England didn't have enough for the Aussies at Twickenham, going down 22-2, but qualified for the quarter-finals by thrashing Russia and Fiji. This time, New Zealand weren't troubled in winning their group, disposing of Wales, Cook Islands and Lebanon but the excitement came in the other groups. France did themselves justice on the international stage for the first time in a long while by qualifying from a tough group in front of great crowds, behind Papua New Guinea, and ahead of Tonga, for whom Willie Mason starred, and South Africa. And in group four, Ireland and Samoa qualified from the predictably-clichéd Group of Death, ahead of New Zealand Maoris and Scotland.

While the 2000 World Cup is regularly panned for its low crowds and disastrous financial results, it is often overlooked that there were many good games, but not enough of the entertainment came in the big games; the notable exception being a truly stunning Welsh display in the semi-finals against a sleepy Australia. Ireland and England produced an excellent quarter-final, but England were never really in danger of losing, while Wales's win over Papua New Guinea was easier than expected. Australia and New Zealand predictably blitzed Samoa and France.

The biggest disappointment of the World Cup came at Bolton as England were absolutely massacred in front of a Saturday-afternoon BBC audience by New Zealand. A scoreline of 49-6 was truly embarrassing with Kear left to rue his decision to play an unfit Paul Sculthorpe. The Kiwis were magnificent, and the only crumb of comfort for the disbelieving English fans was that their conquerors would at least provide some credible opposition for Australia, who would surely hammer Wales with ease the next day.

Sport, though, isn't always predictable and that is its fundamental beauty. While Australia did indeed win through to the final, anybody lucky enough to be at the World Cup semi-final in 2000 between Wales and Australia, at Huddersfield, will never forget it. With a team made up of semi-pros and rugby union players, along with a smattering of Super League stars, Wales scored three quick-fire first-half tries to lead 18-8 after 23 minutes. When Lee Briers added two long-range drop goals in a matter of minutes, an atmosphere of disbelief hung in the night air. Fittler pulled one back, but Wales led at half-time. They clung on for another fifteen minutes, before Australia took over to win 46-22, but in a game where people were predicting a defeat by as much as 80 points, Wales's performance was awe-inspiring.

Like five years earlier, a tougher-than-expected semi-final simply served to sharpen up the Kangaroos for the final. New Zealand gave their all, but Australia enjoyed enough of a cushion throughout the first 50 minutes before easing into overdrive to hit the 40-point mark. Their dominance was undisputed; they were the greatest rugby league team on the planet.

Great Britain needed to improve significantly as they prepared to welcome the 2001 Kangaroos and they did, under the coaching of an Australian, David Waite - an announcement which was greeted with horror by many of the traditionalists. "Decades of mismanagement by the men who run rugby league finally caught up with the game yesterday when Australian David Waite was named as head coach of England and Great Britain," wrote John Ledger in the Yorkshire Post.

With Waite in the first of a three-year contract as head coach, the side appeared to have the sort of professionalism and experience at the top that it had lacked since the days of Malcolm Reilly, although, of course, Waite would only be judged on results. The 2001 Ashes may have been lost, but at least, unlike in 1996, 1998, 1999 and 2000, a victory over a major Southern Hemisphere rival was produced and the fact that it came against Australia made it all the sweeter.

Waite was able to select many of the players who had played in the World Cup for the Celtic nations so Great Britain were immediately stronger than England had been a year earlier but, crucially, Waite struggled in the key scrum-half and hooker roles, with injuries to Sean Long, Keiron Cunningham and Terry Newton. The fact that those roles were subsequently filled by loose forwards Kevin Sinfield and Mike Forshaw, spoke volumes for Super League's lack of home-produced depth.

The tour was very nearly cancelled. After the terrorist attacks on the United States of America on 11 September 2001, panic and uncertainty gripped the world. The Kangaroos initially chose not to tour, but when Australia's rugby union team, the Wallabies, decided to fulfil their tour to England, public opinion began to turn on the rugby league team, and eventually on their captain, Brad Fittler. "Doubts were being expressed by officials, and I stress that point," he wrote in his autobiography. "ARL chief executive Geoff Carr made the first public statement, saying that the fate of the tour depended on future international developments." On 1 October, a 24-man squad was announced with Fittler the captain. "We were due to leave in a week. It began to get very, very ugly. The ARL [then] announced that the tour was cancelled because half the squad were unwilling to go. There was a huge public backlash. The Daily Telegraph in Sydney broke the story that I'd been sent white feathers anonymously in the post. I didn't know at the time what that meant. I was told that white feathers were sent to men who refused to enlist in the two World Wars to let them know they were considered cowards."

Under immense public pressure. and the late interjecion of former League boss Maurice Lindsay, the ARL reversed their decision and the squad - apart from Brisbane Broncos prop Shane Webcke, who chose to stay at home - departed for England. The four tour matches against Bradford, Wigan, St Helens and Leeds were shelved; just the three Tests with Great Britain would be on the agenda.

Considering their halfback and hooker crises, Great Britain's first-Test performance at Huddersfield was fabulous. Waite played a few tricks when he named his seventeen in midweek, different compared to what actually took to the field, and with Australia under-prepared due to no warm-up games, Great Britain were able to win, thanks to a superb display from Paul Sculthorpe, whose two tries and drop goal helped seal a 20-12 win. British fears of a significant Australian improvement were unfortunately realised in the second Test, played on the national side's bogey ground at Bolton Wanderers. The Kangaroos absolutely annihilated Andy Farrell's men. In danger of losing the Ashes for the first time in 31 years, they led 40-0 midway through the second half, until a couple of late British tries gave them some impetus for the decider at Wigan.

Undeterred by the Reebok Stadium massacre, a capacity 25,011-strong crowd turned up at Wigan praying for a miracle and although they didn't get it, they were treated to a great start and much closer game. The final score of 28-8 flattered the visitors, while some second-half physicality and British pressure, with Keith Senior in rampaging form, maintained interest until the closing stages. This was a blood-and-thunder Test match for the most part, and Great Britain could take some pride from a Test series for the first time since 1994.

Pride, though, was absent without leave on 12 July 2002 as Great Britain, in a one-off Test match in Sydney, were beaten 64-10 by a rampant Australia. Andrew Johns, man of the match, claimed after the game that he didn't need to take a shower, while some journalists wondered whether they had just witnessed the death of Test football. The first and last seventeen minutes were even scoreless, so Australia racked up 64 points in 46 minutes, scoring at will, and slicing through the jet-lagged tourists with embarrassing ease.

The fixture had been announced after Great Britain had beaten Australia at Huddersfield the previous autumn, so confidence was high, and in previewing the match, Rugby League World's July 2002 front cover boasted: "Dear Australia, the Brits are back and this time they mean business!" But former Lions captain Garry Schofield savaged the apparent stupidity of staging the match and predicted a 40-point hammering for the Lions. "It could be quite embarrassing," he said. "We saw last November when the Aussies came to England and lost the first Test at Huddersfield that you need more than a week to acclimatise. But the Great Britain boys will have even less time to prepare themselves for the game, whereas the Aussies are coming off a State of Origin series and bang into their season. I really can't understand why we're playing this one-off fixture at all." Schofield, in turn, was heavily criticised for his comments, but he was proved right, and the margin of defeat was even higher than he had predicted.

Andy Farrell, Great Britain's beleaguered captain, offered no excuses: "It was embarrassing," he said. "I was sinking with every try. We just have to learn from it. We have to be hungrier." Australian TV pundit Phil Gould blamed Australian coaches in Super League working to their own agenda rather than the good of British Rugby League, while Maurice Lindsay, the former RFL supremo, led the many calls for Waite to be replaced by Malcolm Reilly.

The visit of the 2002 Kiwis, however, gave Waite's men the chance to restore some credibility and, after an awful second-half first-Test performance at Blackburn, they took it. Leon Pryce gave Great Britain a 10-6 half-time lead at Ewood Park but the collapse which saw a 30-16 Kiwi win was dreadfully disappointing. That, though, made the turnaround in performance in the second Test all the more pleasing. Great Britain were the better side but had to settle for a 14-all draw, and fluffed some promising late field position to win the game. The key for Britain was the call-up for James Lowes, often third choice to Keiron Cunningham and Terry Newton, and a welcome return to form on the international stage for captain Andy Farrell. It was no coincidence that he was playing in the second row and not loose forward, able to concentrate on making a couple of hundred metres with the ball with handling skills an added bonus, rather than being the principal playmaker, a role with which he often struggled at the highest level.

The photographs show that Great Britain lifted the inaugural Albert Baskiville Shield in 2002, but there was an element of farce lingering in the background. The series was tied after the hosts won 16-10 at Wigan with Gary Connolly saving Britain's bacon with a late tackle on a marauding Stacey Jones, but it was announced prior to the match that Great Britain would win the Shield if they won the match on the questionable basis that they had inaugurated the silverware and New Zealand should win it from them if they wanted to take it home. Cynics may have suggested that it was a clever attempt to attract a much-needed big crowd to the game and given that 22,247 turned up, they may have had a point. "Lift Off" screamed the front of Rugby League World. Great Britain were back.

If ever a Test series had 'what if?' stamped all over it, it was 2003 as Great Britain welcomed the Kangaroos for what would prove to be the last Ashes series played to date. Heavily weakened by the losses of Andrew Johns, Jamie Lyon, Gorden Tallis, Brent Tate, Shaun Timmins, Luke Bailey, Shane Webcke, Bryan Fletcher, Jason Ryles, Mark Gasnier, Trent Barrett, Matthew Gidley, Ben Kennedy, Timana Tahu, Jason Stevens and Scott Hill, levels of hope and expectation shot through the roof and when Adrian Morley flattened Robbie Kearns straight from the kick off in the first Test at Wigan, fans cheered as though a try had been scored. With Kearns down there was a break in play and the referee, Steve Ganson, was able to listen to the fourth official in his earpiece. As replays of the incident were shown on the big screen, it was clear that Morley had caught his opponent slightly high. Ganson was advised accordingly and sent Morley off. The JJB Stadium was stunned; Great Britain were a man down - their best forward at that - after just twelve seconds. It had happened before - in 1989 against the Kiwis when Greg McCallum marched Steve Hampson early on, Great Britain still won; and they beat the Kangaroos five years later with Shaun Edwards off the field for 50 minutes.

What they subsequently produced may have been compared to the 1914 Rorke's Drift Test or the 1958 Battle of Brisbane, two occasions when the Lions beat Australia in the most unlikely of circumstances, but, despite leading 18-16 with less than ten minutes to go, Darren Lockyer, the Australian captain, went over for a cruel, late try to win the game for his side. So near, yet so far - one down with just two to play.

It was a similar story at Hull where Great Britain, boosted by the news that Morley had escaped suspension, built a commanding 20-8 lead after 23 minutes with tries from Terry Newton from a magnificent Morley offload, Kris Radlinski and Gary Connolly - surprisingly his first-ever try in Test football. But Britain took their foot off the gas, allowing Australia to level up at 20-apiece, and parity remained until deep into the game. Brett Kimmorley's drop goal inched them ahead and Craig Fitzgibbon's late penalty handed the Kangaroos the game and the series at 23-20. The Ashes were gone. Incredibly, the same thing happened at Huddersfield in game three. With British rugby league fans already depressed that England's rugby union side, which included former Great Britain wing, Jason Robinson, had won their World Cup that morning, their day got worse. Nursing a 12-6 lead late into the game, Australia scored tries in the 76th and 79th minutes to snatch the game 18-12. Those crazy four minutes were a microcosm of the entire wretched series.

Perhaps Great Britain were wrong to bemoan their luck. They had chances, but couldn't take them. In the critical periods, Australia were the smarter side by a distance and in Lockyer and scrum-half Brett Kimmorley they had a couple of matchwinners who seemed to create a try just when it was needed. Britain, on the other hand, tended to score early and hope to cling on. It didn't work. "2003 was unbelievable," said Paul Sculthorpe. "We were leading every game after 75 minutes and lost them all. It was so frustrating to be so near yet so far but it just goes to show the mentality of the Australians. They play right to the end and we suffered for it."

Progress had been made under David Waite. The Australian was never popular with some fans and ex-players as a result of his nationality, while much of the media failed to warm to him. His selections - notably three of four loose forwards chosen together, or Hull halfback Richard Horne on the wing in the 2003 Ashes series - were often criticised, but for the first time in the Super League era, the national side began to inspire genuine hope. There were some low moments like the one-off Test shellacking in 2002, but Waite handed over a much better side and, more importantly, a much more professional set up than the one he had inherited. His assistant Brian Noble succeeded him and, again, while there were a few forgettable moments, he took things, on the whole, to the next level, culminating in his 2006 team emulating Malcolm Reilly's 1988 and 1992 sides by winning in Australia.

Jamie Peacock had no doubts that Waite had been an excellent coach. "I was new to the Great Britain set-up when he came in but the older players couldn't believe the changes that he made and how he ran the Great Britain side in such a professional way. He might not have been the greatest communicator with the press, but I have the utmost respect for him and what he did for us. He took some flak when we were whitewashed in the 2003 Ashes series but, over the

entire series, we were only behind for about eleven minutes. He took us to a level where we could compete for much longer periods than before."

Noble's first year coincided with the birth of the Tri-Nations, and in 2004, 2005 and 2006, he led Great Britain through the seven-match tournament. Credit for the concept was given to Wayne Bennett, although the Australian coach was critical of its length, with each side playing each other twice, compared to just once in 1999, the only recent year when such an experiment had been tested. The tournaments, though, were well received and criticism of the format was virtually non-existent. In 2004, Great Britain recovered from a last-gasp loss to Australia at Manchester to win their next three games and top the group. This was the most consistent run of results Great Britain had put together in years. Andy Farrell, now at prop, was at his marauding best. Paul Sculthorpe, too, was in magnificent form and joining them in the forwards were Adrian Morley, Terry Newton, Gareth Ellis, Stuart Fielden and Peacock, making a top-notch pack. Behind them were Sean Long and Danny McGuire, who in a couple of weeks looked like being Britain's most effective halfback pairing for many a year, although the recently returned-from-union, Iestyn Harris, was waiting in the wings. Keith Senior, Martin Gleeson and Brian Carney were strike three-quarters who could score and create while, at fullback, the defensively-sound Paul Wellens always seemed to win the first collision when returning the ball. It was an effective team, and hopes were high going into the final against Australia. Some even dared to suggest Noble's men were slight favourites.

Eighty minutes later, those claims looked absolutely absurd as Australia produced one of the best 40 minutes in the history of the game to lead 38-0 at half-time despite a pre-match fitness scare for prop Shane Webcke. Lockyer, blighted by injury problems throughout the tournament, was utterly spellbinding. Noble had caused a stir by dropping McGuire to the bench for Harris, but nobody could have lived with the Australian captain that night. The second half fizzled out, and British Rugby League, having witnessed such credible progress over the last month, had to pick the bones out of a 44-4 humiliation.

In a hint of the problems they would have two years later, Long later blamed Noble: "We did OK in the Tri-Nations, finishing top of the group but got spanked in the final. I started with Iestyn but got taken off after 25 minutes for Mags (Danny McGuire). Then Iestyn came off with ten left for me. It was stupid. You don't mess around with your halves like that." On Harris's selection, Long said: "There were better players in form than him but Nobby was the coach at Bradford. He probably thought, 'I've got to pick him because I paid so much money for him.'"

Although there were some moments of promise in 2005, Great Britain never really recovered from that 2004 defeat. It seemed to instil the belief in some of the players that no matter how good they thought they were, Australia would always be far too good when it mattered. It appeared far more than an on-field defeat - it obliterated any justified optimism over the next couple of years that Great Britain could really compete. They failed to make the final, winning only one of their four matches - although, that win came in fine fashion. Having lost their first two games, Great Britain produced a virtuoso display to hammer New Zealand 38-12 - a scoreline that actually flattered the vanquished tourists, but they couldn't follow it up with another win over Australia in Hull and bowed out of the tournament, leaving everybody in no doubt that Australia would extend their domination by another year by beating the Kiwis.

What happened in the final deserves to be recognised among the great rugby league achievements. The pope was still catholic, but by nightfall on 26 November 2005 Australia were no longer at the top of the game's international tree, a position they had occupied for over quarter of a century. New Zealand not only surprised the sporting world by beating their fearsome opponents, but they nilled them, scoring 24 points of their own. Australia's proud record of not having lost a Test series since 1978, when they were beaten by the French, was over. The Kiwis stripped them bare in the most stunning fashion thanks to tries by Paul Whatuira, Manu Vatuvei (two) and Brent Webb.

In 2006, Great Britain warmed up for the Tri-Nations by beating New

Zealand at Knowsley Road 46-14 although no-one seemed to know whether it was a genuine Test side that Great Britain were facing, as only three NRL players figured compared to the thirteen Southern Hemisphere-based players who turned out for them in the Tri-Nations Final win over the Kangaroos. Their coach, Brian McClennan, said, rather confusingly, before the Test that while Great Britain were playing New Zealand, they weren't facing the Kiwis. With that sort of lack of clarity, it was little surprise that the concept was not repeated. Nevertheless, whatever the make-up of the black-and-white team, they were no mugs and the win was most welcome for Brian Noble. The only downside was it may have led to some undue overconfidence as the next time the two teams met, in the 2006 Tri-Nations, New Zealand won 18-14, with the Lions too far behind for much of the game. The aftermath of the game provided international rugby league with one of its great controversies. Nathan Fien, the Kiwi fullback, it was discovered, had no right to be playing for them, as it was his great-grandmother, not his grandmother, who provided his New Zealand heritage. New Zealand were docked the two points but, crucially, and perhaps unfairly, Great Britain weren't awarded them. Both sides, therefore, took zero points from the game - a handy result for Australia, who were desperate to get their hands back on the trophy.

When it comes to talking points, Great Britain's second game, against Australia at the Sydney Football Stadium, produced an abundance of them. Willie Mason flattened Stuart Fielden with a cracking punch early on and then later wiped out Sean Long with a late hit, but still there was no sin bin or red card for a man who was clearly playing on the edge. It was rumoured that he had been fired up by a pre-tournament interview that Fielden had done with the Australian magazine Rugby League Week, which was subheaded: "Firebrand Fielden gives the Aussies an absolute gobful." Fielden's comments in reality were pretty tame but it was the headline 'Arrogant' and the accompanying subheading that got everybody talking.

Britain had their own reasons to be psyched up. Their stand-off, Leon Pryce, was vilified throughout the Australian media for daring to suggest that Bondi beach wasn't as good as Blackpool's. All hell broke loose, and in comical fashion, news bulletins actually went to the length of obtaining footage of Blackpool beach in the winter. Pryce quickly became public enemy number one, with photographers and cameramen following him everywhere. Pryce refused to submit and played his part in Great Britain hitting Australia where it hurt. Four tries were posted in a sensational win that deserves to rank up there among the Lions' finest. The tryscorers in that 23-12 win were Paul Wellens, Jamie Peacock, Lee Gilmour and Gareth Raynor, but the star was Sean Long, who finally came of age in the Test arena with a magnificent game-breaking performance.

Great Britain were back in the tournament and needed to beat New Zealand in Wellington, but, as has been the norm in the Super League era, everything went pear-shaped when the pressure was on. Great Britain lost 34-4, a scoreline that may have been down to a touch of over-confidence after Sydney, but bad luck also played its part with New Zealand scoring a couple of fortuitous tries at crucial times and Great Britain being denied at least one that should have stood. What happened in the days that followed, though, stunned everybody. On the Monday evening (Australian time) it was announced that Sean Long was on a plane back home. No-one outside the camp knew why. People speculated, using Long's past misdemeanours as a barometer, with the BBC website desperately trying to put two and two together, and failing miserably. It wasn't until an interview with Rugby League World six months later, that Long put across his side of the story.

"I've no regrets in my life," he said. "I knew the tour would be tough because we'd had such a tough season, but it was my last chance to play the Aussies and beat them. I did that in one of the games so I've no regrets. I'd watched games as a kid when Henderson Gill did 'a bit of a boogie' and when Steady scored against them in 1992. I wanted to achieve that and I did. Those guys won games but not the series, just like us. Older guys might have gone on tour for three months, when they went by boat, but things were different then. They probably didn't spend too much time at home because of their job anyway. We have great jobs in Rugby League now and sometimes we're home at 2pm. We spend a lot of time at home and when I was away I missed it, especially with Claire being pregnant. I was tired and missing my family. I'd spoken about going home even before the first game in Christchurch so it wasn't an overnight decision. I never settled in over there and had had enough by the time I came home. The game in Sydney that we won took a lot out of me both physically and mentally. Looking back, my head had gone.

"We weren't allowed to drink on the flight from Wellington to Sydney but we did have some in the airport. The behaviour on the plane has been magnified and maybe it was a bit boisterous, but if we'd been in a pub no-one would have heard us. We got back to Sydney on the Sunday and I knew I was going home. The boys thought I was crazy. I told Brian and he asked me to sleep on it but I told him nothing would change. Jamie Peacock and Brian Carney tried to as well, which was a good gesture but my mind was made up. I couldn't have contributed anymore. One thing I was upset about was people bringing up the betting thing and making out that I'd been sent home for having a bet. Who on earth would I have had a bet on?"

Other players saw it differently, including Britain's captain, Peacock. "I always enjoyed playing alongside him and he's a great bloke, but it made things difficult for us. Him and Brian didn't have the best of relationships on that tour but they both got on with it while Sean was there. I think Sean backed himself into a corner by telling Brian he was going home when he probably didn't mean it. I think pride got in the way and he wouldn't change his mind."

With Long gone, and morale shot to pieces, it was little surprise that Noble's men lost to Australia and exited the competition, leaving the Southern Hemisphere sides, again, to contest the final. This time the Aussies matched the Kiwis step for step and a thrilling game went to golden-point extra time where Johnathan Thurston put Darren Lockyer in for the winning try for a 16-12 win. Australia were back on top of the rugby league world.

By the time the 2007 Kiwis landed, it had been announced that the Great Britain jumper was to be retired, and after fourteen years without a series win, it was claimed there was a steely determination to put it to bed in the best possible fashion, although the cynics wondered why the same desire hadn't always been there. That goal was helped by the absence of a number of New Zealand's best players including the retired Stacey Jones, Ruben Wiki and Nigel Vagana, as well as the injured Sonny-Bill Williams, Benji Marshall, Manu Vatuvei, Nathan Cayless and Jerome Ropati. David Fa'alogo was suspended while Brent Webb withdrew, exhausted from his season with Leeds.

New Zealand still fielded a strong side, but Great Britain whitewashed them with wins at Huddersfield, Hull and Wigan. The second Test was one-sided with Jamie Peacock and Leon Pryce in excellent form in a 44-0 cakewalk, but the first and third Tests were entertaining games with the home side prevailing by just six points on each occasion. A couple of props made the headlines in the first Test: Sam Burgess, at eighteen, enjoyed a wonderful debut, scored a try and absolutely hammered the Kiwis' crack forward Fuifui Moimoi in the 75th minute with the mother of all big hits, and Samoan Maurie Fa'asavalu hit the news by being selected in the squad by coach Tony Smith under the residency rule. He also scored. Smith denied other overseas players like Clint Newton the opportunity to play for the national side, but was fine with the Samoan on the basis that Fa'asavalu had learned his rugby league trade in England, having played the game nowhere else before his arrival.

Smith not only defended that decision, but also protested against claims that Britain's task was made much easier because the Kiwis had been so weakened by player withdrawal. "The series will be remembered as a Test series," he told the press. "I don't get it otherwise. Why talk about what wasn't here or wasn't available? Do you just list your best seventeen down on paper and not play? Do you just cross them off and say mine is better than yours and never get to do battle on the field, so you just have the paper exercise?" He had a point. Great Britain had been similarly weakened in the past, with the 1996 tour to New

Zealand being an obvious example, yet few people were prepared to use it as such a prominent excuse.

The series win provided British rugby league with a rare summer-era boost, but it may also have instilled some complacency ahead of the 2008 World Cup, which was to be played in Australia. The Kiwis were obviously much stronger in that competition, and throughout most of it Australia were as formidable as ever. As England found out in their opening game, Papua New Guinea weren't bad either.

The 2008 World Cup is the nadir of post-1996 British or English fortunes, despite considerable competition for that dubious title. Going into the code's thirteenth World Cup optimism was high, but a month later the credibility of English rugby league was in tatters after a narrow win over the Kumuls, who led 16-12 at the break, followed by humiliations against New Zealand, twice, and Australia. The Australian massacre in Melbourne was particularly hard to stomach, with England capitulating 52-4. England looked to have turned a corner when leading the Kiwis 24-8 a week later, before conceding 28 unanswered points, largely down to a humiliating inability to defend out wide. As for the semi-final, England only lost by ten points to the Kiwis, but New Zealand were clearly the better side en route to their showdown with the seemingly invincible Australians in Brisbane.

The final at Suncorp Stadium - or Lang Park to the traditionalists - richly deserves its place in rugby league folklore. The two sides played out a stunning match which left its 50,599 attendees in awe. Australia led 10-0 and could have gone further ahead had a Darren Lockyer effort counted. Instead it was rightly disallowed by the video referee and the Kiwis could breathe again. By half-time, the deficit was down to just four points at 16-12, before 40 of the most thrilling minutes of international football. Lance Hohaia's converted try had the Kiwis ahead by two before Billy Slater, on the hour mark, produced an incredible faux pas as he flung the ball in-field, near his own line, after flirting with the touchline, for Benji Marshall to swoop and score. Greg Inglis pulled one back, but Hohaia was awarded a penalty try by the video referee, Steve Ganson, and Adam Blair wrapped up the World Cup with a try five minutes from time. 34-20 was a convincing score - the Kiwis were crowned the world's best.

Ricky Stuart, the Australian coach, was enraged with the vital refereeing decisions. It was reported that he had verbally abused Geoff Carr, the ARL chief executive, before turning his anger the next morning on Ashley Klein, the referee, in a hotel lobby. He was fined $20,000 and he resigned his post in December.

Overall, the World Cup was regarded as a success, far better than the dismal 2000 version. Its format was immediately criticised as Papua New Guinea were placed in a pool with Australia, New Zealand and England, with three to qualify. Having made the knock-out stages in 2000, it appeared they had no chance of doing so again and their former winger Marcus Bai was enraged. "I reckon its crap, I am furious about this," he stormed. But Stanley Gene reasoned that it would give his country maximum exposure and they won plenty of new admirers with their performances.

Fiji was almost taken over with rugby league fever, one television company selling out of satellite dishes during the tournament. The Batis reached the semi-final before they eventually lost 52-0 to Australia in the last four.

As in 2000, Ireland won many admirers, crushing Samoa 34-16 to top Pool Three, before losing to Fiji in the quarters. Samoa and Tonga's much-anticipated group match went the way of the Samoans 20-12 in front of a five-figure crowd at Penrith.

"The goal of the tournament was to re-establish the World Cup as a viable event in its own right and to raise funds to support the international game," said Colin Love of the Rugby League International Federation. £2 million was subsequently earmarked to aid international development before the next World Cup in 2013.

Eight days into the 2009 Four Nations, England looked as far behind Australia and New Zealand as ever, but they gained some redemption by reaching the final of the inaugural Four Nations. Tony Smith's men opened the competition against France and trailed Bobbie Goulding's side 12-4 at half-time. A couple of Richie Myler tries early in the second half got them back in it and they went on to win 34-12 although the moral victory went to the French. In London 24 hours later, Australia and New Zealand played out a stunning exhibition of international rugby league at The Stoop that was up there with anything that had gone before it in years. The Kiwis led 20-14 with just two minutes left but Cameron Smith backed up Greg Inglis to score near the posts. Johnathan Thurston's conversion secured the draw and brought the curtain down on a breathless game.

A week later Australia were 26-0 up at half-time against a terribly disjointed England who had given the 23,122 crowd at Wigan nothing to cheer about. Greg Inglis was having a field day down the left and England looked to be on the end of a cricket score, but regrouped at half-time and while there was never any danger of them hauling back the Kangaroos, tries to Sam Burgess, Gareth Ellis and Lee Smith restored some English credibility. Later that day, New Zealand led a weakened France by just 16-12 in the early stages of the second half before a late whirlwind saw them top the 60-point mark.

France won a few more admirers against Australia in week three with a decent first-half performance after which Australia led just 8-0, but the 'Roos hit top gear to win 42-4. England's game against New Zealand was as good as a semi-final and Tony Smith had whetted the appetites of the public during the week by pairing together the twenty-year-old halves Kyle Eastmond and Sam Tomkins. It was a bold move that paid off as Eastmond opened the scoring with a breathtaking try before Peter Fox, the Hull Kingston Rovers wing, added two more before half-time for an 18-6 lead. Despite an early Kiwi try in the second half, England held on to set up an eagerly anticipated rematch with the green and golds in the final.

If South Sydney Rabbitohs fans didn't know much about Sam Burgess prior to kick off, they certainly did 40 minutes later as their club's new signing from Bradford produced a stunning display from loose forward to have the Kangaroos on the ropes early in the Elland Road final. His wonderful long-range tenth-minute try, which saw him step past Billy Slater, opened the scoring. A couple of minutes later he ignored the supporting Sam Tomkins as he tried to skin Slater again but was brought down, and Brett Morris scored at the other end almost straightaway. Fox and Inglis exchanged tries as Australia led 14-10 at half-time.

England regained the lead on 50 minutes with Burgess scoring his third try against Australia in two weeks before the Kangaroos turned on the style to produce six tries in a breathtaking 23-minute passage of football. The star was Slater who scored three of them and he also set up Cameron Smith with a sublime in-goal flick and knock back of a Darren Lockyer kick. England had done as much as they could, but they just couldn't live with the Kangaroos in the crucial phase of the game - and that tended to sum up much of the modern era.

Papua New Guinea were the next side to enter the Four Nations as a result of them winning the 2009 Pacific Cup which also involved Cook Islands, who made the final, Fiji, Tonga and Samoa. Presented with the same opposition, however, the Kumuls, without Stanley Gene, didn't perform quite as well, although they only conceded a half-century once in a 76-12 defeat to New Zealand. Australia beat them 42-0 in week one and England beat them 36-10 thanks to four Tony Clubb tries.

The group stage of the competition was disappointing with little doubt after week one who the finalists would be. England and New Zealand opened the tournament and the Kiwis won a below-par match 24-10. That meant England had to beat Australia, something they never looked like doing, while Australia and New Zealand didn't have to produce anything in game six, with both sides

understandably saving themselves for their showdown the following week. Compared to the six-week group stage of the 2004-2006 Tri-Nations, it was enormously anti-climactic.

But the final more than made up for it! For the fourth time since 2005, New Zealand and Australia treated the public to a magnificent final and, worryingly for the Aussies, the Kiwis had now won three of them. Nathan Fien scored a dramatic last-minute try to snatch victory from the jaws of defeat, finishing off a superlative, last-tackle 60-metre move which was engineered by the Golden Boot winner Benji Marshall. Earlier, Shaun Kenny-Dowall had cancelled out an early Brent Tate try before Billy Slater and Jason Nightingale swapped scores, although Australia led 12-10 in the closing stages as a result of an extra conversion before Fien had the last word.

The 2011 Four Nations saw Australia regain their crown in very similar circumstances to 2009. Wales, this time, were cast into the role of plucky outsider and, like their predecessors, made a reasonable fist of not embarrassing themselves, losing 42-4 to England, 36-0 to New Zealand and 56-14 to Australia in a game where they scored the first two tries. England and New Zealand were kept apart until week three with Australia already in the final having disposed of both. At Hull, a clinical England knocked out the champions with an excellent 28-6 win with Canterbury Bulldogs-bound James Graham having a great game. Seven days from a decent showing against Australia at Wembley, Steve McNamara's reign finally had legs after the disappointments of 2010.

Once more, England competed in the first 40 minutes of the final, trailing only 8-6 after Ryan Hall was awarded a penalty try. Hall had enjoyed a magnificent tournament scoring world-class tries for fun against the best players in the game but, apart from a penalty goal, England couldn't trouble the scorers further and four tries in the last 23 minutes saw Australia win 30-8. Fittingly, Darren Lockyer scored a last-minute try, although he fluffed the easiest of conversions, as he ended his career with another trophy. Weeks later he was named in the annual World XIII by Rugby League World for the twelfth time in fourteen years. One of the great rugby league careers was over.

As the sport geared up for the 2013 World Cup, the calendar year which preceded it saw no significant international series. Australia beat New Zealand in both their ANZAC Test and in another at the end of the season - as they tend to do away from the major-tournament finals. Elsewhere, England accounted for Wales and France with ease to win a new triangular competition. The fourteenth Rugby League World Cup certainly won't make or break the sport, but it will provide both the international game and the sport in England a wonderful opportunity to progress to another level. England appear to have more strength in depth and more matchwinners in the backs for the first time in a long time, with Wigan superstar Sam Tomkins at the forefront of everybody's thoughts. Again though, they appear to lack the right combination in the key ballplaying positions. Can they put that right in time?

Ten reasons why Great Britain and England have fared so dismally in the Super League era.

1. The national side has consistently lacked the right players to play in the key positions and have subsequently lacked direction, while last-tackle options have generally been inferior to Australia's and New Zealand's. Too many players in the six, seven and nine shirts in Super League rely on footwork and pace, but the NRL continues to breed playmakers in the classical mould who can pass, kick, create and organise. It might not be too hard to play well for the league leaders in Super League, but being asked to prise open an Australian defence in a tight game on a freezing-cold November evening is a totally different task, and our halves have consistently failed to meet that challenge since the retirements of Andy Gregory and Garry Schofield. Too many Super League players in the key positions have not been British while the continued omission of top-class creative players and organisers like Tommy Martyn and Lee Briers, who were always overlooked in favour of those with mainly individual skills, puzzled many. Of those who have been selected regularly in the key positions, too many players who have dominated in Super League have not performed well enough for the national team. Andy Farrell enjoyed some good Test performances at the start and end of his career, but produced little for the national side between the second Tests of 1997 and 2002, and even though he was regularly used as a main ballplayer, his best Test performances came as an out-and-out forward. Iestyn Harris was one of the most convincing winners of the Man of Steel in 1998 but only had a couple of individual tries to show for his efforts in a Great Britain jersey. Despite his phenomenal success in a Leeds jersey, Kevin Sinfield has, at the time of writing, never played well against Australia or New Zealand at loose forward or stand-off, his favoured positions, while Keiron Cunningham, named by Rugby League World in 2007 as the greatest-ever Super League player, was all too frequently missing from the Great Britain line-up, injured. Sean Long, Leon Pryce, Rob Burrow and Danny McGuire are others who have excelled domestically but disappointed internationally. As well as that, the national side has rarely had stability in the halves. In sixteen competitions (of at least three games) since 1996 against Australia or New Zealand, only on two occasions (1997 and 2011) was the same halfback pairing used throughout.

2. Australia have been far too good in the latter stages of the first and, in particular, the second half, of tight games. As well as superior fitness, perhaps this is down to their players experiencing golden point on a regular basis in the NRL - they know how to approach the closing minutes of a finely balanced game. Great Britain lost four consecutive Tests to the Kangaroos in 2003 and 2004 with late scores, something which can't have been down to bad luck alone.

3. Super League is far less intense than the NRL, which means that Great Britain and England have struggled to match Australia and New Zealand. The standard of the lower teams in Super League is often blamed for this but another factor must be considered. To get into the NRL play-offs, teams have to be at their best for most of the season as shown by the pre-season favourites for the NRL title in 2012, Wests Tigers, failing to make the top eight; and the 2004 Grand Finalists, Canterbury Bulldogs and Sydney Roosters, both winning a wooden spoon within five years. In contrast, it is far easier for the bigger clubs in Super League to make the knock-out stages of the competition. Leeds, who were widely criticised for being so poor for much of 2011 and 2012, were still able to secure play-off football and even went on to win the competition in both years. The leading clubs in Super League are virtually guaranteed a play-off spot which has reduced the importance and intensity of the weekly rounds. "The Super League is not strong," said Ellery Hanley in Australia in

2012. "There's only four teams in the competition. You can't really compare it with the NRL because there are no easy games here."

4. The NRL boasts far greater strength in depth than Super League. The unavailability of top players has rarely hurt Australia and with around twenty players missing from the 2003 Kangaroo Tour, including Andrew Johns and Gorden Tallis, they were still able to produce the first Ashes whitewash since 1986. Great Britain, on the other hand, have regularly bemoaned injuries to players like Keiron Cunningham or Sean Long simply because they haven't been able to replace them. In 2001, Kevin Sinfield and Mike Forshaw, two loose forwards, played scrum-half and hooker, unfamiliar positions to both players. In 2003, Richard Horne played in the unfamiliar position of wing. For the 2008 World Cup, only one scrum-half, Rob Burrow, made the journey. The second choice in the warm-up games was a lower-league player, as he was at the time, Richie Myler.

5. While Brian Noble and Tony Smith earned the Great Britain coaching job by winning Super Leagues and David Waite coached in a couple of Australian Grand Finals, three coaches of the national side in the summer era - Phil Larder, Andy Goodway and Steve McNamara - got the job despite not coming close to any club success. The latter two were very inexperienced club coaches at the time of their appointments, which is in sharp contrast to Australian Test coaches like Wayne Bennett and Tim Sheens.

6. The British game has never been able to come even close to replicating State of Origin as a viable stepping stone between club and international football. In the summer era, six options have been tried. The War of the Roses was revived but discarded after three seasons; a one-off match between England and Wales was played in 2001 but never repeated despite it being a competitive game; the one-off Test in Sydney in 2002, which caused huge embarrassment to the British game, was understandably not repeated; a one-off 'Test' with New Zealand was binned after Great Britain racked up 40 points at St Helens in 2006; Tests with the French lasted four years but were given the elbow as they were too one-sided despite France twice having a half-time lead against Great Britain or England between 2007 and 2009; while the Exiles concept, inaugurated in 2011, came in for heavy criticism in 2012.

7. Rugby league's diminishing profile in the UK has resulted in less support for the national team both in numbers, and from outside investment. Gone are the days when Great Britain would play Australia in front of a 45,000-plus crowd in front of a massive BBC audience. Such a crowd occurred half a dozen times before 1996 (with the highest being 73,631), but never during the Super League era. "We felt like the whole country was behind us in 1990 and 1992, whereas now, only die-hard league fans seem to know that Tests are being played," said Garry Schofield. The best players are no longer household names and sponsors and supporters are subsequently harder to come by. With less than six months to go before the 2013 World Cup, the competition still had no sponsor.

8. Leading British players have regularly criticised the vast number of games they have to play. Long seasons mean shorter off-seasons which, in turn, means less preparation. After the 2009 Tri-Nations Final, England captain Jamie Peacock told Rugby League World: "It's a massive issue. If an outsider looked into Rugby League and why we get beaten by the Australians, they'd think we were stupid playing the amount of games we do. It's ridiculous; it's far too many. "

9. Not only is pre-season too short, but in the Super League era it occurs in the winter. While NRL players can prepare for their new season in perfect conditions, freezing temperatures often play havoc with British preparations, often causing them to train indoors. Most clubs travel abroad for a week, but it isn't enough.

10. The differences in rule interpretations between the NRL and the Super League have been a constant problem in the summer era and the thoroughly impotent Rugby League International Federation continue to do little about it. For instance, in 1999, Great Britain had to face an Australian side making 40 substitutions in the days of unlimited interchange which was implemented in the NRL but not the Super League, and Great Britain, as they later admitted, didn't seem to have a clue how to utilise the system. Differences in the speed of the play the ball, the ten metres and endless arguments of which competition's referee is to take charge of the latest Test have been a constant headache. When it comes to which referees to use, and which rules to implement, Australia seem to be experts at winning the argument.

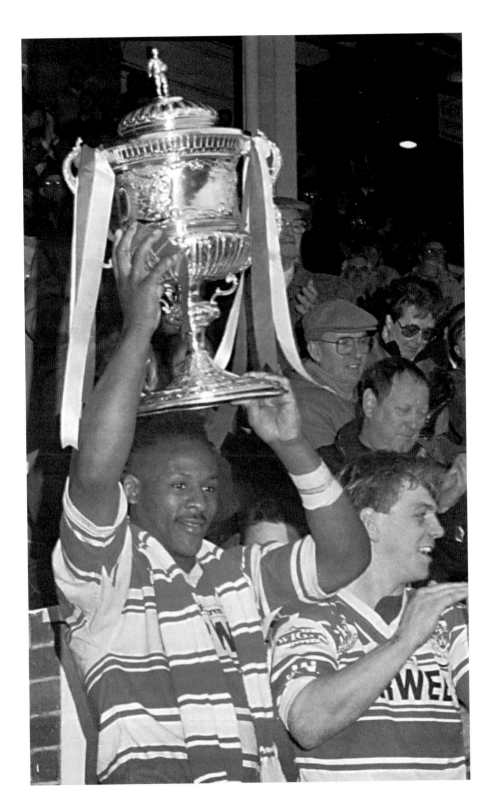

CHAPTER THREE
BRITISH RUGBY LEAGUE (1980-1995)

"If we had slipped back into the second division,
we would have sunk without a trace."
- *Wigan director Jack Robinson, 1981*

Even Manchester United were relegated once - six years after being crowned champions of Europe. So when Wigan, nine times champions and seven times Challenge Cup winners, were consigned to the lower reaches of the professional game in April 1980, it wasn't quite the end of the world. Unless you listened to the club itself, that is. According to former player turned director Martin Ryan, the game and its beleaguered clubs like Wigan, needed a return to the single division, which had been abolished in 1973. "Clubs like Huddersfield, Barrow and Swinton will never come back under the present system, and I think Wigan will soon be in the same boat," he said. "Only Humberside clubs can exist on their gate money these days."

In 1980, as Ryan indicated, English rugby league was in a parlous state. The 1970s had been a damaging decade something that is well illustrated by Great Britain beating Australia at Wembley in November 1973, in front of just 9,874 people. At least Great Britain, who were then the World Champions, were capable of beating Australia at that time. By 1979 they weren't and the Ashes series that year, held in Australia, illustrated how far we had fallen over the course of the decade as the Lions were soundly thrashed in the series.

Domestically, less than 5,000 people were turning up, on average, to watch top-flight games and, as Ryan pointed out, the decision to scrap the single division of 30 clubs in 1973 had emasculated a club like Swinton who had dominated the sport in the 1920s and 1930s and who had been competitive again in the ten years leading up to the divisional split. Wigan, in particular, were doing it tough, averaging just 4,665 at the turnstiles in the season they fell through the trapdoor, and even that was an improvement on the year before.

Ryan's words looked particularly prophetic when his side, who were expected to bounce back up to the first division with ease, lost their opening Division Two match, to York by 22-17, and two games later were famously subjected to a clinical filleting at Craven Cottage in Fulham's inaugural match, which the hosts won 24-5 amid scenes of jubilation among the 9,552 crowd. Under player-coach George Fairbairn, Wigan did manage to gain promotion, but it wasn't as easy as expected and their only goal at the beginning of the 1981-82 season was to avoid a second relegation. "Even with a toe-hold in the first division it was the hardest thing in the world to turn the club round," said another director, Jack Robinson. "If we had slipped back into the second division, we would have sunk without a trace." Back then, it seemed unlikely Wigan would win any major honour in the 1980s.

Even with Wigan's relegation, 1980 is remembered best for its Challenge Cup Final. For the first time, the finalists were Hull Kingston Rovers, the 1979 champions, and Hull FC, who had enjoyed a commendable first season back in the top flight, finishing four places above Rovers in third. The match was anything but a classic, but it was low-scoring, gripping and tense with 30 players battling for lifelong bragging rights for the fans. The Robins went into the match with an injury cloud over Phil Lowe and Len Casey while legends Roger Millward, the player-coach who had twice broken his jaw earlier in the season, and Clive Sullivan would be playing in their first Wembley finals at the ages of 32 and 37. In a measure of how different match preparation was back then, the Rovers players were in the pub 24 hours before kick-off. "Our coach Roger Millward said he was taking us for a walk into nearby Windsor where we happened to pass a pub," said Casey. "So Roger said 'OK, if you want a couple of pints so be it - but two, no more'. And that's all we had."

Steve Hubbard scored the game's first try following a deft pass from Lance Todd winner Brian Lockwood. The referee, Fred Lindop, awarded a possible seven-point try after a foul on the tryscorer. Hubbard missed the conversion but scored with the free shot for a 5-0 lead. He kicked another goal when Millward was taken out by Ronnie Wileman, and it was later confirmed that the Robins general had broken his jaw again. Tim Wilby crossed for Hull but Lloyd missed the conversion and Millward, bravely playing on, slotted a drop goal on half-time for an 8-3 lead. Lloyd reduced the arrears with a penalty but it was his only successful attempt from five. Hubbard's late penalty secured the Cup and a 10-5 scoreline which has been immortalised in East Hull. The other side of the city was shrouded in disappointment, but, in an incredible show of support, the Hull supporters welcomed their beaten players back home as heroes. At the Boulevard, a devastated Lloyd wouldn't get off the bus and join his teammates in the stadium. When the supporters sang his name, demanding his presence, he appeared to a rapturous reception, but was soon back on the bus in tears.

Coached by Peter Fox, brother of Don and Neil, Bradford Northern won the first two league titles of the decade, beating Widnes to the title by a point in 1980 and Warrington by two points twelve months later. Captained by Jimmy Thompson during the first triumph, the club had centre David Redfearn to thank for nineteen tries in 25 appearances while Les Gant weighed in with eleven in 22 from the wing. Northern also picked up the John Player Trophy, beating Widnes 6-0 in a tight final at Headingley with Derek Parker scoring the game's only try. Nigel Stephenson, who had won the title with Dewsbury in 1973, took over the captaincy the following campaign and produced a superb season of performances ably assisted by Alan Parker, Alan Redfearn and Keith Mumby. They clinched the Slalom Lager Championship with a 38-18 win over Hull with Dennis Trotter scoring three tries. But, despite what was up for grabs, only 8,565 people turned up to watch, symptomatic of the game's malaise. They were grateful for a Warrington collapse as the Wire inexplicably failed to win any of their last four games, and their 11-4 defeat at Leigh confirmed Bradford's coronation. In fairness to Warrington, their trip to Hilton Park had been their ninth match in just 23 days. Billy Benyon's men could at least console themselves with the John Player Trophy and the Lancashire Cup, with Tommy Martyn enjoying an excellent season. Down in London, meanwhile, on the morning of the Challenge Cup Final, nineteen-year-old Andy Gregory found himself in a dentist's chair having emergency surgery. Hours later, in just his nineteenth professional game, he scored a try and was instrumental in Widnes beating holders Hull KR 18-9. Fullback Mick Burke won the man-of-the-match vote ahead of Gregory by four votes, with a splendid display which saw him score a fifth-minute try and four goals. The Chemics' other try came from centre Mick George, with their captain, Mick Adams, dropping a goal. Rovers' only try came from Chris Burton.

Average gates broke through the 5,000 barrier in the top flight and in Division Two were a healthy 2,005, a figure which was boosted significantly by new boys Fulham bringing in over 6,000 on average. That Division One figure may look poor now, but the game's chief executive, David Oxley, was in an ebullient mood: "The battle for people's time, attention and money has never been tougher but these latest figures confirm my conviction that our game is marching inexorably forward to the ultimate goal which will see rugby league firmly established as a leading national spectator sport during the course of the current decade." Much of Oxley's optimism will have been based on the heartening emergence of Fulham, giving the capital its first professional team since 1937. News of Fulham FC's intentions to set up a rugby league side broke on 9 June 1980 and just eighteen days later the Rugby League Council had voted them in and their opening-day win over Wigan will live long in the memory. Iain MacCorquodale scored their first points with a penalty goal and Adrian Cambriani scored the club's first try, which helped him become the Observer newspaper's sport's personality of the week. Even the BBC sent along the Match of the Day cameras, as incredible as that seems now. "Rugby league has never enjoyed such widespread and complimentary media coverage in the south of England before," concluded the next issue of Open Rugby. "The almost criminal damage done to the game's image by its portrayal on television was, at long last, shown up to be the sham that it is," it continued, pointing to another issue that the game faced.

Crowds rose again in 1981-82 and they witnessed a thrilling finale to the Championship race. On the final weekend of the season, four teams could still lift the prize and were all paired with one of their title rivals. Going into those games, Widnes led the way by two points ahead of Hull, Hull KR and Leigh in that order. Crucially Leigh, who were coached by Alex Murphy, had a game in hand three days later at already-relegated Whitehaven. Widnes travelled to Hull and lost 21-3, a wide enough margin for the Airlie Birds to go above them on points difference. The result also put Rovers out of contention. The match at Hilton Park between Leigh and Rovers kicked off an hour later and, in wonderful scenes, around 8,000 Hull fans sat on the Boulevard turf listening to the match over the public-address system, cheering on their great rivals as a Robins win would secure them their team the title - but it was Leigh who emerged 18-10 to keep their hopes alive. Now all they had to do was travel to the Recreation Ground and avoid defeat against the side who had been bottom of the league all season, in order to win their first title since 1906. There was still more drama to come as they trailed 4-1 at half-time but tries from Des Drummond, David Dunn and Mick Hogan brought scenes of jubilation from their 4,000 travelling fans as they added the league title to the Lancashire Cup they had won earlier in the season. Drummond, signed by the club for a mere £25 and twice the game's young player of the year, was their star player and already regarded as one of Great Britain's best hopes of beating the 1982 Kangaroos. Bradford came fifth, but their supporters will remember the season for the emergence of Ellery Hanley who scored fifteen tries and kicked 41 goals in 39 matches, although Northern's season ended bizarrely as the players walked off in the 56th minute of a Premiership clash at Hull KR. With six players sent off by referee Robin Whitfield, including four from Bradford, the Northern players left the field and were subsequently banned from three competitions in 1982-83, although the ban was later suspended for three years. The result stood, and elsewhere in an eventful first round, Leigh and Warrington produced a 1-1 draw before Wire won the replay 10-9.

Despite their title heartache, Hull enjoyed a tremendous season. They beat their arch-rivals Rovers 12-4 to win the John Player Trophy at Headingley with an 18-year-old Lee Crooks kicking four goals. They edged out Castleford 15-11 in the Challenge Cup semi-final at Leeds to play Widnes at Wembley, just six days after that final-day drama in the league. Under the Twin Towers, the two sides drew 14-all with Hull rescuing an eight-point deficit in the final fifteen minutes when Steve Norton and Dane O'Hara scored tries. Eddie

Cunningham, who had been ruled out for the season earlier in the campaign, won the Lance Todd trophy with two tries earlier in the match for Widnes. The two sides had to play another final before the replay which was scheduled for 18 days later at Elland Road. The Premiership tournament was played in that period and Widnes won the final 23-8 at Headingley. But David Topliss steered Hull to victory in the big one, scoring twice in an 18-9 win as Hull won only their second-ever Challenge Cup.

By 1982, the league's expansion plans were going well. Following Fulham's excellent inaugural season of 1980-81 in which they achieved promotion, Carlisle replicated their success by winning 28 games from 32 to finish runners-up to Oldham and achieve promotion to Division One. Playing out of the city's soccer ground, Brunton Park, Carlisle's playing roster boasted a couple of young Kiwis in Dean Bell and Clayton Friend, while John Risman, son of Gus, also joined to experience rugby league life at another new outpost, having played for Fulham. In perhaps the club's greatest achievement, Mick Morgan not only walked off with the Division Two player of the year, but also the Man of Steel - an award which was given to the game's biggest personality in its early years. Their first league match against Workington had attracted just under 6,000 and an average of 2,950 represented an admirable beginning for the north Cumbrians. Cardiff were the other newcomers, and drew 9,247 to Ninian Park for the visit of Salford in their first match and settled for a mid-table finish.

After being one of the few club sides to test the 1982 Kangaroos, Hull FC went on to lift the league championship trophy in the 1982-83 season, emerging as the winner of a three-horse race involving Hull KR and a rejuvenated Wigan, now coached by Alex Murphy. A 9-9 midweek draw at Featherstone in their penultimate match eventually derailed his side and Hull wrapped up their first championship in a quarter of a century with a 31-13 home win over Barrow before 16,967 ecstatic supporters. At the bottom, sadly, were Carlisle who endured a campaign from hell, unable to fulfil any fixtures between mid-January and mid-February. Four directors quit, but they just managed to remain in business.

The Airlie Birds also picked up the Yorkshire Cup but were sensationally beaten at Wembley by 33/1 pre-season outsiders Featherstone Rovers. The story of the West Yorkshire side's Cup success was quite incredible, poignantly reaching Wembley in the midst of a recession which had cruel repercussions on the tiny pit village - around 20,000 mining jobs were lost in Wakefield, Castleford and Featherstone in the 1980s. In the first round, they beat Batley 12-5 even though their coach, Allan Agar, had had the most unusual preparation for the game after playing for Carlisle in a 52-0 defeat at St Helens the night before - the Cumbrians were struggling badly and still held his playing registration from the season before. In the next round, Rovers saw off Salford at The Willows 17-11 before they overcame St Helens 11-10 at Knowsley Road in front of the BBC cameras. Against Bradford in the semi-final at Headingley, they were on the wrong end of a 90-metre Ellery Hanley wonder try but prevailed 11-6 thanks to John Gilbert and Terry Hudson tries in the second half. 12-5 down in the final with twenty minutes to play, they snatched the Cup with two David Hobbs tries and a penalty goal from Steve Quinn with three minutes to play. Rovers had only finished a point ahead of the relegation zone, but had beaten the champions on the biggest of stages. It remains one of the game's best David against Goliath stories and Agar was rewarded with the Man of Steel, the only time it has been awarded to a non-player - unless, of course, you count his solitary appearance for Carlisle!

If ever a season signalled the beginning of a new era, it was 1983-84. For the first time a try was worth four points, but more importantly the self-defeating six-year-old international transfer ban was abolished. Some of the greatest names in the game flocked to the north of England with particular focus on Belle Vue on 4 December as Wally Lewis and Peter Sterling, the Australian halfbacks, made their debuts for Wakefield and Hull, a game in which Sterling's Hull triumphed 32-16. A glorious era ensued for the British game which would see Brett Kenny, Mal Meninga, Gene Miles, Eric Grothe, John Ferguson, Gavin Miller, Chris Anderson and many other Australian stars over the next couple of years. It was also a season of the young British player as Joe Lydon's two tries for Widnes lit up Wembley against Wigan, and BARLA under-19s captain Garry Schofield turned professional at Hull, scoring 37 tries in 33 matches. The duo were two of many talented young players who toured Australia and New Zealand with the British Lions at the end of the season. Another young star - although he didn't make the tour - was Wigan's Shaun Edwards. Seconds after midnight on 17 October 1983, the dual-code schoolboy international signed professional forms for Wigan for a record fee of £35,000 and footage of the signing in the player's living room was played to the nation on the BBC's Breakfast Time show just a few hours later. The profile of the game was blossoming.

It was also announced that another new club would soon be welcomed to the professional fold and Sheffield Eagles got off to a dream start the following September by beating Rochdale Hornets 29-10. One of their points came from the boot of Gary Hetherington, who just happened to run the club as well. Hetherington had missed out on a coaching job at York in 1982 and decided instead to form his own club. He had hoped the Eagles would be born a year earlier but plans to play at the city's Bramall Lane ground fell through. Instead, Hetherington went off to enjoy a season with another new club, Kent Invicta.

Second-division Barrow caused a stir by beating Widnes 12-8 to win the 1983-84 Lancashire Cup with David Cairns, who made his Great Britain debut four months later, man of the match. The club won promotion with ease, scoring well over 1126 points in their 34 matches and losing just twice. Hull Kingston Rovers won the first-division title after winning just two games from their first six, before picking up a superb haul of 41 points from 44. With new signings from overseas Mark Broadhurst and John Dorahy in fine form, they also won the Premiership Final, 18-10, against Castleford, with Dorahy man of the match.

A year later they retained the title, winning it by three points from St Helens who, in turn, had Mal Meninga to thank for their push for honours. Rovers could point to Gary Prohm's tryscoring efforts of 34 in 30 league games for helping them across the line. They also won the John Player Trophy, beating Hull 12-0 in front of 25,326 at the city's soccer stadium, Boothferry Park. Sheffield Eagles, meanwhile, came fourth bottom in Division Two, two places ahead of Southend Invicta, the new name for the Kent club who had relocated - sadly they were no more successful there and folded. Hetherington's wife Kath also made the news when she became the first woman to be elected to the Rugby League Council.

The game that everybody remembers from that season involved Wigan and Hull FC who played in the 50th Challenge Cup to be played at Wembley, and who produced one of the most extraordinary afternoons in the code's proud history. It is largely remembered for the sensational midfield duel between Brett Kenny and Peter Sterling who had emerged at a similar time at Parramatta Eels, a club still to win its first Premiership - but with this halfback pair won three in a row. They were now lining up on the biggest stage in British rugby league. Sterling had first played at Hull the season before, 1983-84, and enjoyed his time on Humberside so much that he was only happy to come back for a much longer stint in 1984-85. Kenny, meanwhile, helped his new side to a third-placed finish in the Slalom Lager Championship, with Sterling's Hull finishing sixth but they also made the finals of the Yorkshire Cup, where they beat Hull KR and the John Player Special Trophy where they lost to the same opposition.

Wigan held the upper hand going into the Wembley final, having twice thrashed the black and whites in the fortnight prior to the game. They beat them 40-4 in the league, with Kenny scoring twice, and 46-12 in the first round of the Premiership Trophy. But with men like Sterling, Lee Crooks, Steve 'Knocker' Norton and a wonderful quartet of Kiwis - Gary Kemble, James Leuluai, Dane O'Hara and Fred Ah Kuoi - in their backline, no-one was writing off Hull FC. The game was preceded by a parade of star guests - one player from each of the previous 49 finals dating back to 1929 (war-time finals weren't played at Wembley), and in front of men like Gus Risman, Trevor Foster, Brian Bevan, Lewis Jones, Ike Southward, Eric Ashton, Neil Fox, Vince Karalius, Billy Boston and Roger Millward, Kenny attracted fierce criticism as he sauntered onto the field, hands in his pockets, but one man, above all, knew how to read that sort of body language.

"He did get criticism for being a bit too laid back about the whole occasion," remembered Sterling, "but that's just him all over. I was more worried seeing him that relaxed before the game thinking, 'Shit, we're in trouble here.'" Sterling was spot on. After Hull took an early 6-0 lead through a Kevin James try in which Sterling played no small part, Kenny produced a first-half performance which as good as sealed him the Lance Todd trophy as man of the match, playing a major role in all of Wigan's three first-half tries. On the last tackle he

kept the ball alive for Ian Potter to send over another famous Australian, John 'Chicka' Ferguson who produced a great finish, and then he scored a spectacular long-range try himself, beating Kemble to the corner with a beautiful, precise, curving run. And a minute before half-time, his long pass to David Stephenson saw the centre free Henderson Gill for a superb 75-metre try up the touchline with Kemble trying in vain to halt him.

Kenny set up another at the start of the second half, producing a run-around move that opened up the Hull defence, allowing him to send a jubilant Shaun Edwards to the line. Two minutes later, Sterling produced some great play of his own, breaking through 30 metres out and offloading out of the tackle on the tryline to the supporting Steve Evans. Finally Wigan scored a try without Kenny's assistance when a Sterling pass went to ground on the halfway line and Gill swooped to run in the try. Sterling later told how he passed the ball, hit the ground, heard the cheers and assumed his team had scored only to get to his feet and realise the opposite had happened. At 28-12, surely the game was up for Hull.

They needed three converted tries to win and with Sterling and Leuluai in great form, they scored those three tries. Crucially, however, they converted none of them and, on the scoreboard, that proved to be the difference in the end as they lost 28-24. According to Sterling, there were two other reasons his side came up just short: "Arthur Bunting, who I had great respect for as a coach and who is a very, very close friend, would probably look back and say he made the wrong choice because he left Garry Schofield on the bench, which probably wasn't the best thing he's ever done." And the other reason? "I truly believe that if Brett Kenny hadn't played that day, we would have won by ten or fifteen points. I guess that softened the blow of losing; the fact it was Brett who proved the real difference. I coped with the loss a lot better because I just had incredible admiration for him. And if you're going to get beat, you might as well get beat by one of the champions of the game."

Things were starting to happen at Central Park. The Cup win and the accompanying profile that it brought emboldened their board further as all the game's great players appeared to be in Maurice Lindsay's sights. Five years earlier, South African winger Green Vigo, a member of Open Rugby's inaugural World XIII in 1978, had walked out on the club after they had refused to pay for the food of non-playing reserves on the way home from a game. But the purse strings had been loosened with Lindsay in charge. Greg Dowling and Steve Ella came in from Australia while Lindsay also signed Andy Goodway who had been enjoying a short stint at Manly, but it was the signing of rugby league's Man of Steel, Ellery Hanley, in September 1985 that best signalled their intentions. Even after a 55-try season, Bradford Northern didn't have many clubs queuing up to take their prize asset, and Wigan managed to pick him up for song. In a deal valued at £150,000, Phil Ford and Steve Donlan went to Odsal along with £85,000. "It was probably the best deal we ever struck," said Lindsay. "They took two of our least indispensable players and even agreed to take the £85,000 in instalments." Bradford wasted much of that cash on rugby union's Terry Holmes, who played just 37 times for them before retiring. Joe Lydon was the next big name to come to Wigan later in the season, sold by cash-strapped Widnes for £100,000, and although Wigan failed to win league or Cup in 1986 - although they still won the Charity Shield, the Lancashire Cup and the John Player Trophy - they were laying the foundations for a dynasty that would shape the sport for years to come.

The big trophies were shared by Halifax, who pipped Wigan to the league title by a point, and Castleford, who beat Hull Kingston in a thrilling Wembley final. 100/1 outsiders Fax got off to a poor start, failing to win any of their first four games, but recovered in style to leave themselves requiring just a point from their last game against relegation-threatened Featherstone, who still had a further match to play. The game finished 13-all (Halifax's sixth draw of the season - a record in two-division football), amid controversy that time had been blown three minutes early with both sides supposedly satisfied with a point. The RFL dismissed the claims and, in reality, Featherstone had needed a win and their relegation was confirmed when they lost their last game at Warrington.

The destiny of the Cup relied on the usually reliable boot of Hull KR's stand-off, John Dorahy. A last-minute try from substitute John Lydiat reduced Rovers' deficit to just a point, leaving the Australian with a sideline conversion to win the Cup, but he missed and Malcolm Reilly's Castleford were victorious, with scrum-half Bob Beardmore winning the Lance Todd Trophy.

Having already collected the Charity Shield at the start of the season, Halifax got their hands on another major trophy in 1987 when they beat St Helens in a game that served up one of the most sensational climaxes Wembley has ever witnessed. Looking to overturn a 19-18 deficit, St Helens centre Mark Elia looked a certain tryscorer in the closing moments until John Pendlebury produced the most magnificent of trysaving tackles, punching the ball to safety as Elia dived for the line. There was still time for Elia to cross the line again but Andy Platt's pass to him was correctly ruled forward by John Holdsworth. The win capped a marvellous twelve months for Halifax, who had been close to bankruptcy just four years earlier. Their veteran Australian fullback, Graham Eadie, collected the Lance Todd for a series of trysaving tackles and a try, although Pendlebury must have pushed him close. "I remember that tackle like it was yesterday," said the Halifax winger Wilf George. "I was on the opposite wing and all I could see was Mark Elia was diving in at the corner. My heart sank - I thought that was it - and even when I saw John knock the ball out, I didn't think the referee would have seen it."

Wigan recovered from a shock Cup defeat at Oldham to otherwise sweep the board in 1986-87. With Dean Bell and Andy Gregory added to their ever-growing list of world-class players, and with former New Zealand coach Graham Lowe in the boss's seat, they were far too good for everybody else. Ellery Hanley scored a quite unbelievable 59 tries in 39 appearances as The Riversiders won the Lancashire Cup (beating Oldham 27-6 in the final), the John Player Special Trophy (overcoming Warrington 18-4) and the Premiership Trophy (also against Warrington, 8-0). In the first season of Stones Bitter's sponsorship of the league championship they were devastating, losing only twice in 30 games, both against Warrington, and beating St Helens to the punch by fourteen points, even though Saints didn't lose a match until Boxing Day.

The big event of Wigan's 1987-88 season came on 7 October as they entertained Manly in the first official World Club Challenge match in the code's history - St Helens had played Eastern Suburbs on an unofficial basis in 1976. Lindsay firstly had to persuade the RFL and then the Australians that the fixture was worth playing at all. In order to achieve the latter, he offered a winner-takes-all cash prize which he knew they wouldn't be able to resist. A crowd of 36,895 crammed into Central Park to watch a tryless thriller which finished 8-2 to the home side with prop Shaun Wane named man of the match.

Four days later, Wigan beat Warrington 28-16 to win the Lancashire Cup.

Despite an achievement as admirable as Wigan's, the man who made the headlines that season was an uncapped Rosslyn Park rugby union winger who went to Widnes whose coach, Doug Laughton, had only seen him play on television. Martin Offiah was an instant hit in the 13-man game, which sees its three-quarters get the ball far more that the often-turgid union game. Former dual-code forward Ray French was tipped off about Offiah's abilities and duly alerted his former club St Helens, but one of their directors went to watch him play and returned with a negative report. French then gave the same advice to the other club he played for and even they didn't act straightaway, but managed to convince Offiah that a career in league was worth the sacrifice of a possible England union cap. Offiah signed just before the start of the season and went straight into the team, although he failed to score in his first two games. He broke his duck at Runcorn in the Lancashire Cup, one of fifteen consecutive matches in which he scored, which was just two shy of the record of seventeen set by Leeds' Australian import Eric Harris in 1935-36. He also equalled the first-division record of scoring in eleven consecutive games. At the end of the season, he had bagged 42 in 35 games and walked off with the Man of Steel as well as league-title and Premiership-winners' medals. Rugby league had barely seen a debut season like it.

Steve Hampson won the Division One player-of-the-year award but once again picked up an injury which saw him miss out on a Wembley Cup Final, a repeat of the bad luck which kept him out of the 1984 and 1985 finals. Without him, Wigan were still far too good for Halifax, with five tries between the 27th and 46th minutes blowing the holders away. Kiwi centre Kevin Iro scored twice with Andy Gregory winning the Lance Todd. In just two seasons, Graham Lowe had picked up every cup going.

Widnes retained the championship in possibly the most dramatic fashion, beating Wigan in a winner-takes-all fixture on the last Sunday of the league season, and it was a Martin Offiah hat-trick that proved the difference. The Chemics led the table by a point on the morning of the match but went into the match without their multi-talented playmaker Tony Myler. But Wigan also had injuries and had to make do without their Great Britain halfbacks Shaun Edwards and Andy Gregory. The away team made the better start with Andy Platt dummying over through some weak defence in the first minute, although Offiah got Widnes on the board with his first try. Andy Goodway extended Wigan's lead with an individual try down Offiah's wing but some opportunism at a Wigan play-the-ball by Darren Wright, who kicked the ball through, as the rules allowed you to do back then, for Offiah to score his second, saw Widnes trail by just two at half time. An Alan Tait break resulted in Phil McKenzie setting up Kurt Sorensen for the game's next try before Offiah stole the show with a magnificent solo try to put Wigan two scores ahead. Paul Hulme was next over before Emosi Koloto was sent off for a high tackle on Ian Potter. Ellery Hanley put some doubt in Widnes minds by pulling a try back but McKenzie's dummy bought him a try as Widnes tied the game and the title up, winning 32-18.

"There's a photograph in my book of me taking a conversion," Jonathan Davies later recalled. "I'm bleeding from both knees and my socks are rolled down. Every time I look at the book, I just think that picture says it all. We had players playing on with injuries, David Hulme was off and later on Koloto was sent off. It was a great team effort and at the end I was just knackered."

Thirteen days later, Wigan made up for the most painful of league defeats by winning a Cup Final in the most satisfying fashion. Having lost 4-2 to St Helens at Central Park in the Premiership a week after Widnes, they got to grips with the old enemy underneath the Twin Towers and skewered them by rattling up 27 points to a humiliating nil. In front of a capacity crowd of 78,000 (Wembley's capacity had been reduced from 94,273 the previous year), Kevin Iro put Wigan ahead in the third minute, from which point they dominated, and a joyous Steve Hampson, finally at Wembley, scored the final try on 76 minutes. Ellery Hanley capped a glorious twelve months in which he won the Golden Boot and a third Man of Steel by winning the Lance Todd Trophy and scoring a wonderful individual try. St Helens became the first side to be nilled in the Cup Final since Barrow in 1951.

Hanley had also been man of the match as Wigan beat Widnes 12-6 in the John Player Special Trophy Final in January although his brilliant display played second fiddle in the newspapers to the Chemics' signing, two days earlier, of the Welsh rugby union international Jonathan Davies, who was presented to the 20,000-strong Burnden Park crowd. With Wigan ahead 8-6 ahead, the gamebreaking score came in the 69th minute when Hanley took an Andy Gregory pass to score in the corner. A week later Davies made his Rugby League bow by coming on as a substitute in Widnes's 50-8 league win over Salford at Naughton Park, and he went on to win the title at the first attempt. They then backed that up by beating Canberra Raiders at Old Trafford to be crowned world champions in early October 30-18 with Offiah bagging another two in front of 30,786 spectators. Having trailed 12-0, they clawed their way back magnificently with David Hulme the pick of the players on show.

As the decade drew to a close, Division One attendance figures reached their highest point in that period at 7,292 per game, up from 5,826 twelve months earlier. Wigan led the way, pulling in 14,543 while Leeds, with Garry Schofield and Lee Crooks now on board, following world-record transfers from Hull, smashed through the 10,000 barrier for the only time in the 1980s. With Great Britain ending their losing run against Australia in 1988 and Ellery Hanley named the world's best player, British rugby league entered the 1990s with plenty of reasons to be optimistic.

Wigan became the first team since St Helens in 1966 to complete the league-and-Cup double by beating Leeds - who had earlier signed rugby union's John Gallagher for £350,000 - to the title, and by overcoming Warrington at Wembley 36-14, with Andy Gregory becoming only the second player to win a second Lance Todd. With home-produced talent like Denis Betts and Phil Clarke now complementing their vast array of star players, Wigan's domination didn't look like ending any time soon even though Graham Lowe had left. He had been replaced by John Monie, the man who led Parramatta to the 1986 Premiership, and the transition was seamless, even though Monie was reluctant to come at first. "He told me he had only been out of Australia once, on holiday to Bali," Maurice Lindsay is quoted as saying in a book called The Best Years of our Lives. "He asked me if Wigan was anything like Bali. I must admit I was stumped for a minute. I'm quite a salesman, but I don't think I could have pulled that one off. But I didn't give up, I kept on at him, and eventually he said yes." Monie also won the Regal Trophy (the new name for the John Player Special Trophy), as his side beat Halifax 24-12 with the newly-crowned MBE, Ellery Hanley, man of the match again after scoring a hat-trick.

Wigan's domination was turning into a dynasty by the time they won another double in 1990-91, prevailing in another title race and beating St Helens again at Wembley. The facts, however, don't even begin to tell the full story - even hyperbole might come across as an understatement - as they were forced to play eleven matches in 35 days in a crazy schedule at the end of March and in April. The only match they lost in that time was a Premiership encounter with Featherstone as they did enough to win the Championship by four points. Their last match of the season came at Wembley and although the scoreline of 13-8 was a vast improvement for a St Helens club which was still haunted by the events of two years earlier, Shaun Edwards didn't quite see it like that. "How we managed to stay on our feet, never mind beat St Helens, I'll never know," he said. "About eight of us were on pain-killing injections ... Saints were quite pleased with themselves afterwards, because it had been a close game ... but the truth is that they were beaten by a team of cripples." 1990-91, incidentally, was the first season that the Monday-morning newspaper League Express reported on the game, joining the Rugby Leaguer which was then a Thursday paper.

Warrington, captained by Des Drummond, won the Regal Trophy Final, beating Bradford 12-2 and Hull broke the Lancashire clubs' habit of hogging

the trophies by beating Widnes 14-4 in front of a crowd of 42,043 which remained the highest crowd in the history of the competition by the time it was disbanded in 1997. Martin Offiah scored Widnes's only try, his 49th of the season, and little did their fans know that it was to be his last game for the first team. He had scored 181 tries in 145 appearances for the clubs, but claimed to have simply stopped enjoying his rugby there. "I couldn't say it was one specific thing or one incident. It was just the simple fact that I'd been there for four years and done the same thing over and over again. I had topped the tryscoring charts in all those four years and thought the only thing left to do at Widnes on a personal level was fail, and I didn't want to do that." Widnes were determined not to let him go and with Offiah claiming he was injured, the player didn't play any rugby for the rest of the year, apart from half an hour in a reserve-team game. Eventually Widnes accepted defeat and transfer-listed him, but the £700,000 fee was wholly unrealistic for a sport whose world-record had just been set at £250,000 with Ellery Hanley joining Leeds from Wigan who, naturally, were favourites to sign the winger. But, despite the fee they received for the Great Britain captain, the erection of their new stand had set Wigan back enormously with it going way over budget and opening late. Eventually a fee of £440,000 was agreed with the newly-crowned world champions on the Challenge Cup deadline day, and Offiah was back in business.

Having regularly been a guest summariser for the BBC on Cup Final day, Offiah was finally there on centre stage, stealing the show with a brace of magnificent tries that had the Prime Minister John Major drooling. "Faster than a camera shutter" was how he described Offiah, although how he described Billy McGinty after a alleged pineapple-ring changing-room incident is anybody's guess. Offiah added the winner's medal and subsequent Lance Todd Trophy to his ever-growing list of honours. He played sixteen matches for the cherry and whites in 1991-92 and closed the campaign with 30 tries (half came in two matches with five in the Cup semi-final with Bradford and an astonishing ten against hapless Leeds in a Premiership match) as the side won yet another double, winning the league by eight points from St Helens, and added the Premiership Trophy too. They also entered, and won, the World Sevens in Sydney with Offiah scoring all four tries as they beat Brisbane Broncos in the final in monsoon-like conditions.

Off the field, the game's health was ever improving as the RFL and BARLA finally declared unification, BSkyB announced a new four-year deal for league-match television rights and launched their first magazine programme, Boots 'n' All, and the BBC paid £2.5 million for a four-year Challenge Cup deal. Even the Soviet Union got in on the act, with Moscow Magicians and Tiraspol of Moldova touring England to play Huddersfield and Batley. Trafford Borough (who were Blackpool Borough via Springfield Borough and Chorley Borough, before another club called Chorley Borough started up just to confuse everybody) boasted four Russians in Oleg Zotov, Alexander Diatlov, Valerie Medwedj and Valerie Savikhine, scoring four tries between them in little over half-a-dozen games. Sadly it proved to be Trafford's last season, and Scarborough Pirates went the same way after just one year with chairman Geoffrey Richmond, later the chair of Bradford City in soccer's Premiership, reporting debts of £60,000.

The following season saw three more clubs leave the professional ranks in rather more controversial circumstances after Maurice Lindsay, now the chief executive of the Rugby Football League, announced in March that the bottom three sides in division three would be for the chop as the game would, again, be reverting to two divisions. With five clubs in danger, Highfield beat all four of their rivals in the final five matches to survive while Barrow, one of the game's great clubs, only survived by the skin of their teeth, on points difference. The three unfortunate clubs were Chorley Borough, whose chairman was Lindsay Hoyle, a future deputy speaker of the House of Commons; Blackpool Gladiators and Nottingham City (previously Mansfield Marksman). After a late-season game between Chorley and Highfield which was marred by brawling and three red cards dished out by referee Colin Morris, who later claimed that no-one else wanted to officiate the game, Chorley official Andy Seddon said: "What they have done to us is ludicrous, immoral and shabby. We were voted into the Rugby League and told to formulate a five-year plan. This is the fourth year and we're not being allowed to complete the job." Lindsay had been invited to the game but declined. Even Nottingham, who only won one game all season were incensed. "Any true fan of rugby league must surely agree that this outrageous idea to rob the bottom three clubs of their league status, so late in the season, is wrong, immoral and hopefully to be proved illegal," wrote Julie Burgess, rather poignantly signing her letter to League Express: "wife of Nottingham City coach [Mark], mother of four boys and lover of rugby league." She did at least have the consolation of winning a League Express T-shirt for the quality of her letter and of watching those four boys - Luke, Sam, George and Tom - grow up to play for South Sydney Rabbitohs two decades later.

At the other end of the professional scale, Wigan won the championship and the Challenge Cup in John Monie's last season, meaning that the Australian had won the double in each of his four seasons at the club. They won the title on points difference from St Helens, effectively securing it with an 8-all Good Friday draw with their rivals in which Saints' Kevin Ward broke his leg, an injury that ended a magnificent career. Saints scored two tries to one, but had to hope Wigan would slip up against either Warrington or Castleford, but their prayers weren't answered. At Wembley, they received an almighty first-half scare from Widnes, when a blockbusting Kurt Sorensen try put the Chemics six ahead, but they hit back through Lance Todd winner Dean Bell and Sam Panapa to win their sixth-straight Challenge Cup. They also won the last-ever Lancashire Cup, the Regal Trophy but lost the World Club Challenge to Brisbane and both the Charity Shield and the Premiership Final to Saints. Wakefield Trinity won the last Yorkshire Cup, beating Sheffield Eagles 29-16 at Elland Road. The demise of the County Cups were the other part of the shake-up of the professional game's structure.

That season also saw a rule change introduced midway through the season with little fanfare. From 23 November 1992, the defensive team had to retire ten metres rather than five from the play the ball. Little was made of the alteration at first, with Lindsay later claiming it would make the players fitter. In time, it would alter the whole face of the on-field product, with dummy-half running becoming far more prominent as the years rolled on.

In the first year of the post-Monie era, Wigan's new coach, John Dorahy appeared to do just as well by winning the club's fifth consecutive double. The title was again won on points difference, this time over two clubs - Bradford and Warrington - with one of the key moments of the season coming at Wilderspool in January as Frano Botica kicked Wigan to victory with a late penalty. In the Cup Final, Martin Offiah scored one of Wembley's great tries, as he ran 90 metres, bamboozling Leeds fullback Alan Tait to score a sensational try en route to a 26-16 win for the Riversiders. Offiah's try was so good that

Wembley later dedicated a burger bar to it. Another big story was brewing behind the scenes as the unpopular Dorahy - who had recently been told by his captain, Dean Bell, on behalf of the squad, that 80 per cent of the players were against the coach - was reported to have scuffled with club chairman, Jack Robinson, on the team bus the day after the final. He was sacked the next day. Despite the league-and-Cup double, there was unrest in the camp and the team had been humiliated 33-2 by Castleford in January's Regal Trophy Final. "I would say his man-management skills let him down," said Robinson. "He tried to change too much in too short a time. Whatever he did he put the players' backs up and that wasn't a situation we could tolerate."

Reserve-team coach and former club captain Graeme West took over for what was remaining of the season and put two more trophies on the sideboard in less than a month as his side avenged the Regal Trophy defeat by beating Castleford 24-20 at Old Trafford in the Premiership Final, although their enforcer Kelvin Skerrett broke his jaw. That, along with Andy Platt's departure to the Winfield Cup, left them short of props as they travelled down under to face the mighty Brisbane Broncos in their own backyard in the first official World Club Challenge to be played on Australian soil, and the first to be played midway through the Australian domestic season. But with second-rower Billy McGinty, who had already signed for newly-promoted Workington, producing a magnificent early spell as an emergency front-rower, Wigan produced one of their greatest performances to stun Wayne Bennett's men 20-14 with Denis Betts, Barrie-Jon Mather and Jason Robinson scoring to let Shaun Edwards lift the trophy in front of 54,220 largely disbelieving supporters.

Wigan's efforts were suitably rewarded when they were crowned Team of the Year at the BBC's Sports Personality of the Year ceremony in December 1994 - a richly deserved accolade. It also made up for the fact they had not won it twelve months earlier when the broadcaster outrageously gave it to the England rugby union team for beating New Zealand in a tryless borefest of a friendly at Twickenham, having earlier in the year come third in the Five Nations; but given the BBC's questionable treatment of rugby league, they had done well to win it at all.

In terms of league and knockout football excitement, 1994-95 failed to live up to the previous couple of seasons as Wigan showed that the cracks that had appeared in Dorahy's reign were merely temporary. In West's first full season, they won the title by seven points from Leeds, losing just twice, they thrashed Warrington 40-10 in a lopsided Regal Trophy Final and they beat the Loiners 30-6 in a one-sided Wembley Cup Final. In Jason Robinson, Gary Connolly, Va'aiga Tuigamala (who had signed from rugby union in a huge deal the previous season) and Martin Offiah, they boasted a three-quarter line to rival their greatest; that of their champion side of the early 1910s - James Leytham, Bert Jenkins, Lance Todd and Joe Miller. Their eight successive Challenge Cups would surely never be matched and in the spring of 1995, they stood alone as the greatest team rugby league this country had ever seen.

Their domination had done so much good for the game in terms of the players they produced for Great Britain and for the sport's profile, but it seemed that the public were beginning to tire of the same team lifting most of the silverware. The 7,000-plus average for league games that was reached in 1988-89 wasn't maintained. By 1993-94 it had fallen to under 6,000 and by the end of 1994-95 it stood at a meagre 5,543. Something needed to change - and on 8 April 1995 everything did.

Nobody was quite prepared for the storm that was about to blow through rugby league, on both sides of the world.

CHAPTER FOUR
THE SUPER LEAGUE WAR

"... with thy brawls thou hast disturb'd our sport."
- *Titania (A Midsummer Night's Dream), 1594.*

Ian McCartney, the MP for Makerfield, near Wigan, summed up the feelings of many rugby league supporters when he said in a House of Commons debate on the future of the game in April 1995: "For the first time in Britain's history, a media magnate has bought not just a sporting event but a sport and, with that purchase, he will manipulate that sport on an international stage for the long-term aspirations of his company at the expense of the short and longer-term aims of rugby league, both here and internationally."

David Hinchcliffe, the MP for Wakefield, who instigated the debate, added: "Why should a battle between two Australian media magnates result in my constituents losing something very important which we have had for 122 years - Wakefield Trinity Rugby League Football Club? Why should a power struggle on the other side of the world mean that I should lose the team that I have supported through thick and thin since I was a small child?"

Whatever the merits of the debate, Rugby league was changed forever after a meeting of the clubs and the Rugby Football League at Central Park in Wigan on 8 April 1995. Super League was coming. So was summer rugby. And so were mergers, to which Hinchcliffe was referring.

Warrington and Widnes; Hull FC and Hull Kingston Rovers; Wakefield Trinity, Featherstone Rovers and Castleford; Workington Town, Whitehaven, Carlisle and Barrow; Oldham and Salford; and Sheffield Eagles and Doncaster would no longer exist in their own right. Instead Cheshire, Humberside, Calder, Cumbria, Manchester and South Yorkshire would participate in the new competition, which was scheduled to kick off in March 1996.

Wigan, Leeds, St Helens, Bradford Northern and Halifax would retain their identities while London Broncos, Paris and Toulouse were to be fast-tracked into the competition. The top two sides in Division Two, who would have otherwise been promoted, were to miss out. Keighley Cougars and Batley were in the driving seat when the announcement was made and the Cougars had just spent £135,000 on Great Britain's Daryl Powell as they prepared for life in the Big League. "Keighley deserve to be in the Premier League, and I joined them to be in the Premier League," he said.

The top four clubs from the English and Australasian Super League clubs would play each other at the end of every season in an expanded World Club

Championship competition. Underneath Super League would be Division One, made up of Batley, Bramley, Dewsbury, Highfield, Huddersfield, Hunslet, Keighley, Leigh, Rochdale Hornets, Swinton and Ryedale-York. They were to be joined by a new side to be based in south Wales and each club in this tier would receive a one-off payment of £100,000.

The proposals were voted in unanimously by the 32 existing professional clubs, although some claimed later they didn't really have a choice, with Keighley immediately threatening legal action. Leeds chief executive Alf Davies accused the RFL of "holding a gun to the heads of clubs." The three clubs who were demoted from the league with two months' notice in 1993 - Nottingham City, Blackpool Gladiators and Chorley - also had a vote. The first two also voted positively with Chorley abstaining. Eight days later, even they - by now a National Conference League club - were threatening to sue the RFL.

Rupert Murdoch's News Corporation would be putting £75 million - a fabulous lifeline for a sport with many clubs in financial dire straits - into the game over the next five years (£1.1 million per year being given to each club), in order to secure exclusive television rights for Sky Sports. According to Maurice Lindsay, the chief executive of the Rugby Football League: "Anyone can see that we have just joined forces with one of the richest men in the world. Rupert Murdoch is totally committed to the development of rugby league as a major sport, as his investment shows and once he had made that decision his people have moved with astonishing speed, and great dynamism. If I never do anything else for rugby league I will have at least given the game financial security with this deal. What people should realise is that this was a once-in-a-lifetime offer that may not have been on the table for very long. Think about it - the BBC currently pays around £500,000 per season for their coverage of the game. We have been offered a fortune compared to that figure."

Lindsay had support from Oliver Heald, the MP for Hertfordshire North: "In the past three or four years Wigan has been something very special. I believe that the reasons are that it picks the best athletes, it is able to have them as full-time players and it is able to train them at the highest level. Many rugby league clubs cannot do that. If we could have a league in which everyone could reach the standard of Wigan, what a spectacle it would be." Mr Heald, despite admitting he was a union man with little knowledge of league, had a point. Wigan needed to be challenged, and Super League would perhaps give Wigan's rivals the tools to dethrone them.

The momentous meeting was described in League Express as "significant as the breakaway from rugby union in 1895" but supporters of the affected clubs were immediately mobilised, and demonstrated vociferously at the following day's games. Powell's debut at Keighley was marked by a pitch invasion. There was a sit-in at Castleford, banners galore (including one at Keighley which read: 'Murdoch and Lindsay for the electric chair') and abuse aimed at directors of various clubs. The Cas chairman, Eddie Ashton, needed a police escort to address unhappy fans while emergency meetings were set up by supporters at a number of clubs. The scenes were repeated and intensified at the Easter fixtures a week later, with a memorable banner at Post Office Road, which was hosting Featherstone and Castleford, being unfurled. 'Fev is Fev, Cas is Cas, Stick your merger up your ass', seemed to represent many of the feelings rather well.

Lindsay was unsympathetic. "The merger proposals are down to the clubs themselves, " he said. "No club has to disappear. I'm sure that Wakefield, Featherstone and Castleford will merge, for example, and I think that the new club easily has the potential to be one of the strongest in the game, I can't imagine that the fans wouldn't want to see that. It makes me feel tremendously excited, so if I was a fan of one of those clubs I would be ecstatic."

David Hinchcliffe held the opposing view, and read out a quote from a newly-published book on the subject, Merging on the Ridiculous, in Parliament. "It's a bit like coming home one day and finding that your walls have been knocked through, and from now on you and your neighbour are all sharing one house," he said in a House of Commons debate on 26 April 1995. "What do you say? 'Thanks very much. Another time, perhaps you'd like to ask me first."

This particular argument was far from over.

The roots of the battle belonged in Australia and surrounded pay-TV rights. The Sydney Premiership was first televised in the mid-1970s on Channel Seven and, with the popular ex-Manly player Rex Mossop commentating, it pulled in huge ratings. By 1983 they had lost those rights to Channel Ten, who had outbid them but they filed for receivership in 1990, leaving the ARL panicking about the rest of the deal. Channel Nine rode to the rescue and the game's chief executive, Ken Arthurson, described the broadcaster's boss, Kerry Packer, as a 'true friend of rugby league'. In 1993 the deal was renewed with little publicity with pay-TV rights bolted on. Pay-TV didn't exist in Australia at the time but with Rupert Murdoch buying rights to the NFL in America and to soccer's Premier League in England, both he and Packer knew their real worth.

Murdoch's News Corporation was determined to buy the pay-TV rights for his Foxtel network but Packer wasn't going to let him have them without a fight - a fight which lasted for nearly three years.

Murdoch's company responded to Packer's lack of co-operation by snapping up as many players and clubs as he could and by convincing them that his Star League, as it was first known, would breathe new life into the sport which, they claimed, was going stale under the tired administration of the Australian Rugby League. News had plenty of success in attracting big names and on April Fools' Day 1995, Sydney's Daily Telegraph carried the pictures of twelve leading players on its front page, including Laurie Daley, Bradley Clyde, Allan Langer, Steve Renouf and Andrew Ettingshausen. These were the first to jump ship; the first of many.

With league popularity reaching great heights in 1994 with a State of Origin clash that saw 87,161 people attend the Melbourne Cricket Ground to watch the second game, rugby league was almost growing too fast for the Australian Rugby League administration to cope. From the early 1980s the Sydney competition had become national with Canberra Raiders, Newcastle Knights and Brisbane Broncos, among others, coming to the party, and in 1995 there was to be further expansion with Auckland, North Queensland, South Queensland and Perth making up a 20-team competition.

The Broncos, who had won won two Premierships in their first six years, were growing frustrated at the sport's commercial performances which they believed could be vastly improved and in May 1994 their chief executive, John Ribot, began to examine the possibility of a breakaway competition with News Corporation financing rugby league and being responsible for marketing the game both in Australia and abroad. Arthurson, having threatened Brisbane with expulsion in October 1994, then managed to persuade all of the Winfield Cup clubs to sign a loyalty agreement, which forbade them to play under a rival banner, and when the ARL won in the federal court and Super League was banned from Australia until 2000 at the earliest, it looked like he had masterminded a stunning victory.

Unfortunately for them, there was a right to appeal and in October 1996 the decision was reversed. 1997 would see the game split into two - an ARL competition and a Super League competition, both played amid a backdrop of acrimony, sniping and endless bitterness. In 1995 Super League players had been denied the chance to play State of Origin and internationals. In 1997, Super League players again missed out on Origin and the ARL players missed out on Tests against Great Britain. With everybody weary, peace was eventually agreed upon after the 1997 seasons and the National Rugby League (the NRL) was formed, kicking off in 1998.

At the start of that war, one of News's strategies was to sign up the other league-playing nations in order to isolate the Australian Rugby League. They believed that if they could offer international competition, they would gain an advantage on Arthurson and his men. That is why Murdoch was willing to present Lindsay with such a generous cheque and, within a matter of weeks, another £12 million was added on to it. Suddenly, it was £87 million that was finding its way into British coffers. By the time that piece of good news was announced, the RFL's plans had changed again.

Within days of the initial Central Park meeting, the idea of mergers began to fall apart. At a meeting in Doncaster, which Sheffield owner Gary Hetherington attended, just sixteen out of the 400 present were in favour of the South Yorkshire venture. By 12 April, Salford and Oldham had failed to come to any agreement on the new Manchester club. A couple of days after that, the Widnes-Warrington amalgamation was called off with each club being allowed access to Super League in their own right - instead there was to be just one French club. Tony Gartland resigned as chairman of Halifax as a result of the hostile reaction he faced for suggesting that his club could merge with Bradford Northern. Castleford then pulled out of the Calder merger in order to go it alone and by the time Featherstone members voted against it too, it was clear that new plans would have to be drawn up. Those plans were announced on Sunday 30 April, the day after Wigan beat Leeds at Wembley to win their eighth consecutive Challenge Cup - a timely reminder, if one was needed, that changes of some sort were required.

Even so, did they have to be rushed through so quickly, many supporters were asking. Why were the RFL prepared to force every professional club into taking a decision that would change not just the sport itself for good, but also each club? The answer, according to Lindsay, was that the offer was only open for a few days and a quick decision was demanded. Many were unconvinced.

Mergers were officially off the table, and this time there would be three divisions as there had been up to 1993. Super League would be the top tier and would be made up of the top ten teams from the 1994-95 season - Wigan, Leeds, Castleford, St Helens, Halifax, Warrington, Bradford Northern, Sheffield Eagles, Workington Town and Oldham - along with London Broncos, who were to be fast-tracked from Division Two, and new club Paris. The rest of the clubs were split between the next two divisions - named Division One and Division Two - with Chorley back in the professional fold, in the third tier. The Welsh experiment was back off the table - although not for long as South Wales would eventually take their place in Division Two. Promotion and relegation on a one-up-one-down basis was planned. The extra money meant that the annual share-out had to be recalculated. Over a five-year period, £900,000 annually would now go to each Super League club, between £200,000 and £700,000 to each Division One club on a sliding scale, and £150,000 to the Division Two clubs.

This meant that instead of two clubs being relegated from the top flight, six were being booted out. While bottom two Hull and Doncaster could have no complaints (The Dons had gone bust and weren't included in any of the three divisions for 1996), Featherstone Rovers, Salford, Wakefield Trinity and Widnes suddenly became victims. Keighley Cougars and Batley, who would have been promoted in usual circumstances, were now officially excluded. Widnes, world champions just five-and-a-half years earlier, were particularly upset as they had been under the impression since 14 April that they were to be included as a stand-alone club since the Cheshire merger was binned. They were the only club to vote against the latest proposals, while Keighley were absent from the vote, talking to their lawyer. Peter Roe, who had coached Keighley throughout much of the Cougarmania era, recalled: "They were hard done to, there's no doubt about it, but there was still another side to it. They overspent massively in an attempt to get into the top division and were full time in 1994-95. When the RFL looked at their books, they weren't happy with what they saw and to go a stage further, they'd have still had to treble their wage bill. There was the News Corporation money, but they still had to put more of their own in and there was no significant benefactor to convince the rugby league authorities. But what the RFL did still set a dangerous precedent. The vibe it sent out was before long Super League would be a closed shop. It was as if people who were running the top clubs were running the game. It sent the wrong messages out and it was the beginning of the end for lower-division clubs with ambitions."

"It was all politics," said Widnes fullback Stuart Spruce a few years later. "If you had said to Widnes 'you have to finish in a certain position to get into Super League', they would have done." On 26 May, Widnes lost their court battle against the RFL and faced costs of around £50,000. Mr Justice Jonathan Parker concluded that the 30 April vote of 32-1 in favour of the latest proposals was indicative of the overwhelming wish of rugby league.

Once the merger controversy had dispersed, it was the move to summer that probably created the most interest. The issue had been debated for years. The Rugby Leaguer newspaper had splashed the debate on their front page in an issue as far back as March 1979, with the chief executive of the Rugby Football League, David Oxley, quoted as describing the idea as a "certain recipe for swift and certain disaster." The writer of the article, David Hodgkinson, didn't seem too keen either, saying: "Summer rugby - just a lot of hot air, blowing fast and furious and blowing nowhere. The great debate leaves me cold. And in the end it will come to nothing."

The Leaguer eventually had some competition in 1990 when League Express was first published, a newspaper which regularly campaigned for a move to summer and when it finally happened, there were plenty of other media members delighted with the news. More importantly, it was reported that the players were overwhelmingly in favour of the move.

According to an RFL report entitled 'Summer Rugby', there were seven principal benefits of changing the time of the year that rugby league in Britain was played. They were:

1. Climate - 37 matches had fallen victim to adverse weather in the 1992-93 season.
2. Travel - teams and their supporters could travel to and from matches in daylight.
3. Marketing - pre-match entertainment could be fully embraced in better weather.
4. Upkeep of playing surfaces - it was believed that a better standard of play would result from firmer pitches.
5. No competition from soccer and rugby union for the summer months.
6. Income streams - better pre- and post-match entertainment will result in people spending more in club shops and bars.
7. International competition - the alignment of the English and Australian seasons will help restructure international competitions.

Just as summer rugby was accepted by most - although there were dissenters - what had not been in doubt was the fact that British rugby league was in dire need of money. A document called Framing the Future, written by Bradford-based sports marketing company GSM following a 12-month survey, had been published on 30 August 1994, and it painted a bleak picture. Only four of the sixteen top-flight clubs were profitable with many in severe financial difficulties. The report made several recommendations, with the game's public affairs executive, Harry Gration, warning: "If we don't have the courage to take those decisions there will, I'm convinced, be moves to form a breakaway league." On the other hand, the Highfield chairman Geoff Fletcher said: "The problem in rugby league has been caused by overspending but now they are proposing to kick the smaller clubs out to make us pay for their mistakes."

The Rugby Football League's board of directors was charged with three points:

1. To create a 'Premier League' with an agreed number of clubs and the intention of maximising the marketing and commercial potential of the top flight - not least by increasing their share of central distributions.
2. To create a minimum-standards charter, to decide the criteria by which clubs would qualify or otherwise for promotion into the Premier League - this charter to include factors such as ground facilities, income generation, attendance record, catchment area, management structure as well as other factors.

3. To research the means by which the central authority can operate an increased financial control over clubs, with the especial aim of regulating overspending within the shortest possible period of time.

Maurice Lindsay talked openly about mergers, seven months before he put them on the table so emphatically. "We have two options," he said. "Either we can do nothing and stay where we are which I don't think is an option, or we can look at our game and its structure and make changes. Clubs two miles apart are killing each other with financial pressures. Do we have to stick with tradition all the way?"

In January 1996 the document was updated, dictating the following:

1 Stadia were to have a minimum capacity of 10,000 with 6,000 under cover and 2,500 seats.

2 Clubs were to appoint: a chief executive, a football manager, a media & marketing manager, a commercial manager, an Academy youth development manager and the relevant medical staff.

3 Half of the News Corporation funds were to be spent on facility development, until minimum standards for grounds were met.

4 A salary cap of 40 per cent was to be introduced from 1 January 1997.

Minimum standards suggested improvements to many grandstands, terraces, floodlights, public-address systems, disabled facilities, media facilities, dressing rooms, scoreboards and toilet facilities, as well as the implementation of crèches and first-aid points. It also stated that clubs should be able to provide hospitality boxes that would house 500 people, and there should be at least twenty computerised turnstiles at each ground.

Many of the required stadia improvements were necessary in the wake of the Valley Parade and Hillsborough tragedies in 1985 and 1989 that had claimed 152 lives between them. The subsequent reports into those disasters - The Popplewell Inquiry and The Taylor Report - demanded numerous health-and-safety measures, and impacted on rugby league's finances.

Ian McCartney also said in that 1995 Commons debate: "It is an outrage that the Taylor report has bankrupted the game of rugby league. As a result of horrific incidents that took place in soccer, there was a need to change the law in Britain to make sporting stadiums safer. We all supported that. The report also covered rugby league, but no resources were given to bring its clubs up to the standards set out in that report. In the intervening years, football has received £130 million ... Until a few weeks ago, rugby league had been given a paltry £2 million. Yet the accumulated debt of the sport as a whole is less than the cost of implementing the report. That left rugby league unable to resist the way in which the Murdoch organisation moved in."

With so much money offered by News Corporation, it was little wonder that the RFL snapped their hands off.

With the 1994-95 season ending in May and Super League not due to kick off until March 1996, an interim season was required to plug the gap. It also happened to be the sport's centenary, and so 100 years was 'celebrated' with one of the strangest seasons in the game's history, as rugby league limped into its new beginning.

When the fixtures were announced, there was widespread surprise that the eleven sides - Paris weren't ready to start until Super League kicked off - would play each other twice, thus cramming a full season, albeit with five fewer teams, into just four months. The 1995-96 Stones Bitter Centenary Championship kicked off at Derwent Park in Workington and a crowd of 5,960 crowd, entertained by a Queen tribute band before the game, watched Wigan beat Town 48-6. On 1 October, the domestic season went into hiatus for a month so that the World Cup could be played. It started again on 1 November and ended on 21 January. A full Regal Trophy competition - the last ever - was also squeezed in, with the final on 13 January.

In short, the players were flogged, often playing twice a week. The 1996 Challenge Cup began in February, meaning that the players enjoyed no real off-season, or pre-season preparation for the big Super League kick-off. Rugby league would be rebranding and relaunching in March 1996, with dozens of fatigued players in the spotlight. The Wigan squad, in particular, having had most of their players in the World Cup and having won the final winter Championship and the Regal Trophy, in hindsight, must have been on their last legs. And so it was proved as they travelled to Salford for a fifth-round Challenge Cup tie against the Centenary Division One champions, who were coached by Wigan legend Andy Gregory. They also fielded ex-Wigan players Scott Naylor, Scott Martin, Sam Panapa and, most intriguingly of all, Steve Hampson, who had been unceremoniously dumped by Wigan just months short of his ten-year service mark, which would have seen him awarded a lucrative testimonial.

Gregory was confident enough to predict his team would come up trumps and Welsh prop David Young, the man of the match, opened the scoring in the fourth minute by touching down Mark Lee's grubber. Naylor then sent the Red Devils into dreamland by doubling the lead just before the half-hour mark and the hosts produced a wonderful effort in the second half to win 26-16 in front of 10,048 spectators and send shockwaves through the world of rugby league. "We've worked hard all season and this is one of my finest moments. Everybody kept talking about this Wigan run but it had to come to an end sometime," said Gregory, who had played in the first five of those eight Cup-winning sides.

It was the first Challenge Cup tie Wigan had lost since 1987, when they were surprisingly beaten at the Watersheddings by Oldham, and they were widely predicted to struggle without what had become a large annual income. As for the bigger picture, it was probably the most defining club match that took place anywhere in the world in the time period that this book covers. 11 February 1996 was the day that the great Wigan team lost its invincibility.

Another historic event occurred in the 1995-96 season, and that was rugby union finally becoming a fully professional sport. Whilst it was common knowledge that their players had been paid many years, in what was known as shamateurism, the knock-on effect for rugby league was that union would now accept league players into their sport. It was likely that many ex-union players would return to their first code, and that rugby league clubs would struggle to entice players from the 15-man game. Reckless spending on players who had never tasted rugby league would cease. Failures like Terry Holmes and John Gallagher would no longer be a huge drain on league resources, while even many of those deemed to be a success cost a fortune and left clubs like Widnes, Wigan and Leeds feeling the pinch as rugby league entered its new dawn. On the other hand, the increased profile and crowds that resulted from signings like those of Jonathan Davies and Va'aiga Tuigamala were gone for good.

In so many ways, everything was changing and that was demonstrated in no better way than the fact that the new rugby league season was kicking off not just in March, but in Paris.

CHAPTER FIVE
THE SUPER LEAGUE YEARS

"Some reporters came for a funeral and had to write about a party."
- *Rugby Football League chief executive, Maurice Lindsay, 1996.*

Maurice Lindsay's reaction to Super League's glorious opening night on the banks of the Seine remains one of the most apt quotes of rugby league's summer era. Paris St Germain, the club whose Super League existence so many people questioned - and rightly so, as time would prove - had just beaten Sheffield Eagles, who had ended the last winter season in such fine form, in front of a crowd 17,873, which had wildly exceeded expectations. Paris fielded plenty of French internationals and in their giant Polish prop and playing in squad number four, Gregory Kacala, had an eye-catching figure who represented much of the game's ambitious expansion plans for Super League franchises further afield than France.

In contrast, the second night of Super League was a stark reminder that the game still had a long way to go - the match in Paris had sounded a few alarm bells but, amid the optimism, no-one could hear them. Oldham v Wigan demonstrated at least three things: firstly, that the lower teams were miles away from the top sides as Wigan racked up a half-century of points; secondly, that in the Bears' homely but ramshackle Watersheddings, a few of the competition's stadia were woefully inadequate; and thirdly, in the pre-match stakes, a dubious Tina Turner impressionist represented many of the clubs' half-hearted efforts in the marketing department - although a half-time pillow fight at Halifax was to take the biscuit on that score later in the season. The other interesting result in round one was Warrington's 22-18 win at Headingley. Wire, as they were still known, went on to put the dark days of January 1996, when they lost a Regal Trophy semi-final 80-0 to St Helens, behind them, but Leeds endured a terrible season and were close to being sucked into a relegation battle with Paris and Workington Town. The club's days of spend, spend, spend had finally caught up with them and their rookie coach Dean Bell was left badly exposed.

For most of the season, though, the focus was at the top end of the competition. In the post-1998 era of play-off football, it is easily forgotten just how exciting a first-past-the-post title race could be. Wigan and especially St Helens approached almost every game in 1996 like it was a Cup Final, and rugby league supporters were royally entertained by their fight for Super League. The sight of Bobbie Goulding, the Saints captain, firing up his troops behind the posts for one last hurrah before they nicked another game in the closing stages, became an enduring image of the season. The crucial games in the 1996 league season included St Helens laying down an early marker by beating Wigan on Good Friday 41-26, with new Australian signing Derek McVey producing a magnificent display. When Martin Hall strolled in unopposed for an all-too-easy try to put Wigan 16-4 up, it was microcosmic of their decade-long dominance that didn't look like ending anytime soon. The Super League concept needed St Helens to hit back, and they did that emphatically in a game that had 'Made in England' stamped all over it, with wonderful attacking skills executed at pace, amid questionable defence. Paris v Sheffield is the Super League launch that everybody remembers, but St Helens' victory over Wigan six days later was far more representative of what lay ahead. They wouldn't have admitted it, but Super League officials and Sky must have been delighted with the outcome.

Another side contributed heavily to the quality of the competition both on and off the field, and their presence at the top table was as unexpected as it was welcomed. Bradford Bulls kicked off their season with a 10,027 crowd, an increase of nearly 7,000 on their last league game at Odsal two months earlier. They invested £150,000 of their first News Corporation instalment into a wonderfully successful marketing campaign headed by Peter Deakin, who wasn't a marketing graduate but a former policeman who once told how he would spend his time on the beat in Brighouse, on a quiet shift, thinking how he would improve his beloved sport should he ever get the chance. Under the guidance of a first-rate coaching team in Brian Smith, Matthew Elliott and Brian Noble, the Bulls were good enough to hammer Leeds in the Cup semi-final and get to Wembley, where they narrowly lost one of the great Cup Finals to St Helens, although in hat-trick scorer Robbie Paul they had the afternoon's outstanding player. They finished in third place in Super League, beating Saints and Wigan in a memorable eight-day spell in July.

After that Saints defeat, Wigan had won eight on the bounce (and had also trounced Bath RUFC at rugby league before losing at union by a much smaller margin at Twickenham), before entertaining London Broncos in early June. London were the competition's other expansionary gamble and enjoyed an excellent campaign with some promising home crowds. They frustrated Wigan and although they found themselves 18-4 down just after half-time, they forced their way back into the game and Graham Strutton's late try left Terry Matterson with the unenviable task of having to kick a touchline conversion to snatch a draw. To the delight of everybody on the other side of Billinge Hill, the toe-ended kicker popped it over and it proved to be the kick that cost the cherry and whites the title.

St Helens had to beat Warrington in the final match of the season to lift the Super League trophy. The Wire had come so close to beating Saints on their own patch in May, losing 25-24 and they had enjoyed a commendable season, but any hope they could do Wigan the ultimate favour was soon blown away as Saints scored in the first minute and hammered them 66-14, with Alan Hunte scoring a hat-trick. Having already triumphed at Wembley, the club were no longer the bridesmaids. The key, perhaps, was the signing of Paul Newlove halfway through the Centenary Championship season. Newlove scored 28 Super League tries in twenty games and set up several more for his wing partner, Anthony Sullivan, in a three-quarter partnership which would terrorise Super League defences for years. St Helens were worthy champions.

Wigan's downfall was far from spectacular at first, although that would change. They still boasted an excellent team in 1996 and were good enough to hammer Saints at Old Trafford to win the Premiership Trophy. Chinks in the armour had been evident when their eight-year grip on the Challenge Cup was finally loosened in February by Salford, and their failure to get to Wembley meant a large regular financial income was lost, which led them to sell Martin Offiah to London. From there, things got steadily worse. Their recruitment for 1997 remains possibly the worst by any big club in Super League history. From overseas, in came the unheralded David 'Doc' Murray, Paul Koloi and Stuart Lester - who were all flops - while £30,000 was paid to Oldham for Ian Sherratt who didn't manage to play for Wigan, £70,000 went to Workington Town for Stephen Holgate and, most baffling of all, Lee Hansen came in from Widnes in a swap deal for young playmaker Sean Long - a decision which would haunt Wigan for more than a decade. After a humiliating Challenge Cup defeat to a twelve-man St Helens, Shaun Edwards and Va'aiga Tuigamala didn't play for the club again while coach Graeme West was sacked soon after ,with Eric Hughes taking over.

In what would prove to be an annus horribilis for the club, the club's downfall was now accelerating, but most embarrassingly of all, chairman Jack Robinson found himself in court accused of perverting the course of justice. Prior to that Cup defeat to Salford a year earlier, several Wigan players had gone on holiday and the Wigan Observer reported that several of them were drinking to excess and named Neil Cowie as one of the culprits. Cowie, however, was on a different holiday and it was subsequently alleged that Robinson and fellow director John Martin (Cowie's father-in-law) attempted to profit from the situation by making out that Leeds had been interested in signing the prop for £150,000, only to pull out when they read the story. Wigan would then attempt to sue the paper and split any financial gain with Leeds. But the Loiners' chief executive Alf Davies refused to get involved and although Robinson admitted making him the offer, he was found not guilty of the charges brought against him. The whole episode was enormously embarrassing for the Wigan club and Robinson eventually left the club in August after a home defeat to Salford.

The Sky cameras chose the right venue to kick off the 1997 season - Odsal, where Bradford entertained Warrington. A 58-20 win wouldn't have pleased the purists but it was emblematic of the season the Bulls would go on to have. Robbie Paul stole the show with a fabulous hat-trick while the 15,017-strong crowd - most of whom were given a carton of Super League milk at the turnstile! - knew they were witnessing the start of something special. The Wolves, on the other hand, were sent back to the drawing board and one of their big-name, pre-season recruits, the former Great Britain hooker Martin Dermott, didn't play for the club again. Nor did Iestyn Harris, who had been transfer-listed at an eye-watering £1.35 million and forced to train on his own in the middle of the night. It seemed he would go to St Helens, but ended up at Leeds to help launch the Gary Hetherington era.

In the early stages it was Saints who kept pace with the Bulls, but they lost an astonishing match at a rejuvenated Leeds, who were giving Harris his first start. Trailing by five points, Bobbie Goulding, who had received torrents of abuse from the Leeds fans all night, scored next to the posts with just a couple of minutes to go. A simple conversion would win the game, but he slapped it against the upright with the South Stand just about exploding with euphoria. In the league, Saints were never quite the same. Their impregnability seemed to vanish that night and later in the season lost 65-12 at home to Wigan. Wigan, despite that result, just didn't get going in 1997 as their pre-season had been badly disrupted by a number of their top players - Va'aiga Tuigamala, Gary Connolly, Henry Paul and Jason Robinson - playing rugby union on short-term contracts and when they played St Helens in the Challenge Cup in their first competitive fixture, a few, in particular an out-of-shape Tuigamala, were off the pace. The Warriors regularly lost games and were never in the title hunt.

That Cup match at Knowsley Road produced one of the talking points of the season which, inadvertently, resulted in a great Super League career being launched. Neil Cowie, in bringing the ball out of defence, was poleaxed by a reckless high tackle from Goulding, who was sent off - although Saints went on to win with surprising ease. Goulding was banned for six games, paving the way for a skinny eighteen-year-old halfback by the name of Lee Briers to make his first-team debut. Briers helped Saints get back to Wembley but after Goulding returned, he was sold to Warrington where he has since remained. At Wembley, Saints beat Bradford again, this time 32-22 with Tommy Martyn winning the Lance Todd Trophy. Ten days later, Martyn's season was over as he was injured on Ireland duty in France, a game in which he also scored twice and was named man of the match. Without him, Saints struggled.

The Bulls hit back as impressively as they possibly could and eight days later, in front of a huge crowd, they hammered the Saints in Super League and went on to win their first 20 games in order to secure the title with little opposition from the rest of the field. Strangely, though, they were poor in the other competitions, losing every match in the World Club Championship and bowing out of the end-of-season Premiership play-offs at home to eighth-placed Castleford. For the second year in a row, that competition was won by Wigan at Old Trafford against St Helens.

1997 is the year that the Northern Hemisphere teams were humiliated by their Australian counterparts in that hugely ambitious World Club Championship, which involved Super League clubs on both sides of the world - this was the year that the Super League and the ARL's Optus Cup ran independently of each other in Australia. With routine thrashings every weekend, the occasional European win was celebrated like an Ashes victory, even though they were few and far between. The questionable format, which guaranteed the presence of four teams from each competition in the quarter-finals, meant that St Helens and Bradford qualified without winning a group match whereas Penrith Panthers were eliminated having won all six of their games. Only Wigan - who had earlier completed an impressive double over Canterbury - were competitive in their last-eight game going down to Aussie new boys Hunter Mariners. The Mariners, coached by future Leeds coach Graham Murray, reached the final but were beaten 36-12 by Brisbane Broncos. The competition damaged the Super League brand in Australia, and their strategy of boasting that they, unlike the ARL, could offer their players international competition had been badly undermined by the Northern Hemishpere clubs' lack of ability.

The season was to be the last in Paris's brief history. After their glorious beginning, it was quickly apparent that the club had no foundations, no structure and no money. Players were still playing in the French domestic competition as well as turning out in Super League, giving them the horrendous schedule of three or even four games a week in 1996. In their second year, many were prevented from playing by the French clubs, much to Maurice Lindsay's ire, and Paris became a club stacked with unheralded Australian players, living for most of the year in a hotel outside Paris and using tourist visas, instead of working visas. In both seasons they came second bottom, with Workington Town and Oldham Bears respectively relegated, but the decision was taken to put the Parisians on a two-year sabbatical, which apparently meant they would reappear in the future, being replaced by Huddersfield. Paris were a two-year shambles played out before a background of chaos, but had the club been managed properly and been based in the south of the country, things would have been so different, as Catalan Dragons were later to prove.

For the 1998 season, rugby league introduced its salary cap, which is now regarded as something which helps to even up playing standards, but originally it was introduced to save clubs from their own reckless spending.

In the spring of 1997, Wigan had agreed to sell their Central Park home to Tesco for £12 million, despite local businessman Dave Whelan wanting to buy it. A look at the Wigan accounts in 1996 and 1997 demonstrate just why they had to sell. From a turnover of £5,545,560 in 1996, they had paid out £4,241,718 in wages, salaries and national insurance en route to a total financial loss for the year of £356,355. Although they successfully got the wage bill down in 1997 to just £2,526,541, their turnover had also fallen to £3,432,277 - due to gate and sponsorship income more than halving - and after other expenditure had been factored in, they had made an annual loss of £1,112,964. Over a fifteen-year period, the salary cap has reined in clubs overspending on wages to the extent that no club can spend more than £1.65 million on wages (before various add-ons which are comparatively small). Wigan's near-suicidal spending of 1996 is now not possible.

Despite the embarrassment of the 1997 World Club Championship, the major advantage of the competition was that it drove home just how far behind the Australian clubs the British were, and 1998 saw a significant improvement in the areas that the Australian teams prided themselves on - fitness and defence. Leading the way were Wigan and Leeds, who had finished fourth and fifth in 1997. Both had new coaches from Australia with John Monie returning to Central Park and Graham Murray joining Leeds. The two sides dominated the Super League scene, and played out four matches of the sort of intensity that the British game had not seen for some time. Leeds had set the tone when beating champions Bradford at Odsal in round two with a brutal display of forward power and, in Adrian Morley and Darren Fleary, they had at least two players hell bent on legitimately hurting the opposition with their aggressive style of defence.

Leeds had strengthened from their nightmare 1996 by bringing in a group of steady players. Their Australian signings for 1997 were Wayne Collins, Damian Gibson, Jamie Mathiou and Martin Masella, four players who were miles off representative standards back home, but all of whom came to England with a point to prove and did an admirable job. A year later, Brad Godden and Marc Glanville, better players, were signed, but were still not regular representative players. From Sheffield came Andy Hay, Ryan Sheridan, Dean Lawford and Anthony Farrell and from Keighley, Darren Fleary and Daryl Powell, whose best days had appeared to be behind him, but who went on to do a great job at Headingley. To that solid and unspectacular base, Leeds added one matchwinner, Iestyn Harris, and his spellbinding individual performances were the hallmark of Murray's time at the club. He was the outstanding talent in the British game and walked off with all of the game's individual awards in 1998 with no-one questioning any of them.

By contrast, Wigan rebuilt from their awful 1997 by dusting off the chequebook and, despite their financial problems, they brought Denis Betts home on a sizeable deal, and added some real quality from Australia in Danny Moore and Robbie McCormack. They cleared out the substandard players who had clogged up their 1997 squad, and put together a great side that only lost two league matches all season. In Jason Robinson, Gary Connolly, Kris Radlinski and Andy Farrell, they still had a nucleus of players who had experienced some of the glory years.

One of the defeats was in the first game of the Leeds-Wigan quartet which finished 16-8 to Leeds in front of a capacity 18,000 fans at Headingley in May with Andy Hay scoring the clinching try in an enthralling match. The bar was set even higher at Wigan in August. From the opening kick-off McCormack was left dazed after a challenge from Adrian Morley and had to leave the field. Morley was the victim of subsequent retribution from Mick Cassidy who, uncharacteristically, smashed his forearm into the face of the Leeds youngster who was sprinting at full tilt towards him. It was reminiscent of Les Boyd's ugly challenge on Darryl Brohman in a 1983 State of Origin match for which Boyd was banned for twelve months, but Cassidy received just a six-week suspension, allowing him to return for the Grand Final. Amazingly, Morley returned to the field with one eye shut and Leeds, easily the better team on the night, wrapped up a 15-8 win with a superb try from their centre Brad Godden. In the second week of the Super League play-offs, which had been introduced for the first time, the soon-to-be-crowned Young Player of the Year, Lee Gilmour, stole the show by scoring a long-range try for Wigan as they turned the tables on Leeds with a 17-4 victory, but it was rather immaterial as the two sides were to meet again in the Old Trafford Grand Final. On that occasion, the two sides produced a low-scoring match with aggressive defence the recurring theme in a game that reminded many of the low-scoring mid-1980s Winfield Cup Grand Finals in Australia. Other than Richie Blackmore's first-half try, Leeds couldn't convert their promising early field position into points and were punished as Jason Robinson found the tiniest of holes in their defence on the stroke of half-time to give Wigan a 6-4 lead, before two second-half Andy Farrell penalties won the trophy for Wigan. The inaugural Grand Final had been deemed a success with 43,553 people turning up in atrocious weather to watch a quite superb match.

The real heroes of the season were Sheffield Eagles. Having beaten Leigh and Cumbrian amateurs Egremont, they found themselves in the Challenge Cup quarter-finals, drawn away at Castleford, the club whom the Eagles coach, John Kear, had represented as a player. The Tigers had beaten Leeds and Bradford so were justifiable favourites, but failed to get on top of the visitors who led 16-8 at half-time. Barrie-Jon Mather's second try got them back into it, but he was inexplicably flattened by a wild punch from Keith Senior and could play no further part in the game - the crowd were incensed when Senior was allowed to remain on the pitch. Ironically, it was Senior who scored two late tries to seal his side's passage to the semi-finals, which was unchartered territory for a club who had only been in existence since 1984 and who had spent a significant portion of their time in the lower divisions.

They drew Salford, who were coached by the former Wigan and Great Britain scrum-half, Andy Gregory, in the semi-final at Headingley. Again, the Eagles were underdogs, and this time found themselves 18-10 behind with just twelve minutes to play, but a Mark Aston try closed the gap and when Dale Laughton barged over three minutes later, it sparked wild scenes of jubilation among the Eagles fraternity. They managed to hold on for the final nine minutes as the final hooter drew a close on a remarkable game of rugby league, although, sadly, Stuart Cummings, the referee, was assaulted by a disgruntled supporter at the end of the match.

Few gave the Eagles a chance at Wembley, with almost everybody writing them off as Kear remembered later: "Paul Broadbent and myself went down to London for the press conference in the week of the final. Phil Clarke, Wigan's chief executive, and Andy Farrell were there too. Nobody asked Paul and I any questions apart from whether we wanted tea or coffee when we got there. The journalists asked Andy and Phil all the questions, wanting to know was how many Wigan were going to win by and what it would do for their club." Famously though, the Eagles limited Wigan to just one try, and scored three of their own as they pulled off a 17-8 victory. "The final was a sensational performance. It was 33 minutes before we made an error and we were 10-2 up by then," said Kear. Nick Pinkney, Matt Crowther and Darren Turner scored the tries with scrum-half Mark Aston being awarded the Lance Todd Trophy.

Eighteen months later, the Eagles weren't even in Super League. They were effectively taken over by Huddersfield Giants, in what was passed off as a merger. The Giants had struggled badly since coming into Super League at the expense of Paris for the start of 1998. With relegation scrapped, they finished bottom in their first three years with high-profile names in the coaching job like Garry Schofield, Malcolm Reilly and then Kear himself with the merged club in 2000, all struggling to make an impact. They were finally relegated in 2001 when they came last again and bounced back a competitive side in 2003. Back at Sheffield, Kear had seen the writing on the wall after Wembley:

"The big realisation for me that we were still struggling to make an impact was when we came back for the civic reception and I compared it to Cas in 1986 when there were thousands and thousands of people lining the streets. Sadly, in Sheffield that day there were hardly any people there. The council paid lip service to it, without realising the significance of what we'd done. I knew that if people didn't acknowledge our Cup win then we were going to struggle."

After a disappointing 1998, both Bradford Bulls and St Helens were much improved in 1999 and in the case of the latter, it was largely down to the coaching appointment of one of the most famous names in the game. Ellery Hanley had ended his magnificent playing career with Balmain Tigers and, having already coached Great Britain, he was seen as a big coup for Saints. With Bobbie Goulding gone - sacked after an unsavoury incident after an on-the-road game in Wales in 1998 - the team was rebuilt around its formidable playmakers Tommy Martyn, Sean Long, Keiron Cunningham and Paul Sculthorpe, who had joined in a big-money deal from Warrington a year earlier. They started the season with thirteen wins from their first fourteen Super League games but lost their way as the regular-round season came to an end. Their place at the summit was taken by the Bulls, who had bounced back superbly from a Challenge Cup semi-final defeat at the hands of Leeds, and who lost just four of 30 regular-season matches.

Both clubs benefited from Wigan and Leeds falling away from the standards they had set twelve months earlier. From their Grand Final team, Wigan lost Henry Paul to Bradford and replaced him with Greg Florimo, but the North

Sydney Bears legend failed to settle. And at hooker, Robbie McCormack, who had enjoyed a fabulous 1998, was replaced by Florimo's mate, Mark Reber, who just wasn't in the same class. The Warriors occupied fourth place for much of the year and exited the play-offs in week one at home to Castleford, although they enjoyed a wonderful highlight in beating St Helens 28-20 in the final match ever to be staged at their iconic Central Park home, with legends from the glory days, Denis Betts and Jason Robinson, putting in superb performances. Financial pressures, accrued from their reckless spending, had led the club to sell their home to Tesco for £12 million in 1997, although they remained in place for two more full seasons before moving to the JJB Stadium at Robin Park.

St Helens were hammered 40-4 at Bradford in the play-offs, and with the Bulls having won the Minor Premiership by five points, most seemed to think that their coronation in Manchester was a mere formality. Hanley's men, however, having beaten Castleford to reach the final, turned in a superb defensive performance and Bradford were unable to convert a handful of clean breaks. Henry Paul's first-half try had given them a 6-2 lead, but their inability to put the game to bed bit hard - although they were blameful of the video referee's decision to rule out a second-half try for an apparent knock on. Kevin Iro's late try, converted by Sean Long, left them heartbroken as they lost 8-6.

The first trophy of the season had been joyously picked up by Leeds in the last Challenge Cup Final at the old Wembley. Having beaten Wigan in the fourth round, when handicapped by the first-half sending off Barrie McDermott, they beat St Helens, Widnes and lastly Bradford in a tremendous semi-final en route to the Twin Towers. There they met an emotionally charged London Broncos, who had beaten Castleford in the most enthralling semi-final for years. Steele Retchless's last-gasp try remains one of the Cup's greatest moments, but on the biggest stage of all, they were too weakened by injuries to be a realistic chance of winning. They did, however, lead early in the second half before McDermott's try gave the Rhinos the lead. Leroy Rivett ended up with four tries and Leeds won 52-16. As with Sheffield, the prediction that an appearance on the big stage would kick start big interest in the club failed to come true. Ever since, they have failed to scale the heights of their first four summer seasons, on and off the pitch.

Gateshead Thunder were the other outpost story in 1999 and, again, a decent start was totally undermined by poor management. Thunder made a reasonable local impact with some promising crowds and finished sixth out of fourteen in their debut season but, the end-of-season news that they were to 'merge' with Hull FC signalled the end of the Super League dream in the north-east. The club had been much more stable than Paris so few people saw their demise coming. If was good for Hull though, who were sidelined for the first two years of Super League before finishing fourth bottom and second bottom in 1998 and 1999. This gave them the standard of player to help bring some enthusiasm back to the Boulevard, and from 2000, Hull would be a threat again.

Bradford, Saints and Wigan were far too good for the rest in 2000, with the Bulls, red-hot for most of the season, taking the Challenge Cup, Wigan winning the Minor Premiership and St Helens successfully defending their Super League title at Old Trafford against the Warriors.

The season started in the most controversial fashion for Saints, who sacked their coach Ellery Hanley after just one Super League match - a 32-10 home defeat to Bradford. They had also lost heavily to Melbourne Storm in the World Club Challenge and gone out of the Challenge Cup to holders Leeds, in a humdinger of a match settled by Adrian Morley's late try. But it was off-field issues that stretched back into the 1999 season that did for Hanley. Back then he had been suspended by the club after an interview he did with Total Rugby League newspaper in which he accused the club's directors of being 'ignorant' and 'disgraceful'. An uneasy truce was reached but the cracks resurfaced in March 2000 and the club sacked him for breach of contract, citing the fact that he failed to attend the official Super League launch, he made comments at a sponsors' lunch that harmed the reputation of the club, and that he refused to give an interview with BBC television before the Cup match at Leeds. The fall-out from the sacking was enormous, and it became one of the biggest sensations in Super League's brief history, but Saints moved on to even greater success by appointing Leigh's Australian coach, Ian Millward. Little was known about him at first, but that would change over the course of the year.

Leeds started poorly as they struggled to deal with the departure of Graham Murray. In came another Australian in Dean Lance, who failed to replicate Murray's quiet authority in the role. The club lost their first five Super League games, before losing in the Challenge Cup Final to Bradford at Murrayfield. Their Super League form turned round but their season ended with winger Paul Sterling taking the club to an industrial tribunal, claiming racial discrimination. Lance was found guilty of unconscious racism and it was decided that the club had not investigated Sterling's allegations properly. They were hammered at Bradford in the play-offs, and parted company with Adrian Morley, who left for Sydney Roosters. In just a year, it looked like much of Murray's good work had been unpicked.

St Helens entered the play-offs on a humiliating note after a 42-4 home defeat to Wigan, which had been a Minor Premiership decider. A week later they trailed Bradford 11-10 in a play-off match at Knowsley Road when the hooter went, but they kept the ball alive to score the most famous try in domestic football's modern history. The try, which became known as "Wide to West" due to the wonderful commentary of Eddie Hemmings on Sky Sports, saw the ball travel from one side of the field and back again before Dwayne West broke down the left touchline and found his captain Chris Joynt on his inside, who went over for the winning try to leave the Bulls stunned. They were still in the competition but after such a great start to the season were a broken team and were duly hammered at Wigan a week before the Grand Final.

Saints were favourites to retain the title, largely on account of a 54-16 play-off win at the JJB Stadium, which was now Wigan's home, and they were too good for the Warriors again at Old Trafford, winning 29-16 with man-of-the-match Joynt scoring twice. Unlike the two which had preceded it, this Grand Final was quite high-scoring. Two Wigan tries around the three-quarter mark of the game reduced a 17-4 deficit to just one point, but Saints found the resolve to pull clear again and finally emerge in a breathtaking game.

After the terribly disappointing 2000 World Cup, British rugby league badly needed a pick-me-up and St Helens provided it when they beat Brisbane Broncos on a memorable night in Bolton to win the World Club Challenge. Not only did they breathe some much-needed life back into the credibility of the British game, they helped cement the World Club Challenge as an annual event. It had lacked a consistent format and had St Helens been beaten by Brisbane, in the manner they were beaten by Melbourne twelve months earlier, the concept may have been scrapped. 18-6 down in the second half, Saints roared back with Sean Long and Chris Joynt tries adding to Paul Sculthorpe's first-half effort to win 20-18.

Saints carried the momentum into their domestic campaign, and were too clinical for Wigan in the fourth round of the Challenge Cup. They went on to pip Leeds in a thrilling semi-final and in the final met Bradford at Twickenham, prevailing 13-6 in a dull game played in atrocious conditions. Tommy Martyn and Keiron Cunningham scored the tries, with Sean Long winning his first Lance Todd Trophy. But, gunning for a third straight league title, they were badly derailed by Long's season-ending knee injury sustained in a 44-26 win at Huddersfield and limped into fourth place, despite tremendous personal performances over the course of the season from Australian import David Fairleigh and Man of Steel, Paul Sculthorpe. Their season ended miserably, beaten in the play-offs 44-10 at Wigan. Millward's honeymoon was over.

Dusting themselves off after that early-season Cup disappointment at Knowsley Road, Wigan enjoyed an excellent Super League campaign, despite sacking their popular Kiwi coach Frank Endacott after a 31-30 defeat at Salford, which kept up their record of having a different coach in every Super League season - Graeme West, Eric Hughes, John Monie, Andy Goodway, Endacott and his successor, Stuart Raper, whom the club brought in from Castleford. Despite the lack of stability at the top of the organisation, they had assembled a very good team, with Adrian Lam, the crafty Papua New Guinean scrum-half, pulling the strings behind a fearsome pack of forwards. In Kris Radlinski, Brian Carney, Gary Connolly and Steve Renouf, they had no shortage of matchwinners in the backs.

The season, though, belonged to Bradford Bulls. With Brian Noble having taken over from Matty Elliott at the end of 2000, little changed other than they came strong when it mattered late in the season. With their back three Michael Withers, Tevita Vaikona and Lesley Vainikolo so powerful in returning the ball from deep and a quartet of props often called the Awesome Foursome in Brian McDermott, Paul Anderson, Joe Vagana and Stuart Fielden, they were a formidable outfit, especially with wily hooker James Lowes and the multi-talented Paul brothers pulling the strings. They recovered from their Twickenham disappointment to win the Minor Premiership on points difference over Wigan, beating Leeds 62-18 along the way. Having lost twice to Wigan in the last dozen games of the regular season, their play-off encounters were highly anticipated. Bradford won the first at Odsal 24-18 but when they met Wigan in the final, they blew them away with the greatest Grand Final performance to date. A Withers hat-trick helped the Bulls to a 26-0 lead at half-time and they ran out 37-6 winners with Lowes, Fielden and Graham Mackay providing the other four-pointers. Maurice Lindsay, the Wigan chairman, was so incensed with his players that, according to Terry Newton's autobiography, he refused to pay them their end-of-season bonuses.

Without sacking a coach in 2002, Wigan were rewarded with a third-place finish after another respectable and consistent season. Even better than that, they produced one of the great Challenge Cup Final performances to stun the favourites St Helens, their great rivals, in the final at Murrayfield. The story revolved around their international fullback, Kris Radlinski, who was all but ruled out in the days leading up to the game with a foot infection that had hospitalised him. On the morning of the match, having told coach Raper he couldn't play, the club doctor Ansar Zaman had one last go at getting him right, sliced his foot open and squeezed out as much of the infection as he could. Radlinski passed a fitness test and went on to produce a classic fullback display to help his side to a 21-12 win, and was an almost unanimous choice as man of the match.

Saints' preparation for the final was questionable as they fielded a weakened team in a match at world champions Bradford, the aftermath of which dominated their Murrayfield build-up. They were later fined £25,000 for the stunt. Back in Super League, they built steadily for the season's end and, after winning the Minor Premiership on points difference from Bradford, they won the Grand Final against the Bulls in the most dramatic fashion. Paul Deacon and Paul Sculthorpe had missed with late drop goals to break the 18-all deadlock before, in the game's final minute, Sean Long kicked a drop goal. There was more to come. Saints gathered a short kick off and Chris Joynt went to ground - too easily, claimed the Bulls. Their screams for a voluntary tackle were ignored by referee Russell Smith and Saints were champions. Joynt's actions were debated for months, and if anybody could kick a 40-metre penalty from near the touchline, it was the metronomic Deacon.

At the bottom, Super League waved goodbye to relegated Salford who had steadily declined from the excellent progress made under the coaching of Andy Gregory in the mid- to late-1990s. Wakefield only survived by a point, whereas newly promoted Widnes finished a highly credible seventh, earning Neil Kelly the coach-of-the-year title.

2003 saw a welcome return to form for Leeds, under the tutelage of their former player Daryl Powell. Having struggled for consistency since losing Graham Murray, Powell's faith in the club's youth resulted in a move up the Super League table. Kevin Sinfield had become the team's focal point after the departure to rugby union of Iestyn Harris, and around him were fellow club products Rob Burrow, Danny McGuire, Matt Diskin, Chev Walker, Mark Calderwood, Ryan Bailey, Jamie Jones-Buchanan, Richie Mathers and Danny Ward. When the Rhinos did bring in players from outside, they tended now to get it right. David Furner and Matt Adamson were a marked improvement on previous big-name flops like David Barnhill, Bradley Clyde and Brett Mullins, while the signing of 31-year-old Gary Connolly proved to be a masterstroke. Leeds spent all season in the top two, and lost the Challenge Cup Final by just two points, with Sinfield criticised afterwards for turning down a kickable late penalty. Their campaign was turned upside down when Walker and Bailey were sent to a young offenders' institute as a result of a fight in Leeds city centre and they exited the play-offs after a thrilling home semi-final with a Brian Carney-inspired Wigan; but, as a Super League force, Leeds were back.

The season was dominated by the Bulls, who won the Minor Premiership by three points. They were too strong for Leeds in the qualifying semi-final, beating them for the fifth time out of five in 2003, and they then dismantled Wigan at Old Trafford. It wasn't quite as convincing as in 2001, but after Danny Tickle scored the game's first try for Wigan, Bradford were immense, and ended up on the right side of a 25-12 scoreline, with the retiring James Lowes fittingly scoring the final try of the match. Stuart Reardon, who had just celebrated his 22nd birthday, won the Harry Sunderland Trophy as man of the match. Five of

the Bulls regulars were over 30 and they had been written off in pre-season, but they confounded the critics by becoming the first team to win the Challenge Cup and Super League Grand Final in the same season.

After some excellent seasons in Super League, particularly in its early years, Halifax came a cropper in 2003 being relegated with zero points on the board. They did win one match, their opener against London, but were later deducted two points (along with St Helens and Hull) for salary-cap discrepancies. Financial problems had been at the heart of their demise, but since then they have become a formidable club in the division below Super League. Saints endured a miserable 2003, hammered by Sydney Roosters in the World Club Challenge, beaten by Leeds in a thrilling Cup semi-final and off the pace in Super League.

For the first time since 1972, Leeds were crowned champions in 2004. Daryl Powell had provided a suitable platform and when Tony Smith took over after reviving the fortunes of Huddersfield, the players took that final couple of steps. They were top of the league after round one, having beaten London 58-14, and stayed there all season, taking out the Minor Premiership with ease, nine points ahead of Bradford.

The story of the season came, not for the only time in the Super League era, at St Helens. Once again, Ian Millward fielded a weakened team for a trip to Odsal, this time an Easter Monday fixture three days after a gruelling match with Wigan which had ended 21-21 and which had featured a memorable all-in brawl. Against Bradford, who had regained their world-champion crown against Penrith Panthers at the start of the season, Martin Gleeson was one of the few recognisable names in the side, and scored the game's first try before they collapsed to a 54-8 defeat, but it was later revealed that Gleeson and Sean Long, who didn't play, had placed bets on Bradford to win the match, having known before the bookies that Saints were going to be heavily weakened. At June's hearing, Gleeson was banned for four months, meaning that he missed the rest of Saints' season, and Long for three. Without them, the club tumbled from second to fifth and were eliminated from the play-offs at the hands of Wigan. Before their ban, though, they had won the Challenge Cup, beating the Warriors in the final, with Long collecting his second Lance Todd Trophy.

That final centred more around a figure from the losing camp. Mike Gregory had been appointed the Wigan coach in July 2003 and took them to the Grand Final by going undefeated in his first 11 games. 2004 was more of a struggle, amid a mounting injury crisis, but they won through to the Cup Final in Cardiff in mid-May. A week after their semi-final win over Warrington, however, the club announced that Gregory had developed a chronic bacterial condition which would require treatment in America. The Cardiff final was to be his last game before he would depart and tragically he died in November 2007.

A couple of intriguing stories materialised in West Yorkshire in 2004. Firstly, after ten straight defeats from the start of the season, Castleford pulled off what seemed to be a remarkable coup when they unveiled Ellery Hanley, the former Great Britain and St Helens coach, as assistant to Gary Mercer. "Castleford do have some deficiencies that need to be rectified quickly," he said as he arrived on 20 May but he was gone by 6 July and the Tigers went on to be relegated. Another big announcement came from Bradford Bulls when they signed Iestyn Harris, who was returning to the code from Welsh rugby union. But the whole deal was clouded by the fact that Leeds claimed Harris was due to return to them and that they still held his registration. Harris was cleared by the Rugby Football League to play for the Bulls - although an ugly three-way legal fight between the player and the two clubs was only just beginning - and he played a key role in a gritty play-off win over his old side that saw them reach a fourth consecutive Grand Final. The legal wrangle, though, would have huge financial repercussions for Bradford for years to come, and it played a part in their fall from grace in the latter part of the decade.

After Leeds demolished Wigan in the last play-off match, the West Yorkshire sides served up a tight, defensive Grand Final which the Rhinos won 16-8. Matt Diskin won the official man-of-the-match award, but Richie Mathers, from fullback, was also superb. Danny McGuire scored the clinching try, capping a memorable year which had seen him score 39 tries.

Buoyed by such an emotional win, Smith's men continued their good form for the first three-quarters of 2005. They beat Canterbury in the World Club Challenge and hogged the top spot from February until August by producing some quite scintillating rugby. A 42-12 Easter win at Odsal was one of the great summer-era performances and a 70-0 win over a struggling Wigan was the third time in a year and a half that Leeds had won by that score. But, like Bradford in 2000, they had peaked too soon and it was the Bulls who derailed their season at Headingley in August by beating them 42-10, a week before the Challenge Cup Final with Hull. More serious than the score, however, was an ankle injury sustained by the Great Britain centre, Keith Senior, and it was to prove to be the big talking point of Leeds' season. Desperate for him to play in the final they worked on Senior all week and eventually declared him fit, but after enduring an uncomfortable first half, he was withdrawn from the field. By now, Leeds were a shadow of their early-season selves and were second best all afternoon, apart from a ten-minute spell in the second half. Hull deservedly won the Cup with a late Paul Cooke try and Danny Brough conversion, which reminded several people as he lined it up, including the kicker himself, of Don Fox's infamous missed kick from 1968.

Hull's renaissance has been one of Super League's success stories. Initially excluded from Super League on account of failing to finish in the top ten in the 1994-95 season, Hull rebuilt in the lower divisions and won promotion after a splendid 1997. For two years they struggled in the top flight, but were the fortunate recipients of a bizarre merger with Gateshead Thunder. Ultimately it meant that Thunder's squad, who had finished sixth in 1999, became the Hull FC squad. Directors Shane Richardson and Kath Hetherington as well as coach Shaun McRae also moved to Hull and, at the stroke of a pen, the black and whites could again boast a competitive team. They also had good juniors of their own in Paul Cooke and Richard Horne, who blossomed around the Aussie hard-heads from the north-east. 2000 saw the side reach the Challenge Cup semi-final although, unfortunately, a section of supporters embarrassed themselves with a post-match pitch invasion during which a set of goal posts were pushed over. In 2001, the signings of Australian Jason Smith and England international Tony Smith helped elevate them to third, where they also finished in 2004, McRae's last season before John Kear took over.

There was more drama at St Helens where Ian Millward was sensationally dismissed for 'gross misconduct', with three charges of swearing brought against him, including an incident with the club's own media manager. It was reminiscent of the club's decision to sack Ellery Hanley in 2000 where the directors were obviously keen to dispense with the services of someone they perceived to be difficult. Millward ended up at Wigan and in his fourth game in charge lost 70-0 at Leeds - a club record defeat. Embarrassingly that record only stood for eight days as Millward's men lost 75-0 at Knowsley Road in the quarter final of the Challenge Cup. Wigan recovered to win seven of their last ten, but missed out on play-off football.

At the foot of the table sat Leigh Centurions, a club hopelessly out of their depth in the upper echelons of the game. In 2004 they had beaten Whitehaven in a magnificent National League Grand Final, but Tommy Martyn, their playmaker, retired after the game. Their recruitment for Super League was poor and they went on to win just two matches. Their relegation was never in doubt, but, like Halifax, they have since been a threat most years in the second tier. Widnes were also relegated, becoming the only club in Super League history to lose their top-flight status from the second-bottom position. It was desperately sad for the Vikings as it was a one-off arrangement to accommodate new club Catalan Dragons into the 2006 competition.

Keith Senior's injury didn't just cost Leeds the Cup - he failed to appear again for the club in 2005. With momentum shot, they lost three of their next five including the Grand Final to the Bulls, whose own achievement was absolutely remarkable. Thumped 66-4 at home to St Helens in June and beaten 44-34 by Wakefield in July, it appeared that the fifth-placed club was going nowhere, but they picked up a few wins before their impressive August showing at Headingley, and grew as the season went on. They beat the Cup winners Hull 71-0 in the first round of the play-offs and won 23-18 at St Helens to become only the second team from outside the top two to make the Old Trafford decider. The score in the final was 15-6, but they were better than the nine-point margin suggested. Leon Pryce scooped the Harry Sunderland Trophy and joined Jamie Peacock, Paul Johnson, Rob Parker, Robbie Paul and Lee Radford in ending their Bradford careers on the ultimate high. One interesting name among the Bulls Grand Final personnel was Adrian Morley, the Sydney Roosters forward, who had joined the club on a short-term deal on account of the fact that his side had missed out on the NRL play-offs. Newcastle Knights' Andrew Johns and New Zealand Warriors' Sione Faumuina joined Warrington and Hull on similar deals before the loophole was closed for future years, but given the high-profile nature of Johns' move to Cheshire, perhaps blocking future moves wasn't the right decision.

Hull enjoyed another very good season in 2006; in terms of performances and consistency, their best in Super League. They may have ended it trophyless, but they became the first team from outside the traditional top four, which had dominated Super League since its inception, to reach the Super League Grand Final. They did it without John Kear who was dumped by the board after a shaky Super League start and after the Bulls had loosened their grip on the

Challenge Cup. Parramatta' assistant Peter Sharp took the job and, after losing his first game at home to Leeds, won seventeen of his next eighteen games including a thrilling 27-26 win at leaders St Helens. They finished second and beat Bradford in the final eliminator to qualify for Old Trafford.

There they met St Helens. With Paul Wellens winning the Man of Steel, Jamie Lyon still showing that he was one of the world's best centres, Sean Long and Keiron Cunningham as good as ever and James Graham and James Roby well on their way to becoming international-class players, Saints were simply irresistible in 2006. They won the Challenge Cup, beating Huddersfield in the final, and lost only four Super League matches - by a combined total of just ten points. And in one of those games - away to Catalans - they had fielded a weakened side. They beat Hull 12-8 in their first play-off match, before demolishing them in the Grand Final a fortnight later 26-4. Their achievements saw them achieve a memorable double at the BBC TV Sports Personality of the Year ceremony. Daniel Anderson was named coach of the year and the club were named team of the year, attracting 70 per cent of the public vote to Sussex cricket club's twenty and Europe's Ryder Cup's ten, much to the displeasure of the chattering classes.

Despite Saints' heroics, the biggest stories of the year came at the bottom. Catalan Dragons made an encouraging start to life in Super League having been notified of their inclusion to the competition three years earlier, giving them adequate time to prepare - unlike the ill-fated Paris St Germain. They may have come last, but they were good enough to win eight matches - including a wonderful opening day win over Wigan - and they attracted healthy crowds. Their star player and captain, Stacey Jones, missed twelve matches, a statistic which ultimately consigned them to the wooden spoon. However, they were exempt from relegation, with that fate to befall the lowest-placed English club. Unthinkably, for much of the year it looked likely that Wigan could end up relegated as they occupied the bottom rung from April until the start of July. They had sacked Ian Millward after a 40-14 reversal at Wakefield in April and appointed Bradford's Brian Noble, who left the Bulls just two and a half months after guiding them to a third World Club Challenge triumph in five years against Wests Tigers. Noble shelled out big money for Bulls prop Stuart Fielden and, from June, put together a winning run that saw Wigan challenge for a play-off spot although, in the end, they came eighth. The Bulls, on the other hand, went into decline over the coming seasons after losing their coach on the back of so many key players over the previous year.

The other great story at the bottom involved West Yorkshire rivals Wakefield and Castleford. In their first season back in Super League following their 2004 relegation, the Tigers sat on the cusp of a play-off slot after a 31-30 win over Leeds in July. Wakefield, meanwhile, looked doomed to relegation before John Kear came in to take over from the dismissed Tony Smith. In Kear's first game, they won 18-0 at Cas and the great escape was on. They beat Catalans and Bradford in their next four matches to set up a season-ender to match any Grand Final in the tension stakes. With Wakefield enjoying home advantage, they overturned an early deficit to win 29-17 in front of an 11,000-strong crowd to ensure their safety. Castleford, having played so well for much of the season, had to face another season out of the top flight.

2007 was relatively controversy free apart from Wigan plummeting from fourth place to ninth in July courtesy of having four points deducted for a salary-cap transgression, having had two points deducted twelve months earlier as well. They still scraped into the play-offs after beating table-topping St Helens 20-12 in the final round and they became one of the only sides in Super League play-off history to shake things up from one of the lower places. They went to Odsal and trailed third-place Bradford 30-6, before producing a most remarkable comeback in the last 25 minutes to win 31-30 with Mark Calderwood scoring a hat-trick and Pat Richards kicking a late, match-winning drop goal. They then travelled to Hull and won another nailbiter, this time by 21-18, to set up a final eliminator with Leeds Rhinos.

For most of the season, Saints looked on course to replicate their glorious 2006 as they won another Challenge Cup - against Catalan Dragons in the first final to be played at the new Wembley - and they won the Minor Premiership.

The highlight of their campaign had come early on as they beat Wayne Bennett's Brisbane Broncos 18-14 with pre-match injury doubt Paul Sculthorpe coming off the bench to score a crucial try and win man-of-the-match honours. When they beat Leeds 10-8 in a bruising qualifying semi-final, they went into the Grand Final, once again, as big favourites but Jamie Peacock, the Great Britain captain who had joined the Rhinos from the Bulls in 2006, later claimed that he and his teammates had taken great heart from that defeat. Leeds won the forwards battle, with Gareth Ellis and Peacock magnificent, but with strangely subdued performances from halfbacks Rob Burrow and Danny McGuire, were unable to score the points to win the game. After hammering Wigan in the final eliminator, Leeds produced a virtuoso Grand Final display to beat Saints 33-6. Their forwards were just as good again, but this time the playmakers, in particular Harry Sunderland Award winner Burrow, were on song and St Helens had absolutely no answer to the second-half blue-and-amber onslaught. Tony Smith's Leeds reign ended on the perfect high.

The 2008 season was remarkably similar to the campaign that preceded it. The Super League champions won the World Club Challenge - this time Leeds were too good for Melbourne Storm, winning 11-4 on a wet and cold night at Elland Road. Saints won the Cup again, beating Hull in the final at Wembley and after Wigan again made a go of things in the play-offs after another disappointingly inconsistent season, the final two left standing were St Helens and Leeds who again had finished first and second in that order. The champions were now coached by the New Zealander Brian McClennan, one of the game's great motivators who had ended Australia's domination of the international game in 2005 by winning the Tri-Nations for New Zealand. McClennan gave his players a rousing talk the night before the Grand Final and, having again lost at Knowsley Road in the qualifying semi-final, but beaten Wigan at Headingley in the elimination semi-final, Leeds maintained the symmetry with 2007 by beating Saints 24-16 with Lee Smith winning the Harry Sunderland. Twenty-year-old winger, Ryan Hall, one of the few players to have played both National Conference open-age football (with Oulton Raiders) and Super League, scored a memorable try from his own grubber to give his side a valuable six-point lead at the break, before a Danny McGuire double in the second half brought the bacon home.

On 13 October 2008, the league world was stunned to hear that the Wakefield and Cook Islands prop Adam Watene had collapsed during a gym session and had later died. He was 31. The same club suffered another harrowing tragedy on 22 March 2009 when their twenty-year-old second-rower Leon Walker died during a reserve-team match against Celtic Crusaders in Maesteg, as a result of a heart defect. The Super League match between the two sides, scheduled for later that evening, was postponed.

There was more critical focus on Super League than ever before after England's ignominious World Cup campaign which had seen them humiliated at the hands of Australia and New Zealand over three horrible weekends for long-suffering English rugby league fanatics. Between 2000 and 2004, Super League had boasted a 'big five' of Bradford, St Helens, Leeds, Wigan and Hull FC. By 2007 three of those five sides had fallen away, with nobody replacing them in the quality stakes. Super League badly needed a new challenger but it didn't get one in 2009 as, for the third year in a row, the same sides finished first and second, the same sides made the Grand Final and the same side won it. The "best-ever-season boasts", which had always been commonplace on Sky Sports, were beginning to dissipate. The lack of quality at the top of the competition was becoming harder to deny.

Nevertheless, Leeds' achievement of winning three straight Grand Finals was an indication of their remarkable consistency. After their disappointments in 2005 and 2006, they kept faith with the nucleus of their 2004 title-winning side. Jamie Peacock was the notable addition, but in Brent Webb and Danny Buderus, proven Southern Hemisphere internationals were added to the already numerous top-class players in the Rhinos squad. Happily for the English game, Academy players were still on the production line and Ryan Hall, after his moment of glory at Old Trafford in 2008, topped the tryscoring charts with 31 in 29 Super League games. The transition from the thoughtful Smith to the old-school McClennan was seamless and their 18-10 win in the 2009 Grand Final was more convincing than the score suggested.

Fortunately for the competition, Warrington and Wigan put themselves among the leading pack in 2010. Tony Smith had taken over at Warrington in 2009, combining the role with his last year in charge of England. The club had been the big underachievers in the summer era after a promising 1996. A succession of coaches failed to come even close to silverware and the team were in dire straits before Smith became coach. After a difficult start, he guided them to Challenge Cup success when they beat Huddersfield 25-16 in the final. Although they missed the play-offs, their league form improved dramatically in 2010 as they won 20 games from 27 to finish third in the table and they retained the Cup hammering Leeds 30-6 at Wembley. But it was Wigan who impressed the most in 2010. Brian Noble, who had taken them from last place midway through 2006 to a number of semi-finals, didn't have his contract renewed, largely for failing to win any of those semis and, after considerable speculation over who would get the job, with New Zealand's Stephen Kearney claiming he had turned it down, Michael Maguire, the Melbourne Storm assistant coach, became the club's eleventh coach of the summer era.

The Warriors were grateful that he brought with him the lucky charm that new coaches often do in Super League. In 1996, 1997, 1998, 1999, 2000, 2001, 2004 and 2008 the competition had been won by an incoming coach and Maguire became the ninth man to achieve that feat when he led the Warriors to Grand Final success via the Minor Premiership. He introduced some of Melbourne's questionable defensive tactics, which involved wrestling techniques to slow down the opposition's play-the-ball, much to the chagrin of the purists; but no-one at the DW Stadium cared when he delivered their nineteenth league title. On the back of immense forward power was Sam Tomkins, rapidly becoming the Super League's big star, whose move to fullback during the season was a major catalyst in the side's triumph, while Thomas Leuluai, the veteran Paul Deacon and Sean O'Loughlin pulled the strings. Sadly for St Helens, it was they, again, who lost the final, and were on the wrong end of two tries scored by their former centre, Martin Gleeson. For Keiron Cunningham, the long-serving St Helens hooker, it was a unfortunate way to end a trophy-laden career but at least he had the honour of a statue being erected at the club's new ground, Langtree Park.

The saddest news imaginable broke on 26 September 2010 when it emerged that the Wakefield Trinity hooker Terry Newton had been found hanged at his Wigan home. Earlier in the year, the former Great Britain hooker had tested positive for a banned human growth hormone and was suspended for two years. After releasing an autobiography and doing some media interviews, it seemed that he had been successful in getting his life back on track until this desperately sad news filtered through.

Leeds appeared to be in for a difficult 2011 when Brian McClennan decided to head home. In three years he had won the title twice and was only 80 minutes away from a third Old Trafford appearance in 2010. A month after their season ended at Wigan, it was announced that Brian McDermott, who had initially returned to the club to be McClennan's assistant, would take the top job. Few seemed impressed at the appointment - the former Bradford prop had left his role as Leeds assistant coach to take over at Harlequins in July 2006 and had led them to finishes of seventh, ninth, ninth, eleventh and thirteenth. He was best known for his inability to handle the media, something that was no better illustrated than during a post-match press conference after their defeat to Catalans at the 2008 Millennium Magic. Asked what his overriding emotions were after the game, he fired back: "Are you a psychologist? Do you want to ask about the game?" before responding to several questions with: "I have no opinion on that question," and most worryingly saying: "I am asking some questions whether the whole bit of being in London works." He backtracked later, and said: "If you could see what is happening at grassroots level in London, you would be blown away. There's going to be an explosion down here soon." The explosion is yet to happen.

At the Rhinos, he fared little better in his first five months with the club languishing in eighth place after a 38-18 defeat at Catalans in July with many fans demanding he be dismissed, but what occurred after that was the stuff of legend. They lost the Challenge Cup Final to Wigan, but produced a stirring fightback from 16-0 down to be within a score of lifting the Cup before Thomas Leuluai's late try settled the game. They took that moral victory back into Super League and ended the regular season with two wins from two. In the play-offs, they demolished Hull, and won narrowly at Huddersfield and Warrington to book a fourth Old Trafford appointment with St Helens in five seasons. Leeds led 8-2 at half-time against Mick Potter's men but Tom Makinson and Michael Shenton tries in a five-minute spell gave Saints the lead with 25 minutes to play. Leeds hammered away and when Brent Webb scored with quarter of an hour left, the dam opened. Tries by Ryan Hall, Carl Ablett and Zak Hardaker in the last ten minutes gave the score a flattering look of 32-16, but it could not hide the fact that the sides had produced an absolutely pulsating affair. Leeds had pulled off the seemingly impossible and won the competition from outside the top four. McDermott was vindicated, not that he needed to prove anything to anybody within the club. Their loyalty towards him in the tough times had paid off.

Despite that, when the club found themselves outside the play-off places in June 2012 after a shellacking at Warrington, there was just as much pressure on McDermott and his players. Some considered the happenings of October 2011 as a one off and pointed out that for much of his reign, McDermott boasted a winning record of only around 50 per cent. Again, a Challenge Cup run galvanised them and even though Warrington hammered them in the final for the second time in three years, they gained momentum in the play-offs which saw them home. From another fifth-placed finish, they beat Wakefield at home 42-20 with Ben Jones-Bishop posting a hat-trick, then overcame a tricky trip to Perpignan to prevail 27-20 against the Dragons before beating Wigan 13-12 at the DW Stadium with a late Kevin Sinfield penalty goal the difference. Sinfield didn't miss a kick at goal throughout the play-offs and even though they were paired up with Cup-winners and second-placed Warrington in the final few pundits could split them. Richie Myler's fourth-minute score put Leeds on the back foot before both Sinfield and Jones-Bishop hit back. A try late in the first half to Joel Monaghan, Warrington's Australian winger, restored parity at 14-all and when Ryan Atkins scored after five minutes of the second half, the travelling Wolves were jubilant. With Sinfield having taken a serious head knock, Leeds were going to have to do it tough, even though he bravely continued. But as they had done in the 2011 Grand Final and in the 2012 World Club Challenge against Manly who they beat 26-12, Leeds took control in the latter stages of the game with a devastating late blitz that demonstrated their champion class. With three-quarter time approaching, Carl Ablett scored the crucial try before he set up the clincher for Ryan Hall.

With five titles in six years and six in the entire Super League era, the nearly men of the mid-1990s had finally come good. Leeds, with their stunning Academy set-up in Super League's first decade and solid business structure, have set the standards high. They aren't as dominant as the Wigan of old, but in a salary-cap era, their achievements have been quite extraordinary. They are one of many clubs who have made Super League a far more dynamic brand than the old Stones Bitter Championship, but after seventeen years - how successful has it really been?

CHAPTER SIX
SUMMER RUGBY - HAS IT WORKED?

"Rugby league used to be a winter sport until we moved it to summer.
That transformed it from a game of muddy players on
boggy pitches to the fast, spectacular, skilful game you see today."
- *RFL Executive Chairman, Richard Lewis, 2010.*

Super League continues to bring millions of pounds of much-needed television revenue into the sport and paved the way for the clubs to employ full-time players. Accepting the £87 million from a company that already owned the domestic game's broadcasting rights seemed the obvious thing to do.

Financial security was just one aim of Super League, though. Others would have included: producing a successful structure throughout the professional game, increasing attendances, maintaining a successful international structure, providing the players and coaches to improve Great Britain's performances, expanding the game from its traditional already-strong areas in the north of England (and the south of France), building on its strength in those heartlands, achieving a higher profile for the sport, improving and increasing rugby league's television exposure and enlarging the column inches afforded to the game in the newspapers.

Seventeen years on, how has it done?

What we now call a winter season kicked off in August, went through the autumn, winter and spring and ended in May. Super League kicks off early in the calendar year, goes through the seasons, with its Grand Final and end-of-season internationals played in early winter. December and January, therefore, have been replaced by June and July, achieving two months of better weather for the game. The immediate sacrifices were the Boxing Day and New Year's Day programmes, while pre-season training, so crucial to how a team will go on to perform, now takes place in the depth of winter rather than the height of summer.

Super League and summer rugby were designed to make the sport's domestic league stronger, but it must be asked whether the subsequent weakening of both the international game and the Challenge Cup was justified. It will be demonstrated later that while Super League has increased domestic league crowds, Test and Cup crowds have fallen away significantly. Both have struggled to maintain any real identity since 1996, but previously they provided the sport with the most prominent dates in its calendar, many of which were watched by huge audiences on the BBC. Paradoxically, fewer showpiece occasions now take place in summer. Pre-1996 saw the start of the season, the title run-in, the Challenge Cup Final and the Premiership Final all scheduled in April, May or August. Now, the Challenge Cup Final is the only big occasion to be played in the summer months.

In terms of the structure of the professional game, a summer schedule appears to have caused more problems than it had solved. Before 1996, the Stones Bitter Championship consisted of sixteen teams. The season ran from August to May, with the teams playing each other twice. The champions were the team with the most points and the bottom two were relegated with the best two sides from division two replacing them - all very easy for the casual spectator to understand. Compare that to Super League which, in different years, has kicked off in January, February, March and April. It's gone from twelve teams to fourteen to twelve again and back to fourteen, with many then clamouring for a reduction to ten. Teams have played each other twice - most of the time - but occasionally three times and in some years selected teams faced each other four times in what was sometimes a very irregular league programme. Even the play-offs series, which was introduced in 1998, has gone from five teams to six and then eight. And yes, you've guessed it - few are happy with eight (understandably so, as attendances and match quality have declined) and are demanding a reduction. Super League has enjoyed no structural stability and even on the field - there are regularly a minimum of five rule changes brought in every season, with a number of them subsequently reversed when they haven't worked.

Happily though, league-match attendances have headed in the right direction in the summer era, with Super League crowds in 2012 averaging 9,431 compared to 5,543 in the last full winter season (1994-95), 5,515 in the shortened 1995-96 Centenary Season, and 6,571 in the inaugural summer season of 1996 - although there was a sizeable decline in the first half of the 2013 season (at the time of writing). Bradford Bulls initially led the way, increasing their average from 4,593 at the conclusion of the winter era to 15,163 by the second summer season on the back of aggressive marketing campaigns and a champion team on the pitch. Grand Finals, too, have seen a steady rise in audience numbers from 43,553 in 1998 to 70,676 in 2012.

Summer rugby, however, appears to have had a negative impact on crowds in other areas of the game. Home internationals against Australia since 1996 have, on average, been watched by 11,062 less people than in the 1980 to 1995 period, for reasons discussed in chapter two. In the Challenge Cup, average fourth-round crowds fell from 4,986 in the 1994-95 competition to a disappointing 2,665 in 2012, with the competition average falling (fourth round to semi-final) from 9,606 to 6,488, while semi-final crowds have decreased alarmingly from 1996. From 1980 to 1995, 26 different semi-finals (including replays) attracted a crowd of over 15,000 people compared to only eleven between 1996 to 2012. Fourteen games from the first period attracted a 20,000 crowd compared to just one afterwards. The lowest last-four crowd between 1980 and 1995 was the 12,430 that attended the Castleford-Oldham clash in 1986, but eleven in the summer era have fallen below that mark.

From summer rugby's beginnings, the Challenge Cup has struggled. Previously, top-division clubs would enter it in the new year with the final played at the end of the season, in April or May, but between 1996 and 2004 some of the early rounds involving top-division clubs were even played before Super League kicked off, giving the competition a distinct pre-season feel. In 2005, the final was moved from that spring slot to late August with the preceding rounds moving as well, but competition attendances have continued to fall. The 2004 fourth-round average was 3,029 - 364 higher than in 2012 - and the competition average (round four to semi-final) was 504 higher than eight years later.

With league matches and cup games thrown into the mix, the sport has actually seen a drop in the number of matches that have attracted a crowd of over 20,000 since 1996, compared to the 16 seasons prior. Taking domestic matches only, there was an average of five games per year that drew such a crowd between 1980 and 1995, compared to four and a half in the seventeen years since.

With the Super League Grand Final introduced in 1998, focus has been taken away from traditional knockout Cup football, although play-offs were not a new thing in rugby league. They have always existed in Australia, and were first used in England in 1898 and were used on and off for many years. A top-four system was introduced in the 1906-07 season and remained until 1962. After two seasons of no play-offs, a top-sixteen system was used from the 1965 until 1973, after which it was scrapped.

The Super League Grand Final has been a success with its gripping theatre and huge crowds, but of concern to the Rugby Football League should be the poorly attended matches in the three weeks that precede it. In fifteen years, three different play-off systems have been implemented - top five, top six and top eight. In order to pep up interest, they invented 'club call' in 2009, whereupon the highest ranked team after week one chooses their week-three opponents. In fairness to the RFL, it attracts an abundance of publicity, but most of it is negative.

The two principal drawbacks of the play-offs are attendances and the effect is has on the regular rounds of Super League. Regarding the former, Super League play-off matches have attracted disappointing attendances from the start. St Helens v Bradford in 1998 - Super League's first-ever play-off match - was memorable for referee Stuart Cummings' bizarre decision to red card the Bulls' Graeme Bradley in his final professional match, but the game was watched by just 8,973 people. A week later, Halifax against Saints pulled in 5,451 and even St Helens and Wigan on fourteen occasions between them have, over the years, posted sub-10,000 attendances for play-off matches, and that includes one of their derbies played in 2011. The famous Wide-to-West game of 2000 between Saints and Bradford could only pull in just 8,864 and just one play-off series since has managed to boast a five-figure crowd in every game. That came in 2004, the best supported play-off series, where the five games (excluding the final) pulled in an average of 17,635. On four occasions (three times under the top-eight system), the average has been under 10,000.

The move to a top-eight system looks to have been a mistake. It was brought in for the 2009 series, possibly as a knee-jerk reaction to the poorly-attended 2008 series (9,970 average), although compared to previous years, that was very much a one-off figure. The official explanation was that it would give the lower teams more to play for in the post-relegation era. "It should be judged over a two or three-year period," said RFL chief executive Wood prior to the first top-eight series. "But I still firmly believe that eight places from fourteen clubs is fine because it puts equity deep into the regular season. We're trying to get to a position where the number of dead-rubber games is minimised." In attempting to revitalise the bottom half of the table, though, the RFL have diluted the quality of the actually play-offs themselves. The change to eight teams has resulted in some poor crowds and a multitude of one-sided games, especially in the opening fortnight of the competition. Scores of 44-8, 42-18, 47-0, 56-6, 42-10, 44-0, 46-6, 28-6, 42-20, 46-10, which occurred between 2009 and 2012 are far removed from what play-off football should be. In fact, since the top-six was introduced in 2006, too many of the early games haven't had enough riding on them. Only the top-five system came close to delivering intense matches throughout. There was always at least one gripping match in the first weekend of games which stopped being the case under top six.

The other area where the play-off system is detrimental to the game is admittedly more subjective. From the moment St Helens allowed Wigan to invade their territory and win a Minor Premiership decider in 2000 by 42-4, only to sweep through the play-offs in sensational fashion and beat the Warriors in the Grand Final, players have known that the Super League regular rounds are ultimately the equivalent of Formula One's qualifying laps. Unlike in Australia where teams have to be at their best just to get into the top eight,

Super League's leading sides are almost guaranteed entry and - should they so desire - can relax for large parts of the season, saving their energy levels for the play-offs. Leeds coming fifth in 2011 and 2012, only to win the Grand Final in both seasons provided wonderful drama but also set a dangerous precedent. Super League players have always been subjected to fewer intense matches compared to the NRL because of the gulf in playing standards, but if teams are going to ease off as Leeds appeared to for two seasons, then there is a risk that England will enter major tournaments with their players barely having experienced any high-quality football at all.

In terms of the closeness and unpredictably of Super League, the general consensus is that Super League, over the years, has moved in the right direction - that is the message often conveyed by the Sky Sports commentators, as well as the sport's then-executive chairman, Richard Lewis, in 2010. "There's more equality between teams," he said. "There's a level playing field where everyone can win. You get uncertainty of outcome and surprise results." As Lewis pointed out, Wigan were dominant in the final years of winter rugby league, but there were still seven different clubs who won the league championship between 1980 and 1995, but only four have won Super League between 1996 and 2012, and there have been eight different runners-up compared to seven.

Looking at the average result of the top side in each Super League season and the average result of the bottom side, in order to compare equality, it is hard to find a discernable pattern. The year when the gap was at its smallest was actually 1997, when there was only a difference of 24.6 points per game between runaway leaders Bradford (who wrapped up the title before they lost a game) and relegated Oldham. By 2012, the difference had moved out to over 40 points per game between Minor Premiers Wigan and wooden-spoonists Widnes - but RFL boss Nigel Wood in early 2013 was claiming that Super League was closer than ever. The fact that Super League is a more equal competition than the 1990 to 1995 period when Wigan dominated is undeniable, but their reign would have ended even if summer rugby hadn't come along - in fact, their incredible Challenge Cup domination ended at The Willows in Salford in February 1996, when the game was still under its winter umbrella. By comparison, between 1999 and 2004 there was a recognised 'big four' or 'big five' (Bradford, St Helens, Wigan, Leeds and sometimes Hull), which led to a number of very competitive Super League seasons, although standards at the bottom remained poor. Unfortunately Wigan, Bradford and Hull fell away over the next few years, leaving an unhealthy St Helens and Leeds duopoly until 2009, although in 2006 Leeds were off the pace so Saints were able to wrap up an easy treble, winning the Minor Premiership by eight points, and the two big finals 42-12 and 26-4. Wigan and Warrington have since come into the picture and with Leeds' remarkable triumphs from fifth in 2011 and 2012, a new dynamic has been woven into the fabric of the competition, but there still appears to be fewer genuine Super League contenders midway through 2013 than between 2000 and 2004.

After the international game and various cup competitions, the third area of the game that has failed to grow in the Super League era is the lower divisions. In a 1995 House of Commons debate on rugby league, shortly after the Super League bombshell was announced, Ian McCartney, the MP for Makerfield, said: "If we are serious about a Super League, why will the first division [the second tier] be starved of capital resources, sponsorship and income, as well as the right, even if teams are successful, to apply to join the Super League? A head cannot survive if the body is destroyed." His words over the years have proved rather prophetic.

The five-month Centenary Season saw a tier-two average of 2,146 which was only bettered in 1996 and 1997 with impressive figures of 2,405 and 2,522. By 2012, the average for the division was just 1,185. However, it should be pointed out that average figures since 1996 have always topped 1,000 whereas they didn't in three seasons in the 1980s, but, still, summer rugby hasn't given the lower-division clubs the boost they might have hoped for. A third tier hasn't always been in operation - either before or after 1996 - as the Rugby Football League have regularly moved the professional game from two divisions to three and back again - since 1990 there have been five such alterations. In the three seasons of three-tier rugby league before 1996 and in the ten seasons after it, a four-figure average has only been achieved once. That was in 1992-93 with a 1,027 average in a season when the top two teams, Keighley Cougars and Workington Town, both averaged over 2,000. By 2011, coincidentally, those same sides were the division's grand finalists but were only averaging 830 and 583 respectively despite similarly successful seasons to two decades earlier, and the competition average in 2011 was a mere 595. It rose to 704 in 2012, but is likely to fall heavily in 2013 with four well-supported teams promoted to the Championship and new clubs Gloucestershire All Golds, Hemel Stags and Oxford coming in. After five rounds of the 2013 season, as the book went to print, the average was down to 427.

There is no obvious correlation between the presence of promotion and relegation and tier-two crowd increases or decreases. It was known at the start of 1995-96 that there would be no promotion that season but crowds still increased from the previous season by 57 per-cent compared to 1994-95. Crowds topped 2,000 in 2007 for the last season of automatic promotion and relegation, but stayed at a similar level for the first season of licensing being introduced in 2008, although clubs at that level knew that at least one of them were most likely going to receive a key to Super League, and in the end two did. Over the following two seasons, fans may have felt there was little to play for and crowd averages dropped to 1,720 and 1,596. In 2011, it was widely anticipated that Widnes would be awarded a licence so there was no increase at the turnstile, but the sharp drop off in 2012 is a worry.

The lower-level competitions have struggled to develop a strong brand for another reason. From 1995 it has had all manner of daft names foisted upon it, perhaps in an attempt to convince potential spectators that standards are higher than in reality. What was called Division Two has since been called Division One, the Premiership, the National League, the Championship and possibly soon Super League Two, yet none of those gimmicky names have paid dividends. If an organisation's name continually changes, it cannot develop an identity, and without one it will suffer commercially.

The scrapping of promotion, which was replaced by licensing, remains one of the most divisive measures introduced by the sport. It hadn't always happened in the summer era - Hunslet and Dewsbury were denied in Super League as it was believed they would have been unsuccessful on and off the pitch, and it is hard to argue with that viewpoint. Nevertheless, they had earned promotion and to deny them a place at the top table set a dangerous precedent. The team that was kept in Super League on those occasions was Huddersfield, who actually finished bottom of Super League each season between 1998 and 2001, but were only relegated on the final occasion.

Another thing to consider is the idea that promoted sides tended to struggle in the Super League era, a theory which was largely mythologised by the media. Salford were the first up and finished fifth in 1997, completing a double over Wigan and reaching the semi-finals of the Challenge Cup. Hull came up a year later and won eight games to come ninth and then Wakefield won ten games in 1999, with three sides finishing below them. After no promotion for two seasons, Widnes won the 2001 Northern Ford Premiership Grand Final and went on to enjoy a marvellous time in Super League, only missing out on a top-six play-off spot by a point, winning fourteen and drawing one of their 28 matches. Huddersfield's 2003, under Tony Smith, was highly commendable as they won eleven and drew one before newly promoted Salford came ninth out of twelve in 2004 with eight wins.

Leigh in 2005 were actually the first promoted team to go straight back down (Huddersfield were fast-tracked into Super League for the 1998 season to replace the defunct Paris, not having 'won' promotion). Having recruited poorly, the Centurions were out of their depth, winning just two and drawing one from 28 matches. Castleford suffered the same fate a year later, but it is not fair to include them for these purposes as they didn't finish last and were only relegated because Catalans were exempt from relegation. Hull Kingston Rovers were next up, avoided relegation by seven points, had the temerity to win twice against Hull FC and even pinched their best player, Paul Cooke. Rovers went on to become a play-off team in 2009, 2010 and 2011, proving that promoted sides could be competitive.

Promotion and relegation was scrapped in favour of a licensing system which was implemented in 2009, with the recipients of the first batch of licences announced in 2008. It was believed that this would rid the game of the yo-yo syndrome that had dogged clubs like Castleford between 2004 and 2008 and that clubs would be able to achieve more stability with a three-year licence in their pocket and without the annual threat of relegation and, in turn, they would not panic and sack coaches just because their team was struggling. In hindsight, the Rugby Football League chose poorly in 2008. The selection of Celtic Crusaders, as Super League was expanded to fourteen clubs, raised eyebrows. They were hopelessly out of their depth as a club, and the experiment crashed and burned within three years. Widnes were overlooked on the questionable basis that their previous board of directors had led the club into administration - a strange decision given Steve O'Connor's financial backing was in place at the time of the decision. They were duly handed their licence three years later.

Fans of lower-league clubs tend to believe that a drawbridge has been pulled up and that the system is consequently unfair and it could be scrapped if rumours of a two-tier Super League with promotion and relegation between them come to fruition.

Perhaps if the RFL didn't burden itself with new concepts like the annual Magic Weekend from 2007, for example, it could put extra resources into marketing Cup matches, internationals, play-offs or the lower divisions. The Magic Weekend, which saw a whole round of fixtures taken to Cardiff in 2008, 2008 and 2011, to Edinburgh in 2009 and 2010, and to Manchester in 2012 required a gargantuan marketing effort to fill even a third of those stadia at any one time. In that time, marketing of the Challenge Cup appears to have declined, as have its attendances. In 2011, the RFL couldn't even fill the Halliwell Jones Stadium for a Challenge Cup semi-final between Wigan and St Helens, which attracted less than half the attendance compared to the corresponding fixture between the same teams in 1990 at Old Trafford.

The RFL's official review paper of the 2007 Millennium Magic, as it was originally called, showed that their marketing campaign for the event began six months in advance in December 2006. From then until May, they pursued the campaign in the following ways: direct mail to 65,000 homes and an e-blast

to 41,000 customers who had previously attended rugby at the Millennium Stadium; the game's trade press with two months of half-page adverts; the regional press via five South Wales titles and thirteen across the M62 corridor; on their own websites; on five radio stations; and on 66 bus sides and shelters in South Wales. As well as that, a story per day was sent to the national and regional press in the week and a half leading up to the event and, of course, Sky Sports promoted the concept as enthusiastically as one would expect, telling everybody how brilliant it would be whilst being apparently unwilling to at least debate the merits of the concept. In short, it was a mammoth promotional exercise, even though it is recognised in the review that budgets were limited. Had that sort of effort been concentrated on the Challenge Cup instead, the decline in its fortune could have been arrested and the public at large may have been drawn again, via the nation's primary terrestrial channel, to a sport that could fill stadia for its most famous tournament. Instead, the sport lumbered itself with an event whose financial performance was "at the lower end of expectations", according to the review paper. Three years later, nearly 7,000 less people attended the event in Edinburgh, although moving the event to Manchester improved attendances and feedback seemed to be more positive.

Moving on to the game's efforts to expand out of its traditional northern enclaves, this has been a constant goal of Super League, as it had been at regular intervals beforehand.

In the 1980s, a number of soccer clubs decided to maximise the financial potential of their facilities by starting rugby league teams. Fulham were first in the 1980-81 season, and regular professional rugby league in London was alive for the first time since 1937 when the Streatham and Mitcham team was disbanded after 26 matches into their second season, even though they had won fourteen of them. Fulham beat Wigan in their first match in Division Two and were promoted at the end of the season. Carlisle and Cardiff were next, and the Cumbrians emulated the Londoners by winning promotion at the first attempt, but their second season was horrific with money troubles blighting the club and soccer clubs perhaps began to realise that inaugurating a rugby league club might not be the passport to riches that they had hoped. Throughout the 1980s other clubs were born, but with limited success in the case of Sheffield, and no success elsewhere.

In London, rugby league is played throughout the city in all of its boroughs, which is a remarkable statistic and a huge credit to the development officers and selfless volunteers who have helped that happen. In Championship One, London Skolars look more and more like an impressive club with a competitive team and homegrown players throughout the squad. It is above them, though, where all is not well. The city's Super League club has been renamed, rebranded and dragged around several venues over the years, in an attempt to bring its off-field performance up to a required standard. Since their Wembley appearance in 1999, they have performed poorly on and off the pitch and now often play home games before crowds of 2,000 or less, attracting only 652 people to a Challenge Cup tie against Dewsbury in 2012. Other than a pin in a map, it is hard to see what the club are bringing to the competition.

Paris and Gateshead were planted into Super League in 1996 and 1999 with little other rugby league presence in either city - certainly no amateur competition that could provide players of sufficient ability to make the step up. Paris lasted two seasons. Gateshead's demise was farcical as they supposedly merged with Hull FC, but in reality they were closed down because they were haemorrhaging cash as a result of the prerequisite spadework not being done before they started. At least, though, their agony wasn't prolonged as it has been with other expansion projects. Catalan Dragons, of course, have been a success, but they don't really count as rugby league expansion as the game has been played in the south of France since before World War Two. They have been able to draw on the talents provided by the French Elite Championship, whose clubs have often beaten England's professional teams in the Challenge Cup. Nevertheless, it was a brave decision by the RFL to include them in their flagship competition and they have been handsomely rewarded.

The last roll of Super League's expansionary dice was the ill-fated Celtic Crusaders. Having learned the lessons from the Paris and Gateshead debacles, the RFL, sensibly it seemed at the time, started them in the bottom tier of the professional game, although it is likely they were earmarked for Super League from day one. They spent two years in National League Two and were awarded a Super League licence midway through their first year in National League One in 2008. They demonstrated their on-field qualities by qualifying for the National League Grand Final, only losing in extra-time to Salford. From a playing point of view, they appeared to have a base on which to build, but as ever the harsh world of top-flight rugby league took its toll and after their first Super League season, in which they beat Bradford and Wigan but finished bottom, the cracks started to appear. It was announced that due to financial problems, the club had been sold to Wrexham FC and would be relocating to north Wales. 2010 was an excellent year on the field, under the coaching of Brian Noble, as they took the last play-off place, but not even the signing of Welsh union legend Gareth Thomas had the necessary impact on crowds, which plummeted to just 1,122 for an August game with Harlequins. They struggled in 2011 and withdrew their bid for a Super League licence on the eve of the announcement being made. They finished the season bottom of the table and completed the circle by entering Championship One in 2012.

The conclusion appears to be that top-down expansion rarely works in rugby league in the UK, but a bottom-up method can produce some decent results, although even with good amateur and junior bases there appears to be little evidence to support a theory that a Super League can thrive outside the north of England or the south of France. Welshmen, Londoners and those from the north-east can still find their way into the professional game with local clubs, and more and more are finding their way into Super League with the northern clubs. With clubs from Oxford and Gloucester entering the professional ranks in 2013, that base has expanded. That in itself is an achievement to be proud of.

Sadly though, some traditional league territories have been neglected since 1996. Incredible as it seems now, Super League actually kicked off without a Hull club showing how far the game had declined since Wigan director Martin Ryan's 1980 quote that only those two clubs could survive on their gate figures. However, both clubs were subsequently promoted and have demonstrated that they deserve to be in the competition.

At least, though, there was a representative from another of the game's strong heartlands - Cumbria. In December 1992 third-division Workington Town had taken on the mighty Wigan in the quarter-final of the Regal Trophy. At 18-0 up, the English champions were coasting until tries from Mark Mulligan and Paul Penrice stopped them in their tracks. Just six points down and with nearly 8,000 fans cheering them on, Town searched in vain for the equalising score until a Wigan drop-goal attempt hit a post and the clinching try followed a few tackles later. They may have lost the game, but it sparked a wonderful few years on the north-west coast. Two promotions and two Old Trafford appearances later, Town found themselves in the Big League and a mid-table finish saw them book a place in the game's first season of Super League.

Unfortunately, it all fell apart at just the wrong time. With coach Peter Walsh and many of the best players departing in the summer of 1995, they were relegated after Super League's first season amid a financial crisis which almost saw the club disappear altogether. They were also relegated from the middle tier in 1997, going on to spend many years in the bottom tier of the professional game. They have since rebuilt and were promoted, along with Barrow and Whitehaven, to the Championship in 2012, but a Super League presence in Cumbria looks a long way off, which is a shame for the game at the highest level as so many talented players are slipping through the net. For every Shaun Lunt who goes from Workington Town to the England team in just a few years, as he did in 2010, there are plenty of others in the game's third county who would be capable of gracing Super League, but who don't get spotted by Super League's questionable scouting network.

Oldham is another example. They were the club who pushed the touring Kangaroos so close in 1986 and who beat Wigan in the Challenge Cup three months later. In later years, the town produced Paul and Danny Sculthorpe, Iestyn Harris and Barrie McDermott but the club finds itself struggling in Championship One and only just continuing to exist. Perhaps before looking to expand Super League again, the game could help to revive these once prolific breeding grounds of top-class players.

Away from the field of play, the biggest problem that faces British rugby league is its lack of a significant profile which, in turn, leads to an absence of blue-chip sponsors queuing up to invest in the game, as it discovered in 2013. The names of cyclists, swimmers and darts players are better known throughout the country than rugby league players. Profile is something that's hard to measure, but today's stars appear to be far less well-known than Ellery Hanley, Garry Schofield, Martin Offiah and many others from the pre-Super League era.

There are many reasons for this which this section of the chapter will explore.

Great Britain's and England's poor international performances in most of the years since 1996 are clearly a contributory factor, as is the absence of live internationals on the BBC throughout most of that period, while the popularity of the Challenge Cup has also declined. The lack of major rugby union signings like Jonathan Davies and Va'aiga Tuigamala and many others is another feasible reason and the absence of transfer speculation these days is a major cause for the decline in column inches afforded to the game. Whatever the reasons, Super League was supposed to deliver a higher profile for the sport and has failed badly.

The lack of acceptable rugby league coverage in the national newspapers has been a conundrum for the game's governing body long before Super League, but it was understood that Super League would improve matters. In Australia, Super League salesmen claimed that it would make its players recognisable in China. In England, Maurice Lindsay was more realistic but the Super League concept has only seen a further decline in the sport's exposure in the media.

Why is this?

In the game's last full-length winter season (1994-95), five Regal Trophy matches, six Challenge Cup matches and four Kangaroo tour matches were televised by the BBC, spread quite evenly throughout the nine-and-a-half month season, giving a total of fifteen televised matches. Using 2011 as a comparison, as it was the last time Australia toured, the BBC showed nine matches in the year - two games from the Four Nations (it actually showed no live internationals between 1996 and 1999, as well as between 2001 and 2008) and seven Challenge Cup matches (between 1997 and 2011 they increased their televised matches in the fourth and fifth rounds and the quarter-finals from one to two, but in 2012 they televised only one match in the fourth and fifth rounds). Therefore, in the summer rugby era, rugby league has enjoyed a lot less live terrestrial exposure - and that is its own fault, not the BBC's, for handing internationals to Sky Sports and for scrapping the Regal Trophy.

The fact that only two Super League games a week are televised by Sky remains a disappointment because that is actually a decrease from 1996. In the final winter seasons, Sky Sports showed a Stones Bitter Championship match live on a Friday night and also extended highlights of another match on Sunday nights - a game which was pretty much shown in its entirety. From 1996, a second live match was added on a Saturday evening and Sunday's delayed game was maintained, but it was later dropped and despite there now being four sports' channels, less Super League is now televised. Whereas other sports have received a substantial increase in televised matches in the last twenty years - a round of Premier League soccer matches has four live games, compared to one in the old first division up until 1992 - rugby league has not, despite regularly pulling in impressive viewing figures.

Along the way in the summer era, Sky have also flirted with Academy matches, Australian rugby league and lower-division rugby. The latter two have been lost to another broadcaster, while Academy matches bit the dust a long time ago, despite tremendously favourable feedback from viewers. They tried to introduce a Friday-night red-button feature too, in order to show more than one fixture on a Friday night, but the idea floundered and wasn't developed.

The Regal Trophy was scrapped when Super League began, and although it is rarely mentioned these days, its final provided a further showpiece occasion which was televised on the BBC's flagship Saturday-afternoon programme, Grandstand. Inaugurated in the 1971-72 season as the Player's No.6 Trophy, only one of the first six finals attracted a five-figure crowd, but crowds were markedly higher throughout the '80s and '90s. Twice the 25,000 barrier was broken, with two more over 20,000. The last final came in January 1996 between St Helens and Wigan and was one of the most exciting matches for years. The game at Huddersfield attracted 17,590 spectators and was won by Wigan 25-16 with Saints' Keiron Cunningham winning man of the match. Writing in the Rugby League Weekend newspaper in January 1995, Radio Five's Dave Woods, now the BBC's primary rugby league commentator, pleaded for the competition to remain, and discussed "the access it gives rugby league to national exposure. Without it, outside the period between January and May, we'd have no [club] rugby league on terrestrial TV." That was a sacrifice the RFL were willing to take in moving to a summer calendar.

Television coverage for rugby league has improved in one area - magazine shows. The BBC's Super League Show has run for much of the summer era, despite their refusal to broadcast it nationally for many years and also screening its only repeat between 3am and 6am. Sky have also done the game proud in terms of the hours it devotes to the game with match highlights and discussions, but their programmes compare unfavourably with the NRL equivalents.

The modern game's attitude towards its history has been quite regrettable in the Super League era and this is something that has perhaps impacted upon its commercial performance and media exposure. Super League barely recognises the greats of yesteryear, whereas the NRL actively markets its game, especially State of Origin, around its past. Every NRL television show - Monday Night with Matthew Johns, NRL360, The Footy Show, Sterlo and the Sunday Footy Show - regularly contains clips from before the mid-1990s, a feature which is rare here. English soccer, too, is in tune with its past and the leading clubs show classic games ad nauseum on their television channels but, sadly, the principal marketing strategy of Super League and summer rugby appears to have been: "The game used to be crap, now it's great." The proof of that came in Richard Lewis's words in 2010 to commemorate twenty years of Sky Sports: "Rugby league used to be a winter sport until we moved it to summer. That transformed it from a game of muddy players on boggy pitches to the fast, spectacular, skilful game you see today." For 100 years of phenomenal rugby league to be written off as 'muddy players on boggy pitches' by the game's top administrator was a desperately sad state of affairs and an illustration of a complacent anti-older-generation stance. In 2012 Garry Schofield and Ellery Hanley were flown to Australia by Wests Tigers to be inducted into their Hall of Fame. Neither the RFL nor any of the many clubs that those two greats represented recognised the achievement. English rugby league is often accused of plagiarising the Australians, but this is an area where it badly needs to check out what they're doing.

In terms of newspaper coverage, the game struggled years before Super League came along and, if anything, things are now worse.

Transfer speculation, which newspapers will always be attracted to, is a fraction of what it used to be because the dynamics of the transfer market have altered in recent years. The Iestyn Harris and Shaun Edwards moves in early 1997 and the dozens of speculative stories in the years that preceded Super League attracted plenty of column inches and airtime, but as Super League has progressed such coverage has all but vanished. Transfers now tend to occur in the off-season and even when surprising mid-season deals are done, clubs do their best to keep any speculation out of the newspapers. In other sports, whispers are drip-fed to the media by whichever party has the most to gain from that, but few in rugby league know how to play that game. When Martin Gleeson and Richard Mathers swapped clubs in 2009, nobody had an inkling of what was on the cards until Warrington and Wigan announced the moves. A glance at the 'Memories' section of any of the 19 Rothmans Yearbooks of the 1980s and 1990s show that a significant percentage of any season's stories were generated from transfers or potential transfers and most that involved top-flight clubs would have been reported in the national newspapers.

Compared to other major sports, particularly soccer, rugby league provides few talking points. Many Premier League encounters between the top clubs have a sideshow involving managers, leading players or fans, which dominates the back pages of the red-top newspapers and the discussions on the Sky Sports News channel. The popular media have even shown that they are often more interested in these than the game itself, but rugby league rarely provides any such topics of interest. Animosities between soccer clubs - in particular, the prominent managers - are regularly played out in the media. In rugby league, they either don't exist or are kept quiet in order to maintain the sport's family image, which, of course, helps to keep the sport's column inches minimised.

Less glamorous signings from Australia have also resulted in a reduction in column inches for the game. When the international transfer ban was lifted in 1983, English clubs were able to bring over the very best Australian talents like Wally Lewis (Wakefield), Brett Kenny and Gene Miles (Wigan), Peter Sterling (Hull FC) and Mal Meninga (St Helens). These players were the cream of the crop, the very best players in the game, and even though they only came over for short stays during the Australian off-season, they raised the profile (and standards) of the British game. But when rugby league in this country moved to summer, it meant that the two seasons ran parallel and it was harder to get Australia's Test stars over at all. In 1996 and 1997, out of well over 100 Australians in the English game, only one - John Cartwright - had been capped and only a couple more had played State of Origin. Clubs like Leeds and Wigan had to settle for players like Jamie Mathiou, Martin Masella, Wayne Collins, Stuart Lester, Paul Koloi and Doc Murray, a far cry from previous years.

From 2000, the standard of import rose significantly with Allan Langer, Jason Smith, Adrian Lam and Tonie Carroll prepared to forsake State of Origin for Super League, but there were still too many expensive buys who were at the end of their careers like Brett Mullins, Bradley Clyde, Greg Florimo and Matthew Johns; players who were a shadow of their former selves. As the years have gone on, Jamie Lyon, Matthew Gidley and many others have represented value for money but with the NRL salary cap increasing and the pound devalued against the Australian dollar, there will only be slim pickings on offer for Super League clubs, just like in those early years. The standard and profile of New Zealand players, it should be pointed out, has generally been more consistent, with them not having to consider the pull of State of Origin, but the respective salary caps and the exchange rate will start to change that too. Short-term, high-profile signings did make a brief comeback with Adrian Morley and especially Andrew Johns creating massive interest in signing for Bradford and Warrington from their NRL clubs at the end of the 2005 Super League season. Johns only played three games for Warrington and failed to get them anywhere near the Grand Final, but he still managed to make a lifelong impact on the town. The RFL, though, shut that loophole down, and the sort of media coverage that welcomed Johns went with it.

Few in rugby league appear to be particularly media savvy, and players don't appear to receive suitable media training. A pundit like Garry Schofield, for example, who possesses a wonderful ability to spark debate and interest, is sadly seen by many as a liability to the sport rather than an asset, despite all other major sports having similar figures passing comment on today's game. Sky Sports are particularly wary of Schofield, yet their soccer and cricket panels are full of ex-players voicing criticisms of today's participants.

From reading his columns in the Monday-morning newspaper, League Express, and his Twitter account, Schofield's chief opinions on the game appear to be: firstly, that Great Britain and England have not performed well enough in the Super League era; secondly, the decision to scrap Great Britain was an enormous mistake; thirdly, the on and off-field performances of the

London club have not been good enough to justify a place in Super League; and fourthly, that promotion and relegation should be re-introduced. If you took a clipboard around professional and amateur grounds on matchday, it is highly likely that most people would agree with all four sentiments, but Schofield has been shunned by the leading clubs, players and media organisations because he has not toed the party line. In 2012, the RFL put pressure on League Express columnist Nick Fozzard, also an employee of Castleford Tigers, to stop criticising them even though he was doing a commendable job in getting people talking about the game. In other sports it is regularly demonstrated that a contrary outlook is welcomed, but criticism, even of the constructive variety, does not appear to be welcome in rugby league, and ultimately it is all the poorer for that strange stance.

Newspapers themselves come in for criticism for their sparse coverage of rugby league, and rightly so. Out of all team sports in the UK, rugby league has often boasted viewing figures that is second only to soccer at club level and it's weekly attendances often surpass club rugby union and cricket. Yet, the dullest of rugby union encounters played in front of two men and a dog get significantly more space than the wonderful fare served up in Super League. It is doubtful that there is an anti-league conspiracy, but there is certainly too much ignorance about the game in London newsrooms.

That, however, does come back to rugby league's inability to market itself. No player who has emerged in the Super League era has had a profile to compare to Hanley or Offiah, and even twenty years on, their names are more likely to resonate with the British public than Sculthorpe, Long and Peacock. No club since Bradford in the late-nineties has had a marketing guru as adept as Peter Deakin and too many clubs appear to rely on television money rather than marketing their own product and players. That failure to establish other income streams is a major problem for the game which needs to be addressed. Crowd increases have been modest on an annual basis, but no club has grasped the nettle and achieved the unexpected since the early days of the Bulls, although Wakefield deserve recognition for their 8,172 average in 2012. With the money that has been sunk into the game in the last seventeen years, it remains a disappointment that Super League clubs, especially the big four of Leeds, Wigan, Warrington and St Helens rarely play to sell-out audiences. If they did that regularly, it would be harder for newspapers to ignore the sport.

Journalists, too, must accept some of the blame for the lack of rugby league coverage in their papers. Only a couple of the national newspaper journalists are ever in the market of breaking stories, and some don't seem to have broken a unique story in years, preferring instead to deal in re-worded press releases and match reports. A sports editor is inevitably going to be attracted to a piece of news that his newspaper can boast it told the world first. In fairness, rugby league journalists are generally paid far less than other sports' press men and women and are perhaps less incentivised to investigate a potential scoop; but if that were to change, column inches would surely increase.

The Rugby League Writers Association could perhaps do more too. The RLWA was formed in 1961 at Swinton's Station Road ground and is run on a voluntary basis by some of the game's unsung heroes who selflessly put many hours of labour into keeping it going. But it appears unwilling to make a stand and constructively tackle the game's media problems, which is in stark contrast to the rugby union equivalent who have in the past had great success in making demands of clubs and forming agreements with them of how they should operate with the media. Since I joined the rugby league media in 2005, clubs and players have become far less accommodating to journalists, yet nothing is being done to tackle that by either the RLWA or the RFL's media department.

Very few Championship clubs have any sort of media or marketing set-up and a lot of what there is, is performed on a voluntary basis. This results in regional-newspaper coverage becoming a problem, especially in a year like 2013 when World Cup matches are being played in some of these areas. The RFL appear to have a number of media officials who churn out regular press releases. If they provided, or if they paid journalists to provide, unique material for the newspapers in these areas, that would solve this particular problem. For example, no articles previewing the Rugby League World Cup had appeared in any Cumbrian newspaper by the spring of 2013. The RFL should have been providing that material for them free of charge in the autumn of 2012.

Rugby league will be dogged by media problems for decades to come, but there is much that the sport can do, collectively, to make a difference. Ultimately, Super League hasn't brought about the increase in the game's profile that it was hoped it would. Instead it seems to have declined alarmingly.

A return to winter is out of the question for rugby league, but the governing body must surely look objectively at the game's history and examine what was successful before 1995 that is not now. They must figure out how to ensure that the international and domestic games are compatible as they once were, with a Challenge Cup that was as vibrant as it used to be. Perhaps then, the profile of the game will grow and the media will respect it more.

Instead, rugby league is run, and commentated on, by people who insist that Super League and summer rugby have been unqualified successes - with Richard Lewis's 2010 comments being a prime example of that. Rarely are the issues in this chapter discussed by the game's television pundits, who prefer instead to tell their viewers what they want them to believe - although, on that score, Sky's Back Chat programme is a welcome addition to their schedule and they have finally stopped claiming that each season is the "greatest ever". Acknowledging the many areas of the game that are currently not maximising their potential - and most are nowhere near - would be a start to fixing up some of rugby league's problems, rather than the regular scatter-gun introduction of new gimmicks and new rules which are unveiled in the hope that some pay off.

Super League and summer rugby have ticked some boxes, but not enough. Grabbing Murdoch's cash in 1995 was the right business decision to take, but for seventeen years rugby league has failed to build on that foundation, and the fact that the RFL felt in 2013 that it had to consider another huge restructuring of the professional game proves that after nearly two decades of tinkering, the right answers were never in place.

CHAPTER SEVEN
AUSTRALIAN RUGBY LEAGUE

> "Ding dong, the witch is dead."
> - *Parramatta Eels coach, Jack Gibson, 1981.*

It was the perfect way to launch a new decade.

Canterbury Bankstown scrum-half Steve Mortimer caught the ball at first receiver just inside the Eastern Suburbs half. He passed left to his stand-off Garry Hughes who found his brother, Graeme, the second-rower, in support. The fullback, Greg Brentall, who two-and-a-half months earlier had scored the first-ever try in State of Origin, chimed into the line and took the play further into Easts' territory before launching a speculative left-footed bomb. Steve Gearin, burst into sight from the left wing, stormed past the last two defenders, caught the ball on the fly and as he was tackled just shy of the line, he reached out to score one of the greatest tries in rugby league history.

Australian Grand Finals had a habit of throwing up talking points in the mid to late 1970s. From the saga of Graeme Langlands' white boots in 1975 to Parramatta's rugby union-style flying wedge in 1976 and the replay dramas of 1977 and 1978, it was becoming an occasion that never disappointed, but for sheer, magnificent brilliance, Gearin's try topped all of that and rugby league was able to dine out on it for years. Canterbury won the game 18-4, sparking an era of domination by themselves and Parramatta Eels.

Parramatta had won the midweek knock-out competition in 1980 - previously the Amco Cup, but now known as the Tooth Cup - although they were still without a Premiership success. They reached the 1981 final with renewed optimism on the basis that young players like Steve Ella, Eric Grothe and, in the halves, Brett Kenny and Peter Sterling were now in their side, joining more experienced world-class talent like centre Mick Cronin and loose forward Ray Price, both former union players. There they met Newtown Jets, a famous old club whose glory days were well behind them but who, with wily old halfback Tommy Raudonikis leading them, were desperate for one more shot at glory. They led the Eels 11-7 but four late tries, including two to Kenny, handed the Eels their maiden crown. Their celebrations are stamped into folklore as Jack Gibson addressed a packed Parramatta leagues club with just six words: "Ding dong the witch is dead", while their fans, later in the evening, got so carried away they burned down the club's derelict old stadium, Cumberland Oval. It would be five years before they returned to play there.

Even without a home, they were too good again in 1982, a year which saw the competition expanded out of Sydney. Illawarra Steelers and Canberra Raiders made their bows but finished in the last two places, with the men from the capital taking the wooden spoon. It was also the first year under the sponsorship of Rothmans who had invested $850,000 over three years, with the competition being renamed The Winfield Cup. At the top, the Eels, playing out of Canterbury's Belmore, topped the table from Manly by eight points and beat the same side in the Grand Final 21-8 with Brett Kenny bagging another double. A year later, the same sides contested the final with the same outcome. This time the Eels won 18-6, with Kenny scoring two more, to ensure that their coach, Jack Gibson, had won a title in each of his three years at the club before leaving his post. Their 1983 highlight, though, came in a play-off game against Canterbury when Eric Grothe stormed through six would-be tacklers over 50 metres to score one of the tries of the decade. Manly could at least console themselves with winning the KB Cup, the new name for the midweek competition, in those two seasons. 1983 was also the year that the Four Corners current-affairs television programme unearthed previous financial malpractice relating to Kevin Humphries, who by now was president of the NSWRL and chairman of the ARL. The result of this scandal was that his career was over. Another sad story in 1983 was the demise of Newtown Jets who left the competition amid a financial crisis. Their last game was a 9-6 win over Canberra. Wests were also booted out but reinstated after a court ruling.

With Gibson's assistant, John Monie, in charge, Parramatta went after a fourth-straight Premiership in 1984 but were thwarted by their old foes Canterbury who beat them in a tight, low-scoring final 6-4 with hooker Mark Bugden scoring the crucial try. Elsewhere in 1984, Les Boyd was back after the twelve-month ban he had picked up for the incident involving Daryl Brohman in State of Origin. Three games into his return he gouged the eye of Canterbury's Billy Johnstone and was banned for another fifteen months, which ended his Australian career.

Warren Ryan's Dogs retained their title in 1985, beating St George Dragons 7-6 with Andrew Farrar kicking the vital one-pointer. It was a game that led to a rule change as one of Ryan's tactics was to pepper the Dragons' fullback Glenn Burgess with bombs, most of which led to a goal-line drop-out, thus ensuring the Dogs dominated possession. The laws were subsequently altered so if a player 'defused' a bomb in his in-goal area, his team would be rewarded with a tap restart on the twenty-metre line. The other trophy in 1985, by now called the National Panasonic Cup, went to Balmain Tigers, who fielded the nineteen-year-old Great Britain centre, Garry Schofield.

Ryan's deeply effective defensive football had changed the face of Australian football and that was demonstrated no better than in 1986 when his Bulldogs team and Parramatta produced a Grand Final with an even lower score than two years earlier. In a brutal game, Mick Cronin's two penalties won the Premiership for the Eels by a 4-2 scoreline, although Canterbury fullback Phil Sigsworth had earlier been sent off. Peter Sterling won the inaugural Clive Churchill Medal as man of the match, which was presented in honour of the South Sydney and Australia fullback of the 1950s who had died in 1985. Kenny maintained his record of crossing the tryline twice, but both were disallowed. Matchwinner Cronin had endured a strange year, not actually making his first appearance of the season until the play-offs after suffering a detached retina and then broken ribs on his reserve-grade comeback match. He almost missed the final after getting stuck in traffic behind a six-car pile-up on the F6 freeway. The police escorted him to the game after he had abandoned his car and Australia's all-time record points scorer, along with teammate Ray Price, retired from the game a Grand Final winner.

1987 saw both Parramatta and Canterbury miss out on the top five, highlighting the depth of the Winfield Cup's quality. Canberra Raiders in their sixth season, came good. Nicknamed Canberra Faders in their early years for their inability to last the pace, the signing of Queensland and Australia centre Mal Meninga in 1986 proved to be a pivotal moment in their history. By the time they lined up in the 1987 Grand Final, they had fellow State of Origin players Gary Belcher and Peter Jackson as well as Kiwi Test prop Brent Todd. They were jointly coached by Don Furner and Wayne Bennett. They met Manly in the final, who boasted Great Britain prop Kevin Ward in their ranks. Ward enjoyed a tremendous game and was considered unlucky by some pundits not to win the Clive Churchill Medal, which went to stand-off Cliff Lyons. Manly won the game 18-8.

Manly's next two games are almost as well remembered. Firstly they were beaten at Central Park by Wigan in the first official World Club Challenge match and then at the start of 1988, they were lined up as the first opponents of competition new boys Brisbane Broncos, who were entering the Winfield Cup along with Gold Coast-Tweed Giants and Newcastle Knights, taking the number of participants to sixteen. A combined Brisbane side, led by Wally Lewis, the Australia captain, had won the 1984 Panasonic Cup while, of course, Queensland had dominated State of Origin since its 1980 inception. Boasting Lewis, Gene Miles, Allan Langer and Greg Dowling, and coached by Wayne Bennett, they hammered Manly 44-10 but thereafter failed to live up to expectations and missed the play-offs.

When Ellery Hanley joined Balmain Tigers in 1988 on the back of his excellent performances for the touring Great Britain Lions, the club seemed to have little chance of making the top-five play-offs, which was surprising given they boasted the likes of Wayne Pearce, Garry Jack, Steve Roach, Gary Freeman, Paul Sironen and their Test hooker, the irrepressible Benny Elias who recalled: "Myself and Keith Barnes [the chief executive] picked [Ellery] up from the airport when he arrived from England and I can remember that the first conversation was nothing about the social life or the climate," he said. "It was about football. That's all he wanted to discuss. He could not get to a football field quick enough. He was over to do a job and that was to get us to a Grand Final. We had some super professional players like Steve Roach, Wayne Pearce and Garry Jack but this bloke was a cut above. It was amazing because we thought that Pommy football was just a social kind of football but Ellery Hanley was just an amazing breath of fresh air. He was so committed. He was the first to training and the last to leave. We were 55/1 to win the Grand Final when he came. We needed to win twelve games out of the last thirteen because we were just mid-table. We were no Premiership threat but we got the wins we needed which was an amazing feat." Once in the semi-finals, the Tigers were on a roll and, inspired by their English import, they beat Penrith, Manly, Canberra and Minor Premiers Cronulla to reach their first Grand Final since 1969, but they were beaten 24-12 by Canterbury after Hanley had left the field injured after a late challenge from Terry Lamb.

"Ellery Hanley is the greatest player I ever played with and that includes Wally Lewis," said Elias. "Balmain hadn't been in a Grand Final since 1969 and this bloke came in and made an amazing difference. He did things unknown to Rugby League at the time, but unfortunately we all know what happened in the Grand Final and the rest is history. He was deliberately targeted but a lot of the great players have been deliberately targeted over the years. That's no secret. That's a credit to his ability I suppose. Canterbury's coach was Phil Gould and he probably thought that nobody would be sent off in a Grand Final. I actually recall shaking him at half-time and telling him that we needed him. I told him that it was a Grand Final and he'd get over his concussion later but he just looked at me and told me that he just couldn't go on. I was quietly disappointed because I'd have thought that after all the efforts he'd have played concussed. We'd have rather had a 50 per cent Ellery Hanley than no Ellery Hanley. As soon as he came off, the Bulldogs became more positive and confident. It was unfortunate but that's the way life goes."

A year later the Tigers were back in the final, although without Hanley, who enjoyed a more low-key spell with Western Suburbs along with Garry Schofield and Kelvin Skerrett. Other Brits to grace the Winfield Cup in 1989 included Illawarra's Andy Gregory and Steve Hampson (who came so close to Panasonic Cup glory, losing narrowly to Brisbane), Manly's Hugh Waddell and Bernard Dwyer, Easts' Martin Offiah and Joe Lydon, Cronulla's Paul Bishop,

Penrith's Tracey Lazenby, while Andy Currier and Shaun Edwards played in the Grand Final for the Tigers, although Edwards could only make the bench. That final against Canberra proved to be one of the most thrilling matches in the code's history.

The Green Machine boasted great players like Laurie Daley, Bradley Clyde, Ricky Stuart, Steve Walters and Mal Meninga, their captain, who had recovered from a broken arm sustained earlier in the season. The Tigers had all their big guns in action but it was their former Wallaby winger, James Grant, who scored the game's first try taking an intercept from Brent Todd. Just before half-time, Sironen scored a wonderful try following a speculative hack forward from the Welshman, Currier. Gary Belcher pulled one back for the Raiders before three incidents occured that would come back to haunt the Tigers. Firstly, Meninga produced a miraculous tap-tackle to prevent Michael Neil scoring the clinching try before Tigers coach Warren Ryan withdrew the highly influential Roach and Sironen who, subsequently, couldn't return to the field - Ryan has never escaped the criticism that followed that decision. Then Elias snapped a field-goal attempt against the crossbar, which would have given his side a seven-point lead and sealed the game.

With time running out, the Raiders produced one of the iconic moments in Grand Final history. John 'Chicka' Ferguson, who had starred so memorably for Wigan at Wembley four years earlier, took Daley's basketball pass, stepped inside three defenders and scored a few metres to the left of the posts. With seconds remaining, Meninga kicked the goal to take the game to extra-time. In the first minute of the added period, stand-off Chris O'Sullivan kicked a field goal straight from a scrum. Canberra held out and their win was sealed by the unlikely sight of substitute Steve Jackson beating five defenders in an astonishing show of strength for the try that sealed Canberra's most famous win. Meninga later described it as the greatest moment of his career.

One of the biggest stories in decades erupted during the off-season as Wayne Bennett took the Brisbane Broncos captaincy from Wally Lewis, the most iconic figure in the game. The story was an absolute sensation with the switchboard of Lewis's hotel in America, where he had fled for some peace, bombarded by Australia's media. "Who are you exactly?" they enquired when he returned from a morning stroll. Back home, Bennett knew he had made the right decision. "We were focused on getting things right," he said years later. "Put all the ducks in order and then you can start to fire your bullets and that was part of that process. Wally was a great player, a huge headline player and we had to expect the worse but we were unanimous about it. He wasn't bigger than the club." Still unhappy with the decision, as he remained for many years, Lewis left the club to have a season as captain-coach of the Gold Coast before bringing the curtain down on a magnificent career. Gene Miles took over as captain but it wasn't until Allan Langer's captaincy in 1992 that the Broncos began to realise their enormous potential.

The new decade saw the game's profile boom as it adopted Tina Turner's smash hit, The Best, as its new theme and launched a one-minute advert featuring Turner and many of the game's leading lights. Back on the field, Canberra retained their Premiership, beating Penrith Panthers 18-14 in the Grand Final with Ricky Stuart winning the Clive Churchill Medal. Unfortunately for the Raiders, it was revealed in April 1991 that they had breached the $1.5 million salary cap in winning the title. Even more worrying for the club, they admitted they were close to bankruptcy at $6 million in the red, but they managed to pull through.

The same teams met on the big stage twelve months later with another Raider, Bradley Clyde, voted best on the field, but this time it was Phil Gould's Panthers who emerged triumphant. Club legend and captain, Royce Simmons, had only scored thirteen tries in 232 matches for the club but ended his career on the ultimate high by bagging a double as his side won 19-12. Having been accepted into the competition in 1967, this was the Panthers' maiden Premiership and the second in just the four-year coaching career of Phil Gould. With teenage centre Brad Fittler, the wonderfully talented halfback Greg Alexander and Mark Geyer, a marauding forward, in their side, they were a match for anybody, but things quickly went downhill as they dropped from Minor Premiers to ninth in 1992, well out of semi-final contention. Far worse than that, their young halfback Ben Alexander, brother of Greg, was killed in a road accident on 21 June.

Their place at the top was taken by Brisbane Broncos in just their fifth season. From their first line-up in 1988, only Allan Langer, Chris Johns and Michael Hancock remained but they seemed to be a more balanced side without Wally Lewis, their original captain, and powered to the Minor Premiership by six points and won the Grand Final against St George by the convincing score of 28-8. Two-try Langer, by now the captain, won the Clive Churchill Medal but young centre Steve Renouf stole the limelight with a long-distance try at the end of the game to begin the celebrations. Earlier in the year, former Australia halfback Peter Sterling tearfully announced his retirement from the game after a recurrence of a shoulder injury, which had blighted the latter years of his career. He had initially injured it in a tackle with Great Britain's Roy Powell in a 1988 Test.

A year later Brisbane regained their title, but in entirely different circumstances. They finished fifth in a five-horse race for the JJ Giltinan Shield (awarded to the Minor Premiers) but beat Manly, Canberra and Canterbury, all

in Sydney, in order to reach another final. There they met the same opponents from the year before and again, the Broncos lifted the title with a 14-6 win, but the fall-out was quite remarkable. It later emerged that a copy of the tip-sheet that St George coach Brian Smith had given his players for the 1992 final had been leaked to Bennett before the 1993 final. Bennett decided to embellish it, adding to it words that insulted the Broncos players. He then gave every one of his players a copy of the sheet on the morning of the final telling his charges that Smith was insulting each of their teammates. Fired up, the Broncos won the match and several of their players were critical of Smith in their post-match interviews, including Langer who courted controversy by chanting into a microphone 'St George can't play!' When the truth emerged, Smith was enraged and a lengthy feud between the two coaches ensued.

The Broncos struggled in 1994, losing at home to Wigan in the World Club Challenge and again finishing fifth, although with fewer wins on the board than in 1993. Although they beat Manly again in the semi-finals, they weren't able to repeat their 1993 heroics. The winners this time were Canberra Raiders, for the third time in six seasons, as they beat Minor Premiers Canterbury 36-12 in the final. Mal Meninga, in his final match on Australian soil, brought the house down as he scored a 40-metre interception try to seal the game. With the long-striding Brett Mullins a constant menace at fullback, Laurie Daley and Ricky Stuart in the halves and a devastating back row of David Furner,

Jason Croker and Bradley Clyde, the Raiders had one of the best sides of the modern era.

1995 began amid confusion caused by constant rumours and speculation about Super League but on the positive side, the competition welcomed four new teams in Auckland Warriors, North Queensland Cowboys, South Queensland Crushers and Perth Western Reds. Canberra were still competitive even without Meninga, but were pipped to the top by Manly on points difference, with each side losing just twice out of 22 matches. But hopes of a dream Grand Final were scuppered when the Bulldogs (now called Sydney Bulldogs) beat the Raiders. Manly beat Newcastle, who were now coached by Englishman Malcolm Reilly, to go into the final as favourites but the Bulldogs thwarted them to make up for their 1994 disappointment. Each of their three tries was tinged with controversy and Manly, who had had a brilliant season, had to condede defeat.

The Super League cloud still hung horribly over the game in 1996 and there were few more depressing sights than the Super League-aligned clubs forfeiting their round-one matches, a move which probably cost Brisbane the JJ Giltinan Shield, which eventually went to Manly. The Sea Eagles beat Sydney City Roosters and Cronulla to book a place in the final and, surprisingly, their opponents were David Waite's St George Dragons, who had beaten Canberra, the Roosters and North Sydney Bears. This time the Sea Eagles made no mistake and lifted the trophy, which was now the Optus Cup. The gamebreaking play was provided by Matthew Ridge, the Manly fullback, who collected his own short kick-off just before half-time and was allowed to carry on after Nathan Brown thought he had tackled him. One play later Steve Menzies scored to help his side to a 12-point interval lead. The game ended 20-8.

With rugby league still in turmoil, 1997 saw the Australian game split into two, as the breakaway competition was finally allowed to go ahead. It consisted of ten teams: Brisbane, Cronulla, Canberra, Canterbury, Penrith, Hunter Mariners (a new club based in Newcastle), Auckland, Perth, Adelaide Rams (another new venture) and North Queensland. That was the finishing order after eighteen rounds, and Brisbane, who had an outstanding collection of talents, beat Cronulla in the Grand Final with a Steve Renouf hat-trick.

The remaining twelve sides competed in the Optus Cup, which was run by the Australian Rugby League in what was a more competitive competition than Super League. Unsurprisingly, Manly topped the table at the end with Newcastle beating Parramatta to the runners-up spot on points difference. As with Super League, first met second in the final, and what followed will never be forgotten by those lucky enough to have seen it. Newcastle, 16-10 down with little more than five minutes to play managed to score two late tries, the second of which came with seven seconds remaining, to clinch the most sensational of Premiership triumphs. It was one of the greatest games played for decades, perhaps even eclipsing the incredible dramas of the 1989 final. Robbie O'Davis scored the try that led to Andrew Johns' conversion levelling the scores, before a blind-side run by Johns, who played the match with a punctured lung, saw the supporting Darren Albert go through a huge gap to score the most famous of tries. It was their first-ever Premiership and possibly the greatest achievement in the life of their coach, Malcolm Reilly, who had enjoyed such a successful playing career. By that stage everybody knew that the two warring factions would be coming together again, and such a wonderful contest finally saw rugby league's spirits lifted again.

A proposed Super Bowl between the Broncos and the Knights failed to materialise but round one of the new National Rugby League competition in 1998 paired up the two Minor Premiers. Brisbane won rather too easily for the neutral's liking, but the late sendings-off of Geoff Toovey and John Hopoate for dissent by referee Bill Harrigan created plenty of headlines. Having won three successive Minor Premierships, Manly's drop to tenth was a huge surprise, while Brisbane predictably topped the table, although only on points difference from Newcastle. In third place was a new club, called Melbourne Storm whose existence was down to the bargaining powers of John Ribot, the Super League chief executive, who went on to hold the same role at the Storm. They signed several players from two of the three clubs who became casualties of the Super League War ending (Perth and Hunter - the other club to go was South Queensland) and were competitive from the outset.

The surprise package in the play-offs were Canterbury, who had finished ninth but who were grateful that ten were included in the semis. Having beaten St George and North Sydney, they produced two super-human efforts to overturn significant deficits against Newcastle and Parramatta. The win over the Eels remains one of the most famous matches in the NRL era as an 18-2 deficit with ten minutes to go was whittled down and the Dogs prevailed in extra-time. The final, however, was a step too far for them, even though they led Brisbane at half-time. The Broncos opened up in the second half to win 38-12 and to claim the first title under the National Rugby League banner.

Twenty teams came down to seventeen in time for the 1999 season, and three more were due to go for 2000. For the time being, Gold Coast and Adelaide were cut while St George and Illawarra merged to become St George-Illawarra Dragons. The season began with a world-record crowd of 104,583 at a double header at Sydney's Olympic Stadium which would from now would house the Grand Final. The Dragons' first season as a joint venture was superb as stand-off Anthony Mundine and winger Nathan Blacklock produced some exhilarating football to elevate the club into the Grand Final at their first attempt. They faced Melbourne before a new world-record crowd of 107,961 and led 14-0 but were pegged back and were eventually caught on the line when Jamie Aincough tackled Craig Smith high in the in-goal area and conceded a penalty try for Storm to win 20-18. The Dragons were heartbroken and still without a Premiership since 1979 but Melbourne's achievement in winning a Grand Final in just their second season was phenomenal. At the other end of the table, Manly and champions Brisbane occupied two of the lower places for much of the first half of the season to everybody's surprise. And even more startling was the mid-season departure of Allan Langer, the Broncos' iconic leader, who walked away from the club.

Manly merged with North Sydney at the end of the year to form Northern Eagles while Western Suburbs and Balmain came together to produce Wests Tigers, but the big news was the most successful club in the history of Australian rugby league, South Sydney Rabbitohs, being booted out after 92 seasons. That particular argument was far from over.

Another controversial departure from the game came midway through 2000 when the Dragons' influential stand-off, Anthony Mundine, quit the game and took up boxing. Having played for New South Wales in 1999 he was incensed at missing out on an Australian jumper for the end-of-season Tri Nations despite enjoying a brilliant season. He put his omission from the team down to racism on the part of the selectors and repeated the allegation in 2013.

The Broncos put their disappointing 1999 behind them as they moved into their first full season without Langer in 2000. His halfback partner, Kevin Walters, had taken over the captaincy and led them to the Minor Premiership over Graham Murray's Sydney Roosters by six points, and they beat the same side in the Grand Final 14-6.

In 2001 one of the strangest stories for many a year appeared when Wests Tigers winger John Hopoate, who had been guilty of several indiscretions in his short time at the club, was found guilty of inserting his finger into the backsides of three North Queensland Cowboys players - Glenn Morrison, Peter Jones and Paul Bowman. Hopoate's claim that he had attempted to give the players a 'wedgie' but was dismissed and he was suspended for twelve matches. He left the club and re-appeared in the NRL again with Northern Eagles later in the season.

The NRL was dominated by Parramatta Eels who produced an imperious level of performance on a weekly basis, losing only four games out of 26. Nine points behind them in third were Newcastle Knights who met in the competition finale. Man for man, the Eels had emphatically proven they were the better team, but the Knights had a scrum-half called Andrew Johns who was widely regarded as the best player on the planet. Johns' side blew the Eels away in the final, leading 24-0 at the break. Parramatta, coached by Brian Smith, closed the gap to a final score of 30-24, but it was a misleading score, with their last try coming right at the end. Smith had been foiled again, and given his side's complete domination of the season, this one had to have hurt the most. Nevertheless, what he had built at Parramatta deserves recognition. His six-seven-nine-thirteen quartet of playmakers were Michael Buettner, Jason Taylor, Brad Drew and Daniel Wagon, all unheralded players, but, under Smith's tutelage, they flourished, as did many others.

The Eels were expected to be in the reckoning again in 2002 but they failed to recover from the manner in which they fell at the final hurdle in 2001. They finished in sixth and exited the play-offs in the first week at the hands of Brisbane. Another club who will look back on the year with little fondness was the Bulldogs, who stormed into a huge lead at the top, only to be found guilty of systematically cheating the salary cap. Their 37 points were taken off them, which resulted in them coming last. They would have otherwise won the Minor Premiership by seven points and entered the play-offs as unbackable favourites.

There were a number of feel-good stories in 2002, not least the return to the competition of South Sydney Rabbitohs, now with movie mega-star Russell Crowe backing them. Although they won only five matches from 24, most seemed delighted they were back. Another returnee was Allan Langer after two seasons at Warrington. His astonishing performance in the 2001 State of Origin decider, when he had been recalled from England on a one-off basis, demonstrated he could still perform at the highest level, and Wayne Bennett successfully persuaded him to have one last crack at Premiership glory. In the end, Brisbane finished third and their season ended with the Grand Final a week away.

The JJ Giltinan Shield went to the Warriors, who had dropped 'Auckland' from their name at the end of the 2000 season in favour of 'New Zealand'. The six seasons under the Auckland name had been largely a desperate struggle for survival which culminated in a year of financial strife in 2000. As well as the name change, they also employed Daniel Anderson as coach who masterminded a stunning reversal of their fortunes. In 2001 they competed in the play-offs for the first time before surprising everybody by finishing top in 2002 with mercurial halfback Stacey Jones responsible for much of the good they did.

In the final, they met a team who weren't even in the top eight midway through the season. Ricky Stuart had taken over from Graham Murray as coach of Sydney Roosters in time for the 2002 campaign and ensured they timed their run to glory to perfection. Brad Fittler had retired from representative football in 2001 and was much more of a force, while the excellent performances of Brett Mullins on the wing, after a horror year at Leeds, surprised everybody. But it was another ex-Leeds player who stole the show at the end of the season. Adrian Morley, the only Englishman in the NRL after an injury-hit first eighteen months, justified the club's faith in him as he produced a string of big-hitting displays at the business end of the season. Ably supported by Craig Fitzgibbon and Luke Ricketson in the pack, the Roosters knocked off Cronulla, Newcastle and Brisbane to make the final, where they overturned a second-half deficit to beat the Warriors 30-8. In his trophy-acceptance speech, Fittler singled out Morley for praise. His huge hit on Warriors prop Richard Villasanti had proven to be a significant second-half turning point.

The Roosters reached the final again in 2003, the year that the controversial Golden Point was introduced, by beating Canterbury in the play-offs - a grudge match against a side still smarting from their points deduction. After finishing in last place in 2001, Penrith had rebuilt spectacularly to take out the Minor Premiership by two points from the Roosters with influential players like Craig Gower, Luke Priddis and Rhys Wesser in the key ballplaying positions leading the way. The final was a magnificent spectacle which produced one of those incidents which will live long in the annals. At 6-6 in the second half, Todd Byrne streaked up the left wing and looked a certain scorer for the Roosters until loose forward Scott Sattler scythed him down in full flow with a copybook cover tackle. The Panthers, buoyed by such a superb effort, broke the deadlock with fifteen minutes left when man of the match Luke Priddis scored a close-range try from dummy-half before Luke Rooney scored his second nine minutes later to seal the club's second Premiership. "I thought Byrne would score," said the Panthers' Trent Waterhouse. "You'd think a winger would get a back-rower any day so for Scott to get there was amazing. The game was on the edge at that moment and it gave us the spark to go on with it."

Also in 2003, Manly Sea Eagles returned to the competition after the unpopular and unsuccessful Northern Eagles venture was dissolved and Penrith's Gower was denied the Dally Messenger Medal, which is awarded annually to the competition's best and fairest player, when the ceremony was scrapped as a result of a dispute between the NRL and the players' union. There was another interesting story at the start of 2004 when after just one game, Jamie Lyon walked out on Parramatta citing stress and a desire to get out of the Sydney goldfish bowl. His subdued performance in a 48-14 defeat to the Bulldogs was in stark contrast to that of debutant Sonny Bill Williams who enjoyed a magnificent game in the centres for the winning side. Another Williams who hit the news in 2004 was Melbourne's Danny, who had played for Ireland in the 2000 World Cup. He punched Mark O'Neill in a match when the Tigers player wasn't looking in one of the worst on-field incidents for seen for years. He was banned for eighteen matches and his NRL career was over.

With Sonny Bill Williams repeating that round-one form for much of the season, the Bulldogs finished in second place just behind the Roosters on points difference and the two sides met in the Grand Final, which was to be Roosters' captain Brad Fittler's final game of an illustrious career. His side led 13-6 at the break but second-half tries from Matt Utai and Hazem El Masri brought the Premiership back to Belmore for the first time since 1995. It had been a been a strange year for the club with several of their players questioned over the rape of a woman at Coffs Harbour, where the club had visited in pre-season but with a lack of evidence, charges were dropped.

Brian Smith led the Eels to another Minor Premiership in 2005 in what would prove to be his last full season at the club, but they were trounced 29-0 by North Queensland Cowboys in their preliminary final. The rise of the Cowboys had been admirable. Cellar dwellers more often that not since their 1995 inauguration, the arrival of Graham Murray as coach in 2003 resulted in a swift upturn in performance, thanks in no small part to their fullback, Matt Bowen, one of the most exciting players in the competition and they reached the play-offs for the first time in 2004. At the start of 2005 they signed an even better player in halfback Johnathan Thurston and were quickly a force to be reckoned with. Neither of the 2004 finalists made the 2005 play-offs and when the top three fell by the wayside in the play-offs - St George and Brisbane joining Parramatta on the sidelines - it left two unfancied teams to contest the final. Wests Tigers had beaten the Cowboys 50-6 in the first week of the play-offs but thankfully for the neutral the final was much closer. The Tigers won 30-16 with a Benji Marshall flicked pass setting up a Pat Richards try the undoubted highlight. It was a particularly sweet moment for Tim Sheens, the Wests Tigers coach, who had failed to bring success to the Cowboys between 1997 and 2001. Added to his Canberra triumphs, this was his third Grand Final win as a coach.

2005 was also the last time the NRL saw regular bad-boy John Hopoate in action. Having been dogged by various controversies since his infamous Tigers exit in 2001, his tale of woe at Manly included being caught playing in a rugby union match under a false name and verbally abusing a ball boy. He had to later admit the ball boy had done nothing wrong in how he returned the ball to the field of play. That happened in round one of 2005, and in round two he was sent off for a forearm smash to the head of Cronulla's Keith Galloway. Not only had Galloway already released the ball but the winger also jumped into the collision. It was a sickening clash for which Hopoate was banned for seventeen matches. Manly tore up his contract and he immediately announced his retirement.

There was further controversy before the beginning of the following season when Craig Gower lost the Penrith captaincy, was suspended for four games and was fined heavily after a bizarre afternoon at a charity golf function. He was forced to pay to replace a golf buggy he had destroyed while inebriated and upset league legend Wayne Pearce by groping his daughter and vomiting on his son, Mitchell, the future Roosters halfback. Another negative story appeared when it was announced that the Warriors had been well over the 2005 salary cap of $3.25 million. They were fined heavily and deducted four points before the season started. In the end, that deduction prevented them from making the top-eight.

Melbourne stormed to the Minor Premiership in 2006, winning twenty matches out of 24. Since their 1999 success, they had finished in sixth, ninth and tenth but after the head-coaching appointment of Craig Bellamy, Wayne Bennett's former assistant at Brisbane, they became a regular play-off side with finishes of fifth, sixth and sixth. Inspired by fullback Billy Slater and hooker Cameron Smith, two brilliant young Queenslanders who had been born on the same day in June 1983, the club were back as a Premiership force and led the table from round fourteen but tripped up in the final against Bennett's Broncos - the first ever final to be contested between two non-New South Wales clubs. 10-8 up in the second half, Brent Tate's brilliant try proved crucial before a late Darren Lockyer drop goal wrapped up the title at 15-8. It was Lockyer's fourth Grand Final success, and his first since a hugely successful switch from fullback to stand-off in 2004. The Australia captain was fast becoming regarded as one of the finest players in the game's history.

In the modern era, Lockyer was probably bettered by only Andrew Johns, and 2007 started sadly for the Novocastrian. As the game celebrated the 100th year of professional rugby league in Australia, Johns was injured in round one and after appearing again in round three was sent for a scan after a training-ground knock. It revealed a bulging disc in his neck and he was advised to end his sensational playing career in order to avoid more serious injury. Sadly, he did not adapt well to retirement at first and was arrested in London in possession of an ecstasy tablet before admiiting having taken recreational drugs throughout his playing career. He has moved on to a successful media career, though, and in 2012 was named the eighth Australian Rugby League Immortal by Rugby League Week magazine.

The NRL welcomed its sixteenth club, the Gold Coast Titans, to the party in 2007 and a credible ten wins from 24 matches saw them finish the season just two competition points shy of eighth place. Melbourne again won the JJ

Giltinan Shield and this time they followed it up with Grand Final success by beating second-placed Manly 34-8 in a disappointingly one-sided Grand Final. Greg Inglis, who scored twice to win the Clive Churchill Medal, was another young Queenslander to make a name for himself at the club.

The same clubs occupied the top two slots on the 2008 ladder with Melbourne coming out on top courtesy of their superior points difference (Cronulla also finished on 38 points). Manly breezed into the final again but the Storm found things harder in the semi-final series. They became the first Minor Premiers to lose to the eighth-placed team (New Zealand Warriors) under the current system then, with one minute to go of their match in Brisbane, they faced elimination from the competition, but Greg Inglis scored to set up a heart-thumping 16-14 escape. After 21 seasons in charge, Wayne Bennett left the Broncos coaching role a beaten man in the cruellest of circumstances. The Storm then lost Cameron Smith to a two-match ban for a grapple tackle - a tactic that had blighted the NRL for a couple of years - and would have to do without their most influential player in the final, a decision which enraged Craig Bellamy. It proved too much, although even with their hooker, they wouldn't have won as Manly blitzed them 40-0. Even more surprising than the margin of victory was the fact that free-scoring fullback Brett Stewart wasn't among the scorers, but, fittingly, Steve Menzies was - in his last game for the club after sixteen seasons.

The NRL wouldn't be the NRL without its share of controversy and the 2009 season got off to a terrible start on that score as Brett Stewart, who had just filmed the annual NRL advertisment campaign, was charged with the sexual assault of a seventeen-year-old girl. The NRL unwisely fanned the flames further by suspending him for four matches for drunken behaviour, taking care to state it was offering no judgement on the sexual assault charges. Stewart was found not guilty in September 2010.

Possibly as a consequence of the Stewart furore, Manly lost their consistency in 2009, finishing fifth and exiting the play-offs after a heavy defeat at the hands of Melbourne in week one. Wayne Bennett was now at St George Illawarra, whom he led to the Minor Premiership but they collapsed in the semi-finals, losing to Parramatta before their season ended at Bennett's old club, Brisbane. Having finished fourth, Melbourne hit their straps at the right time and beat Brisbane with ease to make their fourth-straight final. There they met Daniel Anderson's Parramatta who had stunned everybody by reaching the decider from eighth place, beating St George, Gold Coast and Canterbury, with their lowest margin of victory ten points. They fought gamely in the final, too, before going down 23-16 to the Storm after trailing 22-6 with ten minutes remaining.

In sharp contrast to that massive high, Melbourne's world came crashing down in April 2010 when it was revealed they had been cheating the salary cap on a huge scale. Described by The Age newspaper as 'The biggest scandal in Australian sports history', the episode rumbled on for weeks as more revelations came to light. By using a dual-contract system, the club were over a million dollars over the cap in 2009 and 2010 and had been significantly over going back to 2006. As a result, they were stripped of their 2007 and 2009 titles, their 2010 World Club Challenge and their 2006, 2007 and 2008 Minor Premierships - none of which were awarded to the runners-up. They were docked the eight competition points they had accrued in 2010 and told that they would collect no more. With three-quarters of the season to go, they were already consigned to the wooden spoon and a series of meaningless matches. They were also fined an eye-watering Australian sporting record $1,689,000. Forced to come back to the accepted wage levels by 2011, they offloaded their Test three-quarter Greg Inglis, but managed to keep hold of Billy Slater and Cameron Smith.

The year had at least started on a happier note with the first All Stars match between the Indigenous All Stars and the NRL All Stars. With the public voting which players were to play and with innovations introduced such as the 'double try' where a team could have one tackle to score another try rather than kick a conversion, the conept was a hit. The match also marked the final career appearance of Wendell Sailor the former Brisbane winger who had returned to the code with St George Illawarra in 2008. He scored the first try of the match, which his team went on to win 16-12, and celebrated by using the corner post as a didgeridoo. Johnathan Thurston won the Preston Campbell Medal in honour of the player who had organised (and played in) the match.

St George Illawarra repeated their Minor Premiership success of 2009 and this time followed it up by landing the game's big prize. Once more Wayne Bennett beat Brian Smith in a Grand Final, although Smith's achievement in getting the Roosters there was remarkable in itself given that they had won the wooden spoon just a year earlier. Kiwi winger Jason Nightingale scored twice and fullback Darius Boyd picked up the Clive Churchill Medal in a 32-8 win.

Able to compete for points again, Melbourne Storm topped the 2011 table after 24 rounds, two points clear of Manly and Brisbane, who, with Anthony Griffin in charge, had finally started to adapt to life without Wayne Bennett. The trio made it to the third week of the semi-finals where the Sea Eagles beat the Broncos 26-14 to reach their third final in five years and Storm were surprisingly beaten 20-12 by New Zealand Warriors. As in the 1996 final, Manly scored the game's crucial try on the stroke of half-time, this time through Daly Cherry-Evans, and they went on to win 24-10. Glenn Stewart, brother of tryscorer Brett, won the Clive Churchill Medal.

A year later the Storm finally scaled the heights by winning the Grand Final, the club's second legitimate Premiership triumph. They beat Minor Premiers Canterbury in the Grand Final 14-4 in a game in which Englishman James Graham, who had enjoyed such a superb debut season, was reported to have bitten the ear of Storm fullback Billy Slater. Graham was subsequently banned for twelve matches. Cooper Cronk capped a memorable year, which had seen him win Queensland and Australia selection after the retirement of Darren Lockyer, by winning the Churchill Medal. 2012 also saw a welcome return to the right end of the table for Russell Crowe's South Sydney Rabbitohs. With the three Burgess brothers - Luke, Sam and George - on their roster (they were joined by another brother, Tom, in 2013) as well as mega-star Greg Inglis, successfully converted to fullback, Souths qualified for the play-offs for only the second time since their Minor Premiership year of 1989, after finishing in third place. In an illustration of how competitive the NRL is, of the sixteen clubs only two - Souths and Gold Coast - have failed to make a Grand Final since 1996.

2012 was the first year that the NRL was played under the umbrella of the Australian Rugby League Commission, which took over the running of the game from the the Australian Rugby League and News Ltd, who had managed to settle their mid-1990s differences to form the wonderful NRL, a competition that has exceeded all realistic expectations. Rugby league was badly wounded by its Super League War, but no lasting damage was done.

British and Irish first-grade players from 1980
* denotes still playing
(When the book went to print, South Sydney's Tom Burgess and Gold Coast's Matty Russell had not played an NRL match.)

Allan Bateman - Cronulla Sharks (1995-96)
Kevin Beardmore - Canberra Raiders (1985)
John Bentley - Balmain Tigers (1994)
Denis Betts - Auckland Warriors (1995-97)
Paul Bishop - Cronulla Sharks (1988-89), Gold Coast Seagulls (1991)
George Burgess - South Sydney Rabbitohs (2012-13*)
Luke Burgess - South Sydney Rabbitohs (2011-12*)
Sam Burgess - South Sydney Rabbitohs (2010-13*)
Brian Carney - Newcastle Knights (2006)
Gary Charlton - Gold Coast-Tweed Giants (1988)
Phil Clarke - Sydney City Roosters (1995-96)

Gary Connolly - Canterbury Bulldogs (1993)
Lee Crooks - Western Suburbs (1985-86), Balmain Tigers (1987)
Andy Currier - Balmain Tigers (1989-90)
Jonathan Davies - Canterbury Bulldogs (1991), North Queensland Cowboys (1995)
John Devereux - Manly Sea Eagles (1993)
Gary Divorty - Gold Coast Giants (1990)
Paul Dixon - Canterbury Buldogs (1987), Gold Coast Seagulls (1991)
Des Drummond - Western Suburbs (1986)
Bernard Dwyer - Manly Sea Eagles (1989)
Mark Edmondson - Sydney Roosters (2006)
Shaun Edwards - Balmain Tigers (1989)
Gareth Ellis - Wests Tigers (2009-12)
Kevin Ellis - Gold Coast Chargers (1996)
St John Ellis - South Queensland Crushers (1995)
Vince Fawcett - Parramatta Eels (1995)
Mark Flanagan - Wests Tigers (2010-11)
Mike Ford - South Queensland Crushers (1995)
Deryck Fox - Western Suburbs (1986)
Richard Gay - St George Dragons (1993)
Henderson Gill - South Sydney Rabbitohs (1995)
Andy Goodway - Manly Sea Eagles (1985)
James Graham - Canterbury Bulldogs (2012-13*)
John Gray - Manly Sea Eagles (1980), North Sydney Bears (1981-83)
Andy Gregory - Illawarra Steelers (1989)
Mike Gregory - Cronulla (1987)
Steve Hampson - Illawarra Steelers (1989)
Ellery Hanley - Balmain Tigers (1988, 1995-97), Western Suburbs (1989)
James Hasson - Manly Sea Eagles (2013*)
John Henderson - Western Suburbs (1986)
Harvey Howard - Eastern Suburbs (1993), Western Suburbs (1996-99), Brisbane Broncos (2000)
Lee Jackson - South Sydney Rabbitohs (1995), Newcastle Knights (1996-98)
Chris Joynt - Newcastle Knights (1995)
Tracey Lazenby - Penrith Panthers (1989)
Joe Lydon - Eastern Suburbs (1987, 1989)
Andy Kelly - Illawarra Steelers (1984)
Keith Mason - Melbourne Storm (2002)
Barrie-Jon Mather - Perth Western Reds (1995-97)
Richard Mathers - Gold Coast Titans (2007)

James McManus - Newcastle Knights (2007-2013*)
Scott Moore - North Queensland Cowboys (2013*)
Adrian Morley - Sydney Roosters (2001-2006)
David Myers - Manly Sea Eagles (1991), Western Suburbs (1995)
Tony Myler - Balmain Tigers (1986)
Brian Noble - Cronulla Sharks (1985)
Martin Offiah - Eastern Suburbs (1989, 1993), St George Dragons (1991)
Andy Platt - Auckland Warriors (1995-96)
Daio Powell - Perth Western Reds (1995)
Daryl Powell - Balmain (1988), Gold Coast Seagulls (1991)
Gary Price - South Sydney Rabbitohs (1996)
Jack Reed - Brisbane Broncos (2011-13*)
Huw Rees - Western Suburbs (1987)
Dean Sampson - Gold Coast Giants (1990), Parramatta Eels (1995)
Garry Schofield - Balmain Tigers (1985-87), Western Suburbs (1989)
Ian Sibbit - Melbourne Storm (2002)
Kelvin Skerrett - Western Suburbs (1989)
Graham Steadman - Gold Coast Giants (1989)
Jordan Tansey - Sydney Roosters (2009)
Chris Thorman - Parramatta Eels (2004)
Hugh Waddell - Manly Sea Eagles (1989)
Kevin Ward - Manly Sea Eagles (1987-88)
Colin Whitfield - Canterbury Bulldogs (1987)
Gareth Widdop - Melbourne Storm (2010-2013*)

CHAPTER EIGHT
THE HISTORY OF STATE OF ORIGIN

"Bloody Alf! You flew 16,981km to break our hearts.
Now, please go back to England!"
- *Sydney Daily Telegraph front page, 2001.*

When, in 2001, Gene Miles, the great Queensland centre of the 1980s, uttered the words "Number seven, Allan Langer" as he announced the Maroons' line-up for their third game against New South Wales, Rugby League's State of Origin was creating another new life for itself. It had used up about five already, so what was another one? And that's because, for the umpteenth time in its twenty-year history, the Origin concept was, according to the hysterical Sydney media, on the verge of extinction due to their 3-0 series victory a year earlier which had culminated in an embarrassingly easy 56-16 scoreline for the Blues. As we all know, Alfie came back from Warrington at the 'past-it' age of 35, and ran the arrogant Blues ragged to record an absolutely sensational, against-all-odds series victory for the Maroons.

That's not the first time, nor the last, that people have questioned the viability and the validity of State of Origin football. In fact, if New South Wales had won the inaugural game in 1980, it's probable that it would have killed the concept stone dead. That's because the Interstate competition was dying. The age-old best-of-three series between the two states was based upon where a player was currently playing, and most of the best players were based in Sydney. Therefore New South Wales were far too good for Queensland, and everyone knew it. A minor change to the eligibility rules seemed like a last desperate throw of the dice. State of Origin might be the highest standard of Rugby League Football around today, but it's very existence has all too often hung by a thread.

It all began in 1980 as the third Interstate game was scrapped in favour of a new-fangled concept that allowed players to play for their own State, not the State where they had ended up playing. Several Queenslanders were plying their weekly trade for the richer Sydney clubs and were therefore obliged to represent New South Wales. Origin had actually been called for from as far back as 1900 when the New South Wales three-quarter Lonnie Spragg moved north. "Even though residing in Rockhampton, I am of the opinion he should play for New South Wales. The time has arrived , I think, for the observance of [such] a qualification for players in inter-colonial matches," wrote 'the Cynic' in The Referee. And in 1964 the Brisbane-based Courier Mail writer Jack Reardon declared: "While the NSW score was mounting at the SCG last

Tuesday, someone in the press seats suggested that Queensland should be allowed to call on their former players now with Sydney clubs."

Having once again been trounced by New South Wales in the first two matches of Interstate in 1980, it was finally agreed that Queensland could, for the third game, call up John Lang and Kerry Boustead from Easts, Greg Oliphant and Rod Morris from Balmain, Rod Reddy from St George, Allan Smith from Norths and last but not least, the legendary Arthur Beetson from Parramatta Eels. This game wouldn't be part of the Interstate series. It was given its own title - State of Origin.

Arthur Beetson is one of Australian Rugby League's eight 'immortals'; the others being Clive Churchill, Johnny Raper, Reg Gasnier, Bob Fulton, Graeme Langlands, Wally Lewis and, most recently, Andrew Johns. Forget Lewis, the greatest-ever Origin player, for the time being; if it wasn't for the deeds of Arthur Beetson on that fabulous night in July 1980, State of Origin would have died 80 minutes after it had been born. That's because Queensland had to win. For years they had pushed Sydney's governing body to adapt its Interstate rules to Origin's. Senator Ron McAuliffe, the godfather of Queensland Rugby League, sold the concept as hard as he could, and with Interstate on its last legs because of NSW's total domination that had seen them win TWENTY consecutive series, the Origin match was eventually given the go ahead. It was the last shot at keeping the New South Wales v Queensland fixture alive, and few people south of the border thought it stood a chance, including Bobby Fulton, the former Australia captain and future coach, who, incredibly, deemed it 'the non-event of the century'.

Fortunately, 33,210 rabidly passionate Queenslanders thought otherwise and packed out Lang Park. Lewis, to this day, swears that he hasn't heard a noise to rival that of the crowd as Beetson was announced to the crowd. After years of pulling on a Blues jersey just because he played his football in Sydney, the great man had finally come home, right at the end of his career, and, in a moment that saw the birth of the wonderful phrase 'mate against mate, state against state', he was reported to have clobbered his Parramatta mate, and equally iconic legend, Mick Cronin. It was almost like hitting Mother Theresa; surely no-one would hit the gentlemanly Cronin - but with state pride on the line, Beetson got him with a high shot as he stood vulnerable and upright in a tackle. The incident has been exaggerated and mythologised over time as an all-out assault, but if Beetson could swing an arm at Cronin, anything could happen, and with proof that Origin meant the world to at least half of the players on display, Queensland against New South Wales finally had some meaning again, albeit under a new format. The home side won 20-10 with Mal Meninga celebrating his twentieth birthday by kicking seven goals, although the honour of scoring the first-ever Origin try went to the Blues' Greg Brentnall.

1981 saw the continuation of the Interstate series, but again NSW triumphed with minimum effort, so game three, again, was played under Origin rules. The Blues raced into a 15-0 lead, thanks partly to a length-of-the-field Eric Grothe try, but collapsed and lost 22-15. Chris Close, as he was in year one, was named man of the match, but was involved in an ugly incident as he backhanded Grothe, who lay prostrate on the floor, in order to pick up the ball from dummy-half and score. Origin was alive and kicking and common sense prevailed - the old Interstate competition was disbanded and 1982 would see the first best-of-three series played under Origin rules.

Again, few gave the Maroons a chance in 1982, with some south of the border still insisting that each of their one-off successes had been a fluke. There was also a popular theory that it meant more to Queensland and they were only winning because they were trying harder, not because they were better. With Lewis and Meninga developing at a rate of knots, and with Beetson coaching, the Maroons overturned a first-game defeat to win the first proper Origin series with a horrendous in-goal mix-up from Blues pair Phil Sigsworth and Philip Duke in the third match gifting Lewis the try that decided the series.

The following year provided one of Origin's most controversial moments when the fiery Blues forward Les Boyd smashed the cheekbone of the hapless debutant Darryl Brohman with a vicious elbow attack as the Penrith forward was gang-tackled. Incredibly he wasn't sent off, but when the Panthers complained, Boyd was suspended for twelve months. Boyd later said: "It's not that I wanted to do it. [Referee] Barry Gomersall was giving us a friggin' hard time and the penalties were going against us ... it was just one of those spur-of-the-moment things." As well as sidelining Brohman for months and costing him an Australia jumper, the saga was further played out off the field with Brohman suing and receiving around $35,000. State rivalry was cranked up another notch, but, back on the field, Lewis tore New South Wales to pieces with a masterclass in the deciding game which saw his side 33-0 up at one stage before the game finished 43-22.

In 1984, the Blues' agony continued as their opponents won the first two games by margins of seventeen and twelve points. The second game, at the Sydney Cricket Ground, produced possibly Origin's most famous try as Lewis's chipped kick rebounded off the crossbar into the grateful arms of an unlikely tryscorer Greg Dowling, who took the ball from around his ankles in the most dreadful of conditions.

Finally, in 1985, New South Wales got their hands on the Origin shield and Steve Mortimer, their captain and halfback, sunk to his knees in celebration and kissed the famous SCG turf. He was chaired from the field with the chant of "Blues! Blues! Blues!" reverberating around the stadium. Michael O'Connor had enjoyed one of Origin's great debuts, scoring all of his side's points in the game-one 18-2 win before the Blues wrapped up their maiden series win with a 21-14 win in Sydney. During that series, another controversy broke out when Terry Fearnley, who coached both New South Wales and Australia, dropped four Queenslanders from the Kangaroo team to face New Zealand. Maroon fury erupted with McAuliffe calling it 'A football assassination'. In game three of Origin, Greg Dowling, when substituted with Queensland ahead, was quick to let Fearnley, on the NSW bench, know what he thought of him by launching a tirade of abuse in his direction. Queensland won 20-6. Since then, no one has been allowed to coach Australia while coaching Origin.

The Blues even went one better in 1986, whitewashing Queensland, a superb triumph given that two of the games were played at Lang Park. Royce Simmons earned himself no end of praise with a man-of-the-match display in game one, by choosing to play on after he had been knocked out, waving away the trainers even after he lost his balance trying to get back into the defensive line. The Blues won the series with scores of 22-16, 24-20 and 18-16.

The 1987 series is best known for the introduction to Origin of Allan Langer. The tiny halfback was playing for Ipswich Jets in the Brisbane Leagues and a number of Queensland players, most notably Lewis himself, objected to Langer's selection. "[Coach] Wayne Bennett brought it up at a selection meeting and I said to him: 'He struggled in defence at the weekend and he may be a target for the Blues.' Bennett looked at me and just said 'thanks'. Ten minutes later, they'd named the side and Langer was in. My opinion wasn't worth two bob! In training we were going through our defensive patterns and Bennett said Alf would stand behind the line. Paul Vautin came in and said, 'He's playing for Queensland. No-one's going to f***ing hide!' He looked at Alf and said 'You're not going to hide are you?' Alf was too scared to say anything but 'no!'" Langer went on to enjoy a great series and picked up the official man-of-the-match award in the deciding game as his side triumphed 10-8 to get their hands back on the shield for the first time in three years. He would hold onto that number-seven jersey for years with no-one, not even The King, questioning his selection. As a footnote, a fourth game was played in 1987 in California as a promotional exercise and was won 30-18 by NSW, but it didn't count towards the series score.

Two of the most famous Origin moments came in the next two series and both involved Lewis. In 1988, with his state a game to the good thanks to a great performance from Peter Jackson, Lewis was controversially sin-binned for running in by referee Michael Stone. The crowd went ballistic, chucking hundreds of beer cans onto the field in protest. The game was held up as the cans were cleared away while the Blues players, most notably centre Mark McGaw,

were terrified that the fans were going to charge onto the field. 'Sparkles', as he was nicknamed, tried to persuade captain Wayne Pearce to lead his players off the field, but his protests were ignored. When Lewis returned he helped his side to a 16-6 win, which they backed up in the decider at Sydney with a comprehensive 38-22 thrashing of the Blues, with cult hero prop Sam Backo winning consecutive man-of-the-match awards.

Lewis was remembered for the right reasons in 1989 as he scored a sensational try in the most demanding of circumstances to clinch yet another series victory. With game one in the bag, the Maroons travelled south where everything that could have gone wrong did go wrong, as they lost Langer with a broken leg, Meninga with a fractured eye socket, Vautin with an elbow injury and Mick Hancock with a bruised shoulder, while Bob Lindner, incredibly, had to carry on for a period with a fracture in his ankle. In an inspired piece of captaincy, Lewis took his charges past the casualties and urged them to finish the series off for them. With the match crucially poised, and the Blues fancying themselves to win on the basis of the Queensland's problems, Trevor Gillmeister, aptly nicknamed 'The Axe', chopped down Bradley Clyde with a wonderful hit and the ball was seized by the Maroons' stand-in halfback, Michael Hagan, who passed to Lewis. The rest is history. Lewis, barely inside his opponents' half of the field, set off on a mazy, weaving run and ended up carrying defenders over the line for a wonderful individual try. "We were shot to bits - it was probably one of Queensland's greatest moments," he said.

1990 saw Origin move away from the two states as game two went to Melbourne. Going into the series, the Blues had lost eight matches in a row (excluding the 1987 American exhibition), but finally stopped the rot with the lowest score in Origin history in the first game - an 8-0 win in Sydney with Mark McGaw scoring the only try as his side took advantage of the fact that Lewis was missing for Queensland. They sealed the series with a 12-6 win in Victoria helped by a great performance from Ricky Stuart. By this stage Jack Gibson, who in 2008 was named the finest coach in the history of Australian Rugby League, was in charge of New South Wales and nuggety hooker Benny Elias picked up the man-of-the-series award. It was just their third series win.

1991, Lewis's last series, remains one of the greatest State of Origin series with the margin in each game only two points. Game one ended in almost farcical circumstances as Michael O'Connor missed a late conversion to tie the game, but Meninga, inexplicably, booted his kick-off out on the full. NSW had a halfway-line penalty shot to level the scores but Greg Alexander's attempt fell short. Amazingly in game two in Sydney, O'Connor was presented with another late goal attempt and sent a sensational, curling conversion over the posts from tight on the right touchline, as he converted Mark McGaw's try to level the series. The game is also remembered for Mark Geyer's fiery performance which culminated in an infamous spat with Lewis just before half-time. A fortnight later, Queensland triumphed again to send Lewis out a winner. Just after Mal Meninga had converted Dale Shearer's try to give them a 70th-minute lead, it was announced over the public-address system that it was to be the captain's final stand in the state arena prompting the crowd to rise to the occasion and cheer their team to victory. The game was played amid a backdrop of personal emotion for Lewis as he and his wife, Jacqui, had discovered the day before the game that his one-year-old daughter, Jamie-Lee, was deaf.

With Lewis gone, a new era dawned in 1992 and one of Origin's most influential characters took his place in the Blues hotseat. Phil 'Gus' Gould masterminded the first period of New South Wales domination under the Origin rules. As unpopular in Queensland as he is in England, even his fiercest critics would have to admit he was a brilliant coach. He endeavoured to instil a Queensland-like spirit that had worked against the Blues for so many years. He kicked off his reign with a 14-6 win and, after the Maroons had levelled the series in Brisbane with a nailbiting 5-4 win courtesy of a late Langer field goal, saw his team win the decider 16-4.

One of Gould's masterstrokes was to appoint Laurie Daley as his captain. Daley didn't captain his club side, Canberra Raiders, who were led by Meninga. "Laurie often told us how Mal showed him absolutely no mercy," wrote Gould in the foreword to Daley's autobiography. "In game two [of 1993] we led into the final ten minutes but the Queenslanders rallied to score and set up a grandstand finish. We were holding them down their end when a long pass to Mal Meninga sent the big man into the clear. From where I was sitting I could only see one man in pursuit. Coming across in cover was the Blues skipper Laurie Daley. The next few seconds seemed to take an eternity as I watched these two great men eyeball each other and come to terms with the situation. In years gone by Mal Meninga would have not hesitated in going for the corner … [but] … the great man slowed down and waited for support. His respect for the Blues captain had reached the point that he realised Laurie would be too quick for him and too strong to fend. Mal's pass was spoiled by Laurie, who secured possession for the Blues. It was the final play of the game and when the siren sounded, the Blues had scored a sensational series victory. When Laurie came back into the dressing room, I put my hand on his shoulder and said, 'You are the boss now. You got him.'"

Despite New South Wales's three-year domination of Origin, 1994 produced a Queensland moment to eclipse anything Lewis had ever done. With Lewis coaching the Maroons, they trailed game one in Sydney by two points with seconds left and what happened next is firmly embedded in Australian sporting history. Allan Langer found his great mate Kevin Walters, who passed to Willie Carne before the ball ended up with Steve Renouf, who raced upfield. Hancock, Darren Smith, Langer again and Meninga all handled in a sensational, sweeping move before the captain found centre Mark Coyne who stepped inside the challenges of Stuart and Brad Fittler to score. "That's not a try, that's a miracle," shouted Ray Warren in the commentary box. Indeed it was, but Gould went to work on his stunned troops and led them to fourteen- and fifteen-point victories to clinch their third-straight series.

By the time the next series came along, the Australian game was tearing itself apart as Super League tried to wrest control of the sport from the ARL. Regrettably, no Super League-aligned players could play in the 1995 Origin, but, strangely, that short-sighted decision led to one of the most astonishing underdog victories in Australian sport. Queensland's former loose forward Paul Vautin took over the coaching reins and, unable to select players from Brisbane Broncos, was forced to select unheralded players like Terry Cook, Craig Teevan and a young Ben Ikin, whom Vautin mistook for an autograph hunter at the first training session. With the squad manager, Chris Close, admitting that Vautin had the players 'eating out of the palm of his hand' when he first addressed the squad, they stunned the Blues to win game one 2-0, with Wayne Bartrim kicking a penalty. Early emotion got the better of everybody in the early stages of Origin II in Melbourne as the most incredible series of brawls broke out all over the field, including Manly teammates John Hopoate (NSW) and Danny Moore going head to head. When the football restarted, the Maroons wrapped up the series with a 20-12 win with Brett Dallas scoring a late long-range try. Ahead of game three, their captain, Trevor Gillmeister undid his intravenous drip, discharged himself from hospital against medical advice and led his side to a series whitewash. He didn't play 80 minutes but was chaired from the field a hero, before returning to hospital.

In 1996, the Super League players returned, but with a far stronger team on paper, the Maroons couldn't repeat their success and went down to a three-nil drubbing with Andrew Johns and Geoff Toovey leading the way, and Queensland's Craig Greenhill becoming the first red-carded player in Origin history in game two for a high tackle. That alone was something of a shock as it had been widely believed that you had to do something pretty serious to be marched in Origin. The Blues dominated the first two games and led 15-2 in the third before a late Maroon comeback brought the score to 15-14. In the last minute, it looked like Mark Coyne had produced another last-gasp winner, but he was ruled offside following Allan Langer's kick. New South Wales used the same starting team and substitutes throughout the entire series, and remain the only team to do that.

They repeated the dose in 1997, in a dull series memorable only for a brawl which saw Johns sparked out by Queensland hooker Jamie Goddard. As in 1995, there were no Super League players but this time it hurt the series badly and with the game's morale at its lowest ebb, crowds averaged less than 30,000. The first two games were tight, with NSW winning by margins of two points and one, before Queensland hit back to win the dead rubber 18-12. Super League, incidentally, hosted a Tri-Series including New Zealand and the Blues beat the Maroons in a wonderful final decided in golden point by a Noel Goldthorpe field goal, after Brett Mullins had scored a hat-trick of tries.

With League reunited again in 1998, the Maroons got their hands back on the shield with Langer scoring a magnificent and crucial try in the deciding game. Again, as in 1994, they won the opener with a last-minute, length-of-the-field try, with Tonie Carroll this time the hero, although it still needed to be converted after the hooter by a youthful Darren Lockyer on his Origin debut. The Blues levelled the series in Brisbane only to lose it on their own ground a fortnight later. After such a promising start eleven years earlier, this was the arguably first series in which Langer had really made his mark and his state's success effectively counted double because, after a drawn series in 1999,

Queensland held onto the shield as they were the holders and the Blues had failed to win it from them. On that occasion, Mat Rogers scored all of his side's points in game one as Queensland won 9-8 but Laurie Daley hit back with his last Origin hurrah in Sydney scoring the crucial try and winning his first Origin man-of-the-match award. The third game finished 10-all after the Blues blew a late chance to win the game.

In what was a huge controversy at the time, Gorden Tallis was sent off in game one of 2000 for verbally abusing referee Bill Harrigan who had missed a clear knock-on as the Blues pegged back Queensland to win. Andrew Johns, surprisingly on the bench, inspired the Blues to wrap up the series in game two before they massacred Queensland in game three 56-16, after Tallis had called for dead rubbers to be scrapped. It was Origin's biggest win and centre Ryan Girdler could boast the biggest-ever individual haul of 32 points. After every try, the Blues, inspired by the popular TV programme, The Footy Show, went through their repertoire of celebrations with the media later questioning the whole viability of Origin. The Blues, they reckoned, would dominate for years. Queensland were at rock bottom.

How wrong they were! Wayne Bennett, saddened by his state's demise, came back to the coaching role and, giving ten players their debuts, watched on as his side racked up a superb 34-16 win, with debutant Carl Webb scoring a sensational try and Tallis in the form of his life, but the rampaging forward was ruled out for the rest of the series and NSW hit back in game two to win with similar ease; 26-8. Then Queensland dropped their bombshell - Allan Langer would be returning from England to fill their number-seven jersey after Bennett saw some footage of Langer in great Super League form for Warrington. With Sydneysiders deriding the selection as desperate, 'Alfie' rolled back the years, laying on three tries and scoring one himself, as they ran out 40-18 winners. "It was the greatest day of my life," he said later, while the Sydney Daily Telegraph's front page boomed: "Bloody Alf! You flew 16,981km to break our hearts. Now, please go back to England!"

Three years on from the 1999 debacle that saw the Maroons lift the shield despite not having won the series, the ARL had still not changed the rules, and it happened again. A late Dane Carlaw try in game three of 2002, after a Langer pass, tied up the scores and Lote Tuqiri missed the goal. The Blues were furious and fortunately for the concept's credibility, Golden Point extra-time has since been played in drawn matches. Further furore erupted when, in their post-match celebrations, Tallis ran to the crowd gesticulating wildly. It was reported at first that he had given Blues' fans the one-finger salute but it emerged that he had been enraged by a derogatory banner aimed at his mother who had featured on television in the build-up to the game, ensuring that Tallis won plenty of public sympathy - and the finger he had used was his index finger. Game two also served up some controversy with Queensland winger Lote Tuqiri scoring three tries and three goals. After being charged with a dangerous throw after a Brisbane Broncos game, it appeared that the one-game ban would see him miss the match. Bennett, though, was too clever for the judiciary and left Tuqiri off the original Queensland team sheet and named him instead in the Broncos game for the weekend before the Origin match (when Origin players are rested). This resulted in the ban applying to the NRL game, freeing him to take his place in Origin.

The Blues set off on another three-year winning streak from 2003, with coach Gus Gould and scrum-half Andrew Johns the pivotal figures. They took out the first two games with relative ease in a series made memorable by the cameras capturing Michael de Vere stood on the sidelines having a cut on his head treated with a staple gun. "I thought they were just going to tape it up and stop the bleeding and the next thing he [the trainer] had the staple gun!" he said.

Golden Point was first played in an Origin match in the first game in 2004 with Shaun Timmins kicking a drop goal to give the Blues a 9-8 win. In game two, the Maroons hit back with Billy Slater scoring one of the great Origin tries. He gathered a chip through and seeing Blues fullback Anthony Minichiello ahead of him, chipped over him, regathered and scored. Brett Kenny later described it as Origin's finest four-pointer. As far as the series was concerned, though, it was in vain as the Blues won the decider 36-14 with Craig Fitzgibbon man of the match. Fitzgibbon was also the recipient of the Wally Lewis Medal as the player of the series, the first such award in Origin football.

Another Golden Point classic materialised in 2005 with Matty Bowen scoring the deciding try to give Queensland a 24-20 win after an enthralling game. However, inspired by Andrew Johns' greatest individual performance, in the words of the man himself, the Blues hit back in game two and wrapped up the series with a 32-10 win in the decider. Blues fullback Anthony Minichiello won the Wally Lewis Medal as player of the series, and later the Golden Boot. After 2005, there was nothing between the two states: twelve series and 36 wins apiece.

With the Blues seemingly dominating Origin, the biggest turning point in the 30-year history of the concept came in game three of 2006. One game all, they were inching towards victory in the decider and were en route to their fourth-straight series, but in the dying embers of the decider, as the Blues came off their own line, Lockyer pounced on a terrible dummy-half pass from Brett Hodgson to win the game and the series for his state. The Queensland captain was also named player of the series. It was a disaster for the Blues, who haven't won a series since.

What has followed has trumped all of the great Queensland achievements in the 1980s as the modern-day Maroons, coached by one of their greatest players, Mal Meninga, have swept all before them to win an incredible seven straight series and, whereas 2006 certainly needed a degree of luck with Hodgson's late error, they have been thoroughly dominant from 2007 with Lockyer, one of the great players of all time, ably assisted by his halfback partner Johnathan Thurston, and the magnificent Melbourne duo Billy Slater and Cameron Smith. Throw in Greg Inglis, the brilliant three-quarter, and you have five Golden Boot winners who have been far too good for the Blues.

Despite the same side dominating, the controversies and the arguments haven't dissipated. Inglis, say the Blues, should be playing for them, and eligibility laws have subsequently tightened and by 2007 he was a central figure on the inter-state stage as his two tries in the opener played a big part a Queensland comeback from 6-18 at half-time to 25-18 winners in a thoroughly absorbing contest. Game two was comparatively dull but Inglis scored again in a 10-6 triumph in Sydney - Queensland's first-ever win at the Olympic Stadium which was first used for Rugby League in 1999 - which sealed the series. After the game, former Maroons player and coach Paul Vautin said: "This could be the start of a Queensland dynasty," but the Blues restored a little credibility with an 18-4 win in the dead-rubber. Cameron Smith won the Wally Lewis Medal.

New South Wales hopes of preventing a trio of series successes in 2008 were lifted with the appointment of the best club coach in the business. Craig Bellamy had turned Melbourne Storm into a champion team and it was believed that if anybody could implement the tactics to blunt Slater, Smith and Inglis, then it was him. With Queensland's skipper, Darren Lockyer, ruled out of the series, Blues' confidence cranked up another notch and when they won the opening game 18-10 with Greg Bird producing a superb performance, it looked like they had hit upon the right formula. Any optimism, though, was emphatically extinguished as they lost the second game 30-0. The decider, in Sydney, was much closer, and after a second-minute brawl had set the tone, the scores were locked at 10-10 with thirteen minutes remaining. Showing that they could win without Lockyer, Thurston, later named player of the series, broke free and found the supporting Slater who scored under the posts.

Bellamy stayed at the Blues' helm in 2009 but again came up short. For the first time, the opening match was played in Melbourne with Inglis and Slater thriving in familiar territory by providing three of their side's four tries in an 18-10 win. The series was wrapped up with another Maroons win in Sydney, this time by 24-14 in a game best remembered by Trent Barrett, now home from a two-year stint at Wigan, breaking Inglis's jaw, although the powerhouse centre had still done enough to be named player of the series.

The Blues won the meaningless third, but it was by now impossible to deny Queensland's dominance.

Origin in 2010 was unfortunately overshadowed by a race argument in the build-up to game two. Queensland won the opening game 28-24 in Sydney, in a scoreline that didn't do justice to their performance, and in the build-up to the next match, Timana Tahu walked out of the Blues camp, citing personal reasons. It transpired that a member of the coaching staff, Andrew Johns, had used racist language when talking about Queensland's Greg Inglis. Tahu, a former Newcastle teammate of Johns, took offence and the episode was an unnecessary stain on the code's reputation. With the Blues in disarray, they were predictably thrashed 34-6 as another series slipped through their fingers. Israel Folau, whose selection in the aftermath of his announcement that he was to leave the game at the end of the season in order to play Australian Rules Football sparked a big debating point, scored twice. Queensland wrapped up the whitewash with a 23-18 win in Sydney, thanks to late tries from Billy Slater, the man of the match and the series, and Willie Tonga.

Ricky Stuart became the next man to take on Meninga, his old Canberra Raiders captain, and he fared considerably better than Bellamy in his two years in charge of the Blues. Losing to a 73rd-minute Billy Slater try, the Blues produced a wonderful 18-8 win in Sydney with Paul Gallen, in the unfamiliar position of prop, putting in one of the great individual Origin displays. Stuart's side had shown enough to suggest they could win the decider in Brisbane but, once again, Queensland were just too good. They won 34-24, but had led 34-10 going into the last ten minutes. Cameron Smith was named player of the series.

2012 was the first time in six years that a New South Wales series win looked realistic. Having lost game one thanks largely to a controversial Greg Inglis try with seven minutes left (although they were trailing by two points at the time), the Blues again hit back in game two with prolific fullback Brett Stewart scoring twice. 16-8 down at half-time in the decider, the Blues, for once, were strong enough to come back. Stewart scored his third try in as many weeks which reduced the deficit to two, before two Johnathan Thurston penalties made it 20-14. With ten minutes left, Josh Morris added to the try that his twin, Brett, had scored in the first half and when Todd Carney converted, the scores were locked at 20-all. In front of what was later reported to be the second highest Australian TV audience ever, Queensland's Cooper Cronk emerged the hero with a 40-metre drop goal with five minutes to go. The Maroons had prevailed again, but there was nothing to choose between the two states.

After 33 years, State of Origin remains an gargantuan concept on the Australian sporting landscape, and long may that continue. The non-event of the century? Bob Fulton could not have been more wrong!

State of Origin has long become the jewel in the Australian rugby league crown; an event which seems to grind most of the two states to a halt. Attendances have steadily grown throughout the years and most matches are now played before sell-out crowds while TV ratings have become phenomenal in recent years. Once it became fully established, its success has mirrored the popularity of the game as a whole. 1997, for example, was an awful year for the concept with rugby league now an embittered and divided sport, torn apart by the Super League War.

But the speed with which rugby league repaired itself after hostilities ended was remarkable. The National Rugby League brand has been enormously successful and although Australia's national side hasn't been as dominant in the last decade as it had previously been, the Australian game is otherwise in a fantastic position. NRL crowds could be higher (although they are significantly better than Super League's) and occasional front-page scandals have occasional blighted the sport, but they are the only blots on an otherwise perfect landscape. Despite Queensland's post-2006 domination, Origin remains as popular as ever. When New South Wales eventually win back the shield, their success will sit alongside any in Origin's proud history.

The increase in the NRL's salary cap and the strength of the Australian dollar will see more and more English players try their hand down under, which means that the gap between the NRL and Super League won't be closing in the forseeable future, and although that is regrettable from an English point of view, the NRL and State of Origin should be celebrated in their own rights for the thoroughly absorbing and wonderfully entertaining competitions they are.

CHAPTER NINE
THE HISTORY OF THE GOLDEN BOOT

"I remember growing up having posters on my wall of Ellery and his Golden Boot. I couldn't believe it when I won it because it's such a prestigious award."
- *Two-time winner Andrew Johns, 2010*

The Golden Boot is presented annually by Rugby League World magazine to the player adjudged to be the world's best. The roll call of winners throws up a list of some of the finest players ever to lace on a boot, and evokes memories of some of their greatest achievements. It was inaugurated in 1985 by Open Rugby magazine who decided that the Australian captain, Wally Lewis, on the basis of his achievements in 1984, was to be the first recipient. The magazine, published and edited by Harry Edgar, continued to present the award until 1991 when the plug was pulled due to financial and logistical difficulties. In 1999 it was revived by Rugby League World, the new title for the magazine, after it had been sold by Edgar to the publishers of League Express newspaper. After that nine-year hiatus, Andrew Johns was the first winner under the magazine's new ownership, and it continues to be awarded at the end of the rugby league year.

In 2010 Rugby League World, made two significant changes with Edgar's blessing. They decided to recognise that while Lewis, and the other early winners, received the award in one year, it was ultimately awarded for their achievements in the previous calendar year. Therefore Lewis is now recognised as the 1984 winner, Brett Kenny the 1985 winner, through to Mal Meninga, the 1989 winner. Secondly, and more importantly, they retrospectively awarded the Boot to Garry Schofield, the former Great Britain player, for his achievements in 1990. Until then, Schofield had been 'the winner that never was' as the award was ditched before it was presented to him. The reason it was scrapped was that Adidas withdrew their sponsorship. Edgar readily admitted that he had struggled for at least three years with international issues that saw the award move too far from what he had initially intended it to be back in the early 1980s.

Edgar gives a lot of credit for the birth of the Golden Boot to Peter Deakin, who worked for Open Rugby and who later did such magnificent and groundbreaking marketing work at Bradford in the early Super League years. He explained: "It was in the early 1980s that I thought it would be really good to do. A French football magazine called Onze promoted the 'Golden Shoe' which went to the European footballer of the year and it was sponsored by

Adidas - it looked great and I thought it would be fantastic if we could do something like that in Rugby League. I'd always wanted to do something on an international basis. That's how the seed of the idea grew. For credibility it had to be the 'Adidas Golden Boot', so we started talking to them and after a lot of effort we got them on board to sponsor the world ratings, which we'd been doing for a while. Then we asked them to be associated with the world's best - the Golden Boot. This was perfect for Peter. He loved a big event and the razzmatazz involved in something like this, and it was down to him that we managed to get Adidas on board. They were heavily into rugby union and didn't want to touch Rugby League at first."

With Adidas on board and the first Golden Boot made, all that was left was to come up with a winner. By 1984 Lewis was the dominant figure in State of Origin and in 1984, he produced two of his record eight man-of-the-match awards in the first two games. He captained Australia to an Ashes whitewash over Great Britain, and led an Oceania side to an easy victory over the Northern Hemisphere in Paris. He helped his new club, Wynnum Manly, to Grand Final success in Brisbane, and he captained a combined Brisbane side to victory over the Winfield Cup's Eastern Suburbs in the final of the National Panasonic Cup, beating South Sydney, Canterbury and Parramatta along the way with Lewis crowned player of the series. He was as convincing a winner of the Golden Boot as you could get.

"Wally was the man and he was such a genuine winner," said Edgar. "We'd got Australia involved as we had Adidas [the Australian version of the company] and Rugby League Week magazine on board. It worked out perfectly because we wanted the first Golden Boot event to be done around an international match and the only one at the time was Australia against New Zealand in Brisbane. Wally Lewis receiving the award in Brisbane - perfect."

The September 1985 issue of Open Rugby reported: "June 19 was a proud day for Open Rugby magazine – the day an idea first introduced in the magazine some seven years ago came to fruition. The scene was Brisbane's plush Parkroyal Hotel – the morning after the night before when the giants of the League world from Australia and New Zealand had done battle in a great Test match at Lang Park. The Adidas Golden Boot is to be the symbol of excellence worldwide in Rugby League, and it was fitting that the man who stole the show at this gathering of League people, media men and extremely articulate after-dinner speakers was Wally Lewis, the recipient of the inaugural award."

Lewis, whose Golden Boot year began in rather inauspicious circumstances as Wakefield, with whom he was guesting for during the Brisbane off-season, lost 14-12 at Hilton Park, Leigh, said: "Winning the Golden Boot was stunning. Being rated good enough to represent your city (Brisbane), state (Queensland)

and country (Australia) is something that ranks among the proudest moments of your life. But when I was informed that I had won the Golden Boot, it was something very special. It was an individual award, and one that left me in disbelief. To see a list of the players being considered for the award guaranteed plenty of pride."

The next winner was Lewis's Origin rival Brett Kenny, who prevailed from a shortlist of ten contenders. Despite Queensland's domination of the interstate scene in those early days, the Blues won eight of the twelve matches that Kenny started at stand-off, and, along with Peter Sterling, he was the golden boy of Parramatta's four Winfield Cup successes between 1981 and 1986. In 1985 he was hugely instrumental in New South Wales winning the Origin shield for the first time – it was the first series that he played every match in his favoured position. However, it was in England that Kenny enjoyed his finest moments in his Golden Boot year, as he became the first overseas player to win the coveted Lance Todd trophy at Wembley as the stand-out player in the Challenge Cup final with his Wigan side defeating Hull. It wasn't just any Cup Final; it is widely regarded as the greatest-ever Rugby League contest to be played underneath the Twin Towers. Kenny produced a blistering performance, scoring one try and setting up others in a majestic display as Wigan ran out to a convincing half-time lead. In all, Kenny scored nineteen tries in a glorious spell at Wigan, and with Lewis enduring a very difficult 1985, Open Rugby plumped for Kenny as their newest winner, although he had to wait until the Kangaroo tour of late 1986 before being awarded the Boot.

"Finding the right time to present the award wasn't very easy back then," Edgar continued. "Now the internationals are always tagged onto the back end of the year so there's an obvious time to do it, but in the 1980s that wasn't the case. Adidas were keen that we should hold a big event where we could get a lot of media attention but in 1986 we had to wait until the Kangaroo Tour in the autumn, and that's when Brett Kenny won it for what he'd done the previous year." Kenny remembered that he didn't even know what the award was for, due to the fact that it was still yet to be established. "The Golden Boot was something I didn't know too much about – I actually thought it was for goalkickers at first! Two gentlemen from the Open Rugby magazine approached me and explained it was for the best player in the world and that was fantastic to hear. I had to keep it to myself until the presentation function, which was pretty hard to do because when you win something like that you want to tell everybody about it. The Golden Boot is a great achievement for any footballer. To be named the best player in the world is a wonderful honour."

Another Australian was the next recipient and it was another of the Kangaroos' formidable backline. Balmain's Garry Jack was the undisputed number-one fullback at state and national level and played a big role in their respective series whitewash wins in 1986. The Blues pulled off the first-ever 3-0 Origin win with Jack scoring a try in the first game, but it was on the international scene that he shone like a beacon. He played nine Tests in 1986 - a figure that seems incomprehensible now – averaging a try a game. Three of his tries came in the Ashes – one in the first game and two in the second – as Australia wrapped up the series with comprehensive 38-16 and 34-4 wins. Jack, another obvious winner, was the first player to receive the Golden Boot live on television.

"In 1987 I took the Boot to Australia to present it to Garry Jack," said Edgar, "and had some fun and games with Customs! The function was a reunion of the Kangaroos from the year before and all the Queenslanders were there because it was a few days before an Origin game in Sydney - perfect. The Golden Boot award that year was actually made live on television – that's how big it had become. We had to interrupt what we were doing because Channel Ten wanted him live on the news and nothing could stop for the news. The whole evening stopped for Garry to go out of the room to be interviewed live on the news, but that sort of publicity was great for us."

After that Edgar started to experience difficulties with the Australians. "By 1988 I thought it would be great if we could take it to another country," Edgar recalled. "My dream was to do something in France but it was totally out of the question because Adidas there wouldn't touch Rugby League. I think part of their unwritten agreement with French rugby union was that they don't touch rugby league. So France was a no-go area but New Zealand was different. Adidas New Zealand were really keen and they were happy to put on a big event but, of course, it needed a Kiwi winner. Luckily, there was a genuine winner with Hugh McGahan in such great form for his performances in 1987 when he led the Kiwis to victory over the Aussies in the only game they played that year. He was also in great form in the Winfield Cup for Eastern Suburbs. He was the outstanding choice for the Golden Boot.

"That was the first time we encountered a problem. The Aussies couldn't believe that we didn't want to pick an Australian and, in their eyes, it was Sterlo's turn. Now, nobody was a bigger admirer of Peter Sterling than I, but it was simply Hugh McGahan's award that year. However the Aussies insisted that it should be Peter so we had to compromise, and so we had a joint award. Personally, I don't think that works."

McGahan, however, didn't seem too concerned that he had to settle for a half share of the award: "Winning or sharing the boot with Peter Sterling was a proud moment for me - firstly to be rated alongside a 'great' of the game, but it was also recognition that rugby league is played outside Australia and that non-Australian players can aspire to the same heights if they believe in themselves and their abilities. It was also confirmation that hard work and sacrificing some aspects of life will be rewarding in many ways, least of all materially." Sterling, who was outstanding for Parramatta in 1987 and was man of the match in the second Origin encounter, as well as the unofficial 'fourth' Origin game played in America, noted: "It's probably the greatest honour you can achieve in rugby league and one I will treasure for the rest of my life."

The following year saw another non-Australian winner in Britain's Ellery Hanley. His performances for Balmain Tigers in 1988 were so stunning that they are used as a rather unfair and unrealistic barometer for every Englishman who has since plied his trade down under. Hanley arrived in Sydney mid-season with the Tigers languishing far off the pace, but with Hanley in scorching form in the centres, they finished sixth and qualified for the play-offs on the basis that they had the same points total as the team in fifth – back then points difference didn't rule a side out of the semi-finals. Having to do it the hard way, they won an unlikely Grand Final berth in sensational style by winning four sudden-death matches all against sides who had finished higher than them. Hanley was in unstoppable form as Penrith, Manly, Canberra and Cronulla were brushed aside, although in the final against Canterbury he fell victim to a Terry Lamb high tackle that saw him leave the field and not return. The Yorkshireman then backed up those performances in the 1988 Ashes by scoring a superb individual try as Great Britain led 6-0 at half-time in the first match and by playing a leading role as his side won their first match against Australia since 1978 in the third Test.

"In 1989, given that we'd had Aussie winners as well as Hugh from New Zealand, we were keen to see a British winner, and fortunately for us, there was no doubt at all that Ellery was the deserving winner," Edgar pointed out. "He was the one man that the Aussies had no argument over after his performances for Balmain and for Great Britain on the Lions tour. So there was no argument over him being the rightful winner but, again, problems began because Adidas in this country had more or less dropped out. The guy we'd dealt with who we'd managed to persuade to back us had gone and after that it was the usual PR types who didn't understand what it was all about and they weren't sympathetic to us. We couldn't do anything in this country - it had to be done in Australia.

"By then Channel Ten had got involved as a third party and, like with Garry Jack, they wanted to present it live on TV, but this time not at a function but at a game. This was in 1989 and Ellery was back in Australia with Wests. The chosen game was up at Newcastle, where Ellery had to drive there from Sydney to be presented with the award. Channel Ten got their live moment and we got plenty of publicity but I don't think Ellery was too impressed because he'd been at the functions for the other winners, and all he got was a pitchside presentation - and I could sympathise with that."

It was also reported that Hanley accepted the award dressed in Puma gear, something that didn't go down well with the sponsors of the Boot! But irrespective of the side issues, Hanley was delighted to win the Golden Boot, for reasons similar to McGahan's: "I am delighted to have won the Golden Boot, because it might be a long time before a Great Britain player wins it again," he said at the time. "It's always going to be difficult for British players to get this ultimate recognition when Australia dominates our sport in so many ways."

Another iconic League figure was honoured in 1989 and enjoyed a year he will look back on as his finest in the game. Mal Meninga is one of the code's most famous names and faces, and the sight of him in full flight was a thing of beauty. He moved to the still relatively new Canberra Raiders in 1986 after a blistering stint in England with St Helens. Three years later, the Raiders played their part in a truly unforgettable Grand Final as they defeated Balmain in extra-time. Meninga's contribution was immense as he made a match-saving tackle late in the game and then, in the final seconds, after John Ferguson's try reduced the deficit to two points, Meninga had to hold his nerve to tie the scores with the conversion. He did, and his side prevailed in the extra period. At representative level, he was part of two sides who whitewashed their opponents, scoring two tries in the first Origin as his side gained the momentum to record a 3-0 series win before the Kangaroos gained a trio of wins in New Zealand. To cap all that, Meninga had recovered from four broken arms to become the world's best player.

"By this time the Golden Boot had been hijacked from what I wanted it to be," Edgar remembered. "Mal Meninga was the obvious winner for his performances in 1989 but again there was no pomp or ceremony - he was just given the Boot and that was it. The decision makers at Adidas had changed and they weren't sympathetic to us."

Unbeknown to Edgar at the time, Meninga was to be the last winner that he would be responsible for. When, in early 1991, the panel decided that Great Britain's Garry Schofield was the world's best player, on the back of a series of stunning displays for Great Britain against New Zealand and Australia, the Australians wouldn't support the decision, and Adidas refused to support an English-based presentation. Without Adidas, Edgar pulled the plug. "It had very much become an Australian thing and we decided to make one last effort to get it back to what it was and what it should have been," he said. "We wanted to have it in England and after Garry's performances in 1990 - he should have been the rightful winner. He'd been absolutely outstanding on the tour to New Zealand and in the Ashes series against Australia - the closest we've been to them in years. Garry was a brilliant player - no one can deny that. But we couldn't get the backing to do it in this country. We couldn't do it in Australia because Schoey wasn't due to be in Australia. Typically, the Australians believed that an Australian should win it, but we believed that Garry should and that was more or less the last straw. Adidas wouldn't do anything to make it happen in this country and that was it for me. As well as that, Peter [Deakin] wasn't on the scene anymore because he was working in America and he'd been instrumental in getting sponsors and pushing the Aussies. When he wasn't involved, the driving force was gone and that was it."

Sadly, and suddenly, it appeared that the award that Wally Lewis described as "stunning" had seen the light of day for the last time. It ended up being shelved for nine years before League Publications, the new owners of Open Rugby, decided to revive it. Martyn Sadler, chairman of LPL, who wrote for Open Rugby in its early days, said: "I thought it was a great innovation when Open Rugby introduced it, and thought it was overdue recognition for the greatest players in the game. We wanted to find a way to mark the fact that LPL had acquired Open Rugby – something that would make people sit up and take notice."

Graham Clay was the first editor of the newly named Rugby League World and recalled: "When we bought Open Rugby, one of the first things I wanted to do was bring back the Golden Boot because it was a hugely prestigious award. I remember reading Open Rugby when I was a kid and seeing such great players like Wally Lewis and Brett Kenny winning the award and thought it would be great to bring that back. The criteria was simply to judge who had been the best player in the world for each year, with performances in internationals playing a big part in that – but, as Andrew Johns proved in 1999, outstanding domestic performances could still land you the award."

Johns, the brilliant Newcastle Knights scrum-half, who had firmly established himself as one of the world's best since breaking into top-level rugby in 1993. In 1999 he actually missed the Tri-Nations series but played all three Origin games as the series finished tied for the first time in its 20-year history. He was once again fantastic for Newcastle Knights, although they were eliminated in the first round of the play-offs. Johns said: "I remember growing up having posters on my wall of all the big names, and me and my brother had a picture of Ellery and his Golden Boot, so I couldn't believe it when I won it because it's such a prestigious award. When I got mine [in England], the picture went back to Australia and my mum rang me and told me off for picking up an award like the Golden Boot without having a shave!"

In 2000 another of the game's great names got his hands on the award. Brad Fittler had long been one of the game's most recognised faces and in captaining both New South Wales and Australia to Origin and World Cup glory, he did his reputation no harm at all. He also led Sydney Roosters, the club who had broken the bank to entice him from Penrith Panthers at the height of the Super League war, to their first Grand Final in 20 years. "Brad Fittler was another great name, of course," says Clay, "and I actually presented the award to him at the Sydney Roosters Leagues Club. I was out there at the time launching the Australian version of Rugby League World."

Fittler recalled: "It topped off the year. During your career there are always people who put you down, and others who praise you. That's the way it is. So there's nothing wrong with being proud of the accolades that come your way. You get enough kicks where it hurts, on and off the field, and when finally your achievements are recognised, there's no point in hiding your light under a bushel. I was absolutely rapt to get that award. I was at ease with the world."

Johns became the first man to win the Golden Boot for a second time in 2001 when his performances in leading Newcastle Knights to their second Premiership in five years had few people disputing that he was the premier player in the world. He won the Clive Churchill Medal as the best player in their unlikely Grand Final win over Parramatta - Newcastle were huge underdogs that day - before he went on to help Australia win the Ashes on British soil a month later, in particular producing an excellent performance as Australia levelled the series at Bolton with a convincing 40-12 win.

2002 saw a third non-Australian winner with the mercurial Kiwi scrum-half Stacey Jones, recognised for taking the Warriors to their only Grand Final to date, scoring a brilliant try in the final and helping New Zealand earn a share of the spoils in their Test series in Great Britain, picking up the George Smith Medal as player of the series in the process. Jones admitted to being speechless that he had won the Golden Boot before adding: "It's a great honour, a massive honour."

A year later the current Australian captain, Darren Lockyer, won his first Golden Boot largely for inspiring an under-strength Australia to their first Ashes whitewash of Great Britain in 18 years. Lockyer, who hails from Roma, the same Queensland town as Arthur Beetson, had long been a dominant figure on the international scene. With each Test delicately poised in the closing stages, Lockyer's magic touches turned all three in his side's favour from losing positions. By this time Tony Hannan had taken over as the editor of the magazine: "The Golden Boot is one of the great awards - if not the greatest award - in Rugby League, and something it was a huge honour to have a hand in, as editor of Rugby League World. One of the biggest problems we always seemed to have was the awarding of the actual Boot itself, given that ideally the decision is made after the final game of that year's international series and it is usually going to go to an Aussie. 2003 was also the year in which

Darren Lockyer won the award for the first time. He had kindly agreed to pose with the Boot in front of a Christmas tree in the hotel foyer, shortly before the Kangaroos left for the airport. I remember thinking then what a down-to-earth bloke he was and nothing in the handful of times I've met him since has made me change my mind. There's no sport quite like rugby league for that. These lads may be among the best athletes on the planet but they rarely, if ever, have any airs or graces and are genuinely thrilled to join the illustrious list of former winners."

The award caused controversy in 2004 when it was won by another British player. After a magnificent year with Wigan, when he dragged an injury-ravaged side through the toughest of seasons, Andy Farrell's name was added to the list of illustrious previous winners. He won a thoroughly deserved second Man of Steel after figuring for much of the year in the unusual position of prop, producing form that was as good as any in his fourteen-season Wigan career. Internationally, he captained Great Britain once again and was instrumental in them finishing top of the Tri-Nations table after helping them to three wins in four games against Australia and New Zealand - the other game was lost on the hooter as Luke Rooney snatched yet another late winner for the Green and Golds. Farrell remarked at the time: "This is one of the proudest moments of my career. Winning the Golden Boot has been one of the things I have always dreamed of," he said. "Some great players have won this award in the past and to be spoken of in the same breath makes me feel privileged and honoured." Wayne Bennett, the Australia coach, spoke in glowing terms of the British captain: "We were pleased for Andy Farrell - he's been tremendous. I was disappointed at the criticism that has been levelled at home about him winning it. That's pure sour grapes, but not from the Australian team. There was nobody there who didn't think he deserved it."

With the Golden Boot winner decided after those round-robin games and before the final because the presentation was by now tied into the international awards evening, the decision to hand the award to Farrell surprised few in this country, but caused an outcry down under which Bennett refers to. The critics' arguments were strengthened when Great Britain were absolutely annihilated in the final six days later against Australia, who were led by a rampant Darren Lockyer, with the Daily Telegraph in Sydney leading the way. Their writer Dean Ritchie wrote that "Farrell is honest, tough and committed. But it ends there. He has obviously won the award for years of loyal service to Great Britain. It is an award handed out on sentimental grounds." Ritchie claimed that a panel of unnamed journalists, officials and players that he had contacted ranked Farrell as the 28th best player in the world with former Kangaroo great Laurie Daley, who lined up against Farrell at stand-off in the 1997 Super League Test series, adding, "Andy is a good footballer but he's never done anything to put fear into the Australians."

When contacted in 2010 by Rugby League World, Ritchie stood by his remarks: "The NRL is so far ahead of Super League it is embarrassing. Any player who wins the Golden Boot must do so from the NRL competition, not by playing matches against reserve-grade standard Super League sides," before adding: "I was inundated with emails from England. The fans were filthy." Hannan remembers the fuss with some fondness: "You could hear the howls of protest from Bondi to Blackpool. It's always fun when the Aussies whinge, so I enjoyed that very much. Anyway, Faz had won his award fair and square. Although Britain were subsequently turned over in the 2004 Tri-Nations final, at times over that year it seemed as if he was carrying his team single-handedly on his own shoulders. In some ways, though, that did show the pitfall of awarding the prize before the final game. Trying to avoid the last-gasp rush of 2003, we set up a glitzy international awards dinner at the Royal Armouries in Leeds, sponsored by Gillette. Led by Farrell, Britain had enjoyed

a great tournament up until then, but were stuffed 44-4 in the big match. It's a really tough - if not impossible - one to call. I think on balance, though, that waiting, as the magazine has done more recently, is the best approach. There can be no doubt, then, that the right man has won. The funniest thing was the reaction of the notoriously parochial Australian press. Horrified at a non-Australian winning it, they were asking, who votes for this thing? Well, you did you dummies! Every one of them was given a vote although, typically, some of them couldn't be bothered to use it."

A year later Anthony Minichiello, the outstanding Sydney Roosters, New South Wales and Australia fullback, became another Golden Boot winner to be accept the award before the final, only – as with Farrell a year earlier - for it to be undermined by a thrashing on the big stage with Australia losing 24-0 to New Zealand in the Tri-Nations final at Elland Road, their first series defeat since a 2-0 reversal at the hands of the French in 1978.

No-one could really argue with the next winner. Darren Lockyer, by now a stand-off, enjoyed the perfect 2006, leading Brisbane to an unlikely NRL Premiership with a 15-6 win over the much-fancied Melbourne Storm in the Grand Final. He also scored the winning try in the State of Origin series as the Maroons won a series for the first time in five years. In the Tri-Nations, this time held in the Southern Hemisphere, his influence helped Australia win back the trophy from the Kiwis. He was an obvious and undisputed winner, and joined Andrew Johns as a two-time winner.

With 2004 and 2005 in mind, two changes were made to the process of finding the latest Golden Boot winner after I became editor of Rugby League World in 2007. It was decided that the Boot would only be awarded after the last big international of the year and that voting process would be transparent to the public, especially as it came so soon after the controversial Man of Steel awarding to James Roby over Trent Barrett. So, a panel of illustrious ex-players including Sterling, Schofield, McGahan and Mike Stephenson joined various media members like Sadler, Mascord, Malcolm Andrews and myself in voting the Melbourne, Queensland and Australia hooker, Cameron Smith, to be a clear winner of the 2007 Golden Boot, with Jamie Peacock, who had led Leeds and Great Britain to success, coming second. Peacock was the first recognised runner-up of the Golden Boot, with Johnathan Thurston, Steve Price, Gareth Ellis and Roy Asotasi also shortlisted and receiving votes in that order. The first, second and third choices of each voter was published in the magazine for all to see. "I'm quite shocked actually," said Smith on hearing he had won the Boot. "It's capped off a great year and I'm made up to have won it. If you'd told me at the start of the season what sort of year I'd have, I wouldn't have believed you. It's been a quite incredible year and I'm fortunate to be at a club with such a great coach and players. Look at the talent in the Queensland and Australia teams as well. It's a season I will remember for the rest of my life."

The 2008 winner endured the sort of nightmare final game that Farrell and Minichiello did, but the voting was carried out after Billy Slater's disastrous World Cup Final and he still won the Golden Boot at a canter, with only the New Zealand-based Steve Kilgallon out of the fourteen judges not rating him the world's best. Slater was fantastic on a weekly basis for Melbourne and helped the Maroons win their third-straight Origin series before starring in the group stages of the World Cup particularly in their humiliation of England. The big Kiwi winger, Manu Vatuvei, was the runner-up ahead of Greg Inglis, Benji Marshall, Jamie Peacock, Cameron Smith, Brent Kite and Johnathan Thurston. Slater said when I presented him his award in Sydney: "It's a massive achievement to be named the best player in the world and I still can't believe it. You hear the names of previous winners like Andrew Johns and Darren Lockyer. They were my heroes and for my name to be thrown around in that category is massive. I probably won't realise what it means until I'm older."

By this time, the Rugby League International Federation, chaired by Colin Love, had set up its own awards to rival the Golden Boot. They initially tried to bargain with Sadler to gain ownership of the Boot, but were unsuccessful. "The RLIF tried to take over the Golden Boot, but they didn't respond to the conditions we laid down if they were to take over the award." Rugby League World then declined Love's invitation to present the Golden Boot at their awards night on the basis that it was staged before the World Cup Final. Love, in turn, came up with a series of new international awards but, crucially, ones that only reward a individual's achievements from October to October and not January to December - as the Golden Boot does. Therefore, strangely, it does not take into account performances in that year's international competition which led to the farcical situation in 2010 of Todd Carney, the Australian's second-choice stand-off, bizarrely winning an award entitled the 'International' Player of the Year.

Greg Inglis made it a trio of Melbourne Storm Golden Boot winners in as many years when his truly destructive performances in the inaugural Four Nations in 2009 left him the clear winner, especially after he had won the Wally Lewis Medal as the best player in the State of Origin series. And to cap off the perfect year for Inglis, he won his second Grand Final in three years with Melbourne. He won the award ahead of fellow nominees Billy Slater, Gareth Ellis, Cameron Smith, Fuifui Moimoi and Kevin Sinfield in that order. "It's just extremely humbling, especially when I look at the names who have won the Golden Boot in the past," said Inglis upon receiving the award.

The list of great players to have won the Golden Boot continued with Benji Marshall, who did to Australia in the Four Nations final what they have done to New Zealand and Great Britain so many times in the past, in engineering a wonderful last-gasp play that snatched victory from the jaws of defeat. Marshall enjoyed a sensational year with Wests Tigers, impressing most of the voting panel. "That's what the Golden Boot is all about," concluded Edgar. "Benji was head and shoulders above anybody in the Four Nations and I'm delighted that he won it. But I bet there'll be one or two grumbling Australians!"

2011 saw two Golden Boots handed out, although there wasn't a repeat of 1987 where the voting panel couldn't decide between the top two candidates. Instead, Rugby League World decide to right the wrong of 1990 and retrospectively hand Garry Schofield his rightful Golden Boot. The presentation was made at League Express's annual Albert Goldthorpe Medal ceremony with one writer - Ray Fletcher, the joint editor of the nineteen Rothmans yearbooks which spanned Schofield's career - being in no doubt about his talent placing Schofield above Ellery Hanley and alongside Wally Lewis as one of the all-time greats of rugby league. "Garry was a top-class club player, no doubt about it," said Fletcher. "I always felt that Schofield was one of the few players that went above his club form on the international scene, and that's saying something because he was so good for Leeds. Leeds were never the best of teams, but he was the key man and very often he dragged them to victory in many games. He also adapted very well because he started off as a poaching type of centre and ended up as a playmaker and an exceptional team man when he moved to stand-off. I'd put him ahead of Ellery Hanley based on his exceptional Great Britain career. We're talking about a time when we were getting well beaten but he still produced great performances. I recall the 1990 tour when Schoey was the vice-captain and he dictated absolutely everything on the field. In the three Tests he had a hand in or scored every try. I remember from the records I kept around that time that he was involved in 18 out of 20 successive Great Britain tries. That's an incredible feat. I'll accept that Wally was the Emperor, but from what I saw of him, Garry was on a par because Garry never had the great players around him that Wally did."

At the end of the year, the newly-crowned Golden Boot winner was Johnathan Thurston, the Queensland and Australia halfback, who had helped both sides to glory on the representative stage. He narrowly beat Cameron Smith, his teammate from both of those sides, to the award, although very nearly missed the Four Nations Final at Elland Road, in which Australia beat England. "I'm very happy!," he said upon winning the Boot. "2011 for me was a bit up and down. It started very well with the Cowboys and then we won State of Origin again with Queensland. But I injured my knee in the final Origin and was out for five weeks. I came back and my form wasn't great and then we were knocked out of the semi-finals. But I then had four weeks before going into camp with Australia and my body felt good coming into the Four Nations. But on the Wednesday before the final, I felt a pop in my abductor and I didn't finish training. I went to hospital with Matty Scott, who had the same injury, to get some injections, and I didn't train on the Friday. I had a fitness test on the day of the game, and got the all clear. During the final, I could feel it a bit on the kick and chase, but when kicking or moving from side to side, it was OK. We were made up to win the tournament, especially after losing the final in 2010."

After seven straight winners from the NRL, it was no surprise that when another Super League player won the Golden Boot in 2012, there was furore down under - although, in fairness, the unveiling of the Leeds and England captain, Kevin Sinfield, caused a stir in England too. England had no fixtures against Australia and New Zealand so, other than World Club Challenge victory against Manly at the start of the season, Sinfield's only internationals came against France and Wales. But it is most likely that it was for his performances in Super League that he won the award. Having finished fifth again, Leeds came good at the right time to win at Wigan to book a place in the Grand Final where they beat Minor Premiers Warrington. Sinfield kicked every goal he attempted in the play-offs and also scored a crucial try in the final - a game in which he was also knocked out but recovered to lead his team over the line. Martyn Sadler explained the rationale behind the decision: "Kevin can't move as quickly as Ben Barba, or with the elusiveness of Sam Tomkins, while Cameron Smith's ability close to the ruck is surely second to none. But Sinfield is a supreme captain, and only Cameron Smith can rival his leadership, while

Sinfield's goal-kicking success rate in 2012 was 82.84%, compared to 69.64% for Smith. In the Super League Grand Final Sinfield kicked five out of five, from all over the pitch, and that after he had been knocked out earlier by a challenge to the head. What he did in that game goes beyond what could reasonably be expected, even of a Golden Boot winner."

Many in England - even Leeds fans - wondered whether Sinfield was the right winner, with social networking sites debating the issue for days, but the Australian reaction was as unsporting as it was depressingly predictable. As sure as night follows day, the jingoistic Daily Telegraph in Sydney were up in arms, disgusted that one of their own had not been anointed again. Their sports editor, Phil Rothfield, provocatively tweeted "Kevin Who?". At the bottom of a critical article on the newspaper's website, there was a poll for readers to choose between Ben Barba, Canterbury Bulldogs' Dally M Medallist, or Sinfield - which Sinfield won!

Predictably there were calls for the Boot to be scrapped and for the RLIF's flawed International Player of the Year award to be universally recognised as the stand-alone award given to the world's best player. But given the history of the Golden Boot and its wonderful roll call of winners, it is that which stands out as the ultimate individual award that a rugby league player can win. After all, according to 1987 joint winner Peter Sterling it is "the greatest honour you can achieve in rugby league."

CHAPTER TEN
THE 100 BEST PLAYERS FROM 1980 TO 2012*

In order to be able to compare like for like, I have only considered players who were retired from the professional game by the end of the 2012 season.

1 Wally Lewis
AUSTRALIAN IMMORTAL;
1984 GOLDEN BOOT
Captain of Australia, Queensland and Brisbane Broncos, Lewis was absolutely peerless during the 1980s as the world's best player, and is often regarded as rugby league's greatest-ever player. A genius stand-off with wonderful abilities for passing, kicking and running, Lewis was at his best in leading his beloved Queensland on an incredible run of glory, often as underdogs. 'The King' won eight official Origin man-of-the-match awards, easily a record, and helped the Maroons to nine series successes out of 12. He won the inaugural Golden Boot for his performances in 1984.

2 Andrew Johns
AUSTRALIAN IMMORTAL;
1999 & 2001 GOLDEN BOOT
Rated by Peter Sterling, as the best he has ever seen, Johns won a succession of individual awards during a brilliant career. In 1997 he won a Grand Final with a punctured lung and picked up the Clive Churchill Medal four years later. For five successive years, he was Rugby League Week magazine's player of the year. He won four official man-of-the-match awards in Origin, and was great for Australia, but it was his consistent brilliance at club level that was unrivalled. A magnificent scrum-half who revolutionised the art of kicking and defended like a forward.

3 Darren Lockyer
2003 & 2006 GOLDEN BOOT

From 1998 to 2011, Lockyer was included in the annual World XIII on twelve occasions. Pundits wondered whether he was the game's finest-ever fullback, before he went on to become one of the great stand-offs from 2004 where his ability to break the line was in a world of its own. For Brisbane, he won four Grand Finals, and he was the key player in numerous Queensland Origin triumphs, in particular in the successes between 2006 and 2011. Playing for Australia, he was a constant thorn in the side of Great Britain, so often coming up with the crucial play when it mattered most.

4 Ellery Hanley
RFL HALL OF FAME,
1988 GOLDEN BOOT

Hanley's career was launched when he scored an unbelievable try for Bradford Northern against Featherstone in the 1983 Challenge Cup semi-final, swatting off numerous defenders on a 90-metre sprint to the line. Whether, centre, stand-off or loose forward, he was always one of the best players in the world, and picked up the Golden Boot largely for a series of matchwinning displays for Balmain in 1988. He terrorised the Australians at Wembley in 1990 and was superb for Leeds right into his mid-30s in 1995. Rated by Benny Elias as the best player he played with, ahead of Lewis and Sterling.

5 Brett Kenny
1986 GOLDEN BOOT

A sublime runner of the ball, Kenny kept Wally Lewis out of the Australia team on the 1982 Kangaroo Tour having already helped Parramatta to two Grand Final wins, scoring twice on each occasion, before repeating the feat in 1983. In 1985, he guested for Wigan and inspired them to a classic Wembley win over Hull FC, where he won the Lance Todd Trophy and scored a marvellous try. 1986 saw another Premiership and another unbeaten Kangaroo Tour. Kenny's Origin record was excellent too - twelve times he faced Wally Lewis at stand-off, his side winning eight of them.

6 Peter Sterling
1987 GOLDEN BOOT (shared)

A brilliant, scheming scrum-half, Sterling helped Parramatta win Grand Finals in 1981, 1982, 1983 and in 1986, when he won the inaugural Clive Churchill Medal. On the Kangaroo Tour in 1982, he was a surprising choice for the first Test, but kept hold of the jersey with a string of wonderful displays. In 1986 he was magnificent in NSW's Origin whitewash of Queensland, winning man of the match in game two, one of four such awards in his Origin career, and he helped the Kangaroos to another 100 per cent record in their tour of Europe.

7 Mal Meninga

1989 GOLDEN BOOT

A devastating runner of the ball for Brisbane Souths, Queensland and Australia, he moved south in 1986 to play for Canberra Raiders. After suffering numerous broken arms, he re-ignited his career to win three Grand Finals and to captain Australia on the successful 1990 and 1994 Kangaroo Tours, having also toured in 1982 and 1986. Not just a colossus with ball in hand - his tackle on Michael Neil kept the Raiders in the 1989 Grand Final, which they went on to win in extra-time. He was magnificent, also, for St Helens in 1985, twice scoring a brace of tries in finals.

8 Garry Schofield

1990 GOLDEN BOOT

Rated by Rothmans Yearbook editor Ray Fletcher as the best Great Britain player of the modern era, which his eight man-of-the-match awards support. Schofield scored seven of the nine British tries in six losing Ashes Tests in 1984 and 1986 before a move to stand-off saw his performance level rocket. He as good as beat the Kiwis on his own in the 1990 and 1992 series in New Zealand, and came within an ace of masterminding an Ashes triumph in 1990, winning the Golden Boot for his monumental efforts that year. In 1992 he engineered an astonishing 33-10 British Ashes triumph.

9 Laurie Daley

Of all the wonderful playmakers in Australia in the early to mid-90s, Daley was probably the best. His move to stand-off from centre was the making of his career, as he had every attribute needed to fire Canberra, New South and Wales to multiple glories, and his 40-metre try was the crucial play in the 1994 Grand Final. He captained the Blues to their trio of Origin successes between 1992 and 1994 and scored a Wembley hat-trick for Australia against Great Britain in 1997. Daley has been shortlisted as a possible winner of five retrospective Golden Boots between 1991 and 1997.

10 Brad Fittler
2000 GOLDEN BOOT

As a teenager at Penrith, Fittler forced his way on to the 1990 Kangaroo Tour, and was a regular international for the rest of his career. At the height of the Super League War, he moved to Sydney Roosters, whom he eventually led to the Premiership, in 2002. He enjoyed several Origin successes, but perhaps his best came in 2004 when he came out of representative retirement to help the Blues clinch the series. Whether at stand-off or loose forward, or even centre in his early days, Fittler was always one of the best in the world.

11 Wayne Pearce

'Junior' set new standards for fitness during a wonderful time in rugby league that saw him retire regarded as the greatest Balmain player of the lot. His performances on the 1982 Kangaroo Tour were extraordinary as he introduced British crowds to the sort of all-action forward display they had rarely seen before. At club level he led Balmain to Grand Finals in 1988 and 1989, only for them to lose both, in the most heartbreaking fashion on the latter occasion. Captained the Blues to an Origin whitewash in 1986, a year after helping them win in 1985.

12 Eric Grothe

The greatest and most feared winger of his era, Grothe was one of those rarities who revolutionised how his position was played. As an attacking player, he was an absolute sensation as demonstrated by his unbelievable semi-final try against Canterbury in 1983 when he steamrollered around half-a-dozen tacklers to score from more than 50 metres. He also scored a sensational 90-metre try in the 1981 Origin stand-alone match. A year later he terrorised British defences as Australia won the Ashes with ease. He was a magnificent cover tackler too.

13 Allan Langer

The greatest Bronco in their first decade as they won Grand Finals in 1992, 1993, 1997 and 1998, with 'Alfie' at the heart of everything good. At scrum-half Langer was a ceaseless prompter in attacking the line with a world-class short kicking game. His Origin career began as it started, with people questioning his inclusion, but Langer proved the doubters wrong with great performances to help seal the 1987 and 2001 series, before his man-of-the-match performance in the decider in 2002 led to a series draw. He was voted best player in four Origins.

14 Ricky Stuart

Stuart enjoyed a magnificent career, winning three Premierships with Canberra between 1989 and 1994. He won the Clive Churchill Medal in 1990 and gained selection for the Kangaroo Tour. His big moment came in the second Test as he broke free and put Mal Meninga over for the try that turned the series. In 1993 he won the Dally M Medal, but broke his leg towards the end of the season and without him, the Minor Premiers weren't able to make the Grand Final. He made up for it in 1994, enjoying success with club, state and country.

15 Glenn Lazarus

A player who helped take prop-forward play into the new era, Glenn Lazarus, made history by winning Premierships with three clubs - Canberra, Brisbane and Melbourne - playing in successive Grand Finals between 1989 and 1993. He bowed out in the ultimate way by winning again in 1999 in his last match. He was the cornerstone of the New South Wales pack during their three-year Origin domination between 1992 and 1994. He toured twice with the Kangaroos in 1990 and 1994, and also played in the victorious 1992 Ashes series.

16 Cliff Lyons

With competition from Wally Lewis, Brett Kenny and Terry Lamb, Cliff Lyons only played for Australia six times, but his place in Test history is assured after he played a leading role in probably the most famous international of them all. With Australia a game down in the 1990 Ashes, he came into the side and scored a truly wonderful try in game two as his side won 14-10. His club career was the stuff of dreams, as he played 332 games for Norths and Manly between 1985 and 1999, winning Premierships with the Sea Eagles in 1987 (as the Clive Churchill Medallist) and 1996.

17 Gene Miles

As a result of excellent representative performances, including a hat-trick in the first Ashes Test of 1986, Miles, along with Wally Lewis, was regularly targeted by Winfield Cup sides before Brisbane's admission into the competition in 1988. A thoroughbred centre before moving into the second row later in his career, he won six of the seven Origin series he figured in and won three Ashes series. He moved to Wigan in 1992, forming a lethal left-side combination with Martin Offiah.

18 Stacey Jones
2002 GOLDEN BOOT

The greatest Kiwi of the modern era, Jones's pivotal achievement in rugby league was that it was he who, in 2005, masterminded the long-awaited downfall of the Australian team. Jones pulled the strings in the Tri-Nations Final, helping New Zealand to an incredible 24-0 win. A great passer, kicker and runner of the ball, his two tries helped the Kiwis to a 30-16 win over the Aussies in 1997 and he was a regular problem for Great Britain. The genius scrum-half starred for New Zealand Warriors and Catalans, scoring a brilliant solo try in the 2002 Grand Final.

19 Steve Walters

Brilliant Canberra hooker who was at the club throughout the glory years of the late '80s and early '90s. An excellent performer for Queensland and Australia too. Walters was Rugby League Week's Winfield Cup player of the year in 1993, and in 1994 he delivered a truly stunning performance in the deciding Ashes Test at Elland Road to help Australia to victory. His battles with Balmain and New South Wales hooker Benny Elias were a joy to behold. Was shortlisted for Golden Boots in 1991 and 1994.

20 Bradley Clyde

Twice a Clive Churchill Medallist as the best player in a Winfield Cup Grand Final with Canberra, Clyde's signature was one of the most sought after during the Super League War - in fact, it is believed that a huge approach from the Roosters may have sparked league's big split. Between 1989 and 1994, Clyde was peerless as a dynamic, athletic loose forward whose marauding running with the ball was a key factor in Canberra's success during the turn of the decade. Later signed for Canterbury before suffering an injury-hit 2001 at Leeds.

21 Terry Lamb

Lamb made history in 1986 by becoming the first Kangaroo to feature in every tour game. He made his Origin debut at just nineteen in 1981, two years before he won the Dally M Medal when his side, Wests, had come last. He moved to Canterbury in 1984, winning the Rothmans Medal, and helped them end Parramatta's Grand Final dominance with a 6-4 win. One of the game's great support players, he scored 164 tries at club level and helped the Dogs win two more Grand Finals - in 1988 and 1995. He played in a record number of Premiership games until Darren Lockyer passed him in 2011.

22 Shane Webcke

Leader of the pack for Brisbane, Queensland and Australia throughout a hugely successful and consistent career, Webcke's contribution to the modern game cannot be overstated. He forced his way into the Australian team for their (Super League) tour of Great Britain in 1997, having first helped Brisbane Broncos to Grand Final victory over Cronulla. Between 1998 and 2004, he was an ever-present in Rugby League World's annual world XIII, a fitting reward for his admirable consistency and quality. His last-ever game was the 2006 Grand Final win over Melbourne.

23 Andrew Ettingshausen

A one-club player in Australia who enjoyed eighteen seasons at Cronulla, after debuting at eighteen in 1983, Ettingshausen also excelled for New South Wales and Australia, whether at fullback, wing or centre. Strong in defence, quick and a prolific tryscorer who racked up 165 tries for the Sharks, Ettingshausen's tally of 328 first-grade appearances is only bettered by a handful of other players. He made nearly 30 Origin appearances and helped NSW win the Super League Tri-Series in 1997. Also enjoyed a successful spell at Leeds in the late 1980s, winning the Yorkshire Cup in 1988.

24 Gorden Tallis

The 'raging bull' hit the big time as soon as his protracted transfer to Brisbane Broncos from St George went through for 1997. His devastating running and brutal defence were key reasons for the Broncos' successes in 1997 and 1998. Touring England in 1997 and 2000, he was probably the world's best second-rower, while his superb displays for Queensland, especially in 1999, 2001 and 2002, made him public enemy number one south of the border. His incredible tackle on Brett Hodgson in 2002, when he dragged the fullback fifteen metres into touch, was emblematic of his efforts.

25 Ruben Wiki

Legendary Kiwi Test player who earned due reward towards the end of a magnificent Test career with success in the 2005 Tri-Nations Final. Wiki's 55-cap Kiwi career began in 1994 and he went on to enjoy success in two series against Great Britain and in matches against Australia in 1998, 1999, 2003 and 2006 twice, as well as a draw in 2004. Starting out as a centre with Canberra in 1993, he was part of their Grand Final success a year later. He moved to the Warriors in 2005 and eventually hung up his boots in 2008 having spent his latter years as a prop.

26 Steve Mortimer

Mortimer won four Premierships with Canterbury in the 1980s, twice as captain in 1984 and 1985. In 1980, his three trysaving tackles went a long way to securing victory over Eastern Suburbs. A one-club man, he played 272 times for Canterbury - then a record number of appearances for a player at one club. Up against Peter Sterling for representative jerseys, 'Turvey' played nine Origin matches and memorably captained the Blues to their maiden series win in 1985. Dropped from the 1982 Ashes Tests, Mortimer still won eight caps, scoring two tries.

27 Mark Graham

One of the world's best forwards during a sometimes-difficult eight-year spell with North Sydney Bears, Graham is best known for a superb Kiwi career. He became the first man to captain two touring squads to Europe, in 1980 and 1985 and was captain and star player in a side that came so close to a series win over Australia. He led the Kiwis to a much-celebrated 18-0 win over Australia in 1985. An excellent wide runner who often bust the line, and who had great ball skills, Graham had everything in his locker a modern forward needed.

28 Martin Offiah

Almost immediately recognised as one of the game's great tryscorers after switching codes in 1987, Offiah's impact on rugby league was sensational. Within a year of signing for Widnes, Offiah had topped the try charts, was a title winner, a Man of Steel winner and a British Lion. After signing for Wigan for a world record £440,000, he won numerous medals and two Lance Todd trophies, most memorably when his stunning 90-metre try helped beat Leeds in 1994. He'd even put ten past the same opponents in a match two years earlier. Scorer of over 500 tries, the game has never since seen his like.

29 Steve Renouf

An attacking centre of the highest quality, Renouf burst onto the scene as Brisbane's top tryscorer in 1991 before scoring a long-range try to wrap up the 1992 Grand Final for the Broncos. A month later, he broke British hearts with the only try in the World Cup final - on his Test debut. He won another Premiership in 1993 as the tries kept coming. In 1997 he scored a hat-trick in the Australian Super League Grand Final against Cronulla and he ended his career with 40 tries in 55 Super League matches for Wigan in 2000 and 2001. Renouf was named in five World XIIIs.

30 Garry Jack

1986 GOLDEN BOOT

A fullback ahead of his time, Garry Jack was at his best returning the ball and beating tacklers, but he was also a dependable defender and taker of high kicks. The world's best fullback in the mid-1980s, Jack was named the world's best player as a result of his performances in 1986, in particular his flawless displays on the Kangaroo Tour. He started at Wests in 1981, but is best known for his time at Balmain and their runs to consecutive Grand Finals in 1988 and 1989. He played in seventeen Origins, most notably in the 1985 and 1986 series wins.

31 Benny Elias

Elias was one of the first hookers to possess all the skills of a halfback, something that is now commonplace. He came within inches of landing Balmain the 1989 Premiership when his late drop goal rattled the crossbar. He enjoyed a superb New South Wales career, winning three man-of-the-match awards in nineteen games, and being a part of winning series in 1985, 1990, 1992, 1993 and 1994. He only played in five Tests, but, as vice-captain, helped Australia sew up the never-to-be-forgotten 1990 Ashes with outstanding performances in games two and three.

32 Michael O'Connor

A very successful cross-coder, O'Connor's career high came at Old Trafford in the first Ashes Test of 1986 when he scored three tries. He scored seventeen Test tries in as many matches, also kicking 61 goals. For New South Wales, his fabulous touchline conversion on the siren won game two in 1991. His Origin debut had arrived in game one of 1985 and, in stunning fashion, he scored all of the Blues' points in an 18-2 win which set them on their way to their first-ever series win. He won the 1987 Grand Final with Manly against Canberra.

33 Andy Gregory

Wally Lewis rates Gregory as the greatest British player he faced, and his stunning performance in the third Test of 1988 probably had a lot to do with that. In an injury-ravaged side, Gregory produced a blinding performance to help pull off one of Test football's biggest shocks as the Lions won 26-12. He was also exceptional in the 1992 Panasonic Cup Final for Illawarra against Lewis's Brisbane. At home, he won two Lance Todds, among a bucketload of medals for Widnes and Wigan and is widely regarded as the finest British halfback since Alex Murphy.

34 Paul Sironen

An attacking forward of the highest class, Sironen was part of a Balmain side that only fell at the final hurdle in 1988 and 1989, although he scored a superb try on the latter occasion against Canberra. He figured prominently in New South Wales's trio of Origin successes between 1992 and 1994, also playing a part in their victorious 1990 series. Picked on the 1986 Kangaroo Tour, the same year he won the Dally M Rookie of the Year, he didn't figure in any of the Ashes Tests, but he won 21 caps between then and 1994.

35 Paul Sculthorpe

Named by Darren Lockyer as the best Great Britain player he faced, Sculthorpe was magnificent even in a desperately poor era for Great Britain, even standing out in the 10-64 capitulation to Australia in 2002. The highlight of his many great Test moments came at Huddersfield in 2001 when his two tries sealed an Ashes-opening 20-12 win. At Warrington, as a teenager, he was always destined for the top and his move to St Helens enabled him to turn that potential into silverware. He remains the only player to win consecutive Man of Steels.

36 Gary Belcher

After winning two Brisbane Grand Finals with Souths, Belcher travelled south of the border, enjoying wonderful success with Canberra Raiders in a glorious eight-year spell which saw him win two Grand Finals and play in two more. He scored the try that got the Raiders back into the famous 1989 win over Balmain. For Queensland he won successive series in 1987, 1988 and 1989 and finished up with four tries in sixteen appearances for the Maroons. He was Australia's fullback in the 1990 Ashes series and was widely regarded as the world's best custodian.

37 Shaun Edwards

Synonymous with the Wigan glory years more than any other player, Edwards remains rugby league's most decorated man. The medals just poured in - 46 in all. Internationally he often struggled against Australia and didn't start a game against them until 1992, and he was often a substitute for Balmain in the Winfield Cup in his 1989 stint, but he enjoyed two excellent series against New Zealand in 1989 and 1993. He was also superb at London, helping them to second place in 1997 and to Wembley in 1999, but it is as a Wigan legend that he is best known.

38 Kevin Ward

It remains a mystery how the Great Britain prop didn't win the 1987 Clive Churchill Medal as the best player in Manly's Grand Final over Canberra. Ward enjoyed over a decade at Castleford where he won the Challenge Cup in 1986. Towards the end of his time at Wheldon Road, he spent two summers in the Winfield Cup, earning the praise of everybody down under. In 1990 he signed for St Helens but his career ended with a badly broken leg sustained on Good Friday 1993 against Wigan. He played eighteen times for Great Britain, winning three man-of-the-match awards.

39 Wendell Sailor

Sailor was a blockbusting winger whose league career was cut short in 2001 by a move to union. He toured with the Kangaroos in 1994 but hit his peak in 1997 and 1998, helping Brisbane to back-to-back Premierships. He was a mainstay in the Queensland and Australia sides although he sometimes struggled to replicate his devastating club form on the state scene. At times unstoppable, he won another Grand Final in 2000 and a month later the World Cup. After returning to the game, he helped St George to the 2009 Minor Premiership. Four times a World XIII member.

40 Nathan Hindmarsh

One of the most durable forwards in the game, Hindmarsh's levels of consistency and work rate set new standards. A one-club man, Hindmarsh may have played in an unsuccessful Parramatta era, but his exploits have seen him deservedly propelled alongside Sterling, Kenny, Cronin and Price as all-time great Eels. He was an ever present in the Blues winning Origin sides of 2004 and 2005, and was part of the Australian team that won the 2000 World Cup and the 2004 and 2006 Tri-Nations competitions. Rugby League Week player of the year in 2004 and 2005.

41 Brett Kimmorley

Kimmorley was so highly regarded between 1999 and 2001 that even Andrew Johns would often find himself at hooker or on the bench in representative fixtures, behind Kimmorley in the number-seven reckoning. On his day, he was a quite sensational halfback, capable of winning games almost on his own. In the 2003 Ashes, he hurt Great Britain badly, in a series the Kangaroos would have otherwise lost. Always capable of breaking the line, Kimmorley was a great big-game player and won man of the match as a Melbourne player in the 1999 Grand Final.

42 Dean Bell

'Mean Dean' played a big part in New Zealand beating Australia three times in four years between 1983 and 1987, and was skipper on the two biggest rugby league occasions in New Zealand - the 1988 World Cup Final and the Warriors' first match in 1995 - although his 1989 international retirement was far too soon. He was the Wigan captain during an enormously successful period, winning several trophies. His mental toughness matched his physicality, and Bell will be remembered as one of the game's great leaders and a fantastic centre.

43 Gary Freeman

A world-class scrum-half, Freeman enjoyed a ten-year career with the Kiwis, winning a then record 46 caps - nineteen as captain. He was an integral part of Balmain reaching the 1988 and 1989 Grand Finals, and with his next club, Eastern Suburbs, he won the Dally M Medal in 1992. He also played for Penrith and Parramatta. Internationally, he debuted in 1986 and went on to win over 30 caps for New Zealand. He scored twice in a 12-10 win over Great Britain in 1988 to secure a spot in the World Cup Final and captained the Kiwis to a famous 24-8 win over Australia in 1991.

44 Ray Price
Five-time Dally M lock of the year, 'Mr Perpetual Motion' was one of the best forwards in the world at the beginning of the 1980s, if not the best. At the base of the scrum, he played a leading role in Parramatta winning four Premierships in six years, and retired from the game at the top after winning the 1986 Grand Final against Canterbury, although he later had a season at Wakefield. Ex-union international Price didn't win an Origin series as Queensland won the first five, but he played loose forward in the great Kangaroo side of 1982 which swept all before them on their tour of Europe.

45 Steve Roach
One of the most controversial figures of the 1980s, Roach led from the front for club, state and country in a superb eleven-year career. A world-class prop, he was part of the Balmain late-1980's revival that saw them reach two Grand Finals, although 'Blocker' missed the 1988 final through suspension. For New South Wales, he was an ever-present in 1985 and 1986, the first two series in which the Blues triumphed, and lifted the shield again in 1990. He won the World Cup with Australia against New Zealand in 1988 and the Ashes on British soil in 1990.

46 Jason Robinson
Not just a great tryscorer, 'Billy Whizz', unlike many other wingers, possessed magnificent all-round abilities. He was one of the hardest players to tackle when returning the ball from his own territory, and his dummy-half running was top drawer. He possessed a superb eye for the big games, scoring a brace on his Great Britain debut at Wembley in 1993, the winner for Wigan in the 1998 Grand Final, six tries in consecutive Tests for Great Britain in 1997 and 1998, and he tore a superior St Helens side apart in 1999 as Wigan celebrated their last game at Central Park.

47 Keiron Cunningham
While Cunningham's Test career never really got going largely due to injury, his week-in, week-out Super League performances remain unparalleled, and he has been named the competition's best-ever player by three different media outlets. Often dominating the ruck, when coming out of dummy-half, he hit

the ball up like the best prop in the business. Injury caused him to miss several Great Britain games but his best international performance came as Wales led Australia at half-time in the 2000 World Cup semi-final, with Cunningham causing typical havoc.

48 Stephen Kearney

Kearney became New Zealand's youngest captain on the 1993 tour of Europe and went on to enjoy a magnificent domestic and international career. He helped the Kiwis to wins over Australia in 1997 and 1999 and his consistent brilliance saw him make the World XIII for four consecutive years between 1996 and 1999. His club highlight came in 1999 as he helped Melbourne Storm to stunning Grand Final success in just their second season, by adding steel and resolve to the new club's pack. Ended his career at Hull with Challenge Cup success in 2005.

49 Andy Farrell
2004 GOLDEN BOOT

Having debuted for Wigan as a 16-year-old in 1991, Farrell went on to play for Great Britain's Academy, under 21s and full team within the space of three weeks in 1993. By 1996 he was the Wigan and Great Britain captain and remained in those roles until his final game of rugby league in 2004. Farrell was as strong as an ox with great hands and a booming kicking game and his performances in the unfamiliar role of prop in 2004 led to him winning the Golden Boot and Super League's Man of Steel, the latter for the second time. Also a brilliant goalkicker.

50 Steve Ella

A wonderfully flamboyant centre in the magnificent Parramatta side that dominated much of the 1980s, Ella won four Grand Finals and made a name for himself as one of the great attacking players of the decade, although injuries prevented further greatness. He moved to Wigan for the 1985-86 season, when he scored 21 tries in 24 games and even helped them to a 14-8 win over the touring New Zealanders with an excellent stand-off display. 'The Zipzip Man' also scored twice in the Lancashire Cup Final win over Warrington. In 1985, he played for NSW in their first Origin series win.

51 Ian Roberts

One of the great enforcers of the 1990s, Roberts was a central figure in successful Manly, New South Wales and Australia teams. Magnificent at Souths in his early-20s, culminating in them winning an unlikely Minor Premiership in 1989, it was inevitable that the bigger clubs would court Roberts and he duly moved to big-spending Manly in 1990 where he carved out a reputation as one of the world's best props. For the Blues, he won a series at the first attempt in 1990 and enjoyed further success in 1993. He started all three Ashes Tests in 1994.

52 Geoff Toovey

Toovey was the beating heart of a champion Manly side during the mid-1990s. After the disappointment of the 1995 Grand Final loss to Canterbury, the Sea Eagles were too good for St George a year later with captain Toovey winning the Clive Churchill Medal. In 1997, they lost to Newcastle, but Toovey's performance was one of the bravest in finals football. Several times he was injured, but played on. He featured often for New South Wales, winning man of the match in game one in both 1996 and 1997, setting the platform for series wins. He captained Australia once in 1996.

53 Gary Connolly

Connolly had a great all-round game which saw him excel at both fullback and centre. A top-drawer competitor with a strong upper body, he regularly matched the finest Australian centres on the Test stage. Whether at St Helens, Canterbury, Wigan or Leeds, Connolly was always one of the best players around, and even won the Lance Todd Trophy in a beaten Leeds side, as his career was winding down in 2003. He debuted internationally in 1991, but it took him until his last appearance for Great Britain or England in 2003 for him to score his first try.

54 Greg Dowling

Dowling scored possibly State of Origin's most famous try in 1984, stooping low in the heavy rain to take Wally Lewis's kick which had rebounded off the crossbar. That year he also made his Test debut in the Ashes whitewash over Great Britain and followed that up by being picked to face the Kiwis in 1985. In that series he was infamously sent off and, in one of the decade's iconic images, continued fighting with Kevin Tamati on the sideline. He toured with the 1986 Kangaroos and went on to become one of the original Broncos in 1988.

55 Brett Mullins

The Canberra fullback's attacking style in the mid-1990s led to comparisons with the great Clive Churchill. His four-try salvo against Newcastle Knights, including two 100-metre efforts, still features on highlights reels. It was a dream year for the rangy fullback as he made his state and Test debuts and won a Grand Final. He scored a hat-trick against Queensland in the 1997 Super League Tri-Series Final and toured Europe for a second time. He returned from a frustrating year at Leeds to win another Premiership with Sydney Roosters in 2002, this time as a winger.

56 Andy Platt

When interest in Test football peaked in the late 1980s and early 1990s, Platt was one of the best performers around. He won 25 Great Britain caps and a further four for England, with the undoubted highlight coming at Melbourne in 1992 when his brilliant display of hard running and tackling helped lay the platform for a famous 33-10 win. He moved from St Helens to Wigan in 1988, where he won six Challenge Cups and the 1993 Man of Steel, before signing for Auckland Warriors in time for their inaugural 1995 Winfield Cup campaign.

57 Kurt Sorensen

As terrifying as forwards come, opposing forwards rarely got the better of Sorensen. He had made a name for himself well before 1980, but shot to further fame when he returned from international exile to help New Zealand to a series draw with Australia in 1983, enjoying a storming game in the second Test. In 1985, he played in the Kiwis' 18-0 win over Australia and in the drawn series with Great Britain. At club level he enjoyed magnificent careers with Cronulla and Widnes, whom he captained to two titles and world club success over Canberra.

58 Tawera Nikau

Brilliant loose forward who was a phenomenal defender and a big threat in attack, Nikau's finest hour came in the 1999 Grand Final. His Melbourne side were losing 14-0 at half-time to St George, but they fought back to win with Nikau unlucky not to win the Clive Churchill Medal. He helped Castleford to a unbelievable 33-2 win over Wigan in the 1993-94 Regal Trophy Final and was instrumental in Cronulla making the 1997 Australian Super Grand Final. His Kiwi career was ruined at the end by a fall out with Richie Blackmore, but he captained the Maoris in the 2000 World Cup.

59 Noel Cleal

After a Grand Final appearance for Easts in 1980, 'Crusher' came to prominence with a move to Manly in 1983. There he played 124 games, scoring 43 tries, an excellent strike record for a forward, albeit an ex-centre. He was runner-up for the 1984 Rothmans Medal, and won the 1987 Grand Final against Canberra. He won eight Origin matches between 1984 and 1987 (including the unofficial fourth match in 1987), an excellent record considering Queensland's domination in the 1980s. Scored try on Test debut against New Zealand.

60 Kevin Iro

On his day, Iro was one of the game's best attacking players and produced the goods on both sides of the world. He came to prominence in the great Wigan side of the late eighties, scoring a brace of tries in the Wembley Cup Finals of 1988, 1989 and 1990, and enjoyed four excellent seasons at the club. He was just as good at both Manly and Leeds before returning to England with St Helens in 1999 where he scored the winning try in the 1999 Grand Final. For New Zealand, his two tries helped them to a shock win in 1998 over Australia.

61 Paul Newlove

With ball in hand, Newlove was one of the most devastating attacking players in the 1980s and 1990s. He debuted for Great Britain at just eighteen in 1989 and went on to score tries against Australia in the Melbourne win in 1992, at Old Trafford in 1994 and in the 1995 World Cup opener, as well as the final. While he may not have been the best of defenders, he could be relied upon to lay on a try just when it was needed and his big-money move to St Helens led to a trophy-laden spell for the club in the early Super League years.

62 Gavin Miller

In an unbelievable 1989, this prodigiously talented ball-playing forward dominated Australia's individual awards, scooping the Rothmans and Dally M Medals while he was also named Rugby League Week's player of the year. Three years earlier he had won the Man of Steel as a Hull Kingston Rovers player, and it was his stint at Craven Park that helped him fulfil his potential when he returned to Cronulla, having struggled with early-career consistency. In 1988 he played for Australia against the Rest of the World, winning man of the match, and in the World Cup Final.

63 Kevin Walters

Played in two Grand Finals for Canberra before forming a brilliant partnership with Allan Langer that led to four Grand Final wins for Brisbane Broncos in the 1990s. Walters was a majestically talented stand-off who set up the only try in the 1992 World Cup Final for his clubmate Steve Renouf with a beautifully floated ball. For Queensland he played a big role in the 1998 series victory, again partnering Langer, and scoring a clever, crucial try in the decider. He only played eight times for Australia, but faced phenomenal competition for the number-six jumper.

64 Joe Lydon

In 1984, twenty-year-old Lydon won the Lance Todd Trophy after scoring two superb tries for Widnes against Wigan, the Man of Steel and a place on the Lions tour. He became the game's first £100,000 signing when he moved to Wigan in 1986 where he enjoyed a huge amount of success. Lydon also enjoyed two spells for Eastern Suburbs, scoring eight tries in 22 appearances. A hugely talented and versatile back. he won 30 caps for Great Britain, scoring one of their most famous tries against Australia in 1986 when he took on Garry Jack, blitzed him for pace and scored in the corner.

65 Lee Crooks

Rated by Garry Schofield as the most talented British player he played with, Crooks was a ballplaying prop with a great kicking game. He played twice against Australia in 1982 at just 18, before touring in 1984. In 1985 he won man of the match as substitute in the deciding Test with New Zealand, saving the series with a touchline penalty goal in the dying stages. After success at Hull he moved to Leeds for a world-record fee. He was soon at Castleford and also impressed Australian judges with stints at Wests and Balmain.

66 Tony Myler

Genius stand-off whose magnificent skills were all too often curtailed by injuries. He was at his best for Great Britain against New Zealand in 1985 when he played a big part in Garry Schofield's quartet of tries in game two. For Widnes he won numerous medals and had an excellent game against Canberra Raiders in the 1989 World Club Challenge win. Brian Noble, the Lions captain in 1984, said of Myler: "There's Kenny and Lewis but I always threw the Tony Myler argument in there and if he'd stayed healthy, he'd have been one of the world's best."

67 Mick Cronin

Another legend of the 1970s, Cronin eventually retired in 1986 after a truly magnificent career, and he went out at the top, kicking Parramatta's four points in the Grand Final win over Canterbury Bankstown - after missing most of the year with an eye problem. He was such a powerful centre with a devastating hand-off that seemed to clobber anybody who got in his way. He won four Grand Finals with Parramatta and played in the inaugural State of Origin in 1980, kicking two goals. His brilliant Test career ended with a 2-0 series win over New Zealand in 1982.

68 Jonathan Davies

One of the most successful code-switchers in history, Davies belied his small frame to be an instant hit in the brutal world of rugby league whether fullback, wing, centre or stand-off. Within months, he had helped Widnes prevail in a title decider with Wigan and in the World Club Challenge against Canberra. Only in the game for just over six years, Davies played thirteen times for Great Britain, culminating in a wonder try against Australia at Wembley and he led Wales to the World Cup semi-final in 1995. Came so close to guiding Warrington to the 1993-94 league title, when he won the Man of Steel.

69 James Leuluai

Owner of one of the greatest sidesteps in the game, Leuluai's ability to come onto the ball, hit a gap and step the last defender was peerless. His wonderful try at the end of the 1985 Challenge Cup Final exemplified that - it was his trademark - but his try in the 1983 semi-final win over Castleford was probably even better. He signed for Hull after the 1980 Kiwi tour of Britain, and enjoyed a fabulous time on Humberside, scoring 85 tries in 183 appearances. For the Kiwis, he played 29 Tests, scoring fourteen tries including scores in the wins against Australia in 1983 and 1985.

70 Dale Shearer

Excitement machine with a great try record for Manly, Brisbane, Queensland and Australia. Shearer was equally adept at fullback, wing or centre, and even played at stand-off for Queensland late in his career, but is remembered best for his exploits on the flank. After moving south from the Brisbane league, he made his Origin debut in his first Winfield Cup season and went on to win four series and score a dozen tries. He played in the 1986 and 1990 Ashes and played in numerous Tests against New Zealand including the 1988 World Cup Final in which he scored a crucial try .

71 Paul Harragon

Lived the dream in 1997 when he captained his beloved Newcastle to the most dramatic of Grand Final successes of them all as the Knights beat Manly with a try seven seconds from time. His shuddering clashes with Manly enforcer Mark Carroll set the tone for an absolutely incredible afternoon. Harragon was a giant of a prop who was rarely dominated up front and who enjoyed numerous triumphs with New South Wales, for whom he played a then-record twenty consecutive matches between 1992 and 1998. He was a rock for Australia in the 1992 Ashes.

72 Craig Fitzgibbon

The goalkicking backrower enjoyed an eventful start to his career, winning rookie of the year in his first season as an Illawarra player in 1998, and then playing in losing Grand Finals for St George Illawarra and Sydney Roosters. But he made up for it two years later, winning the Clive Churchill Medal in the 2002 decider as the Roosters swept aside the Warriors. That propelled him into the Origin scene where he won his first two series and, for Australia, he won the Ashes in 2003, kicking a superb touchline goal to level up game three in the last few minutes.

73 Tim Brasher

Brasher played for Balmain as an eighteen-year-old in the 1989 Grand Final and went on to enjoy an impressive career whether at wing, centre or his more usual position of fullback. Three years later he made his Australia debut in the World Cup Final, helping his side to a 10-6 win. In 1995 he won another World Cup, this time a conventional competition, and scored in the final, before enjoying an exceptional 1996. For New South Wales, he was part of series wins in 1992, 1993 (when he won man of the match in game two), 1994, 1996, and 1997.

74 Sean Long

Vastly gifted halfback who won a record three Lance Todd Trophies as a St Helens player in 2001, 2004 and 2006. Having not made the grade at Wigan and having had to drop down a division to Widnes, Long had plenty to prove at St Helens, where he also won four Grand Finals in thirteen hugely successful - although at times controversial - seasons at the club. For Great Britain he sometimes struggled, but performed majestically at the Sydney Football Stadium in 2006 as the Lions won 23-12, with Long incontrovertibly man of the match.

75 Darren Smith

Excellent form at Canterbury was marred by a controversial move to Brisbane, which saw him benched for the 1994 Grand Final and miss out on Australian selection. At the Broncos, he was superb in their great sides of 1997 and 1998, touring Great Britain with the Super League Australians in 1997 and playing magnificently at loose forward in the deciding Test, winning the man-of-the-match award. In 1998, he was the NRL's top tryscorer and was later shortlisted for a retrospective Golden Boot. He was excellent in a disappointing 2003 for St Helens.

76 Hugh McGahan
1987 GOLDEN BOOT (shared)
McGahan's brilliant performance when he captained New Zealand to a 13-6 win over Australia in the only game the two countries played that year, went a long way to him winning a share of the 1987 Golden Boot with Peter Sterling. The tall, raw-boned and skilful back-rower once scored six tries in a Test against Papua New Guinea in 1983, in a 60-20 win, one of 32 appearances in a brilliant Test career which saw him a three-time tourist. He also enjoyed an impressive seven-year career with Eastern Suburbs. Played with an Australian philosophy - tough, durable and a great defender.

77 Adam MacDougall
MacDougall was one of the few wingers in the game who regularly kept Brisbane's Wendell Sailor quiet - in fact, he often got the better of him. He played in both of Newcastle's Grand Final triumphs at centre and wing respectively. He scored four Origin tries in four series, winning man of the match in the Blues' controversial win in game one in 2000. He toured England with the Kangaroos in 2000 and 2001, winning the World Cup and the Ashes, and it was his fine defensive performance in the second half of the 2001 decider that got his side home.

78 Steve Price
An 11-year stay at the Bulldogs saw Price win Premierships in 1995 and 2004, and although he missed the latter Grand Final with a knee injury he still lifted the trophy as the club captain. He also played in the 1994 and 1998 finals. The Bulldogs missed him badly when he moved to New Zealand Warriors in 2005 and Price's 91 games for the club saw him smash through the 300 career barrier in total. He flourished late in his career on the representative front and was a Queensland regular by the time they were dominating the Origin scene from 2006.

79 Jason Smith
Smith was a brilliant ball-playing loose forward or stand-off for Canterbury, Parramatta and Hull FC between 1990 and 2004. With the former he played in two Grand Finals, winning in 1995 before controversially walking out on the club with three teammates to sign for bitter rivals Parramatta. He made his Origin bow in 1995, winning man of the match in game two of Queensland's stunning whitewash of the Blues. He was a regular in a brilliant Australia team in 1998 and 1999 before an excellent four-year stay at Hull.

80 Tonie Carroll

One of the strongest runners and biggest hitters in the game, Carroll achieved representative selection as both a centre and a back-row forward. He was superb in Brisbane's Grand Final wins in 1998 and 2000 and scored a famous last-minute winner for Queensland in game one of 1998. He surprised many by turning out for the Kiwis in the 2000 World Cup but produced a sensational performance and maintained his form for Leeds in Super League in 2001. After switching to Australia, he was part of their mouthwatering display in the 2004 Tri-Nations Final, and won another Grand Final in 2006.

81 John Ferguson

Ferguson stole the limelight in the two best finals of the 1980s, scoring crucial tries as Wigan beat Hull at Wembley in 1985 - when he stood up Dane O'Hara magnificently as it seemed like there was nothing on, before scoring a 50-metre interception try - and posting the last-minute four-pointer that sent the classic Australian Grand Final of 1989 into extra-time. After that his Canberra Raiders side were too strong for Balmain. He scored more than a try every other game for Newtown and Canberra, also posting 24 in 25 games in a memorable spell for the cherry and whites.

82 Greg Alexander

A wonderfully talented but slightly inconsistent halfback or fullback, Alexander's big moment in the game came when he captained Penrith Panthers win the 1991 Grand Final against a magnificent Canberra side, having helped them to the final twelve months earlier with a magnificent semi-final performance against the Raiders. He won the Dally M Medal in 1985 and with so much in his armoury, Alexander became the club's first homegrown Test player and was a Kangaroo tourist in 1986 and 1990, despite fierce competition for halfback spots.

83 Nigel Vagana

Played a very significant part in the Kiwis renaissance by enjoying a wonderful nine-year Test career which peaked with Tri-Nations glory against Australia on that unforgettable night at Leeds in 2005. He played in three other finals, including the 1999 and 2006 Tri-Nations, both of which were lost by a whisker to the green and golds. He averaged more than a try every other game for Auckland Warriors and topped the Super League tryscoring charts in his only year in England with seventeen for Warrington in 1997. Prolific also for the Bulldogs and Cronulla.

84 Lesley Vainikolo

The Volcano proved to be an inspired signing for Bradford from Canberra Raiders in 2002, helping them to four consecutive Grand Finals and a Challenge Cup win in 2003. Vainikolo proved to be one of the best attacking players in Super League history with a commendable big-game record. Not just a great tryscorer (136 in the same number of Super League games), but also a player who made so many important metres returning kicks. Big Les was sorely missed by the Bulls, who have struggled to replace him.

85 David Furner

Deservedly awarded the 1994 Clive Churchill Medallist after a superb Grand Final performance for Canberra against Canterbury, Furner was subsequently picked for the Kangaroos tour of Europe and figured at Wembley in the first Test. Regarded as a Raiders legend judging by the way he was farewelled in 2000, Furner left Australia as the greatest pointscoring forward of all time - not just a prolific goalkicker, Furner averaged a try every four games. He made a great impact in Super League with both Wigan and Leeds, enjoying Challenge Cup and Super League success.

86 Mark Gasnier

Nephew of the great Reg Gasnier, if he was weighed down by expectation during his rugby league career it rarely showed. Gasnier was a strong centre with a highly effective fend throughout his eleven seasons at St George Illawarra, scoring and creating tries at will. He played in just one Grand Final, in 2010 after his return from union, and scored the first try in the Dragons' win over Sydney Roosters. He scored twice on his 2004 Origin debut - in the decider - and was the 2005 and 2006 Dally M centre of the year.

87 Trent Barrett

After scoring 30 tries in 46 games in a struggling Illawarra side, Barrett came of age after the Steelers' merger with St George. He gained his favoured number-six jersey after Anthony Mundine's controversial departure in 2000 and went on to win the Dally M Medal later that year. He toured Britain in 2000 and 2001, winning the World Cup and the Ashes, scoring tries in both deciders. He moved to Wigan in 2007, and was deemed unlucky not to win the Man of Steel after an excellent first season. Returned to the NRL and played again for New South Wales.

88 Les Boyd

Boyd is still regarded as one of the most notorious players of all time, having been banned for twelve months following an incident in 1983, and then a further fifteen months shortly after his comeback in 1985. Nonetheless, he was far more than an enforcer and was arguably the stand-out forward in the early 1980s, winning World-XIII selections at both second row and prop, and being a member of the 1982 Kangaroos. He endeared himself to Warrington fans with a successful spell between 1985 and 1989 when he was one of the best forwards in the English game and excelled in the 1986 Premiership final.

89 Denis Betts

A regular in the World XIII between 1991 and 1993, Betts was consistently one of the best forwards in the game in a glorious first spell at Wigan, which saw him win 26 winner's medals. Such a strong-running forward, he was part of the Great Britain team that performed so well in the 1990 and 1992 Ashes series, while he played in three winning series against the Kiwis. He captained England in the 1995 World Cup Final, and was Great Britain's stand-out performer in their 1996 series with New Zealand, scoring a try in each Test.

90 Greg Brentnall

Scorer of State of Origin's first-ever try, Brentnall went on to play at fullback for the all-conquering 1982 Kangaroos. His performances on that tour earned him a place in the World XIII, a position which he kept in 1983. For Canterbury, he began the decade in great fashion as they won the 1980 Grand Final against Easts and Brentnall set up one of the most talked about tries of the decade for Steve Gearin. Two years later, his domestic performances saw him pick up the Rothmans Medal in his penultimate season in the game.

91 Ben Kennedy

One of the best back-rowers of the modern era, Kennedy made the World XIII three times, won the Premiership with Newcastle Knights - scoring a try in the final against Parramatta - and helped New South Wales to four series wins and a draw in a successful seven-year state career. With the national team, he won the World Cup, an Ashes series and a Tri-Nations between 2000 and 2006. Earlier in his career, he had played at Canberra after switching codes, and scored nearly a try every other game over four seasons for the Raiders.

92 Matthew Gidley

Higly skilled centre for Newcastle and St Helens, Gidley excelled on the representative scene when competition for places was particularly fierce. His big year came in 2001 when he helped the Knights, as outsiders, win the Grand Final against a supposedly invincible Parramatta, subsequently earning a spot in the Australia team which won the Ashes. For the Blues he was part of the successful 2003 and 2004 series, and he enjoyed a four-year stint at St Helens, winning the World Club Challenge and two Challenge Cups, but losing four Grand Finals.

93 Keith Senior
A strong-running centre with immense durability who stayed at the top for a decade and a half, Senior is one of the bona-fide stars of the summer game. As a Sheffield player, he made his Great Britain debut against Fiji in 1996, scoring a try off the bench. He scored a further eleven tries for Great Britain, ten of which came against Australia or New Zealand - more than any other player in the Super League era. He won the Challenge Cup with Sheffield in 1998 against Wigan, before moving to Leeds where his 171 tries in 365 games helped them to four titles.

94 Nathan Cayless
New Zealand's World Cup-winning captain in 2008, Cayless enjoyed great longevity with both Parramatta and the Kiwis in a career that spanned fourteen years. He enjoyed Test success over Australia in 1999, 2003, and 2005 before his glorious exit from the Test arena at Suncorp Stadium's World Cup Final, when the Kiwis defied the odds to produce a miracle victory. For the Eels he was a rock in their brilliant 2001 team that stormed to the Minor Premiership but who, infamously, fell in the Grand Final to Newcastle. One of the best forwards of the last decade.

95 Steve Rogers
One of the greatest players of the 1970s and, indeed, all time, The Prince of Centres still had plenty to offer in the '80s. He played in the inaugural Origin and toured with the invincible Kangaroos in 1982, scoring eight matches in nine starts, including tries in the second and third Tests when he formed a brilliant centre partnership with Mal Meninga, having previously partnered Mick Cronin to devastating effect. He ended his Test career scoring against New Zealand in a 16-4 win in 1983. Injuries at Cronulla and Widnes ruined the end of his career. Rogers passed away in 2006.

96 Scott Hill
Classy stand-off or loose forward who helped engineer a stunning 1999 Premiership success for Melbourne in just their second season in the NRL. He was also an integral part of the Hunter Mariners side that went all the way to the Super League World Championship Final in 1997 in the only year of their existence. Hill never looked out of place in the Australian team, despite immense competition for places in the ballplaying positions. He featured at the

back of the scrum in the Kangaroos' impressive World Cup campaign of 2000 and played a big part in NSW's 3-0 series win that year.

97 Mike Gregory

One of the most wholehearted players in generations, Gregory captained Great Britain to successive series successes against New Zealand in 1989 and 1990, the latter with a depleted squad. His most famous Test moment came before that when, in the 1988 third Ashes Test, his long-range try that sealed the game became one of the sport's defining images. For Warrington, his sensational performance in a beaten 1990 Challenge Cup Final team against Wigan, his home-town team, characterised everything that his playing career was about. He later coached Wigan, but tragically lost his life in 2007 after a long illness.

98 Terry Newton

Newton's breakthrough year came at Leeds in 1998 as a key figure in one of the most physical teams in Super League history with Newton characteristically at the forefront. But he had far more to his game than that, as his 92 Super League tries demonstrate. Sixty-two of those came at Wigan, who improved enormously after his signing. His toughness, ball skills and eye for the tryline made him a Great Britain regular, a role in which he never looked out of place. He played in every Super League season between 1996 and 2010 before his untimely death stunned everyone in the game.

99 Kevin Hastings

Regarded by some as one of the greatest players never to have played for Australia, Hastings' pathway to Test and state selection was blocked by Steve Mortimer and Peter Sterling. A consistently brilliant scrum-half or stand-off, the Eastern Suburbs player was both the Rugby League Week player of the year and the Dally M halfback of the year in 1980, 1981 and 1982, but his greatest honour was the Rothmans Medal as the competition's best player in 1981. He also played for first-division side Barrow in 1986-87.

100 Des Drummond

Twice young player of the year, Drummond was instrumental in Leigh's unlikely title win in 1982 and also won medals at Warrington and Workington. For Great Britain he saved the 1980 series against the Kiwis with a superb third-Test performance. He was one of the only players to impress against the 1982 Kangaroos and two years later he played a big part in two scintillating Garry Schofield tries. One of the toughest wingers in the game's history, Drummond was a magnificent defender and a master of the big hit.

CHAPTER 11
STATISTICAL WRAP-UP

1 INTERNATIONAL RUGBY LEAGUE
1.1 GREAT BRITAIN TEST MATCHES

1980 Great Britain 14-14 New Zealand 1st Test
Central Park, Wigan. Att: 7,031. 18 October 1980.
Great Britain: George Fairbairn (c) (4g); Chris Camilleri (1t), John Joyner, Mike Smith (1t), Keith Bentley; Steve Hartley, Kevin Dick; Roy Holdstock, David Watkinson, Trevor Skerrett, Jeff Grayshon, Les Gorley, Len Casey. S: Mick Burke (dnp), Harry Pinner.
New Zealand: Michael O'Donnell; Kevin Fisher, James Leuluai, Bruce Dickison, Dane O'Hara; Fred Ah Kuoi (1t), Gordon Smith (4g); Mark Broadhurst, Alan Rushton, Kevin Tamati, Graeme West, Tony Coll (1t), Mark Graham (c). S: John Whittaker (dnp), Ray Baxendale.
Man of the Match: Fred Ah Kuoi

1980 Great Britain 8-12 New Zealand 2nd Test
Odsal Stadium, Bradford. Att: 10,946. 2 November 1980.
Great Britain: George Fairbairn (c) (4g); Des Drummond, John Joyner, Mike Smith, Chris Camilleri; Ken Kelly, Kevin Dick; Roy Holdstock, Keith Elwell, Glyn Shaw, Jeff Grayshon, Len Casey, Harry Pinner. S: Steve Evans, Les Gorley.
New Zealand: Michael O'Donnell (1t); Gary Prohm, John Whittaker, James Leuluai, Dane O'Hara (1t); Fred Ah Kuoi, Gordon Smith (3g); Mark Broadhurst, Alan Rushton, Kevin Tamati, Graeme West, Tony Coll, Mark Graham (c). S: Kevin Fisher (dnp), Ray Baxendale.
Man of the Match: Mark Broadhurst

1980 Great Britain 10-2 New Zealand 3rd Test
Headingley Stadium, Leeds. Att: 8,210. 15 November 1980.
Great Britain: Mick Burke (2g); Des Drummond (2t), John Joyner, Steve Evans, John Atkinson; John Woods, Arnie Walker; Trevor Skerrett, Keith Elwell, Len Casey (c), Mick Adams, Les Gorley, Steve Norton. S: Ken Kelly (dnp), Roy Holdstock (dnp).
New Zealand: Michael O'Donnell; Gary Prohm, John Whittaker, Bruce Dickison, Dane O'Hara; Fred Ah Kuoi, Gordon Smith (1g); Mark Broadhurst, Alan Rushton, Kevin Tamati, Graeme West, Barry Edkins, Mark Graham (c). S: Kevin Fisher (dnp), Howie Tamati.
Man of the Match: Des Drummond

1981 Great Britain 37-0 France 1st Test
The Boulevard, Hull. Att: 13,173. 6 December 1981.
Great Britain: George Fairbairn (1g); Des Drummond (2t), Mike Smith, John Woods (1t, 7g), Henderson Gill (3t); Steve Hartley (1t), Andy Gregory; Jeff Grayshon, David Ward (c), Trevor Skerrett, Les Gorley, Peter Gorley, Steve Norton. S: Mick Burke, Eddie Szymala.
France: Marcel Pillon; Sébastien Rodriguez, Serge Costals, Hugues Ratier, Laurent Girardet; Eric Walligunda, Christian Scicchitano; Henri Daniel, Christian Maccali, Dominique Verdiere, Jose Gine, Marc Ambert, Joel Roosebrouck (c). S: Michel Laville, Thierry Barnabe.
Man of the Match: Steve Norton

1981 France 19-2 Great Britain 2nd Test
Marseilles. Att: 6,500. 20 December 1981.
France: Andre Perez (3g); Patrick Solal (2t), Jacques Guigue, Guy Delaunay, Sébastien Rodriguez; Michel Laville (1dg), Christian Scicchitano (1t); Carlos Zalduendo, Christian Maccali, Jose Gine, Guy Lafforgue, Marc Ambert, Joel Roosebrouck (c). S: Etienne Kaminski (1t), Thierry Bernabe (dnp).
Great Britain: Mick Burke; Des Drummond, Mike Smith, John Woods (1g), Henderson Gill; Steve Hartley, Andy Gregory; Jeff Grayshon (c), David Watkinson, Trevor Skerrett, Les Gorley, Eddie Szymala, Steve Norton. S: George Fairbairn (dnp), Peter Gorley.
Man of the Match: Joel Roosebrouck

1982 Great Britain 4-40 Australia 1st Ashes Test
Boothferry Park, Hull. Att: 26,771. 30 October 1982.
Great Britain: George Fairbairn; Des Drummond, Eric Hughes, Les Dyl, Steve Evans; John Woods, Steve Nash (c); Jeff Grayshon, David Ward, Trevor Skerrett, Les Gorley, Lee Crooks (2g), Steve Norton. S: Ken Kelly (dnp), David Heron.
Australia: Greg Brentnall; Kerry Boustead (1t), Mal Meninga (1t, 8g), Steve Rogers, Eric Grothe (1t); Brett Kenny (1t), Peter Sterling; Craig Young, Max Krilich (c), Les Boyd (1t), Wayne Pearce (1t), Rod Reddy (1t), Ray Price (1t). S: Steve Ella (dnp), John Muggleton (dnp).
Man of the Match: Wayne Pearce

1982 Great Britain 6-27 Australia 2nd Ashes Test
Central Park, Wigan. Att: 23,216. 20 November 1982.
Great Britain: Keith Mumby (3g); Des Drummond, Mike Smith, David Stephenson, Henderson Gill; John Woods, Ken Kelly; Jeff Grayshon (c), John Dalgreen, Trevor Skerrett, Bob Eccles, Chris Burton, David Heron. S: John Woods, Alan Rathbone.
Australia: Greg Brentnall; Kerry Boustead, Mal Meninga (1t, 6g), Steve Rogers (1t), Eric Grothe (1t); Brett Kenny, Peter Sterling (1t); Craig Young, Max Krilich (c), Les Boyd, Wayne Pearce, Rod Reddy, Ray Price (1t). S: Wally Lewis, Ray Brown.
Man of the Match: Ray Price

1982 Great Britain 8-32 Australia 3rd Ashes Test
Headingley Stadium, Leeds. Att: 17,318. 28 November 1982.
Great Britain: George Fairbairn; Des Drummond, David Stephenson, Mike Smith, Steve Evans (1t); David Topliss (c), Andy Gregory; Mike O'Neill, Brian Noble, Paul Rose, Peter Smith, Lee Crooks (2g, 1dg), Mick Crane. S: John Woods (dnp), Neil Courtney.
Australia: Greg Brentnall; Kerry Boustead (1t), Mal Meninga (7g), Steve Rogers (1t), John Ribot (1t); Brett Kenny (1t), Peter Sterling; Les Boyd, Max Krilich (c) (1t), Rod Morris, Paul McCabe, Rod Reddy, Wayne Pearce (1t). S: Wally Lewis, Ray Brown.
Man of the Match: Brett Kenny

1983 France 5-20 Great Britain 1st Test
Stade Albert Domec, Carcassonne. Att: 3,826. 20 February 1983.
France: Jacky Imbert (1g); Didier Bernard (1t), Jacques Guigue, Guy Delaunay, Etienne Kaminski; Michel Laville, Ivan Greseque; Max Chantal, Christian Macalli, Yves Storer, Marc Ambert, Guy Laforgue, Joel Roosebrouck (c) S: Jean-Jacques Cologni, Herve Guiraud.
Great Britain: Mick Burke (1g); Des Drummond, John Joyner (1t), Ronnie Duane, Joe Lydon (1t, 3g); Tony Myler, Andy Gregory; Mike O'Neill, Brian Noble (1t), Andy Goodway (1t), Len Casey (c), Alan Rathbone, Terry Flanagan. S: John Woods, Peter Smith.
Man of the Match: Brian Noble

1983 Great Britain 17-5 France 2nd Test
The Boulevard, Hull. Att: 6,055. 6 March 1983.
Great Britain: Keith Mumby (4g); Des Drummond, John Joyner, Ronnie Duane (1t), Joe Lydon; Tony Myler, Andy Gregory (1t); Mike O'Neill, Brian Noble, Andy Goodway, Len Casey (c), Alan Rathbone, Terry Flanagan. S: John Woods (dnp), Peter Smith (1t).
France: Jacques Guigues; Patrick Solal (1t), Francis Laforgue, Phillippe Fourquet, Didier Bernard; Herve Guiraud, Christian Scicchitano; Max Chantal, Christian Macalli, Yves Storer, Guy Laforgue, Dominique Baloup (1g), Joel Roosebrouck (c). S: Didier Prunac, Serge Dauphin.
Man of the Match: Peter Smith

1984 France 0-12 Great Britain 1st Test
Parc des Sports, Avignon. Att: 4,000. 29 January 1984.
France: Patrick Wosniak; Patrick Solal, Didier Bernard, Phillippe Fourquet, Hugues Ratier; Andre Perez, Christian Scicchitano; Max Chantal (c), Thierry Bernabe, Pierre Ailleres, Marc Palanque, Guy Laforgue, Dominique Baloup. S: Roger Palisses (dnp), Manuel Caravaca.

Great Britain: Keith Mumby (c); Des Drummond, Ronnie Duane, Des Foy (1t), Garry Clark; Joe Lydon, David Cairns; Keith Rayne, David Watkinson, Andy Goodway (1t), Mick Worrall, David Hobbs, Dave Hall. S: Ellery Hanley, Lee Crooks (2t).
Man of the Match: Keith Rayne

1984 Great Britain 10-0 France 2nd Test
Headingley, Leeds. Att: 7,646. 17 February 1984.
Great Britain: Keith Mumby; Garry Clark, John Joyner, Garry Schofield, John Basnett; Ellery Hanley, David Cairns; Keith Rayne, Brian Noble (c), Kevin Ward, Dick Jasiewicz, David Hobbs (5g), Dave Hall. S: Mike Smith, Peter Smith.
France: Patrick Wosniak; Patrick Solal, Roger Palisses, Phillippe Fourquet, Didier Bernard; Andre Perez, Christian Scicchitano; Max Chantal, Patrick Trinque, Pierre Ailleres, Jean-Louis Meurin, Guy Laforgue, Dominique Baloup (c). S: Joel Conduche (dnp), Bruno Guasch.
Man of the Match: Guy Laforgue

1984 Australia 25-8 Great Britain 1st Ashes Test
Sydney Cricket Ground, Sydney. Att: 30,190. 9 June 1984.
Australia: Garry Jack; Kerry Boustead (1t), Gene Miles, Brett Kenny, Ross Conlon (4g); Wally Lewis (c) (1t, 1dg), Mark Murray (1t); Dave Brown, Greg Conescu, Greg Dowling, Wayne Pearce, Bryan Niebling, Ray Price (1t). S: Chris Close (dnp), Craig Young.
Great Britain: Mick Burke (2g); Des Drummond, Garry Schofield (1t), Keith Mumby, Ellery Hanley; Des Foy, Neil Holding; Lee Crooks, Brian Noble (c), Andy Goodway, Chris Burton, Mick Worrall, Mick Adams. S: Joe Lydon, David Hobbs.
Man of the Match: Wally Lewis

1984 Australia 18-6 Great Britain 2nd Ashes Test
Lang Park, Brisbane. Att: 25,534. 26 June 1984.
Australia: Garry Jack; Kerry Boustead, Gene Miles, Mal Meninga (1t, 3g), Eric Grothe (1t); Wally Lewis (c), Mark Murray; Dave Brown, Greg Conescu, Greg Dowling, Paul Vautin, Bryan Niebling, Wayne Pearce (1t). S: Steve Mortimer, Wally Fullerton-Smith.
Great Britain: Mick Burke (1g); Des Drummond, Garry Schofield (1t), Keith Mumby, Ellery Hanley; Tony Myler, Neil Holding; Keith Rayne, Brian Noble (c), Lee Crooks, Chris Burton, Andy Goodway, Mick Worrall. S: Andy Gregory, Mick Adams.
Man of the Match: Wayne Pearce

1984 Australia 20-7 Great Britain 3rd Ashes Test
Sydney Cricket Ground, Sydney. Att: 18,756. 7 July 1984.
Australia: Garry Jack (1t); Kerry Boustead, Gene Miles, Mal Meninga (4g), Eric Grothe (1t); Wally Lewis (c), Steve Mortimer; Bryan Niebling, Greg Conescu (1t), Greg Dowling, Wayne Pearce, Wally Fullerton-Smith, Ray Price. S: Brett Kenny, Dave Brown.
Great Britain: Mick Burke (1g); Des Drummond, Garry Schofield, Keith Mumby, Ellery Hanley (1t); Tony Myler, Neil Holding (1dg); David Hobbs, Brian Noble (c), Brian Case, Chris Burton, Andy Goodway, Mick Adams. S: Mike Smith (dnp), Keith Rayne (dnp).
Man of the Match: Wayne Pearce

1984 New Zealand 12-0 Great Britain 1st Test
Carlaw Park, Auckland. Att: 10,238. 14 July 1984.
New Zealand: Gary Kemble; Dean Bell, James Leuluai (1t), Fred Ah Kuoi (c) (1t), Dane O'Hara; Olsen Filipaina (2g), Shane Varley; Kevin Tamati, Howie Tamati, Dane Sorensen, Kurt Sorensen, Owen Wright, Hugh McGahan. S: Clayton Friend, Ricky Cowan (dnp).
Great Britain: Mick Burke; Des Drummond, Garry Schofield, Keith Mumby, Ellery Hanley; Mike Smith, Neil Holding; David Hobbs, Brian Noble (c), Brian Case, Chris Burton, Andy Goodway, Mick Adams. S: Andy Gregory (dnp), John Joyner (dnp).
Man of the Match: Kurt Sorensen

1984 New Zealand 28-12 Great Britain 2nd Test
Addington Show Grounds, Christchurch. Att: 3,824. 22 July 1984.
New Zealand: Gary Kemble; Dean Bell (1t), James Leuluai (1t), Fred Ah Kuoi (c) (1t), Dane O'Hara (2t); Olsen Filipaina (4g), Shane Varley; Kevin Tamati, Howie Tamati, Dane Sorensen, Owen Wright, Kurt Sorensen, Hugh McGahan. S: Clayton Friend, Ricky Cowan.
Great Britain: Mick Burke (2g); Des Drummond, Ellery Hanley (1t), Keith Mumby, Joe Lydon; Tony Myler (1t), Andy Gregory; David Hobbs, Brian Noble (c), Brian Case, Chris Burton, Andy Goodway, Mick Adams. S: John Joyner, Kevin Beardmore.
Man of the Match: Dane Sorensen

1984 New Zealand 32-16 Great Britain 3rd Test
Carlaw Park, Auckland. Att: 7,967. 28 July 1984.
New Zealand: Gary Kemble; Dean Bell, James Leuluai (2t), Fred Ah Kuoi (c), Dane O'Hara (1t); Olsen Filipaina (6g), Shane Varley; Kevin Tamati, Howie Tamati, Dane Sorensen, Owen Wright, Kurt Sorensen, Hugh McGahan. S: Clayton Friend (2t), Ricky Cowan.
Great Britain: Mick Burke (4g); Des Drummond, Ellery Hanley (1t), Keith Mumby (1t), Joe Lydon; Tony Myler, Andy Gregory; David Hobbs, Brian Noble (c), Brian Case, Mick Adams, Andy Goodway, Terry Flanagan. S: Steve Donlan, John Joyner.
Man of the Match: Olsen Filipaina

1984 Papua New Guines 20-38 Great Britain (One-off Test)
Rebiamul Oval, Mount Hagen. Att: 7,510. 5 August 1984.
Papua New Guinea: Mathius Kitimun; N Kania, David Noifa (1t), Bal Numapo (2g), Bob Tolik (1t); Gessau Gabob, Poka Kila; Joe Tep (c), F Asarufa, Bob Jakis (1t), Bob Kubak, Roy Loitive, Arebo Taumaku (1t). S: Jimmy Peter, Pora Wek.
Great Britain: Mick Burke (1t, 5g); Des Drummond (2t), Ellery Hanley (1t), Keith Mumby (1t), Joe Lydon; Tony Myler, Andy Gregory; Keith Rayne (1t), Brian Noble (c), Andy Goodway, Terry Flanagan, David Hobbs (1t), Mick Adams. S: Steve Donlan, Wayne Proctor.
Man of the Match: Ellery Hanley

1985 Great Britain 50-4 France 1st Test
Headingley, Leeds. Att: 6,491. 1 March 1985.
Great Britain: Shaun Edwards; Barrie Ledger, David Creasser (8g), Vince Gribbin (1t), Henderson Gill (1t); Ellery Hanley (2t), Deryck Fox (2t, 1g); Roy Dickinson, David Watkinson (1t), Andy Dannatt, Andy Goodway (c), Alan Rathbone, Gary Divorty (1t). S: Carl Gibson, Andy Platt.
France: Serge Pallares; Bernard Jean, Roger Palisses, Phillippe Fourquet, Hugues Ratier; Andre Perez, Ivan Greseque; Max Chantal, Christian Macalli (1t), Jean-Louis Meurin, Pierre Ailleres, Guy Laforgue (c), Dominique Baloup. S: Serge Titeux, Denis Berge (dnp).
Man of the Match: Deryck Fox

1985 France 24-16 Great Britain 2nd Test
Stade Gilbert Brutus, Perpignan. Att: 5,000. 17 March 1985.
France: Serge Pallares (4g); Hugues Ratier, Phillippe Fourquet (1t), Roger Palisses, Didier Couston (3t); Francis Laforgue, Ivan Greseque; Max Chantal, Christian Macalli, Serge Titeux, Pierre Montgaillard, Daniel Verdes, Guy Laforgue (c). S: Thierry Bernabe, Luc Mendes.
Great Britain: Chris Johnson; Garry Clark, David Creasser (1g), Des Foy (1t), Phil Ford (2t); Ellery Hanley (c), Deryck Fox; Roy Dickinson, Nicky Kiss, Shaun Wane, Andy Dannatt, Alan Rathbone, Gary Divorty (1g). S: Paul Harkin, Roy Powell.
Man of the Match: Didier Couston

1985 Great Britain 22-24 New Zealand 1st Test
Headingley, Leeds. Att: 12,591. 19 October 1985.
Great Britain: Mick Burke (3g); Des Drummond, Garry Schofield, Ellery Hanley (1t), Joe Lydon (1t, 2g); Tony Myler, Deryck Fox; Lee Crooks, David Watkinson, John Fieldhouse, Andy Goodway (1t), Ian Potter, Harry Pinner (c). S: David Hulme (dnp), Chris Arkwright.

New Zealand: James Leuluai (1t); Dean Bell (1t), Fred Ah Kuoi, Gary Prohm, Dane O'Hara (1t); Olsen Filipaina (2g), Clayton Friend; Kurt Sorensen (1t), Howie Tamati, Dane Sorensen, Mark Graham (c) (1t), Owen Wright, Hugh McGahan. S: Gary Kemble, Kevin Tamati.
Man of the Match: Harry Pinner

1985 Great Britain 25-8 New Zealand 2nd Test
Central Park, Wigan. Att: 15,506. 2 November 1985.
Great Britain: Mick Burke; Des Drummond, Garry Schofield (4t), Ellery Hanley, Joe Lydon (4g); Tony Myler, Deryck Fox; Jeff Grayshon, David Watkinson, John Fieldhouse, Andy Goodway, Ian Potter, Harry Pinner (c) (1dg). S: Shaun Edwards, Chris Burton.
New Zealand: Gary Kemble; Dean Bell (1t), James Leuluai, Gary Prohm, Dane O'Hara; Olsen Filipaina (c) (2g), Clayton Friend; Kurt Sorensen, Howie Tamati, Dane Sorensen, Graeme West, Sam Stewart, Hugh McGahan. S: Fred Ah Kuoi, Ricky Cowan.
Man of the Match: Garry Schofield

1985 Great Britain 6-6 New Zealand 3rd Test, World Cup Rated
Elland Road, Leeds. Att: 22,209. 9 November 1985.
Great Britain: Mick Burke; Des Drummond, Garry Schofield, Shaun Edwards, Joe Lydon; Ellery Hanley, Deryck Fox; Jeff Grayshon, David Watkinson, John Fieldhouse, Andy Goodway, Ian Potter, Harry Pinner (c). S: Chris Arkwright, Lee Crooks (3g).
New Zealand: Gary Kemble; Darrell Williams, Dean Bell, James Leuluai, Dane O'Hara; Fred Ah Kuoi, Clayton Friend; Kevin Tamati, Wayne Wallace, Dane Sorensen (1g), Mark Graham (c) (1t), Kurt Sorensen, Gary Prohm. S: Olsen Filipaina, Hugh McGahan.
Man of the Match: Lee Crooks

1986 France 10-10 Great Britain 1st Test, World Cup Rated
Parc des Sports, Avignon. Att: 4,000. 16 February 1986.
France: Gilles Dumas (1t, 3g); Didier Couston, Alain Maury, Phillippe Fourquet, Paul Laroche; Dominique Espugna, Patrick Entat; Max Chantal, Patrick Baco, Serge Titeux, Guy Laforgue (c), Marc Palanque, Thierry Bernabe. S: Denis Berge, Jean-Luc Rabot.
Great Britain: Mick Burke; Des Drummond, Garry Schofield, Ellery Hanley (1t), Henderson Gill; Tony Myler, Deryck Fox; Lee Crooks (3g), David Watkinson, Shaun Wane, Ian Potter, John Fieldhouse, Harry Pinner (c). S: Shaun Edwards (dnp), Neil James (dnp).
Man of the Match: Ian Potter

1986 Great Britain 24-10 France 2nd Test
Central Park, Wigan. Att: 8,112. 1 March 1986.
Great Britain: Joe Lydon; Des Drummond (1t), Garry Schofield (1t, 2g), Tony Marchant (1t), David Laws; Tony Myler, Deryck Fox; Lee Crooks (2g), David Watkinson (c), John Fieldhouse, Kevin Rayne, Neil James (1t), Ian Potter. S: Shaun Edwards, Andy Platt.
France: Gilles Dumas (1g); Didier Couston (2t), Denis Berge, Phillippe Fourquet, Paul Laroche; Dominique Espugna, Patrick Entat; Max Chantal, Patrick Baco, Serge Titeux, Guy Laforgue (c), Marc Palanque, Thierry Bernabe. S: Serge Pallares, Jean-Luc Rabot.
Man of the Match: Neil James

1986 Great Britain 16-38 Australia 1st Ashes Test
Old Trafford, Manchester. Att: 50,583. 25 October 1986.
Great Britain: Joe Lydon (1t); Tony Marchant, Garry Schofield (2t), Ellery Hanley, Henderson Gill (1g); Tony Myler, Deryck Fox; Kevin Ward, David Watkinson (c), John Fieldhouse, Ian Potter, Lee Crooks (1g), Andy Goodway. S: Shaun Edwards (dnp), Andy Platt (dnp).
Australia: Garry Jack (1t); Les Kiss, Brett Kenny, Gene Miles (3t), Michael O'Connor (3t, 5g); Wally Lewis (c), Peter Sterling; Greg Dowling, Royce Simmons, Steve Roach, Noel Cleal, Bryan Niebling, Bob Lindner. S: Mal Meninga, Terry Lamb.
Man of the Match: Wally Lewis

1986 Great Britain 4-34 Australia 2nd Ashes Test

Elland Road, Leeds. Att: 30,808. 8 November 1986.
Great Britain: Joe Lydon; Barrie Ledger, Garry Schofield (1t), Tony Marchant, Henderson Gill; Tony Myler, Deryck Fox; Kevin Ward, David Watkinson (c), John Fieldhouse, Ian Potter, Lee Crooks, Andy Goodway. S: Shaun Edwards, Andy Platt.
Australia: Garry Jack (2t); Dale Shearer, Brett Kenny (1t), Gene Miles, Michael O'Connor (1t, 5g); Wally Lewis (c) (1t), Peter Sterling; Greg Dowling, Royce Simmons, Paul Dunn, Noel Cleal, Bryan Niebling, Bob Lindner (1t). S: Terry Lamb, Mal Meninga.
Man of the Match: Noel Cleal

1986 Great Britain 15-24 Australia 3rd Ashes Test, World Cup Rated

Central Park, Wigan. Att: 20,169. 22 November 1986.
Great Britain: Joe Lydon (2g); Henderson Gill (1g), Garry Schofield (2t, 1dg), David Stephenson, John Basnett; Tony Myler, Andy Gregory; Kevin Ward, David Watkinson (c), Lee Crooks, Andy Goodway, Chris Burton, Harry Pinner. S: Shaun Edwards (dnp), Ian Potter.
Australia: Garry Jack; Dale Shearer (1t), Brett Kenny, Gene Miles (1t), Michael O'Connor (4g); Wally Lewis (c) (1t), Peter Sterling; Greg Dowling, Royce Simmons, Paul Dunn, Mal Meninga, Bryan Niebling, Bob Lindner (1t). S: Terry Lamb, Les Davidson.
Man of the Match: Garry Schofield

1987 Great Britain 52-4 France 1st Test, World Cup Rated

Headingley, Leeds. Att: 6,567. 24 January 1987.
Great Britain: Joe Lydon (1t, 8g); Mark Forster (1t), Garry Schofield, David Stephenson, Henderson Gill; Ellery Hanley (c) (2t), Shaun Edwards (2t); David Hobbs, Kevin Beardmore, Lee Crooks, Andy Goodway (1t), Roy Haggerty, Mike Gregory (2t). S: David Creasser, Keith England.
France: Andre Perez (2g); Didier Couston, Roger Palisses, Hugues Ratier, Cyrille Pons; Dominique Espugna, Gilles Dumas; Yves Storer, Yannick Mantese, Jean-Luc Rabot, Daniel Verdes, Marc Palanque (c), Thierry Bernabe. S: Patrick Rocci, Serge Titeux.
Man of the Match: Shaun Edwards

1987 France 10-20 Great Britain 2nd Test

Stade Albert Domec, Carcassonne. Att: 2,000. 8 February 1987.
France: Andre Perez (3g); Gaston Berteloitte, Denis Bienes, Jacques Moliner, Hugues Ratier; Dominique Espugna (1t), Christian Scicchitano; Jean-Luc Rabot, Patrick Trinque, Pierre Ailleres, Daniel Verdes, Marc Palanque (c), Thierry Bernabe. S: Gilles Dumas (dnp), Yves Storer.
Great Britain: Joe Lydon (4g); Mark Forster, Garry Schofield, Ellery Hanley (c) (1t), Henderson Gill (1t); Shaun Edwards, Andy Gregory; David Hobbs, Kevin Beardmore (1t), Keith England, Chris Burton, Roy Haggerty, Mike Gregory. S: David Stephenson (dnp), Paul Dixon.
Man of the Match: Kevin Beardmore

1987 Great Britain 42-0 Papua New Guinea World Cup Rated

Central Park, Wigan. Att: 9,121. 24 October 1987.
Great Britain: Steve Hampson; Des Drummond, David Stephenson (7g), Joe Lydon (1t), Phil Ford (1t); Shaun Edwards (2t), Andy Gregory (1t); Kevin Ward, Paul Groves, Brian Case, Andy Goodway, Paul Medley (1t), Ellery Hanley (c) (1t). S: John Woods, Karl Fairbank.
Papua New Guinea: Dairi Kovae; Kepi Saea, Lauta Atoi, Bal Numapo (c), Arnold Krewanty; Darius Haila, Tony Kila; Joe Tep, Roy Heni, Ati Lomutopa, Mathius Kombra, Bernard Waketsi, Arebo Taumaku. S: Mathius Kitimun, David Gaius.
Man of the Match: Paul Medley

1988 France 14-28 Great Britain 1st Test

Parc des Sports, Avignon. Att: 6,000. 24 January 1988.
France: Jean-Philippe Pougeau; Hugues Ratier (c) (1t), Guy Delaunay, David Fraisse, Cyrille Pons; Dominique Espugna, Gilles Dumas (3g); Marc Tisseyre, Mathieu Khedemi, Pierre Ailleres, Daniel Verdes (1t), Pierre Montgaillard, Jacques Moliner. S: Phillippe Gestas, Denis Bienes.

Great Britain: Steve Hampson; Des Drummond (1t), Garry Schofield (2t), Paul Loughlin (3g), Martin Offiah (1t); Ellery Hanley (c) (1t), Shaun Edwards; Kevin Ward, Kevin Beardmore, Hugh Waddell, Roy Powell, Paul Medley, Andy Platt. S: David Creasser (1g), Paul Dixon.
Man of the Match: Hugh Waddell

1988 Great Britain 30-12 France 2nd Test
Headingley, Leeds. Att: 7,007. 6 February 1988.
Great Britain: Steve Hampson; David Plange (1t), Garry Schofield (1t, 5g), Ellery Hanley (c) (2t), Phil Ford; Shaun Edwards, Andy Gregory (1t); Kevin Ward, Kevin Beardmore, Hugh Waddell, Roy Powell, Paul Dixon, Andy Platt. S: David Stephenson, Paul Medley.
France: Jean-Phillippe Pougeau; Hugues Ratier (c), Phillippe Fourquet, Guy Delaunay, Cyrille Pons (1t); Dominique Espugna, Frederic Bourrel (2g); Marc Tisseyre, Mathieu Khedemi (1t), Pierre Ailleres, Pierre Montgaillard, Daniel Verdes, Phillippe Gestas. S: Jacques Moliner, Denis Bienes (dnp).
Man of the Match: Steve Hampson

1988 Papua New Guinea 22-42 Great Britain, World Cup Rated
Lloyd Robson Oval, Port Moresby. Att: 12,107. 22 May 1988.
Papua New Guinea: Dairi Kovae (2t); Kepi Saea, Mea Morea, Bal Numapo (c) (3g), Arnold Krewanty (1t); Darius Haila, Tony Kila; Isaac Rop (1t), Michael Matmillo, Yer Bom, Mathius Kombra, Tuiyo Evei, Haoda Kouoru. S: Thomas Rombuk, Ngala Lapan.
Great Britain: Paul Loughlin (7g); Phil Ford, Garry Schofield (2t), David Stephenson (1t), Henderson Gill (2t); Shaun Edwards, Andy Gregory; Kevin Ward, Kevin Beardmore, Brian Case, Paul Medley (1t), Mike Gregory (1t), Ellery Hanley (c). S: David Hulme, Paul Dixon.
Man of the Match: Kevin Ward

1988 Australia 17-6 Great Britain 1st Ashes Test
Sydney Football Stadium, Sydney. Att: 24,202. 11 June 1988.
Australia: Garry Jack; Andrew Ettingshausen, Michael O'Connor (2g), Peter Jackson (2t), Tony Currie; Wally Lewis (c) (1dg), Peter Sterling; Phil Daley, Greg Conescu, Sam Backo (1t), Paul Vautin, Wally Fullerton-Smith, Bob Lindner. S: Gary Belcher, Steve Folkes.
Great Britain: Paul Loughlin (1g); Phil Ford, Garry Schofield, David Stephenson, Martin Offiah; David Hulme, Andy Gregory; Kevin Ward, Kevin Beardmore, Paul Dixon, Andy Platt, Mike Gregory, Ellery Hanley (c) (1t). S: Henderson Gill, Roy Powell.
Man of the Match: Kevin Ward

1988 Australia 34-14 Great Britain 2nd Ashes Test
Lang Park, Brisbane. Att: 27,103. 28 June 1988.
Australia: Garry Jack; Andrew Ettingshausen (1t), Michael O'Connor (1t, 5g), Peter Jackson (1t), Tony Currie; Wally Lewis (c) (1t), Peter Sterling; Phil Daley, Greg Conescu, Sam Backo (1t), Paul Vautin, Wally Fullerton-Smith, Wayne Pearce (1t). S: Gary Belcher, Bob Lindner.
Great Britain: Paul Loughlin (3g); Henderson Gill, Phil Ford (1t), Ellery Hanley (c), Martin Offiah (1t); David Hulme, Andy Gregory; Kevin Ward, Kevin Beardmore, Roy Powell, Andy Platt, Paul Dixon, Mike Gregory. S: Darren Wright, Paul Hulme.
Man of the Match: Wally Lewis

1988 Australia 12-26 Great Britain 3rd Ashes Test, World Cup Rated
Sydney Football Stadium, Sydney. Att: 15,994. 9 July 1988.
Australia: Garry Jack; Andrew Ettingshausen, Michael O'Connor (2g), Peter Jackson, Tony Currie; Wally Lewis (c) (1t), Peter Sterling; Martin Bella, Greg Conescu, Sam Backo (1t), Paul Vautin, Wally Fullerton-Smith, Wayne Pearce. S: Gary Belcher, Bob Lindner.
Great Britain: Phil Ford (1t); Henderson Gill (2t), David Stephenson, Paul Loughlin (3g), Martin Offiah (1t); David Hulme, Andy Gregory; Kevin Ward, Paul Hulme, Hugh Waddell, Roy Powell, Mike Gregory (1t), Ellery Hanley (c). S: Darren Wright (dnp), Brian Case.
Man of the Match: Andy Gregory

1988 New Zealand 12-10 Great Britain World Cup Rated
Addington Show Grounds, Christchurch. Att: 8,525. 17 July 1988.
New Zealand: Darrell Williams; Shane Horo, Dean Bell (c), Kevin Iro, Gary Mercer; Shane Cooper, Clayton Friend; Peter Brown (2g), Wayne Wallace, Adrian Shelford, Mark Graham, Sam Stewart, Mark Horo. S: Gary Freeman (2t), Esene Faimalo (dnp).
Great Britain: Phil Ford; Henderson Gill, David Stephenson, Paul Loughlin (1t, 1g), Martin Offiah; David Hulme (1t), Andy Gregory; Kevin Ward, Kevin Beardmore, Hugh Waddell, Mike Gregory, Roy Powell, Ellery Hanley (c). S: Darren Wright (dnp), Paul Hulme.
Man of the Match: Gary Freeman

1989 Great Britain 26-10 France 1st Test
Central Park, Wigan. Att: 8,266. 21 January 1989.
Great Britain: Alan Tait; Phil Ford (1t), Paul Loughlin (3g), Joe Lydon (1t), Martin Offiah (1t); Shaun Edwards (1t), Andy Gregory; Kevin Ward, Kevin Beardmore, Hugh Waddell, Mike Gregory, Roy Powell, Ellery Hanley (c) (1t). S: Peter Williams, Richie Eyres.
France: David Fraisse (1g); Hugues Ratier (c), Eric Verginol, Guy Delaunay, Marcel Criottier; Roger Palisses, Gilles Dumas (1t); Jean-Luc Rabot, Thierry Valero, Pierre Ailleres, Thierry Buttignol, Daniel Verdes, Jacques Moliner (1t). S: Patrick Rocci, Marc Tisseyre.
Man of the Match: Alan Tait

1989 France 8-30 Great Britain 2nd Test
Parc des Sports, Avignon. Att: 6,500. 5 February 1989.
France: Jean Frison; Hugues Ratier (c) (1t), Eric Verginol, Guy Delaunay, David Fraisse; Roger Palisses, Gilles Dumas (1t); Jean-Luc Rabot, Thierry Valero, Pierre Ailleres, Thierry Buttignol, Daniel Verdes, Jacques Moliner. S: Patrick Rocci, Marc Tisseyre.
Great Britain: Alan Tait (1t); Phil Ford (2t), Peter Williams (1t), Joe Lydon (3g), Martin Offiah; Shaun Edwards (1t), Andy Gregory; Kevin Ward, Kevin Beardmore, Lee Crooks, Mike Gregory, Roy Powell, Ellery Hanley (c) (1t). S: Steve Hampson, Keith England.
Man of the Match: Kevin Ward

1989 Great Britain 16-24 New Zealand 1st Test
Old Trafford, Manchester. Att: 18,273. 21 October 1989.
Great Britain: Alan Tait (1t); Phil Ford (1t), Andy Currier, Paul Loughlin (2g), Martin Offiah (1t); David Hulme, Andy Gregory; Kelvin Skerrett, Kevin Beardmore, David Hobbs, Andy Goodway, Andy Platt, Mike Gregory (c). S: Shaun Edwards, Paul Newlove, Roy Powell (dnp), Paul Hulme (dnp).
New Zealand: Darrell Williams; Kevin Iro (1t), Dean Bell, Kurt Sherlock (2g), Gary Mercer; Kelly Shelford (1t), Gary Freeman (1t); James Goulding (1t), Duane Mann, Brent Todd, Kurt Sorensen, Sam Stewart, Hugh McGahan (c) (1t). S: Tony Kemp, Phil Bancroft (dnp), Mike Kuiti (dnp), Francis Leota (dnp).
Man of the Match: Gary Freeman

1989 Great Britain 26-6 New Zealand 2nd Test
Elland Road, Leeds. Att: 13,073. 28 October 1989.
Great Britain: Steve Hampson; Phil Ford, Paul Newlove, Paul Loughlin (5g), Martin Offiah (1t); Shaun Edwards (1t), David Hulme; Kelvin Skerrett, Paul Hulme, Andy Platt, Andy Goodway (2t), Roy Powell, Mike Gregory (c). S: Daryl Powell (dnp), David Hobbs, Deryck Fox, Keith England (dnp).
New Zealand: Darrell Williams; Kevin Iro, Dean Bell, Kurt Sherlock (1g), Gary Mercer; Kelly Shelford, Gary Freeman; Adrian Shelford, Duane Mann, Brent Todd, Kurt Sorensen, Sam Stewart, Hugh McGahan (c) (1t). S: Tony Kemp, Phil Bancroft (dnp), Mike Kuiti (dnp), Esene Faimalo.
Man of the Match: Shaun Edwards

1989 Great Britain 10-6 New Zealand 3rd Test, World Cup Rated

Central Park, Wigan. Att: 20,346. 11 November 1989.

Great Britain: Alan Tait (1t); Phil Ford, Paul Newlove, Paul Loughlin (1g), Martin Offiah (1t); Shaun Edwards, David Hulme; Kelvin Skerrett, Paul Hulme, Andy Platt, Andy Goodway, Roy Powell, Mike Gregory (c). S: Joe Lydon, David Hobbs (dnp), Deryck Fox (dnp), Keith England.

New Zealand: Tony Kemp; Kevin Iro, Dean Bell, Darrell Williams, Gary Mercer; Kelly Shelford (1t, 1g), Gary Freeman; Brent Todd, Duane Mann, Esene Faimalo, Kurt Sorensen, Sam Stewart, Hugh McGahan (c). S: Kurt Sherlock (dnp), Dean Clark, Francis Leota, Mike Kuiti (dnp).

Man of the Match: Martin Offiah

1990 France 4-8 Great Britain 1st Test

Stade Gilbert Brutus, Perpignan. Att: 6,000. 18 March 1990.

France: Jean-Phillippe Pougeau; Hugues Ratier (c), David Fraisse, Guy Delaunay, Cyrille Pons (1t); Gilles Dumas, Patrick Entat; Jean-Luc Rabot, Thierry Valero, Thierry Buttignol, Daniel Divet, Didier Cabestany, Jacques Moliner. S: Pierre Ailleres, Jean Ruiz (dnp), Denis Bienes (dnp), Phillippe Solokow (dnp).

Great Britain: Alan Tait; Joe Lydon, Garry Schofield (2g), Paul Loughlin, Martin Offiah (1t); Shaun Edwards, Andy Gregory; Kelvin Skerrett, Kevin Beardmore, Andy Platt, Mike Gregory, Andy Goodway, Ellery Hanley (c). S: Graham Steadman (dnp), Denis Betts, Daryl Powell, Keith England (dnp).

Man of the Match: Kelvin Skerrett

1990 Great Britain 18-25 France 2nd Test

Headingley, Leeds. Att: 6,554. 7 April 1990.

Great Britain: Alan Tait (1t); Gerald Cordle (1t), Garry Schofield, Carl Gibson, Martin Offiah (1t); Graham Steadman (3g), Shaun Edwards (c); Kelvin Skerrett, Kevin Beardmore, Keith England, Denis Betts, Karl Fairbank, Mike Gregory. S: Deryck Fox (dnp), Shaun Irwin, David Bishop, Roy Powell (dnp).

France: David Fraisse (5g); Hugues Ratier (c), Guy Delaunay, Denis Bienes, Cyrille Pons (1t); Gilles Dumas (1g, 1dg), Patrick Entat; Thierry Buttignol, Thierry Valero, Jean-Luc Rabot (1t), Daniel Divet (1t), Didier Cabestany, Jacques Moliner. S: Marc Tisseyre (dnp), Charles Frison, Jean-Paul Marquet (dnp), Phillippe Solokow (dnp).

Man of the Match: Gilles Dumas

1990 Papua New Guinea 20-18 Great Britain 1st Test

Danny Leahy Oval, Goroka. Att: 11,598. 27 May 1990.

Papua New Guinea: Ipisa Wanega; Arnold Krewanty, Phillip Boge, Bal Numapo (5g, 1dg), Mea Morea; Stanley Haru (1t, 1dg), Gigmai Ongugo; Bobby Ako, Michael Matmillo, Tuiyo Evei (1t), Joe Gispe, Arebo Taumaku (c), Michael Angara. S: Chris Itam (dnp), Noah Kool, Goro Arigai, Max Tiri (dnp).

Great Britain: Alan Tait; Paul Eastwood (1t), Daryl Powell, Jonathan Davies (1t, 3g), Carl Gibson; Garry Schofield, Bobbie Goulding (1t); Roy Powell, Lee Jackson, Paul Dixon, Denis Betts, Karl Fairbank, Mike Gregory (c). S: Deryck Fox (dnp), Phil Clarke (dnp), Shaun Irwin, Keith England.

Man of the Match: Stanley Haru

1990 Papua New Guinea 8-40 Great Britain 2nd Test

Lloyd Robson Oval, Port Moresby. Att: 5,969. 2 June 1990.

Papua New Guinea: Ipisa Wanega; Arnold Krewanty, Phillip Boge, Bal Numapo (2g), Mea Morea; Stanley Haru, Gigmai Ongugo (1t); Ati Lomutopa, Michael Matmillo, Tuiyo Evei, Joe Gispe, Arebo Taumaku (c), Michael Angara. S: Chris Itam, Noah Kool (dnp), Goro Arigai (dnp), Max Tiri.

Great Britain: Alan Tait; Paul Eastwood (1t), Jonathan Davies (6g), Daryl Powell (1t), Carl Gibson (2t); Garry Schofield (1t), Bobbie Goulding (1t); Roy Powell, Lee Jackson, Keith

England, Denis Betts, Paul Dixon (1t), Mike Gregory (c). S: Deryck Fox, Karl Fairbank (dnp), Shaun Irwin (dnp), Phil Clarke.
Man of the Match: Garry Schofield

1990 New Zealand 10-11 Great Britain 1st Test
Show Grounds Oval, Palmerston North. Att: 8,073. 24 June 1990.
New Zealand: Darrell Williams; Tony Iro, Kevin Iro (1t), Tony Kemp, Sam Panapa (1t); Dean Clark, Gary Freeman; Peter Brown (1g), Duane Mann, Brent Todd, Mark Horo, Tawera Nikau, Hugh McGahan (c). S: Mark Nixon (dnp), Morvin Edwards, Dean Lonergan (dnp), George Mann.
Great Britain: Chris Bibb; Jonathan Davies (1t, 1g), Joe Lydon, Carl Gibson, Martin Offiah; Garry Schofield (1dg), Bobbie Goulding; Kelvin Skerrett, Martin Dermott, Keith England, Denis Betts, Paul Dixon (1t), Mike Gregory (c). S: Deryck Fox (dnp), Ian Lucas (dnp), Daryl Powell, Roy Powell.
Man of the Match: Garry Schofield

1990 New Zealand 14-16 Great Britain 2nd Test
Mount Smart Stadium, Auckland. Att: 7,843. 8 July 1990.
New Zealand: Matthew Ridge (5g); Tony Iro, Kevin Iro, Darrell Williams, Sam Panapa; Dean Clark, Gary Freeman; Peter Brown, Duane Mann, Brent Todd, Mark Horo (1t), Tawera Nikau, Hugh McGahan (c). S: Morvin Edwards (dnp), Tony Kemp, George Mann (dnp), Dean Lonergan.
Great Britain: Joe Lydon; Jonathan Davies (2g), Carl Gibson, Daryl Powell, Martin Offiah (1t); Garry Schofield (1t), Bobbie Goulding; Kelvin Skerrett, Lee Jackson, Keith England, Denis Betts (1t), Paul Dixon, Mike Gregory (c). S: Deryck Fox (dnp), Roy Powell, Shaun Irwin, Karl Fairbank (dnp).
Man of the Match: Garry Schofield

1990 New Zealand 21-18 Great Britain 3rd Test, World Cup Rated
Queen Elizabeth Park, Christchurch. Att: 3,133. 15 July 1990.
New Zealand: Matthew Ridge (6g); Sam Panapa, Kevin Iro, Darrell Williams, Tony Iro; Tony Kemp (1t), Gary Freeman; Peter Brown, Duane Mann, Brent Todd, Tawera Nikau (1t), Mark Horo, Hugh McGahan (c) (1dg). S: Morvin Edwards, Dean Clark (dnp), George Mann (dnp), Dean Lonergan.
Great Britain: Joe Lydon; Jonathan Davies (3g), Carl Gibson, Daryl Powell, Martin Offiah (1t); Garry Schofield (1t), Bobbie Goulding; Kelvin Skerrett, Martin Dermott, Keith England, Denis Betts, Roy Powell (1t), Mike Gregory (c). S: Deryck Fox (dnp), Shaun Irwin, Paul Dixon, Karl Fairbank (dnp).
Man of the Match: Garry Schofield

1990 Great Britain 19-12 Australia 1st Ashes Test
Wembley Stadium, London. Att: 54,569. 27 October 1990.
Great Britain: Steve Hampson; Paul Eastwood (2t, 3g), Daryl Powell, Carl Gibson, Martin Offiah (1t); Garry Schofield (1dg), Andy Gregory; Karl Harrison, Lee Jackson, Paul Dixon, Denis Betts, Roy Powell, Ellery Hanley (c). S: Shaun Edwards (dnp), Kevin Ward, David Hulme (dnp), Karl Fairbank.
Australia: Gary Belcher; Michael Hancock, Mal Meninga (c) (1t, 2g), Mark McGaw (1t), Andrew Ettingshausen; Ricky Stuart, Allan Langer; Steve Roach, Kerrod Walters, Martin Bella, Paul Sironen, John Cartwright, Bob Lindner. S: Greg Alexander, Des Hasler, Dale Shearer, Glenn Lazarus.
Man of the Match: Ellery Hanley

1990 Great Britain 10-14 Australia 2nd Ashes Test
Old Trafford, Manchester. Att: 46,615. 10 November 1990.
Great Britain: Steve Hampson; Paul Eastwood (1g), Daryl Powell, Carl Gibson, Martin Offiah; Garry Schofield, Andy Gregory; Karl Harrison, Lee Jackson, Andy Platt, Denis Betts,

Paul Dixon (1t), Ellery Hanley (c). S: David Hulme (dnp), Kevin Ward, Paul Loughlin (1t), Roy Powell (dnp).

Australia: Gary Belcher; Andrew Ettingshausen, Mal Meninga (c) (1t, 1g), Laurie Daley, Dale Shearer (1t); Cliff Lyons (1t), Ricky Stuart; Steve Roach, Benny Elias, Glenn Lazarus, Paul Sironen, Bob Lindner, Brad Mackay. S: Greg Alexander (dnp), Des Hasler (dnp), Mark Sargent (dnp), John Cartwright (dnp).
Man of the Match: Benny Elias

1990 Great Britain 0-14 Australia 3rd Ashes Test, World Cup Rated
Elland Road, Leeds. Att: 32,500. 24 November 1990.
Great Britain: Steve Hampson; Paul Eastwood, Daryl Powell, Carl Gibson, Martin Offiah; Garry Schofield, Andy Gregory; Karl Harrison, Lee Jackson, Andy Platt, Denis Betts, Paul Dixon, Ellery Hanley (c). S: David Hulme (dnp), Mike Gregory, Jonathan Davies, Roy Powell.
Australia: Gary Belcher; Andrew Ettingshausen (1t), Mal Meninga (c) (1t, 1g), Laurie Daley, Dale Shearer; Cliff Lyons, Ricky Stuart; Steve Roach, Benny Elias (1t), Glenn Lazarus, Paul Sironen, Bob Lindner, Brad Mackay. S: Greg Alexander, Des Hasler, Mark Sargent, David Gillespie.
Man of the Match: Ricky Stuart

1991 France 10-45 Great Britain 1st Test, World Cup Rated
Stade Gilbert Brutus, Perpignan. Att: 3,965. 27 January 1991.
France: Christophe Auroy (1t); Eric Remirez, David Fraisse (1t), Guy Delaunay, Cyrille Pons; Gilles Dumas (c), Patrick Entat; Marc Tisseyre (1g), Thierry Valero, Thierry Buttignol, Jean-Pierre Magnac, Daniel Verdes, Jacques Moliner. S: Pierre Chamorin, Michel Roses (dnp), Denis Beines, Abderazach Baba.
Great Britain: Steve Hampson; Paul Eastwood (6g), Daryl Powell, Carl Gibson, Martin Offiah (2t); Garry Schofield (2t, 1dg), Shaun Edwards (2t); Ian Lucas, Lee Jackson, Andy Platt (1t), Denis Betts (1t), Les Holliday, Ellery Hanley (c). S: Mark Aston, Karl Fairbank, St John Ellis, Richie Eyres.
Man of the Match: Denis Betts

1991 Great Britain 60-4 France 2nd Test
Headingley, Leeds. Att: 5,284. 16 February 1991.
Great Britain: Steve Hampson (1t); Paul Eastwood (1t, 8g), Daryl Powell, Paul Loughlin, Martin Offiah (5t); Garry Schofield (3t), Shaun Edwards (1t); Andy Dannatt, Lee Jackson, Andy Platt, Richie Eyres, Karl Fairbank, Ellery Hanley (c). S: St John Ellis, Roy Powell, Kevin Ellis, Keith England.
France: Christophe Auroy; Alain Bouzer, David Fraisse, Pierre Chamorin, Cyrille Pons (1t); Jacques Moliner, Patrick Entat; Pierre Montgaillard, Thierry Valero, Thierry Buttignol (c), Didier Cabestany, Daniel Verdes, Jean-Bernard Saumitou. S: Jean-Pierre Magnac, Marc Tisseyre, Adolphe Alesina, Eric Remirez.
Man of the Match: Garry Schofield

1991 Great Britain 56-4 Papua New Guinea 2nd Test, World Cup Rated.
Central Park, Wigan. Att: 4,193. 9 November 1991.
Great Britain: Steve Hampson; Paul Newlove (1t), Jonathan Davies (8g), Daryl Powell (1t), Anthony Sullivan (1t); Garry Schofield (c) (1t), Shaun Edwards; Karl Harrison, Martin Dermott, Andy Platt, Paul Moriarty (2t), Denis Betts (1t), Michael Jackson (2t). S: Gary Connolly, Karl Fairbank (1t), Deryck Fox, Gary H Price.
Papua New Guinea: Ipisa Wanega; Joshua Kouoru, Richard Wagambie, Philip Boge, Chris Itam; Tuksy Karu (1t), Stanley Haru (c); John Unagi, Kes Kaglipari, Kera Ngaffin, James Naipao, Leslee Hoffman, Joe Gispe. S: Max Tiri, Ngala Lapan, Thomas Daki, Lipirin Palangat.
Man of the Match: Michael Jackson

1992 France 12-30 Great Britain 1st Test
Stade Gilbert Brutus, Perpignan. Att: 5,688. 16 February 1992.
France: Patrick Limongi; Jean-Marc Garcia (1t), Pierre Chamorin, Pascal Fages, Claude Sirvent; Gilles Dumas (c) (2g), Patrick Entat; Bernard Llong, Thierry Valero, Yves Viloni, Guy Delpech, Christophe Bonnafous, Jacques Pech (1t). S: Thierry Matteo, Pascal Bomati, Patrick Torreilles, Lilian Hebert.
Great Britain: Alan Tait; John Devereux (1t), Gary Connolly, Jonathan Davies (c) (3g), John Bentley (1t); Jonathan Griffiths (1t), Bobbie Goulding; Lee Crooks, Lee Jackson, Paul Dixon, Karl Fairbank, Michael Jackson, Les Holliday. S: Daryl Powell, Mark Jones, Graham Steadman (2t), Richie Eyres (1t).
Man of the Match: Les Holliday

1992 Great Britain 36-0 France 2nd Test
The Boulevard, Hull. Att: 5,250. 7 March 1992.
Great Britain: Graham Steadman; Paul Eastwood (1t, 6g), Gary Connolly, Allan Bateman, Alan Hunte (1t); Daryl Powell, Shaun Edwards (c); Lee Crooks, Martin Dermott (1t), Kelvin Skerrett, Denis Betts, Karl Fairbank, Les Holliday (1t). S: John Devereux (dnp), Andy Platt (1t), Deryck Fox (1t), Steve McNamara.
France: Patrick Limongi; Claude Sirvent, Pierre Chamorin, Pascal Fages, Cyrille Pons; Gilles Dumas (c), Patrick Entat; Patrick Aillieres, Thierry Valero, Yves Viloni, Bernard Llong, Christophe Bonnafous, Jacques Pech. S: Francis Lope, Patrick Torreilles, Pascal Bomati, Patrick Marginet.
Man of the Match: Martin Dermott

1992 Papua New Guinea 14-20 Great Britain (One-off Test)
Lloyd Robson Oval, Port Moresby. Att: 7,294. 31 May 1992.
Papua New Guinea: Philip Boge; Joshua Kouoru, Richard Wagambie (1t), August Joseph, Kini Tani (1t); Aquila Emil (1g), Ngala Lapan (c); Ben Bire, Michael Matmillo, Kera Ngaffin, Bobby Ako, Joe Gispe, Matthew Elara (1t). S: Korul Sinemau, Michael Angra, Steven Kapan, Nande Yer.
Great Britain: Steve Hampson; Paul Eastwood (1t), Garry Schofield (c), Paul Loughlin (2g), Martin Offiah (2t); Daryl Powell, Shaun Edwards; Lee Crooks, Martin Dermott, Andy Platt, Denis Betts, Karl Fairbank, Phil Clarke (1t). S: Joe Lydon, Kelvin Skerrett, Paul Newlove, Sonny Nickle.
Man of the Match: Ben Bire

1992 Australia 22-6 Great Britain 1st Ashes Test
Sydney Football Stadium, Sydney. 12 June 1992.
Australia: Andrew Ettingshausen; Rod Wishart (3g), Mal Meninga (c) (2t), Laurie Daley, Michael Hancock (1t); Peter Jackson, Allan Langer; Glenn Lazarus, Steve Walters, Paul Harragon, Paul Sironen (1t), Bob Lindner, Bradley Clyde. S: Brad Mackay, David Gillespie, Brad Fittler, Kevin Walters.
Great Britain: Graham Steadman; Paul Newlove, Daryl Powell, Paul Loughlin, Martin Offiah; Garry Schofield (c), Andy Gregory; Kelvin Skerrett, Martin Dermott, Lee Crooks (1g), Denis Betts, Andy Platt, Phil Clarke. S: Shaun Edwards, Michael Jackson, Joe Lydon (1t), Ian Lucas.
Man of the Match: Bradley Clyde

1992 Australia 10-33 Great Britain 2nd Ashes Test
Princes Park, Melbourne. Att: 30,257. 26 June 1992.
Australia: Andrew Ettingshausen; Rod Wishart, Mal Meninga (c) (1g), Laurie Daley, Michael Hancock; Peter Jackson, Allan Langer; David Gillespie, Steve Walters, Paul Harragon, Paul Sironen, Bob Lindner (1t), Bradley Clyde. S: Brad Mackay, Glenn Lazarus, Chris Johns (1t), Kevin Walters.
Great Britain: Graham Steadman (1t); Paul Eastwood (6g), Daryl Powell, Paul Newlove (1t), Martin Offiah (1t); Garry Schofield (c) (1t, 1dg), Shaun Edwards; Kelvin Skerrett, Martin Dermott, Andy Platt, Denis Betts, Billy McGinty, Phil Clarke (1t). S: Gary Connolly, Paul Hulme, Joe Lydon, Karl Harrison.
Man of the Match: Andy Platt

1992 Australia 16-10 Great Britain 3rd Ashes Test
Lang Park. Att: 32,313. 3 July 1992.
Australia: Andrew Ettingshausen; Willie Carne, Brad Fittler, Mal Meninga (c) (1t, 4g), Michael Hancock; Laurie Daley (1t), Allan Langer; Glenn Lazarus, Steve Walters, Paul Harragon, Paul Sironen, Bob Lindner, Bradley Clyde. S: David Gillespie, Kevin Walters, Chris Johns, John Cartwright.
Great Britain: Graham Steadman; Paul Eastwood (3g), Daryl Powell, Paul Newlove, Martin Offiah (1t); Garry Schofield (c), Shaun Edwards; Kelvin Skerrett, Martin Dermott, Andy Platt, Denis Betts, Billy McGinty, Phil Clarke. S: Gary Connolly, Paul Hulme, Joe Lydon, Karl Harrison.
Man of the Match: Mal Meninga

1992 New Zealand 15-14 Great Britain 1st Test
Show Grounds Oval, Palmerston North. Att: 11,548. 12 July 1992.
New Zealand: Matthew Ridge (2g); Sean Hoppe, Kevin Iro, Tony Kemp (1t), Richie Blackmore (1t); Dean Clark, Gary Freeman (c); Brent Stuart, Duane Mann, Brent Todd, Gavin Hill (1g), Quentin Pongia, Brendan Tuuta. S: Daryl Halligan (1dg), Mike Kuiti, Tea Ropati, Mark Woods.
Great Britain: Graham Steadman; Paul Eastwood (3g), Daryl Powell, Gary Connolly, Martin Offiah; Garry Schofield (c), Shaun Edwards (1t); Kelvin Skerrett, Lee Jackson, Andy Platt, Denis Betts, Billy McGinty, Phil Clarke (1t). S: Joe Lydon, Paul Hulme, John Devereux (dnp), Karl Harrison.
Man of the Match: Gary Freeman

1992 New Zealand 16-19 Great Britain 2nd Test
Carlaw Park, Auckland. Att: 10,223. 19 July 1992.
New Zealand: Matthew Ridge (2g); Sean Hoppe (1t), Kevin Iro, Tony Kemp, Richie Blackmore; Dean Clark, Gary Freeman (c) (1t); Brent Stuart, Duane Mann, Brent Todd (1t), Gavin Hill, Quentin Pongia, Brendan Tuuta. S: Daryl Halligan, Mike Kuiti, Tea Ropati, Mark Woods.
Great Britain: Graham Steadman; Paul Eastwood (3g), Daryl Powell, Gary Connolly, Martin Offiah (1t); Garry Schofield (c) (1dg), Shaun Edwards; Karl Harrison, Lee Jackson (1t), Andy Platt, Denis Betts (1t), Billy McGinty, Phil Clarke. S: Paul Newlove, Michael Jackson, John Devereux, Karl Fairbank.
Man of the Match: Garry Schofield

1992 Great Britain 6-10 Australia The World Cup Final
Wembley Stadium, London. Att: 73,631. 24 October 1992.
Great Britain: Joe Lydon; Alan Hunte, Gary Connolly, Garry Schofield (c), Martin Offiah; Shaun Edwards, Deryck Fox (3g); Kevin Ward, Martin Dermott, Andy Platt, Denis Betts, Phil Clarke, Ellery Hanley. S: John Devereux, Kelvin Skerrett, Alan Tait, Richie Eyres.
Australia: Tim Brasher; Willie Carne, Steve Renouf (1t), Mal Meninga (c) (3g), Michael Hancock; Brad Fittler, Allan Langer; Glenn Lazarus, Steve Walters, Mark Sargent, Paul Sironen, Bob Lindner, Bradley Clyde. S: John Cartwright, David Gillespie, Chris Johns (dnp), Kevin Walters.
Man of the Match: Steve Walters

1993 France 6-48 Great Britain 1st Test
Stade Albert Domec, Carcassonne. Att: 5,500. 7 March 1993.
France: Jean Frison; Jean-Marc Garcia, Pierre Chamorin, Pascal Fages (1g), Claude Sirvent; Gilles Dumas (c) (1t), Lucien de Macedo; Theo Anast, Bernard Cartier, Thierry Buttignol, Ezzedine Attia, Didier Cabestany, David Amat. S: Eric Castel, Pascal Bomati, Richard Clarke, Patrick Torreilles.
Great Britain: Stuart Spruce; John Devereux (1t), Andy Currier (6g), Gary Connolly, Alan Hunte; Garry Schofield (c) (3t), Shaun Edwards (1t); Neil Cowie, Steve McCurrie, Steve Molloy, Richie Eyres (1t), Phil Clarke, Ellery Hanley (2t). S: Mike Ford (1t), Chris Joynt, Allan Bateman, Steve McNamara.
Man of the Match: Garry Schofield

1993 Great Britain 72-6 France 2nd Test

Headingley, Leeds. Att: 8,196. 2 April 1993.
Great Britain: Alan Tait (2t); John Devereux (1t), Paul Newlove (3t), Gary Connolly, Alan Hunte (2t); Jonathan Davies (10g), Shaun Edwards (2t); Karl Harrison, Martin Dermott, Andy Platt (c), Denis Betts (1t), Richie Eyres, Phil Clarke. S: Mike Ford (1t), Karl Fairbank, Daryl Powell (1t), Sonny Nickle.
France: Eric van Brussel (1t); Claude Sirvent, Pascal Mons, Adolphe Alesina, Jean-Marc Garcia; Gilles Dumas (c) (1g), Pascal Fages; Theo Anast, Patrick Torreilles, Thierry Buttignol, Bernard Cartier, Didier Cabestany, Jean-Luc Combettes. S: David Amat, Abdrajah Baba, David Fraisse, Fabien Beranger.
Man of the Match: Paul Newlove

1993 Great Britain 17-0 New Zealand 1st Test

Wembley Stadium, London. Att: 36,131. 16 October 1993.
Great Britain: Jonathan Davies (2g, 1dg); Jason Robinson (2t), Paul Newlove, Gary Connolly, John Devereux (1t); Garry Schofield (c), Shaun Edwards; Karl Harrison, Martin Dermott, Karl Fairbank, Denis Betts, Chris Joynt, Phil Clarke. S: Daryl Powell, Richie Eyres, Alan Tait, Sonny Nickle.
New Zealand: Morvin Edwards; Daryl Halligan, Kevin Iro, David Watson, Sean Hoppe; Gene Ngamu, Gary Freeman (c); John Lomax, Duane Mann, Brent Stuart, Stephen Kearney, Quentin Pongia, Tawera Nikau. S: Jason Williams, Jason Mackie, Whetu Taewa, Jason Lowrie.
Man of the Match: Shaun Edwards

1993 Great Britain 29-12 New Zealand 2nd Test

Central Park, Wigan. Att: 16,502. 30 October 1993.
Great Britain: Jonathan Davies (4g); John Devereux (2t), Gary Connolly, Paul Newlove (1t), Martin Offiah (1t); Garry Schofield (c) (1t, 1dg), Shaun Edwards; Karl Harrison, Lee Jackson, Karl Fairbank, Sonny Nickle, Chris Joynt, Phil Clarke. S: Daryl Powell, Richie Eyres, Alan Tait, Michael Jackson.
New Zealand: Dave Watson (1t); Frano Botica (2g), Kevin Iro, Iva Ropati (1t), Sean Hoppe; Tony Kemp, Gary Freeman (c); Se'e Solomona, Duane Mann, Brent Stuart, Stephen Kearney, Quentin Pongia, Jason Mackie. S: Jason Williams, John Lomax, Whetu Taewa, Gary Mercer.
Man of the Match: John Devereux

1993 Great Britain 29-10 New Zealand 3rd Test

Headingley, Leeds. Att: 15,139. 6 November 1993.
Great Britain: Jonathan Davies (1t, 4g, 1dg); John Devereux, Gary Connolly, Paul Newlove, Martin Offiah (1t); Garry Schofield (c), Shaun Edwards; Kelvin Skerrett, Lee Jackson, Karl Fairbank (1t), Andy Farrell (1t), Chris Joynt, Phil Clarke (1t). S: Daryl Powell, Sonny Nickle, Alan Tait, Michael Jackson.
New Zealand: Dave Watson; Frano Botica (3g), Kevin Iro, Iva Ropati, Jason Williams (1t); Tony Kemp, Aaron Whittaker; Se'e Solomona, Denvour Johnston, Brent Stuart, Stephen Kearney (c), Quentin Pongia, Jason Mackie. S: Richie Blackmore, John Lomax, Whetu Taewa, David Lomax.
Man of the Match: Phil Clarke

1994 France 4-12 Great Britain One-off Test

Stade Albert Domec, Carcassonne. Att: 7,000. 20 March 1994.
France: Jean Frison; Jean-Marc Garcia, Frantz Martial (1t), David Fraisse, Claude Sirvent; Pascal Fages, Patrick Entat (c); Frederic Teixido, Patrick Torreilles, Bernard Llong, Daniel Divet, Didier Cabestany, Georges Grandjean. S: Ezzedine Attia, Theo Anast, Pascal Bomati, Alexander Couttet.
Great Britain: Graham Steadman; John Bentley, Gary Connolly, Paul Newlove (1t), Martin Offiah; Garry Schofield (c), Shaun Edwards (1t); Lee Crooks (1g), Lee Jackson, Steve Molloy, Andy Farrell (1g), Karl Fairbank, Chris Joynt. S: St John Ellis, Paul Moriarty, Daryl Powell, Barrie-Jon Mather.
Man of the Match: Shaun Edwards

1994 Great Britain 8-4 Australia 1st Ashes Test

Wembley Stadium, London. Att: 57,034. 22 October 1994.

Great Britain: Jonathan Davies (1t, 1g); Jason Robinson, Gary Connolly, Alan Hunte, Martin Offiah; Daryl Powell, Shaun Edwards (c); Karl Harrison, Lee Jackson, Chris Joynt, Denis Betts, Andy Farrell, Phil Clarke. S: Bobbie Goulding (1g), Barrie McDermott, Allan Bateman, Mick Cassidy.

Australia: Brett Mullins; Andrew Ettingshausen, Mal Meninga (c), Steve Renouf (1t), Wendell Sailor; Laurie Daley, Allan Langer; Ian Roberts, Steve Walters, Paul Harragon, Paul Sironen, Bradley Clyde, Brad Fittler. S: Ricky Stuart, Tim Brasher (dnp), Dean Pay, David Furner.

Man of the Match: Jonathan Davies

1994 Great Britain 8-38 Australia 2nd Ashes Test

Old Trafford, Manchester. Att: 43,930. 5 November 1994.

Great Britain: Graham Steadman; Jason Robinson, Gary Connolly, Alan Hunte, Martin Offiah; Daryl Powell, Bobbie Goulding (2g); Karl Harrison, Lee Jackson, Chris Joynt, Denis Betts, Andy Farrell, Phil Clarke (c). S: Garry Schofield, Barrie McDermott, Paul Newlove (1t), Mick Cassidy.

Australia: Brett Mullins (2t); Andrew Ettingshausen (1t), Mal Meninga (c), Steve Renouf (1t), Rod Wishart (7g); Laurie Daley (1t), Ricky Stuart; Glenn Lazarus, Steve Walters, Ian Roberts, Dean Pay, Bradley Clyde (1t), Brad Fittler. S: Allan Langer, Tim Brasher (dnp), Greg Florimo, Paul Sironen.

Man of the Match: Brad Fittler

1994 Great Britain 4-23 Australia 3rd Ashes Test

Elland Road, Leeds. Att: 39,468. 20 November 1994.

Great Britain: Gary Connolly; Jason Robinson, Alan Hunte, Paul Newlove, Martin Offiah; Phil Clarke, Shaun Edwards (c); Karl Harrison, Lee Jackson, Barrie McDermott, Denis Betts, Andy Farrell (2g), Chris Joynt. S: Bobbie Goulding, Daryl Powell, Garry Schofield, Sonny Nickle.

Australia: Brett Mullins; Andrew Ettingshausen, Mal Meninga (c), Steve Renouf, Rod Wishart (1t, 3g); Laurie Daley (1t), Ricky Stuart (1dg); Glenn Lazarus, Steve Walters (1t), Ian Roberts, Dean Pay (1t), Bradley Clyde, Brad Fittler. S: Allan Langer, Tim Brasher, Greg Florimo, David Fairleigh.

Man of the Match: Steve Walters

1996 Papua New Guinea 30-32 Great Britain One-off Test

Lae. Att: 10,000. 28 September 1996.

Papua New Guinea: Robert Sio (1t); James Kops, Marcus Bai, Robert Tela, David Gomia (1t); Stanley Gene (1t), Adrian Lam (c) (1t); Ben Biri (2t), Elias Paiyo (3g), Raymond Kahl, Noide Yer, David Westley, Bruce Mamando. S: Simon Kundi, Ruben Ruing, Max Tire, Obert Batia.

Great Britain: Stuart Spruce; Joey Hayes, Kris Radlinski (2t), Alan Hunte, Anthony Sullivan (1t); Iestyn Harris, Bobbie Goulding (1t, 6g); Paul Broadbent, Keiron Cunningham (1t), Terry O'Connor, Denis Betts, Chris Joynt, Andy Farrell (c). S: Tony Smith, Rowland Phillips, Daryl Powell, Paul Sculthorpe.

Man of the Match: Bobbie Goulding

1996 Fiji 4-72 Great Britain One-off Test

Prince of Wales Park, Nadi. Att: 5,000. 5 October 1996.

Fiji: Waisale Sovatabua; Paula Baravilula, Manoa Thompson, Joe Tamani, Stan Tulevu; Inoke Ratudina, Kalavati Naisore; Pio Kumbawe (c), Meli Kaidroki, Malakai Yasa, Joe Dakuitoga, Ian Sagaitu, Livai Nalagilagi. S: Vula Dakuitoga, Sam Marayawa (1t), Waisake Vatabua, Ulaisi Wainidroa.

Great Britain: Stuart Spruce (2t); Alan Hunte (2t), Kris Radlinski, Daryl Powell (2t), Anthony Sullivan (1t); Iestyn Harris, Bobbie Goulding (3t, 10g); Paul Broadbent, Keiron Cunningham, Brian McDermott, Denis Betts, Paul Sculthorpe, Andy Farrell (c) (1t). S: Tony Smith, Keith Senior (1t), Steve Molloy, Mick Cassidy (1t).

Man of the Match: Bobbie Goulding

1996 New Zealand 17-12 Great Britain 1st Test

Ericsson Stadium, Auckland. Att: 7,400. 18 October 1996.
New Zealand: Matthew Ridge (c) (4g, 1dg); Sean Hoppe, Richie Blackmore, John Timu (2t), Richie Barnett; Gene Ngamu, Stacey Jones; Grant Young, Syd Eru, Quentin Pongia, Tony Iro, Stephen Kearney, Tyran Smith. S: Joe Vagana, Ruben Wiki, Marc Ellis, Logan Swann.
Great Britain: Stuart Spruce; Alan Hunte (1t), Kris Radlinski, Daryl Powell, Anthony Sullivan; Iestyn Harris, Bobbie Goulding (2g); Paul Broadbent, Keiron Cunningham, Terry O'Connor, Denis Betts (1t), Paul Sculthorpe, Andy Farrell (c). S: Chris Joynt, Keith Senior, Adrian Morley, Tony Smith (dnp).
Man of the Match: John Timu

1996 New Zealand 18-15 Great Britain 2nd Test

Show Grounds Oval, Palmerston North. Att: 9,000. 25 October 1996.
New Zealand: Matthew Ridge (c) (3g); Sean Hoppe, Ruben Wiki (2t), John Timu, Richie Barnett; Gene Ngamu (1t), Stacey Jones; Grant Young, Syd Eru, Quentin Pongia, Tony Iro, Stephen Kearney, Tyran Smith. S: Marc Ellis, Joe Vagana, Richie Blackmore, Logan Swann.
Great Britain: Stuart Spruce; Alan Hunte (1t), Kris Radlinski, Daryl Powell, Anthony Sullivan; Iestyn Harris, Bobbie Goulding (3g, 1dg); Paul Broadbent, Keiron Cunningham, Terry O'Connor, Denis Betts (1t), Paul Sculthorpe, Andy Farrell (c). S: Barrie-Jon Mather, Steve Molloy, Karle Hammond, Chris Joynt.
Man of the Match: Stephen Kearney

1996 New Zealand 32-12 Great Britain 3rd Test

Lancaster Park, Christchurch. Att: 9,000. 1 November 1996.
New Zealand: Matthew Ridge (c) (1t, 4g); Sean Hoppe (2t), Ruben Wiki (1t), John Timu (1t), Marc Ellis; Gene Ngamu (1t), Stacey Jones; Grant Young, Syd Eru, Quentin Pongia, Tony Iro, Stephen Kearney, Tyran Smith. S: Anthony Swann, Joe Vagana, Richie Blackmore, Logan Swann.
Great Britain: Stuart Spruce; Alan Hunte, Kris Radlinski, Daryl Powell, Barrie-Jon Mather; Karle Hammond, Bobbie Goulding (2g); Paul Broadbent, Keiron Cunningham, Terry O'Connor, Denis Betts (1t), Paul Sculthorpe, Andy Farrell (c). S: Iestyn Harris, Adrian Morley (1t), Chris Joynt, Bernard Dwyer.
Man of the Match: Gene Ngamu

1997 Great Britain 14-38 Australia 1st Test

Wembley Stadium, London. Att: 41,135. 1 November 1997.
Great Britain: Jason Robinson (1t); Alan Hunte, Kris Radlinski, Paul Newlove, Anthony Sullivan; Andy Farrell (c) (3g), Bobbie Goulding; Brian McDermott, James Lowes (1t), Paul Broadbent, Chris Joynt, Mick Cassidy, Paul Sculthorpe. S: Steve McNamara, Paul Atcheson, Adrian Morley, Dean Sampson.
Australia: Darren Lockyer; Brett Mullins (2t), Andrew Ettingshausen, Ryan Girdler (5g), Wendell Sailor; Laurie Daley (c) (3t), Craig Gower (1t); Jason Stevens, Steve Walters, Brad Thorn, Matt Adamson, Gorden Tallis, Darren Smith (1t). S: Robbie Kearns, Craig Greenhill, Ken Nagas, Brett Kimmorley.
Man of the Match: Laurie Daley

1997 Great Britain 20-12 Australia 2nd Test

Old Trafford, Manchester. Att: 40,324. 8 November 1997.
Great Britain: Paul Atcheson; Jason Robinson (1t), Kris Radlinski, Paul Newlove, Alan Hunte; Andy Farrell (c) (1t, 6g), Bobbie Goulding; Brian McDermott, James Lowes, Paul Broadbent, Chris Joynt, Adrian Morley, Paul Sculthorpe. S: Sean Long (dnp), Simon Haughton, Steve McNamara, Mike Forshaw.
Australia: Darren Lockyer (2g); Ken Nagas, Andrew Ettingshausen, Brett Mullins, Wendell Sailor; Laurie Daley (c), Craig Gower (1t); Jason Stevens, Steve Walters (1t), Brad Thorn, Matt Adamson, Gorden Tallis, Darren Smith. S: Robbie Kearns, Craig Greenhill, Brett Kimmorley (dnp), Russell Richardson.
Man of the Match: Andy Farrell

1997 Great Britain 20-37 Australia 3rd Test
Elland Road, Leeds Att: 39,337. 16 November 1997.
Great Britain: Paul Atcheson; Jason Robinson (1t), Kris Radlinski, Paul Newlove, Alan Hunte; Andy Farrell (c) (4g), Bobbie Goulding; Brian McDermott, James Lowes, Paul Broadbent, Chris Joynt, Adrian Morley, Paul Sculthorpe. S: Sean Long, Simon Haughton (2t), Steve McNamara, Mike Forshaw.
Australia: Darren Lockyer (1dg); Ken Nagas (1t), Andrew Ettingshausen, Ryan Girdler (4g), Wendell Sailor (2t); Laurie Daley (c) (1t), Craig Gower; Jason Stevens, Steve Walters, Brad Thorn (1t), Bradley Clyde, Gorden Tallis, Darren Smith (1t). S: Robbie Kearns (1t), Matt Adamson, Brett Kimmorley, Russell Richardson.
Man of the Match: Darren Smith

1998 Great Britain 16-22 New Zealand 1st Test
McAlpine Stadium, Huddersfield. Att: 18,509. 31 October 1998.
Great Britain: Kris Radlinski; Jason Robinson (1t), Gary Connolly, Paul Newlove (1t), Keith Senior (1t); Andy Farrell (c) (2g), Tony Smith; Neil Cowie, Keiron Cunningham, Darren Fleary, Chris Joynt, Lee Gilmour, Paul Sculthorpe. S: Iestyn Harris, Dale Laughton, Simon Haughton, Terry O'Connor.
New Zealand: Richie Barnett; Sean Hoppe, Kevin Iro, Ruben Wiki, Daryl Halligan (3g); Robbie Paul (1t), Stacey Jones (1t); Joe Vagana (1t), Syd Eru, Quentin Pongia (c), Jarrad McCracken, Stephen Kearney (1t), Logan Swann. S: Henry Paul, Tony Iro, Tony Puletua, Nathan Cayless.
Man of the Match: Stephen Kearney

1998 Great Britain 16-36 New Zealand 2nd Test
Reebok Stadium, Bolton. Att: 27,884. 7 November 1998.
Great Britain: Kris Radlinski; Jason Robinson (1t), Gary Connolly, Keith Senior, Francis Cummins; Iestyn Harris (1t), Tony Smith; Neil Cowie, Keiron Cunningham, Dale Laughton, Chris Joynt, Paul Sculthorpe, Andy Farrell (c) (4g). S: Terry O'Connor, Harvey Howard, Simon Haughton, Lee Gilmour.
New Zealand: Richie Barnett (2t); Sean Hoppe (1t), Kevin Iro, Ruben Wiki (1t), Daryl Halligan (6g); Robbie Paul, Stacey Jones, Joe Vagana, Syd Eru, Quentin Pongia (c), Jarrad McCracken, Stephen Kearney, Logan Swann. S: Henry Paul (1t), Tony Iro, Tony Puletua (1t), Nathan Cayless.
Man of the Match: Richie Barnett

1998 Great Britain 23-23 New Zealand 3rd Test
Vicarage Road, Watford. Att: 13,278. 14 November 1998.
Great Britain: Kris Radlinski; Jason Robinson (1t), Gary Connolly, Keith Senior, Francis Cummins; Sean Long (1t), Tony Smith (1t, 1dg); Terry O'Connor, Terry Newton, Dale Laughton, Chris Joynt, Paul Sculthorpe, Andy Farrell (c) (5g). S: Lee Gilmour (dnp), Mike Forshaw, Simon Haughton, Darren Fleary.
New Zealand: Richie Barnett; Sean Hoppe, Kevin Iro, Ruben Wiki, Daryl Halligan (5g); Robbie Paul (2t), Stacey Jones (1dg); Joe Vagana, Syd Eru, Quentin Pongia (c), Jarrad McCracken, Stephen Kearney, Logan Swann. S: Henry Paul (1t), Craig Smith, Tony Puletua, Nathan Cayless.
Man of the Match: Stacey Jones

1999 Australia 42-6 Great Britain Tri-Nations
Suncorp Stadium, Brisbane. Att: 12,511, 22 October 1999.
Australia: Darren Lockyer (2t); Mat Rogers (6g), Shaun Timmins, Matt Gidley (1t), Wendell Sailor (1t); Matthew Johns, Brett Kimmorley (1t); Darren Britt, Craig Gower, Rodney Howe, Bryan Fletcher, Nik Kosef, Brad Fittler (c) (1t). S: Ryan Girdler (1g), Darren Smith, Jason Smith (1t), Mick Vella.
Great Britain: Kris Radlinski; Jason Robinson, Gary Connolly, Keith Senior, Anthony Sullivan; Iestyn Harris (1t), Ryan Sheridan; Dale Laughton, Keiron Cunningham, Barrie McDermott, Denis Betts, Adrian Morley, Andy Farrell (c) (1g). S: Sean Long, Paul Anderson, Paul Sculthorpe, Andy Hay.
Man of the Match: Darren Lockyer

1999 New Zealand 26-4 Great Britain Tri-Nations

Ericsson Stadium, Auckland. Att: 11,961. 29 October 1999.
New Zealand: Richie Barnett (c); Nigel Vagana (2t), Ruben Wiki, Willie Talau, Lesley Vainikolo; Henry Paul (5g), Robbie Paul; Joe Vagana (1t), Richard Swain, Craig Smith, Matt Rua (1t), Stephen Kearney, Logan Swann. S: Gene Ngamu, Jason Lowrie, Nathan Cayless, David Kidwell.
Great Britain: Kris Radlinski; Jason Robinson, Gary Connolly, Keith Senior, Francis Cummins; Iestyn Harris, Ryan Sheridan; Dale Laughton, Keiron Cunningham, Barrie McDermott, Adrian Morley, Chris Joynt, Andy Farrell (c). S: Sean Long (1t), Denis Betts, Mike Forshaw, Andy Hay.
Man of the Match: Stephen Kearney

2001 France 12-42 Great Britain One-off Test

Stade Armandie, Agen. Att: 10,000. 26 October 2001.
France: Renaud Guigue; Michael van Snick, Gilles Cornut, Arnaud Dulac, Sylvain Houles; Laurent Frayssinous (1t, 2g), Fabien Devecchi (c); Romain Gagliazzo, Vincent Wulf, Frederic Teixido, Aurelien Cologni, Adel Fellous, Laurent Carrasco. S: Romain Sort (1t), Julien Gerin, David Collado, Eric Anselme.
Great Britain: Kris Radlinski (1t); Paul Wellens (1t), Paul Johnson, Gary Connolly, David Hodgson; Lee Briers (1t, 1g), Paul Deacon (1t); Terry O'Connor, Kevin Sinfield, Barrie McDermott, Chris Joynt (2t), Paul King (1t), Andy Farrell (c) (6g). S: Richard Horne, Mike Forshaw, Stuart Fielden, Paul Anderson.
Man of the Match: Chris Joynt

2001 Great Britain 20-12 Australia 1st Ashes Test

McAlpine Stadium, Huddersfield. Att: 21,578. 11 November 2001.
Great Britain: Kris Radlinski; Leon Pryce, Gary Connolly, Keith Senior, Paul Johnson; Paul Sculthorpe (2t, 2dg), Kevin Sinfield; Terry O'Connor, Mike Forshaw, Barrie McDermott, Chris Joynt, Jamie Peacock (1t), Andy Farrell (c) (3g). S: Richard Horne, Paul Wellens (dnp), Paul Anderson, Stuart Fielden.
Australia: Darren Lockyer; Adam MacDougall (1t), Matt Gidley, Jamie Lyon, Lote Tuqiri; Trent Barrett, Andrew Johns (1t, 2g); Jason Stevens, Danny Buderus, Robbie Kearns, Dane Carlaw, Ben Kennedy, Brad Fittler (c). S: Braith Anasta, Michael Vella, Petero Civoniceva, Jason Ryles.
Man of the Match: Paul Sculthorpe

2001 Great Britain 12-40 Australia 2nd Ashes Test

Reebok Stadium, Bolton. Att: 22,152. 17 November 2001.
Great Britain: Kris Radlinski; Leon Pryce (1t), Gary Connolly, Keith Senior, Paul Johnson; Paul Sculthorpe (1t), Kevin Sinfield; Terry O'Connor, Mike Forshaw, Barrie McDermott, Chris Joynt, Jamie Peacock, Andy Farrell (c) (2g). S: Paul Wellens, Richard Horne, Paul Anderson, Stuart Fielden.
Australia: Darren Lockyer (1t); Adam MacDougall (1t), Matt Gidley, Jamie Lyon, Lote Tuqiri; Trent Barrett, Andrew Johns (2t, 6g); Jason Ryles, Danny Buderus, Robbie Kearns, Dane Carlaw, Ben Kennedy (1t), Brad Fittler (c) (1t). S: Braith Anasta (1t), Michael Vella, Petero Civoniceva, Brad Meyers.
Man of the Match: Andrew Johns

2001 Great Britain 8-28 Australia 3rd Ashes Test

JJB Stadium, Wigan. Att: 25,011. 24 November 2001.
Great Britain: Paul Wellens; Leon Pryce, Gary Connolly, Keith Senior, Paul Johnson (1t); Paul Sculthorpe, Paul Deacon; Terry O'Connor, Mike Forshaw, Barrie McDermott, Chris Joynt, Stuart Fielden, Andy Farrell (c) (2g). S: Paul Anderson, Kevin Sinfield, Jamie Peacock, David Hodgson.
Australia: Darren Lockyer (1t); Adam MacDougall, Matt Gidley (1t), Jamie Lyon, Nathan Blacklock; Trent Barrett (2t), Andrew Johns (3g); Jason Stevens, Danny Buderus, Robbie Kearns, Dane Carlaw, Ben Kennedy, Brad Fittler (c) (1g). S: Braith Anasta, Brad Meyers (1t), Petero Civoniceva, Jason Ryles.
Man of the Match: Trent Barrett

2002 Australia 64-10 Great Britain One-off Test

Aussie Stadium, Sydney. Att: 31,844. 12 July 2002.

Australia: Darren Lockyer (2t); Timanu Tahu (1t), Chris McKenna (1t), Shaun Timmins (1t), Lote Tuqiri (1t), Trent Barrett, Andrew Johns (c) (10g); Shane Webcke, Danny Buderus (1t), Jason Ryles, Gorden Tallis (1t), Steve Simpson, Scott Hill (2t). S: Brent Tate, Steve Menzies, Willie Mason (1t), Jason Stevens.

Great Britain: Kris Radlinski, Paul Johnson, Paul Wellens, Keith Senior, Karl Pratt (1t); Paul Sculthorpe (1g), Ryan Sheridan; Terry O'Connor, Keiron Cunningham, Barrie McDermott, Jamie Peacock, Stuart Fielden, Andy Farrell (c). S: Martin Gleeson, Terry Newton, Chris Joynt, Kevin Sinfield (1t).

Man of the Match: Andrew Johns

2002 Great Britain 16-30 New Zealand 1st Test

Ewood Park, Blackburn. Att: 16,654. 9 November 2002.

Great Britain: Gary Connolly; Leon Pryce (1t), Martin Gleeson, Keith Senior, Karl Pratt; Kevin Sinfield, Paul Deacon; Stuart Fielden, Keiron Cunningham, Barrie McDermott, Adrian Morley, Andy Farrell (c) (4g), Mike Forshaw. S: Lee Gilmour, Chris Joynt, Paul Anderson, Jamie Peacock (1t).

New Zealand: Robbie Paul; Henry Fa'afili (3t), Nigel Vagana (2t), Clinton Toopi, Francis Meli; Lance Hohaia, Stacey Jones (c) (1t); Jerry Seuseu, Richard Swain (3g), Paul Rauhihi, Ali Lauitiiti, Stephen Kearney, Awen Guttenbeil. S: Monty Betham, David Solomona, Logan Swann, Tony Puletua.

Man of the Match: Robbie Paul

2002 Great Britain 14-14 New Zealand 2nd Test

McAlpine Stadium, Huddersfield. Att: 23,604. 16 November 2002.

Great Britain: Gary Connolly; Leon Pryce (1t), Martin Gleeson (1t), Keith Senior, Lee Gilmour; Paul Sculthorpe, Paul Deacon; Terry O'Connor, James Lowes, Stuart Fielden, Jamie Peacock, Andy Farrell (c) (3g), Mike Forshaw. S: Kevin Sinfield, Richard Horne, Paul Anderson, Danny Orr.

New Zealand: Robbie Paul; Henry Fa'afili, Nigel Vagana, Clinton Toopi, Francis Meli (1t); Lance Hohaia, Stacey Jones (c); Jerry Seuseu, Richard Swain (1g), Paul Rauhihi, Ruben Wiki (1t), Stephen Kearney, Awen Guttenbeil. S: Tony Puletua, Ali Lauitiiti, Monty Betham, Logan Swann.

Man of the Match: Paul Sculthorpe

2002 Great Britain 16-10 New Zealand 3rd Test

JJB Stadium, Wigan. Att: 22,247. 23 November 2002.

Great Britain: Gary Connolly; Leon Pryce, Martin Gleeson (1t), Keith Senior (1t), Lee Gilmour; Paul Sculthorpe (1t), Paul Deacon; Stuart Fielden, James Lowes, Barrie McDermott, Adrian Morley, Andy Farrell (c) (2g), Mike Forshaw. S: Danny Orr, Jamie Peacock, Paul Anderson, Richard Horne.

New Zealand: David Vaealiki; Henry Fa'afili, Nigel Vagana, Sean Hoppe, Francis Meli; Lance Hohaia, Stacey Jones (c) (1t, 1g); Jerry Seuseu, Richard Swain, Paul Rauhihi, Awen Guttenbeil, Ruben Wiki, Monty Betham. S: Tony Puletua, David Solomona, Ali Lauitiiti (1t), Logan Swann.

Man of the Match: Keith Senior

2003 Great Britain 18-22 Australia 1st Ashes Test

JJB Stadium, Wigan. Att: 24,614. 8 November 2003.

Great Britain: Kris Radlinski; Brian Carney (2t), Gary Connolly, Keith Senior (1t), Richard Horne; Paul Sculthorpe, Sean Long (2g); Stuart Fielden, Terry Newton, Adrian Morley, Jamie Peacock, Andy Farrell (c), Mike Forshaw. S: Paul Anderson, Barrie McDermott, Paul Deacon (1g), Lee Gilmour.

Australia: Darren Lockyer (c) (1t); Anthony Minichiello, Phil Bailey (1t), Craig Wing, Shannon Hegarty; Craig Gower (1t), Brett Kimmorley; Shane Webcke, Danny Buderus, Robbie Kearns, Steve Simpson, Craig Fitzgibbon (3g), Luke Ricketson. S: Petero Civoniceva, Willie Mason, Trent Waterhouse (1t), Michael Crocker.

Man of the Match: Brett Kimmorley

2003 Great Britain 20-23 Australia 2nd Ashes Test

KC Stadium, Hull. Att: 25,147. 15 November 2003.
Great Britain: Kris Radlinski (1t); Brian Carney, Gary Connolly (1t), Keith Senior, Richard Horne; Paul Sculthorpe, Paul Deacon (4g); Stuart Fielden, Terry Newton (1t), Barrie McDermott, Jamie Peacock, Adrian Morley, Andy Farrell (c). S: Sean Long (dnp), Kevin Sinfield, Mike Forshaw, Paul Anderson.
Australia: Darren Lockyer (c) (1t); Anthony Minichiello, Craig Wing, Michael de Vere, Matt Sing; Craig Gower, Brett Kimmorley (1t, 1dg); Shane Webcke, Danny Buderus, Robbie Kearns, Steve Simpson, Craig Fitzgibbon (1t, 5g), Luke Ricketson. S: Petero Civoniceva, Willie Mason, Trent Waterhouse, Michael Crocker.
Man of the Match: Darren Lockyer

2003 Great Britain 12-18 Australia 3rd Ashes Test

McAlpine Stadium, Huddersfield. Att: 24,163. 22 November 2003.
Great Britain: Kris Radlinski (1t); Brian Carney, Martin Gleeson, Lee Gilmour, Richard Horne; Paul Sculthorpe (1t), Paul Deacon (1g); Stuart Fielden, Terry Newton, Adrian Morley, Jamie Peacock, Andy Farrell (c), Mike Forshaw. S: Sean Long (1g), Barrie McDermott, Kevin Sinfield, Gareth Ellis.
Australia: Darren Lockyer (c); Anthony Minichiello, Craig Wing, Michael de Vere (1t), Matt Sing; Michael Crocker, Brett Kimmorley; Shane Webcke, Danny Buderus, Robbie Kearns, Steve Simpson, Craig Fitzgibbon (3g), Luke Ricketson (2t). S: Petero Civoniceva, Willie Mason, Trent Waterhouse, Darren Smith.
Man of the Match: Darren Lockyer

2004 Great Britain 8-12 Australia Tri-Nations

City of Manchester Stadium, Manchester. Att: 38,572. 30 October 2004.
Great Britain: Paul Wellens; Brian Carney (1t), Martin Gleeson (1t), Keith Senior, Stuart Reardon; Paul Sculthorpe, Sean Long; Stuart Fielden, Terry Newton, Adrian Morley, Jamie Peacock, Andy Farrell (c), Gareth Ellis. S: Chev Walker, Stephen Wild, Ryan Bailey, Danny McGuire.
Australia: Anthony Minichiello; Matt Sing, Shaun Berrigan, Willie Tonga, Luke Rooney (2t); Craig Gower, Brett Kimmorley; Shane Webcke, Danny Buderus (c), Jason Ryles, Andrew Ryan, Nathan Hindmarsh, Tonie Carroll. S: Craig Wing, Petero Civoniceva, Willie Mason (1t), Shaun Timmins.
Man of the Match: Stuart Fielden

2004 Great Britain 22-12 New Zealand Tri-Nations

Galpharm Stadium, Huddersfield. Att: 20,372. 6 November 2004.
Great Britain: Paul Wellens; Brian Carney, Martin Gleeson, Keith Senior, Stuart Reardon (2t); Danny McGuire, Sean Long; Stuart Fielden, Terry Newton (1t), Adrian Morley, Jamie Peacock, Andy Farrell (c) (2g), Paul Sculthorpe (1g). S: Gareth Ellis, Ryan Bailey, Paul Johnson, Iestyn Harris (2g).
New Zealand: Brent Webb (2g); Francis Meli, Nigel Vagana, Clinton Toopi, Shontayne Hape; Vinnie Anderson, Thomas Leuluai; Jason Cayless, Louis Anderson, Ruben Wiki (c), Logan Swann, David Kidwell, Sonny Bill Williams (1t). S: Robbie Paul, Nathan Cayless, Paul Rauhihi, Ali Lauitiiti (1t).
Man of the Match: Sonny Bill Williams

2004 Great Britain 24-12 Australia Tri-Nations

JJB Stadium, Wigan. Att: 25,004. 13 November 2004.
Great Britain: Paul Wellens; Brian Carney, Martin Gleeson, Keith Senior (1t), Stuart Reardon (1t); Danny McGuire, Sean Long; Stuart Fielden (1t), Terry Newton (1t), Adrian Morley, Jamie Peacock, Andy Farrell (c) (4g), Paul Sculthorpe. S: Paul Johnson, Ryan Bailey, Sean O'Loughlin, Gareth Ellis.
Australia: Anthony Minichiello; Matt Sing, Shaun Berrigan, Willie Tonga, Luke Rooney (1t); Scott Hill, Brett Kimmorley (1g); Shane Webcke, Danny Buderus (c), Petero Civoniceva, Craig Fitzgibbon (1g), Nathan Hindmarsh, Tonie Carroll. S: Craig Wing, Andrew Ryan, Willie Mason, Mark O'Meley (1t).
Man of the Match: Paul Sculthorpe

2004 Great Britain 26-24 New Zealand Tri-Nations

KC Stadium, Hull. Att: 23,377. 20 November 2004.

Great Britain: Paul Wellens; Brian Carney (2t), Martin Gleeson, Keith Senior (1t), Stuart Reardon; Iestyn Harris, Danny McGuire; Stuart Fielden, Matt Diskin, Adrian Morley, Gareth Ellis, Andy Farrell (c) (1t, 3g), Sean O'Loughlin. S: Mickey Higham, Chev Walker, Paul Johnson (1t), Danny Ward.

New Zealand: Brent Webb (4g); Francis Meli, Nigel Vagana (1t), Clinton Toopi, Shontayne Hape (1t); Vinnie Anderson (1t), Thomas Leuluai; Jason Cayless, Louis Anderson, Paul Rauhihi (c), Logan Swann, Ali Lauitiiti, Wairangi Koopu. S: Dene Halatau, Roy Asotasi, Nathan Cayless, Alex Chan (1t).

Man of the Match: Brian Carney

2004 Great Britain 4-44 Australia Tri-Nations Final

Elland Road, Leeds. Att: 39,120. 27 November 2004.

Great Britain: Paul Wellens; Brian Carney, Martin Gleeson, Keith Senior, Stuart Reardon (1t); Iestyn Harris, Sean Long; Stuart Fielden, Terry Newton, Adrian Morley, Jamie Peacock, Andy Farrell (c), Paul Sculthorpe. S: Ryan Bailey, Paul Johnson, Danny McGuire, Sean O'Loughlin.

Australia: Anthony Minichiello (2t); Matt Sing (1t), Shaun Berrigan, Willie Tonga (2t), Luke Rooney; Darren Lockyer (c) (1t, 6g), Brett Kimmorley; Shane Webcke, Danny Buderus, Petero Civoniceva, Andrew Ryan, Nathan Hindmarsh, Tonie Carroll. S: Craig Wing, Willie Mason (1t), Mark O'Meley, Craig Fitzgibbon (2g).

Man of the Match: Darren Lockyer

2005 Great Britain 26-42 New Zealand Tri-Nations

Loftus Road, London. Att: 15,568. 29 October 2005.

Great Britain: Paul Wellens; Brian Carney, Martin Gleeson, Keith Senior (1t), Leon Pryce; Kevin Sinfield (4g), Paul Deacon (1g); Stuart Fielden, Keiron Cunningham, Jamie Peacock (c), Lee Gilmour, Paul Johnson (3t), Gareth Ellis. S: Rob Burrow, Adrian Morley, Chev Walker, Nick Fozzard.

New Zealand: Brent Webb (2t); Jake Webster (1t), Paul Whatuira, Clinton Toopi (2t), Manu Vatuvei (1t); Nigel Vagana, Stacey Jones (7g); Paul Rauhihi (1t), Motu Tony, Ruben Wiki (c), David Kidwell, David Solomona, Awen Guttenbeil. S: Louis Anderson, Roy Asotasi, Frank Pritchard, Ali Lauitiiti.

Man of the Match: Stacey Jones

2005 Great Britain 6-20 Australia Tri-Nations

JJB Stadium, Wigan. Att: 25,004. 5 November 2005.

Great Britain: Paul Wellens; Brian Carney, Martin Gleeson, Keith Senior, Leon Pryce; Iestyn Harris, Paul Deacon; Stuart Fielden, Keiron Cunningham, Adrian Morley (1t), Jamie Peacock (c), Paul Johnson, Kevin Sinfield (1g). S: Lee Gilmour, Chev Walker, Jamie Thackray, Mickey Higham.

Australia: Anthony Minichiello (1t); Matt King, Mark Gasnier, Matt Cooper (2t), Brent Tate; Darren Lockyer (c), Scott Prince; Petero Civoniceva, Danny Buderus, Steven Price, Luke O'Donnell, Craig Fitzgibbon (4g), Ben Kennedy. S: Trent Barrett, Jason Ryles, Mark O'Meley, Willie Mason.

Man of the Match: Anthony Minichiello

2005 Great Britain 38-12 New Zealand Tri-Nations

Galpharm Stadium, Huddersfield. Att: 19,232. 12 November 2005.

Great Britain: Paul Wellens; Brian Carney (2t), Martin Gleeson, Keith Senior (1t), Leon Pryce; Iestyn Harris (5g), Paul Deacon (1t, 2g); Stuart Fielden (1t), Keiron Cunningham, Adrian Morley, Jamie Peacock (c), Paul Johnson, Gareth Ellis. S: Mickey Higham, Chev Walker (1t), Jamie Thackray, Richard Horne.

New Zealand: Brent Webb; Jake Webster (2t), Shontayne Hape, Clinton Toopi, Manu Vatuvei; Nigel Vagana, Stacey Jones; Paul Rauhihi, Motu Tony, Ruben Wiki (c), David Kidwell, David Solomona, Awen Guttenbeil. S: David Faiumu, Roy Asotasi, Louis Anderson, Ali Lauitiiti (1t).

Man of the Match: Chev Walker

2005 Great Britain 14-26 Australia Tri-Nations

KC Stadium, Hull. Att: 25,150. 19 November 2005.

Great Britain: Leon Pryce; Brian Carney (1t), Martin Gleeson, Keith Senior, Gareth Raynor; Iestyn Harris (3g), Richard Horne (1t); Stuart Fielden, Keiron Cunningham, Adrian Morley, Jamie Peacock (c), Paul Johnson, Gareth Ellis. S: Mickey Higham, Chev Walker, Jamie Thackray, Kevin Sinfield.

Australia: Anthony Minichiello; Matt King, Mark Gasnier (1t), Matt Cooper (1t), Brent Tate (1t); Trent Barrett, Craig Gower; Petero Civoniceva, Danny Buderus (c), Jason Ryles, Luke O'Donnell, Craig Fitzgibbon (5g), Ben Kennedy. S: Craig Wing, Willie Mason, Mark O'Meley (1t), Trent Waterhouse.

Man of the Match: Anthony Minichiello

2006 Great Britain 46-14 New Zealand One-off Test

Knowsley Road, St Helens. Att: 10,103. 27 June 2006.

Great Britain: Paul Wellens; Ade Gardner (1t), Martin Gleeson, Keith Senior (1t), Leon Pryce; Danny McGuire (2t), Sean Long (2t, 6g); Stuart Fielden, Keiron Cunningham, Adrian Morley, Jamie Peacock, Gareth Ellis, Paul Sculthorpe (c) (1g). S: Terry Newton, Sean O'Loughlin, Lee Gilmour, James Graham (2t).

New Zealand: Clinton Toopi; Henry Fa'afili (1t), Willie Talau, Shontayne Hape, Lesley Vainikolo (1t); Ben Roberts, Stacey Jones (c) (1g); Alex Chan, Motu Tony, Iafeta Paleaasina (1t), Ali Lauitiiti, David Solomona, David Kidwell. S: Robbie Paul, Harrison Hansen, Vinnie Anderson, Monty Betham.

Man of the Match: Paul Wellens

2006 New Zealand 18-14 Great Britain Tri-Nations

Jade Stadium, Christchurch. Att: 17,005. 28 October 2006.

New Zealand: Brent Webb (1t); Tame Tupou, Nigel Vagana, Iosia Soliola (1t), Manu Vatuvei; Jerome Ropati, Stacey Jones (3g); Ruben Wiki (c), Nathan Fien, Roy Asotasi, David Kidwell, Frank Pritchard, Simon Mannering. S: Motu Tony (1t), Nathan Cayless, Jason Cayless, David Fa'alogo.

Great Britain: Paul Wellens (1t); Brian Carney, Martin Gleeson, Keith Senior, Leon Pryce; Danny McGuire (1g), Sean Long (2g); Stuart Fielden, Terry Newton, Adrian Morley, Jamie Peacock (c), Gareth Ellis (1t), Sean O'Loughlin. S: James Roby, Garreth Carvell, Gareth Hock, Lee Gilmour.

Man of the Match: Brent Webb

2006 Australia 12-23 Great Britain Tri-Nations

Aussie Stadium, Sydney. Att: 24,953. 4 November 2006.

Australia: Karmichael Hunt; Brent Tate, Mark Gasnier, Jamie Lyon, Greg Inglis (1t); Darren Lockyer (c) (1t, 2g), Ben Hornby; Mark O'Meley, Shaun Berrigan, Petero Civoniceva, Willie Mason, Nathan Hindmarsh, Luke O'Donnell. S: Cameron Smith, Anthony Tupou, Brent Kite, Sam Thaiday.

Great Britain: Paul Wellens (1t); Brian Carney, Keith Senior, Kirk Yeaman, Gareth Raynor (1t); Leon Pryce, Sean Long (3g, 1dg); Stuart Fielden, Terry Newton, Jamie Peacock (c) (1t), Gareth Ellis, Gareth Hock, Sean O'Loughlin. S: James Roby, Adrian Morley, Lee Gilmour (1t), Jon Wilkin.

Man of the Match: Sean Long

2006 New Zealand 34-4 Great Britain Tri-Nations

Westpac Stadium, Wellington. Att: 16,401. 11 November 2006.

New Zealand: Brent Webb (2t); Shontayne Hape, Iosia Soliola, Steve Matai, Manu Vatuvei (1t); Nigel Vagana (1t), Stacey Jones (5g); Ruben Wiki (c) (1t), Dene Halatau, Roy Asotasi, David Kidwell, Simon Mannering, David Fa'alogo. S: Motu Tony, Nathan Cayless (1t), Adam Blair, Frank Pritchard.

Great Britain: Paul Wellens; Leon Pryce, Keith Senior, Kirk Yeaman, Gareth Raynor; Danny McGuire, Sean Long; Stuart Fielden, Terry Newton, Adrian Morley, Jamie Peacock (c), Gareth Hock, Gareth Ellis (1t). S: James Roby, Jon Wilkin, Lee Gilmour, Garreth Carvell.

Man of the Match: Stacey Jones

2006 Australia 33-10 Great Britain Tri-Nations

Suncorp Stadium, Brisbane. Att: 44,358. 18 November 2006.
Australia: Karmichael Hunt (1t); Brent Tate (1t), Mark Gasnier (1t), Justin Hodges (1t), Greg Inglis; Darren Lockyer (c) (1t, 1dg), Johnathan Thurston (4g); Brent Kite, Cameron Smith, Petero Civoniceva, Nathan Hindmarsh, Andrew Ryan, Luke O'Donnell. S: Mark O'Meley, Shaun Berrigan, Anthony Tupou (1t), Antonio Kaufusi.
Great Britain: Paul Wellens (1g); Leon Pryce, Martin Gleeson, Keith Senior (1t), Gareth Raynor; Danny McGuire (1t), Richard Horne; Stuart Fielden, Terry Newton, Jamie Peacock (c), Gareth Hock, Gareth Ellis, Sean O'Loughlin. S: James Roby, Adrian Morley, Lee Gilmour, Jon Wilkin.
Man of the Match: Darren Lockyer

2007 Great Britain 42-14 France One-off Test

Headingley, Leeds. Att: 12,685. 22 June 2007.
Great Britain: Chris Melling; David Hodgson, Stephen Wild (1t), Paul Sykes (1t), Ade Gardner; Danny McGuire (1t), Rob Burrow (2t); Adrian Morley (c) (1t), James Roby (1t), Andy Lynch, Gareth Ellis, Andy Coley, Jon Wilkin. S: Sean O'Loughlin, James Graham, Kevin Sinfield (5g), Jamie Langley (1t).
France: Thomas Bosc (1g); Sébastien Planas, Sylvain Houles, Cyril Stacul, Constant Villegas; Maxime Greseque (2t), Christophe Moly; David Ferriol, Julien Rinaldi, Jerome Guisset (c), Olivier Elima, Eric Anselme (1t), Aurelien Cologni. S: James Wynne, Jean-Christophe Borlin, Cyrille Gossard, Gregory Mounis.
Man of the Match: Rob Burrow

2007 Great Britain 20-14 New Zealand 1st Test

Galpharm Stadium, Huddersfield. Att: 16,522. 27 October 2007.
Great Britain: Paul Wellens; Adrian Gardner, Martin Gleeson, Keith Senior, Gareth Raynor (1t); Leon Pryce, Rob Burrow (4g); Adrian Morley, Terry Newton, Sam Burgess (1t), Jamie Peacock (c), Gareth Ellis, Sean O'Loughlin. S: Maurie Fa'asavalu (1t), James Roby, James Graham, Jon Wilkin.
New Zealand: Sam Perrett; Tame Tupou, Shontayne Hape (2t), Paul Whatuira (1t), Taniela Tuiaki; Lance Hohaia (1g), Thomas Leuluai; Roy Asotasi (c), Dene Halatau, Fuifui Moimoi, Simon Mannering, Frank Pritchard, Jeremy Smith. S: Greg Eastwood, Louis Anderson, Sam Rapira, Epalahame Lauaki.
Man of the Match: Rob Burrow

2007 Great Britain 44-0 New Zealand 2nd Test

KC Stadium, Hull. Att: 20,324. 3 November 2007.
Great Britain: Paul Wellens (1t); Ade Gardner (1t), Martin Gleeson, Keith Senior (1t), Gareth Raynor (1t); Leon Pryce (2t), Rob Burrow (1t, 1g); Adrian Morley, Jon Clarke, Jamie Peacock (c) (1t), Gareth Ellis, Sean O'Loughlin, Kevin Sinfield (5g). S: Maurie Fa'asavalu, James Graham, Sam Burgess, Danny McGuire.
New Zealand: Sam Perrett; Shontayne Hape, Clinton Toopi, Paul Whatuira, Taniela Tuiaki; Lance Hohaia, Thomas Leuluai; Sam Rapira, Dene Halatau, Roy Asotasi (c), Simon Mannering, Frank Pritchard, Jeremy Smith. S: David Faiumu, Louis Anderson, Greg Eastwood, Fuifui Moimoi.
Man of the Match: Leon Pryce

2007 Great Britain 28-22 New Zealand 3rd Test

JJB Stadium, Wigan. Att: 21,235. 10 November 2007.
Great Britain: Paul Wellens; Ade Gardner, Martin Gleeson, Keith Senior (1t), David Hodgson (1t); Danny McGuire (1t), Rob Burrow (1t, 4g); Adrian Morley, Jon Clarke, Jamie Peacock (c), Gareth Ellis, Sean O'Loughlin, Jon Wilkin. S: James Graham (1t), Jamie Jones-Buchanan, James Roby, Kirk Yeaman.
New Zealand: Sam Perrett; Chase Stanley (2t), Clinton Toopi, Paul Whatuira (1t), Taniela Tuiaki (1t); Ben Roberts, Jeremy Smith; Sam Rapira, Dene Halatau, Roy Asotasi (c), Louis Anderson, Jeremy Smith (3g), Simon Mannering. S: Lance Hohaia, Fuifui Moimoi, Epalahame Lauaki, Jeff Lima.
Man of the Match: Sean O'Loughlin

1.1.1 GREAT BRITAIN COACHES
1980-1982 Johnny Whiteley
1983-1984 Frank Myler
1985-1986 Maurice Bamford
1987-1994 Malcolm Reilly
1994 Ellery Hanley
1996 Phil Larder
1997-1999 Andy Goodway
2001-2003 David Waite
2004-2006 Brian Noble
2007 Tony Smith

1.1.2 GREAT BRITAIN CAPTAINS 1980-2007
29 matches - Andy Farrell
19 Ellery Hanley
13 Garry Schofield
11 Jamie Peacock
8 Brian Noble, Mike Gregory
4 Harry Pinner, David Watkinson, Shaun Edwards
3 Len Casey
2 George Fairbairn, Jeff Grayshon
1 David Ward, Steve Nash, David Topliss, Keith Mumby, Andy Goodway, Jonathan Davies, Andy Platt, Phil Clarke, Paul Sculthorpe, Adrian Morley

1.1.3 BRITISH MAN OF THE MATCH AWARDS 1980-2007

8 Garry Schofield
3 Shaun Edwards, Kevin Ward, Paul Sculthorpe
2 Ellery Hanley, Bobbie Goulding, Rob Burrow
1 Des Drummond, Steve Norton, Brian Noble, Peter Smith, Keith Rayne, Deryck Fox, Harry Pinner, Lee Crooks, Ian Potter, Neil James, Kevin Beardmore, Paul Medley, Hugh Waddell, Steve Hampson, Andy Gregory, Alan Tait, Martin Offiah, Kelvin Skerrett, Denis Betts, Lee Jackson, Les Holliday, Martin Dermott, Andy Platt, Paul Newlove, John Devereux, Phil Clarke, Jonathan Davies, Andy Farrell, Chris Joynt, Keith Senior, Stuart Fielden, Brian Carney, Chev Walker, Paul Wellens, Sean Long, Leon Pryce, Sean O'Loughlin

1.2 ENGLAND TEST MATCHES
England matches played simultaneously with Great Britain games are not recorded here, as they were effectively second-string sides. Elsewhere, England have been used in European Championship tournaments with France and Wales, in World Cups and, from 2009 onwards, they replaced Great Britain to compete in the Four Nations. They have also played various one-off Tests.

1980 England 26-9 Wales European Championship
Craven Park, Hull. Att: 7,557. 29 February 1980.
England: George Fairbairn (1t, 6g); Stuart Wright, John Joyner (1t), Mike Smith, Des Drummond; Steve Evans, Neil Holding; Roy Holdstock (1t), David Ward (c), Keith Rayne (1t), Len Casey, Peter Gorley, Harry Pinner (2dg). S: John Woods, Jeff Grayshon.
Wales: Harold Box; Brian Juliff (1t), Graham Walters, Bill Francis (c), Paul Prendiville; Paul Woods (3g), Ness Flowers; Mel James, Don Parry, Glyn Shaw, Chris Seldon, John Bevan, Roy Mathias. S: Steve Diamond, Mark McJennett.
Man of the Match: George Fairbairn

1980 France 2-4 England European Championship
Stade de l'Egassiairal, Narbonne. Att: 20,000. 16 March 1980.
France: Francis Tranier; Sébastien Rodriguez, Jean-Marc Bourret (1g), Christian Laumond, Jean-Marc Gonzales; Michel Mazare, Ivan Greseque; Max Chantal, Henri Daniel, Didier

Hermet, Jose Gine, Christian Baile, Joel Roosebrouck (c).
England: George Fairbairn; Des Drummond, Mike Smith, John Joyner, Steve Evans (1t); John Woods, Alan Redfearn (1dg); Roy Holdstock, David Ward (c), Keith Rayne, Jeff Grayshon, Peter Smith, Harry Pinner. S: Peter Glynn (dnp), Peter Gorley.
Man of the Match: Ivan Greseque

1981 England 1-5 France European Championship
Headingley, Leeds. Att: 3,229. 21 February 1981.
England: George Fairbairn (c) (1dg); Des Drummond, John Joyner, Mike Smith, Steve Fenton; Ken Kelly, Arnie Walker; Steve O'Neill, David Ward, Brian Case, Len Casey, Ian Potter, Harry Pinner. S: John Woods, Bill Pattinson.
France: Marcel Pillon; Sébastien Rodriguez, Michel Naudo, Hugues Ratier, Jose Moya (1g); Eric Walligunda, Herme Guiraud (1t); Max Chantal, Christian Maccali, Delphin Castagnon, Manuel Caravaca, Jose Gine, Joel Roosebrouck (c). S: Phillippe Fourquet, Marc Ambert.
Man of the Match: Jose Gine

1981 Wales 4-17 England European Championship
Craven Park, Hull. Att: 4,786. 18 March 1981.
Wales: Steve Rule (2g); Adrian Cambriani, Graham Walters, John Bevan (c), Brian Juliff; Danny Wilson, Paul Woods; Mel James, Don Parry, Gareth Owen, Trevor Skerrett, Colin Dixon, Roy Mathias. S: Clive Griffiths, Martin Herdman.
England: George Fairbairn (c) (4g); Terry Richardson, John Joyner (1t), Mike Smith, Steve Fenton; Ken Kelly (1t), Steve Nash; Roy Holdstock, David Ward, Len Casey, Ian Potter, Bill Pattinson, Steve Norton. S: John Woods (1t), Mick Adams.
Man of the Match: Ken Kelly

1981 Wales 15-20 England One-off Test
Ninian Park, Cardiff. Att: 8,102. 8 November 1981.
Wales: Gordon Pritchard; Adrian Cambriani, Steve Bayliss, Steve Fenwick (4g), John Bevan (c); Danny Wilson (1dg), Ness Flowers (1t); Mel James, Don Parry, Tommy David, Martin Herdman, Glyn Shaw, Paul Ringer. S: Paul Prendiville (1t), Roger Owen.
England: George Fairbairn (1g); Des Drummond (1t), Mike Smith, Les Dyl, Henderson Gill (1t); John Woods (3g), Steve Nash; Jeff Grayshon (1t), David Ward (c), John Millington, Phil Lowe, Peter Gorley (1t), Steve Norton. S: Steve Evans, Les Gorley.
Man of the Match: Henderson Gill

1984 Wales 9-28 England One-off Test
Eugene Cross Park, Ebbw Vale. Att: 2,111. 14 October 1984.
Wales: Lyn Hallett (2g); Chris Camilleri, Paul Prendiville, Mike Davies, Phil Ford; Danny Wilson (1t, 1dg), Ness Flowers; Trevor Skerrett (c), Chris Preece, Glyn Shaw, Mark McJennett, Chris O'Brien, Brian Juliff. S: Graeme Johns, Graham Walters.
England: Mick Burke (1t, 4g); Des Drummond, Garry Schofield, Ellery Hanley (1t), Garry Clark (3t); Steve Donlan (c), David Cairns; David Hobbs, Kevin Beardmore, Hugh Waddell, Andy Kelly, Andy Goodway, Milton Huddart. S: Barrie Ledger, Chris Arkwright.
Man of the Match: Andy Goodway

1992 Wales 11-36 England One-off Test
Vetch Field, Swansea. Att: 10,243. 27 November 1992.
Wales: Phil Ford; Gerald Cordle, Allan Bateman, John Devereux (1g), Anthony Sullivan; Jonathan Griffiths (1t), Kevin Ellis (1dg); Mark Jones (1t), David Bishop, David Young (c), Paul Moriarty, Ian Marlow, Rob Ackerman. S: Adrian Hadley, Rowland Phillips, Gary Pearce, Mark Moran.
England: Stuart Spruce (1t); Alan Hunte, Gary Connolly, Paul Newlove (1t), Martin Offiah (2t); Garry Schofield (c) (1t), Mike Ford; Lee Crooks (1t, 4g), Lee Jackson, Steve Molloy, Richard Eyres, Phil Clarke, Ellery Hanley (1t). S: Daryl Powell, Chris Joynt, Jason Critchley, Dean Busby.
Man of the Match: Richie Eyres

1995 Wales 18-16 England European Championship
Ninian Park, Cardiff. Att: 6,232. 1 February 1995.
Wales: Paul Atcheson; Phil Ford, Allan Bateman, Iestyn Harris, Anthony Sullivan; Jonathan Davies (c) (4g, 2dg), Kevin Ellis (2t); Kelvin Skerrett, Martin Hall, David Young, Paul Moriarty, Mark Perrett, Richard Eyres. S: Adrian Hadley, Daio Powell, Neil Cowie, Rowland Phillips.
England: Richard Gay (1t); Jason Robinson (1t), Daryl Powell, Paul Newlove, Ikram Butt; Garry Schofield, Deryck Fox (1t, 2g); Karl Harrison, Richard Russell, Harvey Howard, Anthony Farrell, Sonny Nickle, Phil Clarke (c). S: Simon Baldwin, Mick Cassidy, Steve McNamara, Steve McCurrie.
Man of the Match: Kevin Ellis

1995 England 19-16 France European Championship
Gateshead International Stadium, Gateshead. Att: 6,103. 15 February 1995.
England: Richard Gay; John Bentley, Nick Pinkney (1t), Richard Goddard, Francis Cummins (1t); Nigel Wright (1dg), Deryck Fox (3g); Paul Broadbent (1t), Lee Jackson, Steve McNamara, Simon Baldwin, Stephen Holgate, Daryl Powell (c). S: Tony Smith, Steve McCurrie, Roger Simpson, Mark Hilton.
France: Laurent Luchesse; Pascal Bomati, Freddie Banquet (2t), Stephane Millet (2g), Jean-Marc Garcia (1t); David Despin, Patrick Entat; Carl Jaavuo, Stephane Tena, Frederic Teixido, Daniel Divet, Didier Cabestany (c), Jacques Pech. S: Ezzedine Attia, Claude Sirvent, Lillian Hebert, Jean-Luc Ramondou.
Man of the Match: Daryl Powell

1995 England 20-16 Australia World Cup Group 1
Wembley Stadium, London. Att: 41,271. 7 October 1995.
England: Kris Radlinski; Jason Robinson (1t), Barrie-Jon Mather, Paul Newlove (1t), John Bentley; Daryl Powell, Shaun Edwards (c); Karl Harrison, Lee Jackson, Andy Platt, Denis Betts, Phil Clarke, Andy Farrell (1t, 2g). S: Bobbie Goulding, Nick Pinkney, Chris Joynt (1t), Simon Haughton.
Australia: Tim Brasher; Rod Wishart (2g), Mark Coyne (1t), Terry Hill, John Hopoate; Brad Fittler (c), Geoff Toovey; David Gillespie, Wayne Bartrim, Mark Carroll, Steve Menzies (2t), Dean Pay, Jim Dymock. S: Robbie O'Davis, Matthew Johns, Jason Smith, Paul Harrogan.
Man of the Match: Andy Farrell

1995 England 46-0 Fiji World Cup Group 1
Central Park, Wigan. Att: 26,263. 11 October 1995.
England: Kris Radlinski (1t); Jason Robinson (2t), Nick Pinkney, Paul Newlove (1t), John Bentley (1t); Tony Smith (1t), Bobbie Goulding (3g); Paul Broadbent (1t), Lee Jackson, Dean Sampson, Denis Betts (c), Mick Cassidy, Andy Farrell (1t, 2g). S: Shaun Edwards, Paul Cook, Simon Haughton (1t), Steve McCurrie.
Fiji: Waisale Sovatabua; Joe Dakuitoga, Livai Nalagilagi (c), Filimoni Seru, Noa Nadruku; Noa Nayacakalou, Save Taga; Malakai Yasa, Iane Sagaitu, Pio Nakubuwai, Apisalome Degei, Iliesa Toga, Sam Marayawa. S: Niumaia Korovata, Ulaiasi Wainidroa, George Vatubua, Kalaveti Naisoro.
Man of the Match: Bobbie Goulding

1995 England 46-0 South Africa World Cup Group 1
Headingley, Leeds. Att: 14,041. 14 October 1995.
England: Paul Cook; John Bentley, Nick Pinkney (2t), Barrie-Jon Mather, Martin Offiah; Daryl Powell, Bobbie Goulding (1t, 7g); Karl Harrison, Mick Cassidy, Andy Platt, Simon Haughton (1t), Chris Joynt, Phil Clarke (c). S: Kris Radlinski (1t), Paul Broadbent (1t), Tony Smith (1t), Dean Sampson (1t).
South Africa: Pierre van Wyk; Guy Coombe, Tim Fourie, Willem Boshoff, Andrew Ballot; Mark Johnson, Berend Alkema; Gideon Watts, Kobus van Deventer, Jaco Booysen (c), Gerald Williams, Jaco Alberts, John Mudgeway. S: Justin Jennings, Elmar Lubbe, Francois Cloete, Jaco Visser.
Man of the Match: Nick Pinkney

1995 England 25-10 Wales World Cup Semi-Final
Old Trafford, Manchester. Att: 30,042. 21 October 1995.
England: Kris Radlinski; Jason Robinson, Nick Pinkney, Paul Newlove (1t), Martin Offiah (2t); Tony Smith, Bobbie Goulding (1g, 1dg); Karl Harrison, Lee Jackson, Andy Platt, Denis Betts (c) (1t), Phil Clarke (1t), Andy Farrell (1g). S: Barrie-Jon Mather, Mick Cassidy, Simon Haughton, Dean Sampson.
Wales: Iestyn Harris; John Devereux, Allan Bateman, Scott Gibbs, Anthony Sullivan; Jonathan Davies (c) (3g), Kevin Ellis; Kelvin Skerrett, Martin Hall, David Young, Paul Moriarty, Scott Quinnell, Richard Eyres. S: Mark Jones, Keiron Cunningham, Rowland Phillips (1t), Adrian Hadley.
Man of the Match: Bobbie Goulding

1995 England 8-16 Australia World Cup Final
Wembley Stadium, London. Att: 66,540. 28 October 1995.
England: Kris Radlinski; Jason Robinson, Gary Connolly, Paul Newlove (1t), Martin Offiah; Tony Smith, Bobbie Goulding (2g); Karl Harrison, Lee Jackson, Andy Platt, Denis Betts (c), Phil Clarke, Andy Farrell. S: Mick Cassidy, Chris Joynt, Barrie-Jon Mather, Nick Pinkney.
Australia: Tim Brasher (1t); Rod Wishart (1t), Mark Coyne, Terry Hill, Brett Dallas; Brad Fittler (c), Geoff Toovey; Dean Pay, Andrew Johns (4g), Mark Carroll, Steve Menzies, Gary Larson, Jim Dymock. S: Jason Smith, Robbie O'Davis, Matthew Johns, Nik Kosef.
Man of the Match: Andrew Johns

1996 England 73-6 France European Championship
Gateshead International Stadium, Gateshead. Att: 6,325. 12 June 1996.
England: Steve Prescott (2t, 7g); Jason Robinson (1t), Gary Connolly (3t), Paul Newlove (2t), Martin Offiah (4t, 1dg); Steve Blakeley (1t), Shaun Edwards (c); Karl Harrison, Johnny Lawless, Paul Broadbent, Chris Joynt, Steve McNamara (1g), Paul Sculthorpe (1t). S: Steve Molloy, Paul Rowley, Matt Calland, Adrian Morley.
France: Laurent Luchesse; Pascal Bomati, Freddie Banquet, Jean-Marc Garcia, Arnaud Cervello; Fabien Devecchi, Patrick Entat (c); Hadj Boudebza, Patrick Torreilles (1g), Frederic Teixido, Pascal Jampy, Didier Cabestany, Jacques Pech. S: Eric van Brussell (1t), Darren Adams, Bagdad Yaha, Jerome Bisson.
Man of the Match: Steve Prescott

1996 Wales 12-26 England European Championship
Cardiff Arms Park, Cardiff. Att: 5,425. 26 June 1996.
Wales: Paul Atcheson; Diccon Edwards, Allan Bateman, Gareth Davies, Jason Critchley (1t); Iestyn Harris (2g), Ian Watson; Mark Jones, Keiron Cunningham, Neil Cowie, Paul Moriarty, Mark Perrett, Chris Morley (1t). S: Rowland Phillips, Richard Webster, Martin Hall, Gareth Stephens.
England: Steve Prescott (1t); Jason Robinson, Gary Connolly, Nathan McAvoy, John Bentley; Daryl Powell, Shaun Edwards (1t); Paul Broadbent, Johnny Lawless, Steve Molloy, Chris Joynt (1t), Paul Sculthorpe, Andy Farrell (c). S: Bobbie Goulding (1t, 5g), Steve Blakeley, Barrie McDermott, Mick Cassidy.
Man of the Match: Bobbie Goulding

2000 England 2-22 Australia World Cup Group 1
Twickenham, London. Att: 33,758. 28 October 2000.
England: Kris Radlinski; Leon Pryce, Scott Naylor, Keith Senior, Chev Walker; Tony Smith, Sean Long; Harvey Howard, Paul Rowley, Stuart Fielden, Adrian Morley, Mike Forshaw, Andy Farrell (c) (1g). S: Paul Wellens, Kevin Sinfield, Darren Fleary, Paul Anderson.
Australia: Darren Lockyer; Mat Rogers (3g), Ryan Girdler, Matt Gidley (1t), Wendell Sailor (2t); Brad Fittler (c), Brett Kimmorley; Shane Webcke, Andrew Johns, Robbie Kearns, Gorden Tallis, Bryan Fletcher, Scott Hill. S: Adam MacDougall (1t), Jason Croker, Darren Britt, Jason Stevens.
Man of the Match: Brett Kimmorley

2000 England 76-4 Russia World Cup Group 1
Knowsley Road, St Helens. Att: 5,736. 1 November 2000.
England: Paul Wellens; Leon Pryce (1t), Chev Walker (1t), Keith Senior, Darren Rogers; Andy Farrell (c) (5g), Paul Deacon (1t); Francis Stephenson (1t), Paul Rowley (2t), Darren Fleary, Jamie Peacock (2t), Andy Hay (1t), Kevin Sinfield (3t). S: Sean Long (2t, 5g), Stuart Spruce, Stuart Fielden, Harvey Howard.
Russia: Robert Iliassov; Mikhail Mitrofanov (1t), Andrei Doumalkine, Craig Cygler, Maxim Romanov; Andre Olar, Igor Gavriline; Ian Rubin (c), Alexander Lysenkov, Robert Campbell, Petr Sokolov, Aaron Findlay, Joel Rullis. S: Paval Kalachkine, Victor Netchaev, Igor Jiltsov, Vadim Postnikov.
Man of the Match: Paul Rowley

2000 England 66-10 Fiji World Cup Group 1
Headingley, Leeds. Att: 10,052. 4 November 2000.
England: Stuart Spruce; Paul Wellens (2t), Scott Naylor (1t), Kris Radlinski (1t), Darren Rogers (2t); Sean Long, Paul Deacon; Francis Stephenson, Tony Smith (1t), Paul Anderson, Jamie Peacock (3t), Andy Hay (1t), Andy Farrell (c) (1t, 9g). S: Kevin Sinfield, Chev Walker, Stuart Fielden, Harvey Howard.
Fiji: Lote Tuqiri (c) (1t); Niko Vakararawa, Seteriki Rakabula, Eparama Navale (1t), Jimi Bolakoro; Waisale Sovatabua, Kalaveti Naisoro Tuiabayaba; Etuate Vakatawa, Fred Robart, Tabua Cakacaka, Peceli Wawavanua, Samu Marawaya, Atunaisa Vunivalu (1g). S: Farosiko Tokarei, Josefa Lasagavibua, Roger Matakamikamica, Peceli Vuniyayawa.
Man of the Match: Jamie Peacock

2000 England 26-16 Ireland World Cup Quarter-Final
Headingley, Leeds. Att: 15,405. 11 November 2000.
England: Paul Wellens; Chev Walker (1t), Kris Radlinski, Keith Senior (1t), Darren Rogers; Sean Long, Paul Deacon; Stuart Fielden, Paul Rowley, Paul Anderson, Adrian Morley, Mike Forshaw, Andy Farrell (c) (5g). S: Tony Smith (1t), Scott Naylor, Jamie Peacock (1t), Harvey Howard.
Ireland: Steve Prescott (2g); Brian Carney, Michael Withers (2t), Michael Eagar, Mark Forster; Tommy Martyn (1t), Ryan Sheridan; Terry O'Connor (c), Danny Williams, Barrie McDermott, Chris Joynt, Kevin Campion, Luke Ricketson. S: Gavin Clinch, David Barnhill, Jamie Mathiou, Paul Southern.
Man of the Match: Stuart Fielden

2000 England 6-49 New Zealand World Cup Semi-Final
Reebok Stadium, Bolton. Att: 16,032. 18 November 2000.
England: Kris Radlinski; Chev Walker, Scott Naylor, Keith Senior, Paul Wellens; Sean Long, Paul Deacon; Stuart Fielden, Tony Smith (1t), Harvey Howard, Paul Sculthorpe, Mike Forshaw, Andy Farrell (c) (1g). S: Jamie Peacock, Andy Hay, Darren Fleary, Paul Anderson.
New Zealand: Richie Barnett (c); Nigel Vagana (1t), Tonie Carroll, Willie Talau (2t), Lesley Vainikolo (2t); Henry Paul (8g, 1dg), Stacey Jones; Craig Smith, Richard Swain, Quentin Pongia, Matt Rua, Stephen Kearney (1t), Ruben Wiki (1t). S: Robbie Paul, Joe Vagana, Nathan Cayless, Logan Swann (1t).
Man of the Match: Henry Paul

2001 Wales 33-42 England One-off Test
Racecourse Ground, Wrexham. Att: 6,373. 31 July 2001.
Wales: Mark Lennon; Damian Gibson (1t), Martin Pearson, Jason Critchley, Jason Lee (2t); Lee Briers (1t, 4g, 1dg), Barry Eaton; Keith Mason, Ian Watson, David Whittle, Chris Morley (1t), Dean Busby, Keiron Cunningham (c). S: Paul Atcheson (1t), Steffan Hughes, Gareth Dean, Gareth Price.
England: Paul Wellens (1t); Leon Pryce, Kris Radlinski, Keith Senior, Chev Walker; Paul Sculthorpe (3t), Paul Deacon; Paul Anderson, Terry Newton, Brian McDermott, Jamie Peacock (1t), Kevin Sinfield, Andy Farrell (c) (1t, 5g). S: Karl Pratt (1t), Paul King, Nathan Sykes, Lee Radford (1t).
Man of the Match: Lee Briers

2008 France 8-56 England One-off Test
Stade Ernest Wallon, Toulouse. Att: 8,326. 27 June 2008.
France: Trent Clayton; Younes Khattabi, Teddy Sadaoui, Sébastien Raguin, Cyril Stacul; Thomas Bosc (2g), James Wynne (1t); Olivier Elima, Julien Rinaldi (c), Adel Fellous, Laurent Carrasco, Eric Anselme, Greg Mounis. S: Remi Casty, Jamal Fakir, Pierre Sabatie, Vincent Duport.
England: Paul Wellens (1t); Ade Gardner, Martin Gleeson (3t), Keith Senior (1t), Peter Fox (1t); Leon Pryce (1t), Rob Burrow (3g); Adrian Morley, James Roby, Jamie Peacock (c), Gareth Ellis, Sam Burgess, Kevin Sinfield (5g). S: James Graham, Maurie Fa'asavalu (1t), Jon Wilkin (1t), Danny McGuire (1t).
Man of the Match: Leon Pryce

2008 England 74-0 Wales One-off Test
Keepmoat Stadium, Doncaster. Att: 11,263. 10 October 2008.
England: Shaun Briscoe (2t); Peter Fox (1t), Michael Shenton, Paul Sykes (2t), Mark Calderwood (1t); Martin Gleeson (c) (2t), Richie Myler (2t); Stuart Fielden, Mickey Higham, Louie McCarthy-Scarsbrook (1t), Gareth Hock (1t), Ben Westwood, Rob Purdham (1t, 9g). S: David Hodgson, Jamie Langley, Darrell Griffin, Tony Clubb (1t).
Wales: Dave Halley; Damian Gibson, Aled James, Lee Williams, Rhys Williams; Mark Lennon, Ian Watson; Craig Kopczak, Sean Penkywicz, David Mills (c), Ben Flower, Geraint Davies, Andy Bracek. S: Rhys Griffiths, Matt Barron, Jordan James, Gil Dudson.
Man of the Match: Rob Purdham

2008 England 32-22 Papua New Guinea World Cup Pool 1
Dairy Farmers Stadium, Townsville. Att: 10,780. 25 October 2008.
England: Paul Wellens; Ade Gardner (2t), Martin Gleeson (1t), Keith Senior, Lee Smith (3t); Leon Pryce, Rob Burrow; Jamie Peacock (c), James Roby, James Graham, Gareth Hock, Gareth Ellis, Kevin Sinfield (4g). S: Danny McGuire, Maurie Fa'asavalu, Adrian Morley, Jon Wilkin.
Papua New Guinea: John Wilshere (c) (3g); George Keppa (1t), Tu'u Maori, Jessie Joe Parker, David Moore; Stanley Gene, Keith Peters; Makali Aizue, Paul Aiton (1t), Trevor Exton, Neville Costigan, James Nightingale, Rod Griffin (1t). S: Rodney Pora, George Moni, Jason Chan (1t), Charlie Wabo.
Man of the Match: Stanley Gene

2008 Australia 52-4 England World Cup Pool 1
Telstra Stadium, Melbourne. Att: 36,297. 2 November 2008.
Australia: Billy Slater (3t); Joel Monaghan (1t), Greg Inglis (3t), Israel Folau, Brent Tate; Darren Lockyer (c), Scott Prince (8g); Steve Price, Cameron Smith, Petero Civoniceva, Anthony Laffranchi (2t), Glenn Stewart, Paul Gallen. S: Karmichael Hunt, Brent Kite, Anthony Tupou, Josh Perry.
England: Paul Wellens; Ade Gardner, Martin Gleeson, Keith Senior, Mark Calderwood; Leon Pryce, Rob Burrow; Adrian Morley, James Roby (1t), James Graham, Gareth Ellis, Jamie Peacock (c), Kevin Sinfield. S: Danny McGuire, Maurie Fa'asavalu, Gareth Hock, Jon Wilkin.
Man of the Match: Greg Inglis

2008 New Zealand 36-24 England World Cup Pool 1
EnergyAustralia Stadium, Newcastle. Att: 15,145. 8 November 2008.
New Zealand: Lance Hohaia (1t); Jason Nightingale (1t), Steve Matai, Jerome Ropati, Manu Vatuvei (4t); Benji Marshall (c), Thomas Leuluai; Adam Blair, Nathan Fien (1t), Evarn Tuimavave, Simon Mannering, David Fa'alogo, Jeremy Smith (1g). S: Issac Luke (3g), Greg Eastwood, David Kidwell, Bronson Harrison.
England: Paul Wellens; Mark Calderwood, Paul Sykes, Keith Senior, Lee Smith; Martin Gleeson (1t), Rob Burrow (2t); Adrian Morley, Mickey Higham (1t), Jamie Peacock (c), Jamie Jones-Buchanan, Gareth Ellis, Rob Purdham (4g). S: Kevin Sinfield, Ben Westwood, Gareth Hock, Jamie Langley.
Man of the Match: Issac Luke

2008 New Zealand 32-22 England World Cup Semi-Final
Suncorp Stadium, Brisbane. Att: 26,650. 15 November 2008.
New Zealand: Lance Hohaia (1t); Sam Perrett (1t), Simon Mannering, Jerome Ropati (2t), Manu Vatuvei; Benji Marshall (1t, 1g), Nathan Fien; Nathan Cayless (c), Thomas Leuluai, Adam Blair, Bronson Harrison (1t), David Fa'alogo, Jeremy Smith (3g). S: Issac Luke, Greg Eastwood, Sam Rapira, Sika Manu.
England: Paul Wellens; Ade Gardner, Martin Gleeson (1t), Keith Senior, Mark Calderwood; Danny McGuire (2t), Rob Burrow (3g); James Graham, James Roby, Jamie Peacock (c) (1t), Ben Westwood, Gareth Ellis, Rob Purdham. S: Leon Pryce, Adrian Morley, Mickey Higham, Jon Wilkin.
Man of the Match: Nathan Fien

2009 France 12-66 England One-off Test
Stade Jean Bouin, Paris. Att: 7,200. 13 June 2009.
France: Constant Villegas; Frederic Vaccari, Jean-Phillipe Baile (1t), Sébastien Planas, Vincent Duport; Thomas Bosc (2g), Mikael Murcia; Remi Casty, Kane Bentley, Jerome Guisset (c), Greg Mounis, Cyrille Gossard (1t), Eric Anselme. S: Romain Gagliazzo, Sébastien Martins, William Barthau, Mathieu Griffi.
England: Shaun Briscoe (2t); Peter Fox (2t), Michael Shenton (1t), Ryan Atkins, Ryan Hall (1t); Danny McGuire (1t), Richie Myler (3t, 9g); Adrian Morley, Scott Moore, Jamie Peacock (c), Ben Westwood, Gareth Hock, Sam Burgess (1t). S: James Graham, James Roby (1t), Eorl Crabtree, Tony Clubb.
Man of the Match: Richie Myler

2009 Wales 12-48 England One-off Test
Brewery Field, Bridgend. Att: 3,249. 17 October 2009.
Wales: Elliot Kear; Rhys Williams, Rhys Griffiths, Anthony Blackwood, Ashley Bateman; Lloyd White (2g), Ian Webster; Jordan James (c), Neil Budworth, Gil Dudson, Craig Kopczak (1t), Ben Flower, Geraint Davies. S: Ian Watson (1t), Lee Williams, Ross Divorty, Matt Barron.
England: Paul Sykes (6g); Tom Briscoe (2t), Michael Shenton, Sean O'Loughlin (1t), Peter Fox; Sam Tomkins (3t), Richie Myler; Adrian Morley (c) (1t), Scott Moore, Garreth Carvell, Gareth Ellis, Ben Westwood, Sam Burgess (1t). S: Louie McCarthy-Scarsbrook (1t), Mickey Higham, Danny Tickle, Chris Bridge.
Man of the Match: Sam Tomkins

2009 England 34-12 France Four Nations
Keepmoat Stadium, Doncaster. Att: 11,529. 23 October 2009.
England: Shaun Briscoe; Tom Briscoe (1t), Lee Smith (1t), Michael Shenton, Ryan Hall (1t); Danny McGuire, Richie Myler (2t); Adrian Morley, Scott Moore, Jamie Peacock (c), Gareth Ellis, Sam Burgess, Kevin Sinfield (1t, 5g). S: James Graham, James Roby, Ben Westwood, Kyle Eastmond.
France: Clint Greenshields; Vincent Duport (1t), Sébastien Raguin, Jean-Phillipe Baile, Dimitri Pelo; Thomas Bosc (2g), James Wynne; David Ferriol, Kane Bentley (1t), Remi Casty, Olivier Elima (c), Julien Touxagas, Jamal Fakir. S: Constant Villegas, Teddy Sadaoui, Sébastien Martins, Romain Gagliazzo.
Man of the Match: Richie Myler

2009 England 16-26 Australia Four Nations
DW Stadium, Wigan. Att: 23,122. 31 October 2009.
England: Shaun Briscoe; Tom Briscoe, Lee Smith (1t, 1g), Michael Shenton, Ryan Hall; Danny McGuire, Sam Tomkins; Adrian Morley, James Roby, James Graham, Jamie Peacock (c), Gareth Ellis (1t), Kevin Sinfield (1g). S: Eorl Crabtree, Sam Burgess (1t), Ben Westwood, Kyle Eastmond.
Australia: Billy Slater (2t); Brett Morris (1t), Greg Inglis (1t), Justin Hodges, Jarryd Hayne; Darren Lockyer (c) (1t), Johnathan Thurston (3g); Ben Hannant, Cameron Smith, Petero Civoniceva, Anthony Watmough, Paul Gallen, Nathan Hindmarsh. S: Brett White, David Shillington, Luke Lewis, Robbie Farah.
Man of the Match: Greg Inglis

2009 England 20-12 New Zealand Four Nations
Galpharm Stadium, Huddersfield. Att: 19,390. 7 November 2009.
England: Shaun Briscoe; Peter Fox (2t), Chris Bridge, Michael Shenton, Ryan Hall; Sam Tomkins, Kyle Eastmond (1t); Adrian Morley, Kevin Sinfield (4g), James Graham, Jamie Peacock (c), Gareth Ellis, Sam Burgess. S: Eorl Crabtree, Jon Wilkin, Ben Westwood, James Roby.
New Zealand: Lance Hohaia; Sam Perrett, Kieran Foran, Junior Sau, Bryson Goodwin (1t, 2g); Benji Marshall (c), Nathan Fien; Frank-Paul Nuuausala, Thomas Leuluai, Fuifui Moimoi, Iosia Soliola, Frank Pritchard, Adam Blair. S: Issac Luke, Jeff Lima, Ben Matulino (1t), Jared Waerea-Hargreaves.
Man of the Match: Kevin Sinfield

2009 England 16-46 Australia Four Nations Final
Elland Road, Leeds. Att: 31,042. 14 November 2009.
England: Shaun Briscoe; Peter Fox (1t), Chris Bridge, Michael Shenton, Ryan Hall; Sam Tomkins, Kyle Eastmond; Adrian Morley, Kevin Sinfield (2g), James Graham, Jamie Peacock (c), Gareth Ellis, Sam Burgess (2t). S: Eorl Crabtree, Jon Wilkin, Ben Westwood, James Roby.
Australia: Billy Slater (3t); Brett Morris (2t), Greg Inglis (1t), Justin Hodges, Jarryd Hayne (1t); Darren Lockyer (c), Johnathan Thurston (7g); Ben Hannant, Cameron Smith (1t), Petero Civoniceva, Luke Lewis, Paul Gallen, Nathan Hindmarsh. S: Kurt Gidley, Brett White, Anthony Watmough, Sam Thaiday.
Man of the Match: Billy Slater

2010 England 60-6 France One-off Test
Leigh Sports Village, Leigh. Att: 7,951. 12 June 2010.
England: Gareth Widdop (1t, 2g); Tom Briscoe (1t), Chris Bridge (1t), Michael Shenton (2t), Ryan Hall; Kevin Brown, Sam Tomkins (4t); Jamie Peacock (c), Kevin Sinfield (6g), James Graham, Gareth Ellis (2t), Sam Burgess, Sean O'Loughlin. S: James Roby, Adrian Morley, Joel Tomkins, Ben Westwood.
France: Constant Villegas; Nicolas Piquemal, Cyrille Gossard, Sébastien Raguin, Frederic Vaccari; Tony Gigot, Nicolas Munoz; David Ferriol, Greg Mounis (1g), Remi Casty, Olivier Elima (c), Jamal Fakir, Andrew Bentley (1t). S: Julien Touxagas, Mathieu Griffi, Michael Simon, William Barthau.
Man of the Match: Sam Tomkins

2010 New Zealand 24-10 England Four Nations
Westpac Stadium, Wellington. Att: 20,681. 23 October 2010.
New Zealand: Lance Hohaia (1t); Jason Nightingale, Shaun Kenny-Dowall (1t), Junior Sau (1t), Manu Vatuvei; Benji Marshall (c) (1t, 4g), Nathan Fien; Greg Eastwood, Thomas Leuluai, Adam Blair, Simon Mannering, Bronson Harrison, Jeremy Smith. S: Ben Matulino, Issac Luke, Frank Pritchard, Frank-Paul Nuuausala.
England: Gareth Widdop (1t, 1g); Darrell Goulding, Michael Shenton, Ryan Atkins, Tom Briscoe; Kevin Brown, Sam Tomkins; Stuart Fielden, James Roby (1t), James Graham (c), Gareth Ellis, Sam Burgess, Sean O'Loughlin. S: Luke Robinson, Darrell Griffin, Ben Westwood, Joel Tomkins.
Man of the Match: Benji Marshall

2010 Australia 34-14 England Four Nations
AAMI Park, Melbourne. Att: 18,894. 31 October 2010.
Australia: Billy Slater (1t); Brett Morris, Brent Tate (1t), Willie Tonga (1t), Lote Tuqiri (1t); Darren Lockyer (c) (5g), Cooper Cronk; Nate Myles, Cameron Smith, Petero Civoniceva, Luke Lewis (2t), Sam Thaiday, Paul Gallen. S: David Shillington, Tom Learoyd-Lahrs, Anthony Watmough, Kurt Gidley.
England: Sam Tomkins; Darrell Goulding, Leroy Cudjoe (1g), Ryan Atkins, Tom Briscoe; Sean O'Loughlin, Luke Robinson (1t); Sam Burgess (1t), James Roby, James Graham (c), Gareth Ellis, Joel Tomkins, Ben Westwood (2g). S: Stuart Fielden, Eorl Crabtree, Ben Harrison, Shaun Lunt.
Man of the Match: Luke Lewis

2010 England 36-10 Papua New Guinea Four Nations
Eden Park, Auckland. 44,324 (part of double header with NZ v Aus). 6 November 2010.
England: Sam Tomkins; Ryan Hall, Leroy Cudjoe, Tony Clubb (4t), Tom Briscoe; Kevin Brown, Luke Robinson (2t); James Graham (c), James Roby, Sam Burgess, Gareth Ellis, Ben Westwood (3g), Sean O'Loughlin. S: Darrell Griffin, Garreth Carvell, Ben Harrison (1t), Gareth Widdop (1g).
Papua New Guinea: Jessie Joe Parker; Michael Mark, Elijah Riyong, Menzie Yere (1t), Richard Kambo; Glen Nami, Dion Aiye (1g); Makali Aizue (1t), Charlie Wabo, Nickson Kolo, Rodney Griffin, David Loko, Paul Aiton. S: Benjamin John, George Moni, Joseph Pombo, Johnson Kuike.
Man of the Match: Tony Clubb

2011 France 18-32 England One-off Test
Parc des Sports, Avignon. Att: 16,866. 21 October 2011.
France: Cyril Stacul; Vincent Duport (1t), Mathias Pala, Jean-Phillipe Baile, Frederic Vaccari; Dane Chisholm, Thomas Bosc (3g); David Ferriol, Greg Mounis, Remi Casty, Olivier Elima (c) (1t), Cyrille Gossard, Jason Baitieri. S: Eloi Pelissier (1t), Jamal Fakir, Sébastien Raguin, Michael Simon
England: Sam Tomkins; Ryan Hall (1t), Jack Reed (1t), Kirk Yeaman (1t), Tom Briscoe (2t); Kevin Sinfield (4g), Rangi Chase; Jamie Peacock (c), James Roby (1t), James Graham, Gareth Ellis, Ben Westwood, Chris Heighington. S: Gareth Widdop, Adrian Morley, Jamie Jones-Buchanan, Jon Wilkin.
Man of the Match: Rangi Chase

2011 England 42-4 Wales Four Nations
Leigh Sports Village, Leigh. Att: 10,377. 29 October 2011.
England: Sam Tomkins (4t); Ryan Hall, Jack Reed (1t), Kirk Yeaman (1t), Tom Briscoe; Kevin Sinfield (5g), Rangi Chase; Jamie Peacock (c), James Roby, James Graham, Gareth Ellis, Ben Westwood, Chris Heighington (1t). S: Gareth Widdop (1t), Adrian Morley, Jamie Jones-Buchanan, Jon Wilkin.
Wales: Danny Jones; Elliot Kear (1t), Ian Webster, Christian Roets, Rhys Williams; Lee Briers (c), Matt Seamark; Jordan James, Neil Budworth, Gil Dudson, Tyson Frizell, Andy Bracek, Ben Flower. S: Ian Watson, Ross Divorty, Aled James, Craig Kopczak.
Man of the Match: Sam Tomkins

2011 England 20-36 Australia Four Nations
Wembley Stadium, London. Att: 42,344. (part of double header with NZ v Wales). 5 November 2011.
England: Sam Tomkins; Ryan Hall (2t), Jack Reed (1t), Kirk Yeaman, Tom Briscoe; Kevin Sinfield (2g), Rangi Chase; James Graham, James Roby, Jamie Peacock (c), Gareth Ellis, Ben Westwood, Chris Heighington (1t). S: Gareth Widdop, Adrian Morley, Jamie Jones-Buchanan, Jon Wilkin.
Australia: Billy Slater; Akuila Uate, Chris Lawrence (1t), Greg Inglis (1t), Darius Boyd (1t); Darren Lockyer (c), Johnathan Thurston (6g); Paul Gallen (1t), Cameron Smith, Matt Scott, Luke Lewis (1t), Sam Thaiday, Anthony Watmough. S: Cooper Cronk, Keith Galloway, David Shillington, Tony Williams (1t).
Man of the Match: Johnathan Thurston

2011 England 28-6 New Zealand Four Nations
KC Stadium, Hull. Att: 23,447. 12 November 2011.
England: Sam Tomkins; Ryan Hall (1t), Jack Reed, Kirk Yeaman, Tom Briscoe (1t); Kevin Sinfield (6g), Rangi Chase; James Graham (1t), James Roby, Jamie Peacock (c), Jon Wilkin, Ben Westwood, Chris Heighington. S: Gareth Widdop, Adrian Morley, Jamie Jones-Buchanan, Garreth Carvell.
New Zealand: Kevin Locke, Jason Nightingale (1t), Lewis Brown, Simon Mannering, Gerard Beale; Benji Marshall (c) (1g), Keiran Foran; Ben Matulino, Thomas Leuluai, Russell Packer, Sika Manu, Adam Blair, Jeremy Smith. S: Alex Glenn, Issac Luke, Jared Waerea-Hargreaves, Elijah Taylor.
Man of the Match: Sam Tomkins

2011 England 8-30 Australia Four Nations Final
Elland Road, Leeds. Att: 34,174. 19 November 2011.
England: Sam Tomkins; Ryan Hall (1t), Jack Reed, Kirk Yeaman, Tom Briscoe; Kevin Sinfield (2g), Rangi Chase; James Graham, James Roby, Jamie Peacock (c), Jon Wilkin, Gareth Ellis, Ben Westwood. S: Gareth Widdop, Adrian Morley, Jamie Jones-Buchanan, Garreth Carvell.
Australia: Darius Boyd; Jharal Yow Yeh (1t), Chris Lawrence, Greg Inglis (1t), Akuila Uate; Darren Lockyer (c) (1t), Johnathan Thurston (1t, 5g); Paul Gallen, Cameron Smith, Matt Scott, Luke Lewis, Sam Thaiday (1t), David Shillington. S: Anthony Watmough, Cooper Cronk, Keith Galloway, Tony Williams.
Man of the Match: Johnathan Thurston

2012 Wales 12-80 England Autumn International Series
Glyndwr University Racecourse Stadium, Wrexham. Att: 4,014. 27 October 2012.
Wales: Craig Moss; Elliot Kear, Michael Channing, Christian Roets (1t), David James; Danny Jones, Matt Seamark (2g); Jordan James, Neil Budworth, Craig Kopczak (c), Rhodri Lloyd, Ben Evans, Ben Flower. S: Gil Dudson, Joe Burke, Daniel Fleming (1t), Steve Parry.
England: Zak Hardaker (2t); Josh Charnley (4t), Kallum Watkins (1t), Leroy Cudjoe (2t), Ryan Hall (2t); Kevin Sinfield (c) (12g), Richie Myler; Adrian Morley, Michael McIlorum, Chris Hill, Jamie Jones-Buchanan (1t), Gareth Ellis (1t), Sean O'Loughlin. S: Rob Burrow (1t), Gareth Hock, Carl Ablett, Lee Mossop.
Man of the Match: Kevin Sinfield

2012 England 44-6 France Autumn International Series
Craven Park, Hull. Att: 7,173. 3 November 2012.
England: Sam Tomkins (2t); Ryan Hall, Kallum Watkins (3t), Leroy Cudjoe, Tom Briscoe (2t); Kevin Sinfield (c) (1t, 6g), Richie Myler; Lee Mossop, Michael McIlorum, Chris Hill, Gareth Ellis, Gareth Hock, Jamie Jones-Buchanan. S: Rob Burrow, Adrian Morley, Carl Ablett, Ben Harrison.
France: Cyril Stacul; Damien Cardace, Mathias Pala, Vincent Duport, Clement Soubreyas; Thomas Bosc (1g), William Barthau; Olivier Elima (c), Kane Bentley (1t), Remi Casty, Kevin Larroyer, Jason Baitieri, Greg Mounis. S: Eloi Pelissier, Mathieu Griffi, Romaric Bemba, Michael Simon.
Man of the Match: Kallum Watkins

2012 England 48-4 France Autumn International Series Final
City of Salford Community Stadium, Salford. Att: 7,921. 11 November 2012.
England: Sam Tomkins (2t); Josh Charnley (1t), Kallum Watkins, Leroy Cudjoe, Ryan Hall (4t); Kevin Sinfield (c) (8g), Richie Myler; Lee Mossop, Michael McIlorum, Chris Hill, Jamie Jones-Buchanan, Gareth Ellis, Sean O'Loughlin. S: Rob Burrow (1t), Carl Ablett, Gareth Hock, Adrian Morley.
France: Clement Soubreyas; Teddy Sadaoui, Kevin Larroyer, Vincent Duport, Mathias Pala (1t); Thomas Bosc, William Barthau; Jamal Fakir, Kane Bentley, Remi Casty, Olivier Elima (c), Sébastien Raguin, Jason Baitieri. S: Romaric Bemba, Tony Gigot, Julian Bousquet, Mathieu Griffi.
Man of the Match: Ryan Hall

1.2.1 ENGLAND COACHES 1980-2012
1980-81: Johnny Whiteley
1984: Reg Parker (manager)
1992: Malcolm Reilly
1995: Ellery Hanley
1995-96: Phil Larder
2000: John Kear
2001: David Waite
2008-09: Tony Smith
2010-12: Steve McNamara

1.2.2 ENGLAND CAPTAINS 1980-2012
16 matches - Jamie Peacock
6 Andy Farrell
3 David Ward, Denis Betts, James Graham, Kevin Sinfield
2 George Fairbairn, Phil Clarke, Shaun Edwards
1 Steve Donlan, Daryl Powell, Martin Gleeson, Adrian Morley

1.2.3 ENGLISH MAN OF THE MATCH AWARDS 1980-2007
4 Sam Tomkins
3 Bobbie Goulding
2 Richie Myler, Kevin Sinfield
1 George Fairbairn, Ken Kelly, Henderson Gill, Andy Goodway, Richie Eyres, Daryl Powell, Andy Farrell, Nick Pinkney, Steve Prescott, Paul Rowley, Jamie Peacock, Stuart Fielden, Leon Pryce, Rob Purdham, Tony Clubb, Kallum Watkins, Ryan Hall

1.3 INTERNATIONAL FINALS NOT INVOLVING GREAT BRITAIN OR ENGLAND

1988 New Zealand 12-25 Australia World Cup Final
Eden Park, Auckland. Att: 47,363. 9 October 1988.
New Zealand: Gary Mercer; Tony Iro (1t), Kevin Iro (1t), Dean Bell (c), Mark Elia; Gary Freeman, Clayton Friend; Peter Brown (2g), Wayne Wallace, Adrian Shelford, Mark Graham, Kurt Sorensen, Mark Horo. S: Shane Cooper, Sam Stewart.
Australia: Garry Jack; Dale Shearer (1t), Andrew Farrar, Mark McGaw, Michael O'Connor (4g); Wally Lewis (c), Allan Langer (2t); Paul Dunn, Benny Elias (1dg), Steve Roach, Paul Sironen, Gavin Miller (1t), Wayne Pearce. S: Terry Lamb, David Gillespie.
Man of the Match: Allan Langer

1999 New Zealand 20-22 Australia Tri-Nations Final
Ericsson Stadium, Auckland. Att: 22,500. 5 November 1999.
New Zealand: Richie Barnett (c); Nigel Vagana (1t), Ruben Wiki, Willie Talau, Lesley Vainikolo; Henry Paul (6g), Robbie Paul (1t); Joe Vagana, Richard Swain, Craig Smith, Matt Rua, Stephen Kearney, Logan Swann. S: Gene Ngamu, Jason Lowrie, Nathan Cayless, David Kidwell.
Australia: Darren Lockyer; Mat Rogers (2t, 3g), Darren Smith, Matt Gidley, Wendell Sailor (1t); Matthew Johns (1t), Brett Kimmorley; Darren Britt, Craig Gower, Jason Stevens, Bryan Fletcher, Nik Kosef, Brad Fittler (c). S: Ryan Girdler, Shaun Timmins, Jason Smith, Michael Vella.
Man of the Match: Mat Rogers

2000 Australia 40-12 New Zealand World Cup Final
Old Trafford, Manchester. Att: 44,329. 25 November 2000.
Australia: Darren Lockyer (1t); Wendell Sailor (2t), Matt Gidley (1t), Adam MacDougall, Mat Rogers (6g); Brad Fittler (c) (1t), Brett Kimmorley; Shane Webcke, Andrew Johns, Robbie Kearns, Gorden Tallis, Bryan Fletcher, Scott Hill. S: Jason Stevens, Darren Britt, Nathan Hindmarsh (1t), Trent Barrett (1t).
New Zealand: Richie Barnett (c); Nigel Vagana, Tonie Carroll (1t), Willie Talau, Lesley Vainikolo (1t); Henry Paul (2g), Stacey Jones; Craig Smith, Richard Swain, Quentin Pongia, Matt Rua, Stephen Kearney, Ruben Wiki. S: Robbie Paul, Joe Vagana, Nathan Cayless, Logan Swann.
Man of the Match: Wendell Sailor

2005 New Zealand 24-0 Australia Tri-Nations Final
Elland Road, Leeds. Att: 26,534. 26 November 2005.
New Zealand: Brent Webb (1t); Jake Webster, Paul Whatuira (1t), Clinton Toopi, Manu Vatuvei (2t); Nigel Vagana, Stacey Jones (4g); Paul Rauhihi, Motu Tony, Ruben Wiki (c), David Kidwell, Louis Anderson, Shontayne Hape. S: David Faiumu, Roy Asotasi, David Solomona, Ali Lauitiiti.
Australia: Anthony Minichiello; Matt King, Mark Gasnier, Matt Cooper, Brent Tate; Trent Barrett, Craig Gower; Petero Civoniceva, Danny Buderus (c), Jason Ryles, Luke O'Donnell, Craig Fitzgibbon, Ben Kennedy. S: Craig Wing, Willie Mason, Mark O'Meley, Steve Price.
Man of the Match: Stacey Jones

2006 Australia 16-12 New Zealand Tri-Nations Final (aet)
Aussie Stadium, Sydney. Att: 27,325. 25 November 2006.
Australia: Karmichael Hunt; Brent Tate (1t), Mark Gasnier, Justin Hodges, Greg Inglis; Darren Lockyer (c) (1t), Johnathan Thurston (4g); Brent Kite, Cameron Smith, Petero Civoniceva, Nathan Hindmarsh, Andrew Ryan, Luke O'Donnell. S: Willie Mason, Mark O'Meley, Shaun Berrigan, Anthony Tupou.
New Zealand: Brent Webb; Shontayne Hape, Iosia Soliola (1t), Steve Matai, Manu Vatuvei; Nigel Vagana, Stacey Jones (2g); Ruben Wiki (c), Dene Halatau, Roy Asotasi, David Kidwell, Simon Mannering, David Fa'alogo. S: Motu Tony, Nathan Cayless, Adam Blair, Frank Pritchard (1t).
Man of the Match: Nathan Hindmarsh

2008 Australia 20-34 New Zealand World Cup Final
Suncorp Stadium, Brisbane. Att: 50,599. 15 November 2008.
Australia: Billy Slater; Joel Monaghan, Greg Inglis (1t), Israel Folau, David Williams (1t); Darren Lockyer (c) (2t), Johnathan Thurston (2g); Petero Civoniceva, Cameron Smith, Brent Kite, Glenn Stewart, Anthony Laffranchi, Paul Gallen. S: Karmichael Hunt, Craig Fitzgibbon, Anthony Tupou, Anthony Watmough.
New Zealand: Lance Hohaia (2t); Sam Perrett, Simon Mannering, Jerome Ropati (1t), Manu Vatuvei; Benji Marshall (1t, 2g), Nathan Fien; Nathan Cayless (c), Thomas Leuluai, Adam Blair (1t), David Fa'alogo, Bronson Harrison, Jeremy Smith (1t). S: Issac Luke (3g), Greg Eastwood, Sam Rapira, Sika Manu.
Man of the Match: Darren Lockyer

2010 Australia 12-16 New Zealand Four Nations Final
Suncorp Stadium, Brisbane. Att: 36,299. 13 November 2010.
Australia: Billy Slater (1t); Brett Morris, Brent Tate (1t), Willie Tonga, Lote Tuqiri; Darren Lockyer (c), Cooper Cronk; Matt Scott, Cameron Smith (2g), David Shillington, Luke Lewis, Sam Thaiday, Paul Gallen. S: Tom Learoyd-Lahrs, Greg Bird, Kurt Gidley, Nate Myles.
New Zealand: Lance Hohaia; Jason Nightingale (1t), Shaun Kenny-Dowall (1t), Simon Mannering, Sam Perrett; Benji Marshall (c) (2g), Nathan Fien (1t); Sam McKendry, Thomas Leuluai, Adam Blair, Bronson Harrison, Ben Matulino, Jeremy Smith. S: Greg Eastwood, Issac Luke, Frank-Paul Nuuausala, Sika Manu.
Man of the Match: Benji Marshall

1.4 THE WORLD CLUB CHALLENGE 1987-2013

The first official World Club Challenge, a game played between the Australian and English champions in order to crown the world's best team, was played in 1987. It was only played five times in ten years before an expanded competition was played in 1997 between the entire European and Australasian Super Leagues although that experiement was never been repeated largely due to the uncompetiveness of the European teams. From 2000, the World Club Challenge has been played in England on an annual basis at the start of the respective seasons.

1987 Wigan 8-2 Manly-Warringah
Central Park, Wigan. Att: 36,895. 7 October 1987.
Wigan: Steve Hampson; Richard Russell, David Stephenson (4g), Joe Lydon, Henderson Gill; Shaun Edwards, Andy Gregory; Brian Case, Nicky Kiss, Shaun Wane, Andy Goodway, Ian Potter, Ellery Hanley (c). S: Ged Byrne, Graeme West, Ian Gildart, Ian Lucas.
Manly: Dale Shearer; David Ronson, Darrell Williams, Michael O'Connor (1g), Stuart Davis; Cliff Lyons, Des Hasler; Phil Daley, Mal Cochrane, Ian Gately, Ron Gibbs, Owen Cunningham, Paul Vautin (c). S: Mark Brokenshire, Jeremy Ticehurst, Mark Pocock, Paul Shaw.
Man of the Match: Shaun Wane

1989 Widnes 30-18 Canberra Raiders
Old Trafford, Manchester. Att: 30,786. 4 October 1989.
Widnes: Alan Tait; Andy Currier, Jonathan Davies (1t, 3g), Darren Wright (1t), Martin Offiah (2t); Tony Myler, David Hulme; Joe Grima, Phil McKenzie, Derek Pyke, Kurt Sorensen (c), Paul Hulme (1t), Richard Eyres (1t). S: Barry Dowd, Paul Moriarty, Brimah Kebbie, David Smith.
Canberra: Gary Belcher; Matthew Wood (2g), Mal Meninga (c) (1t), Laurie Daley, John Ferguson; Chris O'Sullivan (1t, 1g), Ricky Stuart; Steve Jackson, Steve Walters (1t), Glenn Lazarus, Dean Lance, Gary Coyne, Bradley Clyde. S: Phil Carey, Paul Martin, Mark Lowry, Craig Bellamy.
Man of the Match: David Hulme

1991 Wigan 21-4 Penrith Panthers
Anfield, Liverpool. Att: 20,152. 2 October 1991.
Wigan: Steve Hampson; David Myers (1t), Sam Panapa (1t), Joe Lydon (1dg), Frano Botica (6g); Shaun Edwards, Andy Gregory (c); Kelvin Skerrett, Martin Dermott, Andy Platt, Denis Betts, Billy McGinty, Phil Clarke. S: Ian Lucas, Ian Gildart, Neil Cowie, Mike Forshaw.
Penrith: Greg Barwick; Darren Willis (1t), Graeme Bradley, Brad Izzard, Graham Mackay; Steve Carter, Greg Alexander (c); Brandon Lee, Royce Simmons, Paul Dunn, Paul Clarke, John Cartwright, Colin van der Voort. S: Ben Alexander, Grant Izzard, Tony Xuereb, Paul Smith.
Man of the Match: Frano Botica

1992 Wigan 8-22 Brisbane Broncos
Central Park, Wigan. Att: 17,746. 30 October 1992.
Wigan: Andre Stoop; Jason Robinson, Dean Bell (c), Andrew Farrar, Martin Offiah; Frano Botica (2g), Shaun Edwards (1t); Kelvin Skerrett, Martin Dermott, Andy Platt, Denis Betts, Billy McGinty, Phil Clarke. S: Sam Panapa, Ian Lucas, Martin Crompton, Neil Cowie.
Brisbane Broncos: Julian O'Neill (1t); Willie Carne, Steve Renouf, Chris Johns, Michael Hancock (2t); Kevin Walters, Allan Langer (c); Glenn Lazarus, Kerrod Walters (1t), Andrew Gee, Trevor Gillmeister, Mark Hohn, Terry Matterson (3g). S: John Plath, Tony Currie, Brett Plowman, Peter Ryan.
Man of the Match: Terry Matterson

1994 Brisbane Broncos 14-20 Wigan
ANZ Stadium, Brisbane. Att: 54,220. 1 June 1994.
Brisbane: Willie Carne; Wendell Sailor (1t), Steve Renouf, Chris Johns, Michael Hancock (1t); Kevin Walters, Allan Langer (c); Glenn Lazarus, Kerrod Walters, Andrew Gee, Mark Hohn, Alan Cann, Julian O'Neill (1t, 1g). S: John Plath, Peter Ryan, Brett Galea, Chris McKenna.
Wigan: Gary Connolly; Jason Robinson (1t), Sam Panapa, Barrie-Jon Mather (1t), Martin Offiah; Frano Botica (4g), Shaun Edwards (c); Neil Cowie, Martin Dermott, Billy McGinty, Denis Betts (1t), Andy Farrell, Phil Clarke. S: Va'aiga Tuigamala (dnp), Martin Hall, Paul Atcheson, Mick Cassidy.
Man of the Match: Shaun Edwards

1997 Brisbane Broncos 36-12 Hunter Mariners
Ericsson Stadium, Auckland. Att: 12,000. 17 October 1997.
Brisbane: Darren Lockyer; Michael de Vere (3g), Darren Smith (3t), Steve Renouf (1t), Wendell Sailor (1t); Kevin Walters (1t), Allan Langer (c); Shane Webcke, John Plath (1t), Andrew Gee, Brad Thorn, Gorden Tallis, Peter Ryan. S: Michael Hancock, Tonie Carroll, Phillip Lee, Ben Walker (1g).
Hunter: Robbie Ross; Nick Zisti (2t), Brad Godden, Kevin Iro, John Carlaw (1t); Scott Hill, Brett Kimmorley; Troy Stone, Robbie McCormack (c), Anthony Brann, Darrien Doherty, Paul Marquet, Tyran Smith. S: Tim Maddison, Tony Iro, Richard Swann, Keith Beauchamp.
Man of the Match: Darren Lockyer

2000 St Helens 6-44 Melbourne Storm
JJB Stadium, Wigan. Att: 13,394. 22 January 2000.
St Helens: Paul Atcheson; Chris Smith, Paul Newlove, Kevin Iro, Sean Hoppe (1t); Tommy Martyn, Sean Long (1g); Julian O'Neill, Paul Wellens, Sonny Nickle, Chris Joynt (c), Bryan Henare, Paul Sculthorpe. S: Apollo Perelini, Fereti Tuilagi, Tony Stewart, John Stankevitch.
Melbourne: Robbie Ross (2t); Brad Watts (5g), Aaron Moule (1t), Tony Martin, Marcus Bai (1t); Scott Hill (2t), Brett Kimmorley; Wayne Evans (1t), Richard Swain, Robbie Kearns, Paul Marquet, Stephen Kearney, Matt Rua. S: Danny Williams, Russell Bawden, Tasesa Lavea (1g), Dane Morgan (1t).
Man of the Match: Brett Kimmorley

2001 St Helens 20-18 Brisbane Broncos
Reebok Stadium, Bolton. Att: 16,041. 26 January 2001.
St Helens: Paul Wellens; Sean Hoppe, Kevin Iro, Paul Newlove, Anthony Sullivan; Tommy Martyn, Sean Long (1t, 3g, 1dg); David Fairleigh, Keiron Cunningham, Sonny Nickle, Chris Joynt (c) (1t), Peter Shiels, Paul Sculthorpe (1t, 1dg). S: Tim Jonkers, Vila Matautia, John Stankevitch, Tony Stewart.
Brisbane: Darren Lockyer; Wendell Sailor, Stuart Kelly, Michael De Vere (3g), Lote Tuqiri; Shaun Berrigan (1t), Scott Prince; Shane Webcke, Luke Priddis, Petero Civoniceva, Gorden Tallis (c), Dane Carlaw, Phillip Lee (1t). S: Chris Walker (dnp), Shane Walker, Ashley Harrison, Brad Meyers (1t).
Man of the Match: Sean Long

2002 Bradford Bulls 41-26 Newcastle Knights
McAlpine Stadium, Huddersfield. Att: 21,113. 1 February 2002.
Bradford: Michael Withers (2t); Tevita Vaikona, Scott Naylor, Lee Gilmour, Lesley Vainikolo (1t); Robbie Paul (c) (2t), Paul Deacon (8g, 1dg); Joe Vagana, James Lowes, Brian McDermott, Jamie Peacock, Daniel Gartner (1t), Mike Forshaw. S: Stuart Fielden, Paul Anderson, Leon Pryce, Brandon Costin.
Newcastle: Robbie O'Davis; Josh Smith (1t), Matthew Gidley (1t), Mark Hughes, Kurt Gidley; Sean Rudder, Andrew Johns (c) (2t, 3g); Josh Perry, Danny Buderus (1t), Matt Parsons, Daniel Abraham, Steve Simpson, Bill Peden. S: Matt Jobson, Clinton O'Brien, John Morris, Clint Newton.
Man of the Match: Robbie Paul

2003 St Helens 0-38 Sydney Roosters
Reebok Stadium, Bolton. Att: 19,807. 14 February 2003.
St Helens: Darren Albert; Ade Gardner, Martin Gleeson, Paul Newlove, Anthony Stewart; Tommy Martyn, Sean Long; Darren Britt, Jason Hooper, John Stankevitch, Chris Joynt (c), Darren Smith, Paul Sculthorpe. S: Barry Ward, Tim Jonkers, Mick Higham, Mark Edmondson.
Roosters: Anthony Minichiello; Todd Byrne (1t), Justin Hodges, Chris Flannery, Shannon Hegarty; Brad Fittler (c) (1t), Craig Wing; Jason Cayless, Michael Crocker, Peter Cusack, Adrian Morley (1t), Craig Fitzgibbon (1t, 9g), Luke Ricketson. S: Ned Catic, Todd Payten (1t), Chad Robinson, Brett Finch.
Man of the Match: Craig Fitzgibbon

2004 Bradford Bulls 22-4 Penrith Panthers
McAlpine Stadium, Huddersfield. Att: 18,962. 13 February 2004.
Bradford: Michael Withers (3g); Tevita Vaikona, Paul Johnson, Shontayne Hape, Lesley Vainikolo (1t); Leon Pryce (1t), Karl Pratt; Paul Anderson, Aaron Smith, Stuart Fielden, Lee Radford, Jamie Peacock (c), Logan Swann (1t). S: Joe Vagana, Rob Parker (1t), Jamie Langley, Stuart Reardon.
Penrith: Rhys Wesser; Brett Howland, Luke Lewis, Paul Whatuira, Luke Rooney; Preston Campbell, Craig Gower (c); Joel Clinton, Luke Priddis (1t), Martin Lang, Joe Galuvao, Tony Puletua, Trent Waterhouse. S: Ben Ross, Shane Rodney, Colin Ward, Luke Swain.
Man of the Match: Michael Withers

2005 Leeds Rhinos 39 Canterbury Bulldogs 32

Elland Road, Leeds. Att: 37,028. 4 February 2005.
Leeds: Richard Mathers (1t); Mark Calderwood (1t), Chev Walker (1t), Keith Senior, Marcus Bai; Kevin Sinfield (c) (5g, 1dg), Danny McGuire (1t); Ryan Bailey, Andrew Dunemann, Danny Ward, Jamie Jones-Buchanan (1t), Chris McKenna, Gareth Ellis. S: Barrie McDermott, Ali Lauitiiti, Rob Burrow (1t), Willie Poching (1t).
Canterbury: Luke Patten (1t); Hazem El Mazri (2t, 4g), Jamahl Lolesi (2t), Willie Tonga, Trent Cutler; Braith Anasta, Corey Hughes; Chris Armit, Adam Perry, Roy Asotasi, Reni Maitua, Sonny Bill Williams, Tony Grimaldi (c) (1t). S: Ben Czislowski, Adam Brideson, Nate Myles, Brett Oliver.
Man of the Match: Sonny Bill Williams

2006 Bradford Bulls 30-10 Wests Tigers

Galpharm Stadium, Huddersfield. Att: 19,207. 4 February 2006.
Bradford: Michael Withers; Marcus Bai (2t), Ben Harris, Shontayne Hape, Lesley Vainikolo; Karl Pryce, Iestyn Harris (c) (5g); Stuart Fielden (2t), Ian Henderson, Andy Lynch, Brad Meyers, Paul Johnson, Jamie Langley. S: Stanley Gene (1t), Joe Vagana, Matt Cook, Brett Ferres.
Wests: Brett Hodgson (1t, 1g); Shannon McDonnell, Dean Collis, Paul Whatuira, Jamahl Lolesi; Daniel Fitzhenry (1t), Scott Prince (c); Ryan O'Hara, Robbie Farah, John Skandalis, Anthony Laffranchi, Chris Heighington, Ben Galea. S: Liam Fulton, Bronson Harrison, Sam Harris, Bryce Gibbs.
Man of the Match: Stuart Fielden

2007 St Helens 18-14 Brisbane Broncos

Reebok Stadium, Bolton. Att: 23,247. 23 February 2007.
St Helens: Paul Wellens; Ade Gardner (2t), Matt Gidley, Willie Talau, Francis Meli; Leon Pryce, Sean Long (c); Nick Fozzard, James Roby, Jason Cayless, Lee Gilmour, Mike Bennett, Jon Wilkin. S: Paul Sculthorpe (1t, 3g), James Graham, Bryn Hargreaves, Keiron Cunningham.
Brisbane: Karmichael Hunt; Steve Michaels, Justin Hodges, Brent Tate, Darius Boyd (1t); Darren Lockyer (c), Shane Perry; Dane Carlaw, Shaun Berrigan, Petero Civoniceva, Corey Parker (1t, 3g), Brad Thorn, Tonie Carroll. S: Sam Thaiday, Greg Eastwood, Ben Hannant, Michael Ennis.
Man of the Match: Paul Sculthorpe

2008 Leeds Rhinos 11-4 Melbourne Storm

Elland Road, Leeds. Att: 33,204. 29 February 2008.
Leeds: Brent Webb; Scott Donald (1t); Clinton Toopi, Keith Senior, Lee Smith; Danny McGuire, Rob Burrow; Kylie Leuluai, Matt Diskin, Jamie Peacock, Jamie Jones-Buchanan, Gareth Ellis, Kevin Sinfield (c) (3g, 1dg). Subs: Ali Lauitiiti, Ryan Bailey, Nick Scruton, Carl Ablett.
Melbourne: Billy Slater; Steve Turner, Will Chambers, Israel Folau, Anthony Quinn; Matt Geyer, Cooper Cronk (c); Jeff Lima, Cameron Smith, Brett White, Antonio Kaufusi, Ryan Hoffman (1t), Dallas Johnson. S: Russell Aitken, Adam Blair, Sika Manu, Sam Tagataese.
Man of the Match: Kevin Sinfield

2009 Leeds Rhinos 20-28 Manly Sea Eagles

Elland Road, Leeds. Att: 32,569. 1 March 2009.
Leeds: Lee Smith; Scott Donald, Carl Ablett, Keith Senior (1t), Ryan Hall (1t); Danny McGuire (1t), Rob Burrow; Kylie Leuluai, Matt Diskin, Jamie Peacock, Jamie Jones-Buchanan (1t), Ian Kirke, Kevin Sinfield (c) (2g). S: Ali Lauitiiti, Ryan Bailey, Luke Burgess, Kallum Watkins.
Manly: Brett Stewart (2t); Michael Robertson, Jamie Lyon, Steve Matai (1t), David Williams; Chris Bailey, Matt Orford (c) (4g); Jason King, Matt Ballin, Josh Perry, Anthony Watmough (2t), Glenn Hall, Glenn Stewart. S: Heath l'Estrange, Adam Cuthbertson, George Rose, Shane Rodney.
Man of the Match: Anthony Watmough

2010 Leeds 10-18 Melbourne Storm
Elland Road, Leeds. Att: 27,697. 28 February 2010.
Leeds: Brent Webb; Kallum Watkins, Brett Delaney, Keith Senior, Ryan Hall; Danny McGuire (1t), Rob Burrow (2g); Kylie Leuluai, Matt Diskin, Jamie Peacock, Jamie Jones-Buchanan, Ian Kirke, Kevin Sinfield (c) (1g). S: Danny Buderus, Ali Lauitiiti, Greg Eastwood, Ryan Bailey.
Melbourne: Billy Slater; Luke MacDougall (1t), Dane Nielsen, Greg Inglis, Anthony Quinn (1t); Brett Finch, Cameron Smith (c) (5g); Aiden Tolman, Ryan Hinchcliffe, Jeff Lima, Adam Blair, Ryan Hoffman, Todd Lowrie. S: Rory Kostjasyn, Kevin Proctor, Hap Cahill, Jesse Bromwich.
Man of the Match: Cameron Smith

2011 Wigan Warriors 15-21 St George-Illawarra Dragons
JJB Stadium, Wigan. Att: 24,268. 27 February 2011.
Wigan: Sam Tomkins (1dg); Darrell Goulding, Martin Gleeson, George Carmont (2t), Amos Roberts; Paul Deacon (3g), Thomas Leuluai; Paul Prescott, Michael McIlorum, Andy Coley, Harrison Hansen, Ryan Hoffman, Sean O'Loughlin (c). S: Joel Tomkins, Chris Tuson, Lee Mossop, Liam Farrell.
St George-Illawarra: Darius Boyd; Brett Morris (2t), Mark Gasnier, Matt Cooper (1t), Jason Nightingale; Jamie Soward (2g, 1dg), Ben Hornby (c); Dan Hunt, Nathan Fien, Michael Weyman, Beau Scott, Ben Creagh, Matt Prior. S: Michael Greenfield, Trent Merrin, Jon Green, Cameron King (1t).
Man of the Match: Brett Morris

2012 Leeds Rhinos 26-12 Manly Sea Eagles
Headingley, Leeds. Att: 21,062. 17 February 2012.
Leeds: Brent Webb; Ben Jones-Bishop (1t), Kallum Watkins (1t), Zak Hardaker, Ryan Hall (2t); Kevin Sinfield (c) (3g), Danny McGuire; Kylie Leuluai, Rob Burrow, Jamie Peacock, Jamie Jones-Buchanan, Brett Delaney, Carl Ablett (1t). S: Ryan Bailey, Darrell Griffin, Paul McShane, Chris Clarkson.
Manly: Brett Stewart (1t); David Williams, Jamie Lyon (2g), Steve Matai, Michael Oldfield; Kieran Foran, Daly Cherry-Evans (1t); Jason King (c), Matt Ballin, Brent Kite, Anthony Watmough, Tony Williams, Glenn Stewart. S: Jamie Buhrer, Vic Mauro, Darcy Lussick, George Rose.
Man of the Match: Jamie Peacock

2013 Leeds Rhinos 14-18 Melbourne Storm
Headingley, Leeds. Att: 20,400. 22 February 2013.
Leeds: Kallum Watkins; Joe Vickery, Carl Ablett, Joel Moon, Ryan Hall (1t); Kevin Sinfield (c) (3g), Danny McGuire; Kylie Leuluai, Rob Burrow, Jamie Peacock, Stevie Ward, Brett Delaney, Jamie Jones-Buchanan (1t). S: Ian Kirke, Paul McShane, Chris Clarkson, Mitch Achurch.
Melbourne: Billy Slater (1t); Sisa Waqa, Will Chambers, Justin O'Neill, Mahe Fonua; Gareth Widdop, Cooper Cronk; Jesse Bromwich (1t), Cameron Smith (c) (3g), Bryan Norrie, Tohu Harris (1t), Ryan Hoffman, Ryan Hinchcliffe. S: Siosaia Vave, Jason Ryles, Junior Moors, Lagi Setu.
Man of the Match: Cooper Cronk

2 DOMESTIC RUGBY LEAGUE - BRITISH
2.1 CHALLENGE CUP FINALS 1980 - 2012

Challenge Cup Finals were played at Wembley between 1929 and 1999, when the stadium was rebuilt. Between 2000 and 2006 the finals was played at Murrayfield, the Millennium Stadium or Twickenham before returning to Wembley in 2007. The man-of-the-match award is called the Lance Todd Trophy, named after the great New Zealander who played for Wigan and Dewsbury in the early part of the 20th century. In 1982, the award was made to Eddie Cunningham after the drawn game between Widnes and Hull. David Topliss, the man of the match in the replay, is not recognised as a Lance Todd Trophy winner.

1979-80 Hull Kingston Rovers 10-5 Hull
Wembley Stadium, London. Att: 95,000. 3 May 1980.
Hull KR: David Hall; Steve Hubbard (1t, 3g), Mike Smith, Steve Hartley, Clive Sullivan; Roger Millward (c) (1dg), Allan Agar; Roy Holdstock, David Watkinson, Brian Lockwood, Phil Lowe, Paul Rose, Len Casey. S: Phil Hogan, John Millington.
Hull: Paul Woods; Graham Bray, Graham Walters, Tim Wilby (1t), Paul Prendiville; John Newlove, Clive Pickerill; Keith Tindall, Ron Wileman, Charlie Stone, Charlie Birdsall, Sammy Lloyd (1g), Steve Norton (c). S: Brian Hancock, Vince Farrar.
Lance Todd Trophy: Brian Lockwood

1980-81 Widnes 18-9 Hull Kingston Rovers
Wembley Stadium, London. Att: 92,496. 2 May 1981.
Widnes: Mick Burke (1t, 4g); Stuart Wright, Mick George (1t), Eddie Cunningham, Keith Bentley; Eric Hughes, Andy Gregory (1t); Mike O'Neill, Keith Elwell, Brian Lockwood, Les Gorley, Eric Prescott, Mick Adams (c) (1dg). S: John Myler, Glyn Shaw.
Hull KR: David Hall; Steve Hubbard (3g), Mike Smith, Phil Hogan, Peter Muscroft; Steve Hartley, Paul Harkin; Roy Holdstock, David Watkinson, Steve Crooks, Phil Lowe, Chris Burton (1t), Len Casey (c). S: Paul Proctor, John Millington.
Lance Todd Trophy: Mick Burke

1981-82 Hull 14-14 Widnes
Wembley Stadium, London. Att: 92,147. 1 May 1982.
Hull: Gary Kemble; Dane O'Hara (1t), Terry Day, Steve Evans, Paul Prendiville; David Topliss (c), Kevin Harkin; Trevor Skerrett, Ron Wileman, Charlie Stone, Mick Crane, Sammy Lloyd (4g), Steve Norton (1t). S: James Leuluai (dnp), Lee Crooks.
Widnes: Mick Burke (1g); Stuart Wright (1t), Keiron O'Loughlin, Eddie Cunningham (2t), John Basnett; Eric Hughes, Andy Gregory (1g); Mike O'Neill, Keith Elwell (1dg), Brian Lockwood, Les Gorley, Eric Prescott, Mick Adams (c). S: Tony Myler, Steve O'Neill.
Lance Todd Trophy: Eddie Cunningham

Replay: Hull 18-9 Widnes
Elland Road, Leeds. Att: 41,171. 19 May 1982.
Hull: Gary Kemble (1t); Clive Sullivan, James Leuluai, Steve Evans, Paul Prendiville; David Topliss (c) (2t), Tony Dean; Keith Tindall, Tony Duke, Charlie Stone, Trevor Skerrett, Lee Crooks (1t, 3g), Steve Norton. S: Terry Day (dnp), Mick Crane.
Widnes: Mick Burke (3g); Stuart Wright (1t), Keiron O'Loughlin, Eddie Cunningham, John Basnett; Eric Hughes, Andy Gregory; Mike O'Neill, Keith Elwell, Brian Lockwood, Les Gorley, Eric Prescott, Mick Adams (c). S: Tony Myler (dnp), Fred Whitfield (dnp).
Man of the Match: David Topliss

1982-83 Featherstone Rovers 14-12 Hull
Wembley Stadium, London. Att: 84,969. 7 May 1983.
Featherstone: Nigel Barker; John Marsden, Steve Quinn (4g), John Gilbert, Ken Kellett; Alan Banks, Terry Hudson (c); Mick Gibbins, Ray Handscombe, Steve Hankins, David Hobbs (2t), Tim Slatter, Peter Smith. S: Paul Lyman, Gary Siddall.
Hull: Gary Kemble; Dane O'Hara, Steve Evans, James Leuluai (1t), Paul Prendiville; David Topliss (c), Kevin Harkin; Trevor Skerrett, John Bridges, Charlie Stone, Paul Rose, Lee Crooks (1t, 3g), Steve Norton. S: Terry Day, Mick Crane.
Lance Todd Trophy: David Hobbs

1983-84 Widnes 19-6 Wigan
Wembley Stadium, London. Att: 80,116. 5 May 1984.
Widnes: Mick Burke (3g); Stuart Wright, Eric Hughes, Joe Lydon (2t), John Basnett; Keiron O'Loughlin (1t), Andy Gregory; Steve O'Neill (1dg), Keith Elwell, Kevin Tamati, Les Gorley, Mike O'Neill, Mick Adams (c). S: David Hulme, Fred Whitfield.
Wigan: Shaun Edwards; Dennis Ramsdale, David Stephenson, Colin Whitfield (1g), Henderson

Gill; Mark Cannon, Gary Stephens; Kerry Hemsley (1t), Howie Tamati, Brian Case, Graeme West (c), Mick Scott, John Pendlebury. S: Wayne Elvin, Brian Juliff.
Lance Todd Trophy: Joe Lydon

1984-85 Wigan 28-24 Hull
Wembley Stadium, London. Att: 97,801. 4 May 1985.
Wigan: Shaun Edwards (1t); John Ferguson (2t), David Stephenson (1g), Steve Donlan, Henderson Gill (1t, 3g); Brett Kenny (1t), Mike Ford; Neil Courteney, Nicky Kiss, Brian Case, Graeme West (c), Brian Dunn, Ian Potter. S: Nick du Toit, Danny Campbell.
Hull: Gary Kemble; Kevin James (1t), Steve Evans (1t), James Leuluai (2t), Dane O'Hara; Fred Ah Kuoi, Peter Sterling; Lee Crooks (c) (2g), Shaun Patrick, Neil Puckering, John Muggleton, Paul Rose, Steve Norton. S: Garry Schofield, Gary Divorty (1t).
Lance Todd Trophy: Brett Kenny

1985-86 Castleford 15-14 Hull Kingston Rovers
Wembley Stadium, London. Att: 82,134. 3 May 1986.
Castleford: Gary Lord; David Plange, Tony Marchant (1t), Gary Hyde, Jamie Sandy (1t); John Joyner (c), Bob Beardmore (1t, 1dg); Kevin Ward, Kevin Beardmore, Barry Johnson, Keith England, Martin Ketteridge (1g), Ian French. S: David Roockley, Stuart Horton.
Hull KR: George Fairbairn; Garry Clark, Mike Smith, Gary Prohm (2t), David Laws; John Dorahy (1g), Paul Harkin; Peter Johnston, David Watkinson (c), Asuquo Ema, Andy Kelly, Des Harrison, Gavin Miller. S: Gordon Smith, John Lydiat (1t).
Lance Todd Trophy: Bob Beardmore

1986-87 Halifax 19-18 St Helens
Wembley Stadium, London. Att: 91,267. 2 May 1987.
Halifax: Graham Eadie (1t); Scott Wilson, Colin Whitfield (3g), Grant Rix, Wilf George (1t); Chris Anderson (c), Gary Stephens; Graham Beevers, Seamus McCallion (1t), Keith Neller, Paul Dixon, Mick Scott, John Pendlebury (1dg). S: Neil James, Brian Juliff.
St Helens: Phil Veivers; Barrie Ledger, Paul Loughlin (1t, 3g), Mark Elia (1t), Kevin McCormack; Brett Clark, Neil Holding; Tony Burke, Graham Liptrot, John Fieldhouse, Andy Platt, Roy Haggerty, Chris Arkwright (c). S: Paul Round (1t), Paul Forber.
Lance Todd Trophy: Graham Eadie

1987-88 Wigan 32-12 Halifax
Wembley Stadium, London. Att: 94,273. 30 April 1988.
Wigan: Joe Lydon (1t, 1g); Tony Iro (1t), Kevin Iro (2t), Dean Bell (1t), Henderson Gill (1t); Shaun Edwards (c), Andy Gregory (1g); Brian Case, Nicky Kiss, Adrian Shelford, Andy Goodway, Ian Potter, Ellery Hanley (1t). S: Ged Byrne, Shaun Wane.
Halifax: Graham Eadie (c); Martin Meredith, Tony Anderson (1t), Ian Wilkinson, Colin Whitfield (2g); Bob Grogan, Steve Robinson; Neil James (1t), Seamus McCallion, Keith Neller, Les Holliday, Paul Dixon, John Pendlebury. S: Dick Fairbank, Mick Scott.
Lance Todd Trophy: Andy Gregory

1988-89 Wigan 27-0 St Helens
Wembley Stadium, London. Att: 78,000. 29 April 1989.
Wigan: Steve Hampson (1t); Tony Iro, Kevin Iro (2t), Dean Bell, Joe Lydon (3g); Shaun Edwards, Andy Gregory (1t, 1dg); Ian Lucas, Nicky Kiss, Adrian Shelford, Andy Platt, Ian Potter, Ellery Hanley (1t). S: Denis Betts, Andy Goodway.
St Helens: Gary Connolly; Michael O'Connor, Phil Veivers, Paul Loughlin, Les Quirk; Shane Cooper, Neil Holding; Tony Burke, Paul Groves, Paul Forber, Bernard Dwyer, Roy Haggerty, Paul Vautin (c). S: Darren Bloor, Stuart Evans.
Lance Todd Trophy: Ellery Hanley

1989-90 Wigan 36-14 Warrington

Wembley Stadium, London. Att: 77,729. 28 April 1990.
Wigan: Steve Hampson; Joe Lydon (6g), Kevin Iro (2t), Dean Bell, Mark Preston (2t); Shaun Edwards, Andy Gregory; Adrian Shelford, Martin Dermott, Andy Platt, Denis Betts (1t), Andy Goodway, Ellery Hanley (c) (1t). S: Bobbie Goulding, Ian Gildart.
Warrington: David Lyon (1t); Des Drummond, Gary Mercer, Paul Darbyshire (1g), Mark Forster; Martin Crompton, Paul Bishop (2g); Tony Burke, Duane Mann, Neil Harmon, Bob Jackson, Gary Sanderson, Mike Gregory (c) (1t). S: Billy McGinty, Mark Thomas.
Lance Todd Trophy: Andy Gregory

1990-91 Wigan 13-8 St Helens

Wembley Stadium, London. Att: 75,532. 27 April 1991.
Wigan: Steve Hampson; David Myers (1t), Kevin Iro, Dean Bell, Frano Botica (1t, 2g); Shaun Edwards, Andy Gregory (1dg); Ian Lucas, Martin Dermott, Andy Platt, Denis Betts, Phil Clarke, Ellery Hanley (c). S: Bobbie Goulding, Andy Goodway.
St Helens: Phil Veivers; Alan Hunte (1t), Tea Ropati, Paul Loughlin, Les Quirk; Jonathan Griffiths, Paul Bishop (2g); Jonathan Neill, Bernard Dwyer, Kevin Ward, John Harrison, George Mann, Shane Cooper (c). S: Gary Connolly, Paul Groves.
Lance Todd Trophy: Denis Betts

1991-92 Wigan 28-12 Castleford

Wembley Stadium, London. Att: 77,286. 2 May 1992.
Wigan: Joe Lydon (2dg); Frano Botica (5g), Dean Bell (c), Gene Miles, Martin Offiah (2t); Shaun Edwards (1t), Andy Gregory; Kelvin Skerrett, Martin Dermott, Andy Platt, Denis Betts, Billy McGinty, Phil Clarke. S: Steve Hampson (1t), Neil Cowie.
Castleford: Graham Steadman; Jon Wray, St John Ellis, Richie Blackmore (1t), David Nelson; Grant Anderson, Mike Ford; Lee Crooks (c), Graham Southernwood, Keith England (1t), Graeme Bradley, Martin Ketteridge (2g), Tawera Nikau. S: Tony Smith, Dean Sampson.
Lance Todd Trophy: Martin Offiah

1992-93 Wigan 20-14 Widnes

Wembley Stadium, London. Att: 77,684. 1 May 1993.
Wigan: Steve Hampson; Jason Robinson, Joe Lydon, Andrew Farrar, Martin Offiah; Frano Botica (4g), Shaun Edwards; Kelvin Skerrett (1t), Martin Dermott, Andy Platt, Denis Betts, Phil Clarke, Dean Bell (c) (1t). S: Sam Panapa (1t), Andy Farrell.
Widnes: Stuart Spruce; John Devereux, Andy Currier, Darren Wright, David Myers; Jonathan Davies (3g), Bobbie Goulding; Kurt Sorensen (1t), Paul Hulme (c), Harvey Howard, Richie Eyres (1t), Esene Faimalo, David Hulme. S: Steve McCurrie, Julian O'Neill.
Lance Todd Trophy: Dean Bell

1993-94 Wigan 26-16 Leeds

Wembley Stadium, London. Att: 78,348. 30 April 1994.
Wigan: Gary Connolly; Va'aiga Tuigamala, Dean Bell (c), Barrie-Jon Mather, Martin Offiah (2t); Frano Botica (5g), Shaun Edwards; Kelvin Skerrett, Martin Dermott, Andy Platt, Denis Betts, Andy Farrell (1t), Phil Clarke. S: Sam Panapa (1t), Mick Cassidy.
Leeds: Alan Tait; Jim Fallon (1t), Kevin Iro, Craig Innes, Francis Cummins (1t); Graham Holroyd (2g), Garry Schofield (1t); Neil Harmon, James Lowes, Harvey Howard, Gary Mercer, Richie Eyres, Ellery Hanley (c). S: Marcus Vassilakopoulos, Mike O'Neill.
Lance Todd Trophy: Martin Offiah

1994-95 Wigan 30-10 Leeds

Wembley Stadium, London. Att: 78,550. 29 April 1995.
Wigan: Henry Paul (1t); Jason Robinson (2t), Va'aiga Tuigamala (1t), Gary Connolly, Martin Offiah; Frano Botica (5g), Shaun Edwards (c); Kelvin Skerrett, Martin Hall (1t), Neil Cowie, Denis Betts, Mick Cassidy, Phil Clarke. S: Paul Atcheson, Andy Farrell.
Leeds: Alan Tait; Jim Fallon, Kevin Iro, Craig Innes, Francis Cummins; Garry Schofield, Graham

Holroyd (3g); Harvey Howard, James Lowes (1t), Esene Faimalo, Gary Mercer, Richie Eyres, Ellery Hanley (c). S: George Mann, Neil Harmon.
Lance Todd Trophy: Jason Robinson

1996 St Helens 40-32 Bradford Bulls
Wembley Stadium, London. Att: 75,994. 27 April 1996.
St Helens: Steve Prescott (2t); Danny Arnold (2t), Scott Gibbs, Paul Newlove, Anthony Sullivan; Karle Hammond, Bobbie Goulding (c) (4g); Apollo Perelini (1t), Keiron Cunningham (1t), Andy Leathem, Chris Joynt, Simon Booth (1t), Chris Morley. S: Tommy Martyn, Ian Pickavance (1t), Vila Matautia, Alan Hunte.
Bradford: Nathan Graham; Paul Cook (6g), Matt Calland, Paul Loughlin, Jon Scales (1t); Graeme Bradley, Robbie Paul (c) (3t); Brian McDermott, Bernard Dwyer (1t), Jon Hamer, Jeremy Donougher, Sonny Nickle, Simon Knox. S: Karl Fairbank, Paul Medley, Jason Donohue, Carlos Hassan.
Lance Todd Trophy: Robbie Paul

1997 St Helens 32-22 Bradford Bulls
Wembley Stadium, London. Att: 78,022. 3 May 1997.
St Helens: Steve Prescott; Danny Arnold, Andy Haigh, Paul Newlove, Anthony Sullivan (1t); Tommy Martyn (2t), Bobbie Goulding (c) (6g); Apollo Perelini, Keiron Cunningham, Julian O'Neill, Chris Joynt (1t), Derek McVey, Karle Hammond (1t). S: Ian Pickavance, Vila Matautia, Andy Northey, Chris Morley.
Bradford: Stuart Spruce; Abi Ekoku, Danny Peacock (1t), Paul Loughlin (1t), Paul Cook; Graeme Bradley, Robbie Paul (c); Brian McDermott, James Lowes (1t), Tahi Reihana, Sonny Nickle, Bernard Dwyer, Steve McNamara (3g). S: Paul Medley, Matt Calland, Glen Tomlinson (1t), Simon Knox.
Lance Todd Trophy: Tommy Martyn

1998 Sheffield Eagles 17-8 Wigan Warriors
Wembley Stadium, London. Att: 60,669. 2 May 1998.
Sheffield: Waisale Sovatabua; Nick Pinkney (1t), Whetu Taewa, Keith Senior, Matt Crowther (1t); Dave Watson, Mark Aston (2g, 1dg); Paul Broadbent (c), Johnny Lawless, Dale Laughton, Paul Carr, Darren Shaw, Rod Doyle. S: Michael Jackson, Darren Turner (1t), Martin Wood, Lynton Stott (dnp).
Wigan: Kris Radlinski; Jason Robinson, Danny Moore, Gary Connolly, Mark Bell (1t); Henry Paul, Tony Smith; Stephen Holgate, Robbie McCormack, Tony Mestrov, Denis Betts, Simon Haughton, Andy Farrell (c) (2g). S: Lee Gilmour, Neil Cowie, Mick Cassidy, Terry O'Connor.
Lance Todd Trophy: Mark Aston

1999 Leeds Rhinos 52-16 London Broncos
Wembley Stadium, London. Att: 73,242. 1 May 1999.
Leeds: Iestyn Harris (c) (1t, 8g); Leroy Rivett (4t), Richie Blackmore, Brad Godden (1t), Francis Cummins (1t); Daryl Powell, Ryan Sheridan; Barrie McDermott (1t), Terry Newton, Darren Fleary, Adrian Morley, Anthony Farrell, Marc Glanville. S: Jamie Mathiou, Marcus St Hilaire (1t), Lee Jackson, Andy Hay.
London: Tulsen Tollett; Rob Smyth (2g), Greg Fleming (1t), John Timu, Martin Offiah (1t); Karle Hammond, Shaun Edwards (c); Steele Retchless, Robbie Beazley, Matt Salter, Shane Millard, Robbie Simpson (1t), Peter Gill. S: Matt Toshack, Dean Callaway, Chris Ryan, Glen Air.
Lance Todd Trophy: Leroy Rivett

2000 Bradford Bulls 24-18 Leeds Rhinos
Murrayfield Stadium, Edinburgh. Att: 67,247. 29 April 2000.
Bradford: Stuart Spruce; Nathan McAvoy (1t), Scott Naylor, Michael Withers (2t), Tevita Vaikona; Henry Paul (4g), Robbie Paul (c); Brian McDermott, James Lowes, Paul Anderson, Jamie Peacock, Mike Forshaw, Brad Mackay. S: Stuart Fielden (1t), David Boyle, Leon Pryce, Bernard Dwyer.

Leeds: Iestyn Harris (c) (5g); Leroy Rivett, Richie Blackmore, Keith Senior, Francis Cummins; Daryl Powell, Ryan Sheridan; Darren Fleary, Dean Lawford, Barrie McDermott, Adrian Morley, Anthony Farrell, Andy Hay (1t). S: Jamie Mathiou, Lee Jackson, David Barnhill, Marcus St Hilaire (1t).
Lance Todd Trophy: Henry Paul

2001 St Helens 13-6 Bradford Bulls
Twickenham Stadium, London. Att: 68,250. 28 April 2001.
St Helens: Paul Wellens; Sean Hoppe, Kevin Iro, Paul Newlove, Anthony Sullivan; Tommy Martyn (1t, 1dg), Sean Long (2g); Sonny Nickle, Keiron Cunningham (1t), David Fairleigh, Chris Joynt (c), Peter Shiels, Paul Sculthorpe. S: Vila Matautia, Steve Hall, Tim Jonkers, Anthony Stewart (dnp).
Bradford: Michael Withers; Tevita Vaikona, Scott Naylor, Shane Rigon, Leon Pryce; Henry Paul (3g), Robbie Paul (c); Joe Vagana, James Lowes, Brian McDermott, Jamie Peacock, Daniel Gartner, Mike Forshaw. S: Paul Anderson, Stuart Fielden, Lee Gilmour, Paul Deacon.
Lance Todd Trophy: Sean Long

2002 Wigan Warriors 21-12 St Helens
Murrayfield Stadium, Edinburgh. Att: 62,140. 27 April 2002.
Wigan: Kris Radlinski; Brett Dallas (1t), Gary Connolly (1t), Jamie Ainscough, Paul Johnson; Julian O'Neill, Adrian Lam (1t, 1dg); Terry O'Connor, Terry Newton, Craig Smith, Mick Cassidy, David Furner, Andy Farrell (c) (4g). S: Ricky Bibey, David Hodgson, Mark Smith, Brian Carney.
St Helens: Paul Wellens; Darren Albert (1t), Martin Gleeson (1t), Paul Newlove, Anthony Stewart; Tommy Martyn, Sean Long; Darren Britt, Keiron Cunningham, Peter Shiels, Chris Joynt (c), Tim Jonkers, Paul Sculthorpe (1t). S: Barry Ward, John Stankevitch, Sean Hoppe, Mickey Higham.
Lance Todd Trophy: Kris Radlinski

2003 Bradford Bulls 22-20 Leeds Rhinos
Millennium Stadium, Cardiff. Att: 71,212. 26 April 2003.
Bradford: Robbie Paul (c) (1t); Tevita Vaikona, Scott Naylor, Shontayne Hape, Lesley Vainikolo (1t); Leon Pryce, Paul Deacon (5g); Joe Vagana, James Lowes, Daniel Gartner, Lee Radford, Jamie Peacock (1t), Mike Forshaw. S: Paul Anderson, Lee Gilmour, Rob Parker, Karl Pratt.
Leeds: Gary Connolly (1t); Mark Calderwood, Chris McKenna (1t), Keith Senior, Francis Cummins; Kevin Sinfield (c) (4g), Andrew Dunemann; Ryan Bailey, Matt Diskin, Barrie McDermott, Chev Walker, Matt Adamson, David Furner (1t). S: Danny Ward, Wayne McDonald, Rob Burrow, Willie Poching.
Lance Todd Trophy: Gary Connolly

2004 St Helens 32-16 Wigan Warriors
Millennium Stadium, Cardiff. Att: 73,734. 15 May 2004.
St Helens: Paul Wellens (1t); Ade Gardner, Martin Gleeson, Willie Talau (2t), Darren Albert; Jason Hooper, Sean Long (6g); Nick Fozzard, Keiron Cunningham, Keith Mason, Chris Joynt, Lee Gilmour (1t), Paul Sculthorpe (c) (1t). S: Mark Edmondson, Dominic Feaunati, Jon Wilkin, Ricky Bibey.
Wigan: Kris Radlinski; David Hodgson, Sean O'Loughlin, Kevin Brown, Brett Dallas (2t); Danny Orr, Adrian Lam; Craig Smith, Terry Newton (1t), Quentin Pongia, Danny Tickle, Gareth Hock, Andy Farrell (c) (2g). S: Terry O'Connor, Danny Sculthorpe, Mick Cassidy, Stephen Wild.
Lance Todd Trophy: Sean Long

2005 Hull 25-24 Leeds Rhinos
Millennium Stadium, Cardiff. Att: 74,213. 27 August 2005.
Hull: Nathan Blacklock; Motu Tony (1t), Richard Whiting (1t), Kirk Yeaman, Gareth Raynor (1t); Richard Horne, Danny Brough (4g, 1dg); Ewan Cowes, Richard Swain (c), Garreth Carvell, Shayne McMenemy, Stephen Kearney, Paul Cooke (1t). S: Paul King, Chris Chester, Jamie Thackray, Tom Saxton.
Leeds: Richard Mathers; Mark Calderwood (2t), Chev Walker, Keith Senior, Marcus Bai (1t);

Kevin Sinfield (c) (4g), Rob Burrow; Ryan Bailey, Matt Diskin, Danny Ward (1t), Ali Lauitiiti, Chris McKenna, Gareth Ellis. S: Jamie Jones-Buchanan, Willie Poching, Danny McGuire, Andrew Dunemann.
Lance Todd Trophy: Kevin Sinfield

2006 St Helens 42-12 Huddersfield Giants
Twickenham Stadium, London. Att: 65,187. 26 August 2006.
St Helens: Paul Wellens; Ade Gardner, Jamie Lyon (1t, 7g), Willie Talau (1t), Francis Meli; Leon Pryce, Sean Long (c) (1t); Paul Anderson, Keiron Cunningham, Jason Cayless (1t), Jon Wilkin (2t), Paul Sculthorpe (c), Jason Hooper. S: Lee Gilmour, James Roby, James Graham, Maurie Fa'asavala (1t).
Huddersfield: Paul Reilly; Martin Aspinwall (1t), Chris Nero, Michael de Vere (2g), Stuart Donlan; Chris Thorman (c), Robbie Paul (1t); Paul Jackson, Brad Drew, Jim Gannon, Eorl Crabtree, Andy Raleigh, Stephen Wild. S: Steve Snitch, Stuart Jones, Paul Smith, Wayne McDonald.
Lance Todd Trophy: Sean Long

2007 St Helens 30-8 Catalans Dragons
Wembley Stadium, London. Att: 84,241. 25 August 2007.
St Helens: Paul Wellens (1t); Ade Gardner (2t), Matt Gidley, Willie Talau, Francis Meli; Leon Pryce, Sean Long (5g); Nick Fozzard, Keiron Cunningham (c), Jason Cayless, Lee Gilmour, Mike Bennett, Jon Wilkin. S: James Roby (1t), James Graham, Paul Clough (1t), Maurie Fa'asavalu.
Catalans: Clint Greenshields; Justin Murphy (1t), Sébastien Raguin, John Wilson, Younes Khattabi (1t); Adam Mogg, Stacey Jones (c); Jerome Guisset, Luke Quigley, Alex Chan, Jason Croker, Cyrille Gossard, Greg Mounis. S: David Ferriol, Vincent Duport, Remi Casty, Kane Bentley.
Lance Todd Trophy: Paul Wellens & Leon Pryce (shared)

2008 St Helens 28-16 Hull
Wembley Stadium, London. Att: 82,821. 30 August 2008.
St Helens: Paul Wellens; Ade Gardner, Matt Gidley (1t), Willie Talau, Francis Meli (2t); Leon Pryce (1t), Sean Long (4g); Bryn Hargreaves, Keiron Cunningham (c), James Graham, Jon Wilkin (1t), Chris Flannery, Paul Sculthorpe. S: Lee Gilmour, James Roby, Paul Clough, Maurie Fa'asavalu.
Hull: Todd Byrne; Matt Sing, Graeme Horne, Kirk Yeaman (2t), Gareth Raynor (1t); Danny Washbrook, Tommy Lee; Ewan Dowes, Shaun Berrigan, Peter Cusack, Willie Manu, Danny Tickle (2g), Lee Radford (c). S: Richard Horne, Garreth Carvell, Tom Briscoe, Jamie Thackray.
Lance Todd Trophy: Paul Wellens

2009 Warrington Wolves 25-16 Huddersfield Giants
Wembley Stadium, London. Att: 76,560. 29 August 2009.
Warrington: Richard Mathers (1t); Chris Hicks (1t), Chris Bridge (4g), Matt King, Chris Riley; Vinnie Anderson (1t), Lee Briers (1dg); Adrian Morley (c), Michael Monaghan (1t), Garreth Carvell, Louis Anderson, Ben Harrison, Ben Westwood. S: Michael Cooper, Paul Johnson, Mickey Higham, Tyrone McCarthy.
Huddersfield: Brett Hodgson (c) (1t, 2g); Leroy Cudjoe, Jamahl Lolesi, Paul Whatuira, David Hodgson (1t); Kevin Brown, Luke Robinson; Keith Mason, Shaun Lunt (1t), Darrell Griffin, Liam Fulton, Stephen Wild, David Faiumu. S: Eorl Crabtree, Paul Jackson, Scott Moore, Martin Aspinwall.
Lance Todd Trophy: Michael Monaghan

2010 Warrington Wolves 30-6 Leeds Rhinos
Wembley Stadium, London. Att: 85,217. 28 August 2010.
Warrington: Richard Mathers; Chris Hicks (3t), Matt King, Ryan Atkins (2t), Chris Riley; Lee Briers, Michael Monaghan; Adrian Morley (c), Jon Clarke, Garreth Carvell, Louis Anderson (1t), Ben Westwood (3g), Ben Harrison. S: Paul Wood, David Solomona, Mickey Higham, Vinnie Anderson.

Leeds: Brent Webb; Lee Smith (1t), Brett Delaney, Keith Senior, Ryan Hall; Danny McGuire, Rob Burrow; Kylie Leuluai, Danny Buderus, Ryan Bailey, Chris Clarkson, Jamie Jones-Buchanan, Kevin Sinfield (c) (1g). S: Matt Diskin, Greg Eastwood, Ian Kirke, Carl Ablett.
Lance Todd Trophy: Lee Briers

2011 Wigan Warriors 28-18 Leeds Rhinos
Wembley Stadium, London. Att: 78,482. 27 August 2011.
Wigan: Sam Tomkins; Josh Charnley (1t), Joel Tomkins (1t), George Carmont, Pat Richards (4g); Paul Deacon, Brett Finch; Jeff Lima (2t), Thomas Leuluai (1t), Andy Coley, Harrison Hansen, Ryan Hoffman, Sean O'Loughlin (c). S: Liam Farrell, Lee Mossop, Michael McIlorum, Paul Prescott.
Leeds: Brent Webb; Ben Jones-Bishop (1t), Kallum Watkins, Carl Ablett (1t), Ryan Hall (2t); Kevin Sinfield (c) (1g), Danny McGuire; Kylie Leuluai, Danny Buderus, Jamie Peacock, Jamie Jones-Buchanan, Brett Delaney, Weller Hauraki. S: Rob Burrow, Ryan Bailey, Ian Kirke, Chris Clarkson.
Lance Todd Trophy: Jeff Lima

2012 Warrington Wolves 35-18 Leeds Rhinos
Wembley Stadium, London. Att: 79,180. 25 August 2012.
Warrington: Brett Hodgson (1t, 5g); Joel Monaghan (1t), Stefan Ratchford, Ryan Atkins (1t), Chris Riley (1t); Lee Briers (1dg), Richard Myler; Garreth Carvell, Mickey Higham, Chris Hill, Trent Waterhouse (1t), Ben Westwood, Ben Harrison. S: Adrian Morley (c), Paul Wood, Michael Monaghan, Tyrone McCarthy (1t).
Leeds: Zak Hardaker; Ben Jones-Bishop, Kallum Watkins (2t), Carl Ablett, Ryan Hall; Kevin Sinfield (c) (3g), Stevie Ward; Kylie Leuluai, Rob Burrow, Jamie Peacock, Jamie Jones-Buchanan, Brett Delaney, Ryan Bailey. S: Darrell Griffin, Shaun Lunt, Ian Kirke (1t), Jimmy Keinhorst.
Lance Todd Trophy: Brett Hodgson

2.2 SUPER LEAGUE GRAND FINALS 1998 - 2012

Super League began in 1996 and for two seasons was decided on a first-past-the-post basis, with the winners being St Helens (1996) and Bradford Bulls (1997). From 1998, a play-off system would be introduced with the champions being the winner of the Grand Final which has been played at Old Trafford since its inception. The man-of-the-match award is named after Harry Sunderland, the Australian administrator who played a significant role of the birth of the game in France. The Grand Final effectively replaced the Premiership competition which had also seen the man of the match awarded the Harry Sunderland Trophy.

1998 Wigan Warriors 10-4 Leeds Rhinos
Old Trafford, Manchester. Att: 43,553. 24 October 1998.
Wigan: Kris Radlinski; Jason Robinson (1t), Danny Moore, Gary Connolly, Mark Bell; Henry Paul, Tony Smith; Terry O'Connor, Robbie McCormack, Tony Mestrov, Lee Gilmour, Stephen Holgate, Andy Farrell (c) (3g). S: Neil Cowie, Mick Cassidy, Paul Johnson, Simon Haughton.
Leeds: Iestyn Harris (c); Leroy Rivett, Richie Blackmore (1t), Brad Godden, Francis Cummins; Daryl Powell, Ryan Sheridan; Martin Masella, Terry Newton, Darren Fleary, Adrian Morley, Anthony Farrell, Marc Glanville. S: Jamie Mathiou, Marcus St Hilaire, Graham Holroyd, Andy Hay.
Harry Sunderland Trophy: Jason Robinson

1999 St Helens 8-6 Bradford Bulls
Old Trafford, Manchester. Att: 50,717. 9 October 1999.
St Helens: Paul Atcheson; Chris Smith, Kevin Iro (1t), Paul Newlove, Anthony Sullivan; Paul Sculthorpe, Tommy Martyn; Apollo Perelini, Keiron Cunningham, Julian O'Neill, Fereti Tuilagi, Sonny Nickle, Chris Joynt (c). S: Paul Wellens, Sean Long (2g), Sean Hoppe, Vila Matautia.
Bradford: Stuart Spruce; Tevita Vaikona, Scott Naylor, Michael Withers, Leon Pryce; Henry Paul (1t, 1g), Robbie Paul (c); Paul Anderson, James Lowes, Stuart Fielden, David Boyle, Bernard Dwyer, Steve McNamara. S: Paul Deacon, Nathan McAvoy, Mike Forshaw, Brian McDermott.
Harry Sunderland Trophy: Henry Paul

2000 St Helens 29-16 Wigan Warriors
Old Trafford, Manchester. Att: 58,132. 14 October 2000.
St Helens: Paul Wellens; Steve Hall, Kevin Iro, Sean Hoppe (1t), Anthony Sullivan; Tommy Martyn, Sean Long (4g); Apollo Perelini, Keiron Cunningham, Julian O'Neill, Chris Joynt (c) (2t), Tim Jonkers (1t), Paul Sculthorpe (1dg). S: Fereti Tuilagi (1t), Steve Barrow, John Stankevitch, Sonny Nickle.
Wigan: Jason Robinson; Brett Dallas, Kris Radlinski, Steve Renouf, David Hodgson (1t); Tony Smith (1t), Willie Peters; Terry O'Connor, Terry Newton, Neil Cowie, Mick Cassidy, Denis Betts, Andy Farrell (c) (1t, 2g). S: Lee Gilmour, Chris Chester, Tony Mestrov, Brady Malam.
Harry Sunderland Trophy: Chris Joynt

2001 Bradford Bulls 37-6 Wigan Warriors
Old Trafford, Manchester. Att: 60,164. 13 October 2001.
Bradford: Michael Withers (3t); Tevita Vaikona, Scott Naylor, Graham Mackay (1t, 1g), Leon Pryce; Henry Paul (5g, 1dg), Robbie Paul (c); Joe Vagana, James Lowes (1t), Brian McDermott, Daniel Gartner, Jamie Peacock, Mike Forshaw. S: Stuart Fielden (1t), Paul Anderson, Shane Rigon, Paul Deacon.
Wigan: Kris Radlinski; Brett Dallas, Gary Connolly, Steve Renouf, Brian Carney; Matthew Johns, Adrian Lam (1t); Terry O'Connor, Terry Newton, Harvey Howard, Mick Cassidy, David Furner (1g), Andy Farrell (c). S: Paul Johnson, Neil Cowie, Denis Betts, Chris Chester.
Harry Sunderland Trophy: Michael Withers

2002 St Helens 19-18 Bradford Bulls
Old Trafford, Manchester. Att: 61,138. 19 October 2002.
St Helens: Paul Wellens; Darren Albert, Martin Gleeson (1t), Paul Newlove, Anthony Stewart; Paul Sculthorpe, Sean Long (1t, 3g, 1dg); Darren Britt, Keiron Cunningham, Barry Ward, Mike Bennett (1t), Tim Jonkers, Chris Joynt (c). S: Sean Hoppe, Peter Shiels, John Stankevitch, Mick Higham.
Bradford: Michael Withers (1t); Tevita Vaikona, Scott Naylor (1t), Brandon Costin, Lesley Vainikolo; Robbie Paul (c) (1t), Paul Deacon (3g), Joe Vagana, James Lowes, Stuart Fielden, Daniel Gartner, Jamie Peacock, Mike Forshaw. S: Lee Gilmour, Paul Anderson, Brian McDermott, Leon Pryce.
Harry Sunderland Trophy: Paul Deacon

2003 Bradford Bulls 25-12 Wigan Warriors
Old Trafford, Manchester. Att: 65,537. 18 October 2003.
Bradford: Stuart Reardon (1t); Tevita Vaikona, Michael Withers, Shontayne Hape (1t), Lesley Vainikolo; Karl Pratt, Paul Deacon (6g, 1dg); Joe Vagana, James Lowes (1t), Stuart Fielden, Daniel Gartner, Jamie Peacock, Mike Forshaw. S: Paul Anderson, Lee Radford, Leon Pryce, Robbie Paul (c).
Wigan: Kris Radlinski (1t); Brian Carney, Martin Aspinwall, David Hodgson, Brett Dallas; Sean O'Loughlin, Luke Robinson; Quentin Pongia, Terry Newton, Craig Smith, Mick Cassidy, Danny Tickle (1t), Andy Farrell (c) (2g). S: Paul Johnson, Terry O'Connor, Gareth Hock, Mark Smith.
Harry Sunderland Trophy: Stuart Reardon

2004 Leeds Rhinos 16-8 Bradford Bulls
Old Trafford, Manchester. Att: 65,547. 16 October 2004.
Leeds: Richard Mathers; Mark Calderwood, Chev Walker, Keith Senior, Marcus Bai; Kevin Sinfield (c) (4g), Danny McGuire (1t); Danny Ward, Matt Diskin (1t), Ryan Bailey, Chris McKenna, Ali Lauitiiti, David Furner. S: Willie Poching, Barrie McDermott, Rob Burrow, Jamie Jones-Buchanan.
Bradford: Michael Withers; Stuart Reardon, Paul Johnson, Shontayne Hape (1t), Lesley Vainikolo (1t); Iestyn Harris, Paul Deacon; Joe Vagana, Robbie Paul (c); Stuart Fielden, Jamie Peacock, Logan Swann, Lee Radford. S: Paul Anderson, Karl Pratt, Rob Parker, Jamie Langley.
Harry Sunderland Trophy: Matt Diskin

2005 Bradford Bulls 15-6 Leeds Rhinos
Old Trafford, Manchester. Att: 65,537. 15 October 2005.
Bradford: Michael Withers; Leon Pryce (1t), Ben Harris, Shontayne Hape, Lesley Vainikolo (1t); Iestyn Harris (1dg), Paul Deacon (3g); Jamie Peacock (c), Ian Henderson, Stuart Fielden, Paul Johnson, Brad Meyers, Lee Radford. S: Adrian Morley, Jamie Langley, Joe Vagana, Robbie Paul.
Leeds: Richard Mathers; Mark Calderwood, Chev Walker, Chris McKenna, Marcus Bai; Danny McGuire (1t), Rob Burrow; Ryan Bailey, Andrew Dunemann, Danny Ward, Gareth Ellis, Willie Poching, Kevin Sinfield (c) (1g). S: Barrie McDermott, Ali Lauitiiti, Jamie Jones-Buchanan, Matt Diskin.
Harry Sunderland Trophy: Leon Pryce

2006 St Helens 26-4 Hull
Old Trafford, Manchester. Att: 72,582. 14 October 2006.
St Helens: Paul Wellens; Ade Gardner (1t), Jamie Lyon (3g), Willie Talau (1t), Francis Meli (1t); Leon Pryce (1t), Sean Long (c); Paul Anderson, Keiron Cunningham (1t), Jason Cayless, Lee Gilmour, Jon Wilkin, Jason Hooper. S: Maurie Fa'asavala, James Graham, Mike Bennett, James Roby.
Hull: Shaun Briscoe; Motu Tony, Sid Domic (1t), Kirk Yeaman, Gareth Raynor; Paul Cooke, Richard Horne; Ewan Dowes, Richard Swain (c), Garreth Carvell, Lee Radford, Shayne McMenemy, Danny Washbrook. S: Paul King, Graeme Horne, Scott Wheeldon, Richard Whiting.
Harry Sunderland Trophy: Paul Wellens

2007 Leeds Rhinos 33-6 St Helens
Old Trafford, Manchester. Att: 71,352. 13 October 2007.
Leeds: Brent Webb (1t); Lee Smith (1t), Clinton Toopi, Keith Senior, Scott Donald (1t); Danny McGuire, Rob Burrow (1dg); Kylie Leuluai, Matt Diskin, Jamie Peacock, Jamie Jones-Buchanan (1t), Gareth Ellis, Kevin Sinfield (c) (6g). Subs: Ali Lauitiiti (1t), Ryan Bailey, Ian Kirke, Carl Ablett.
St Helens: Paul Wellens; Ade Gardner, Matt Gidley, Willie Talau, Francis Meli; Leon Pryce, Sean Long (1g); Nick Fozzard, Keiron Cunningham (c), Jason Cayless, Lee Gilmour, Chris Flannery, Jon Wilkin. S: James Graham, James Roby (1t), Maurie Fa'asavalu, Mike Bennett.
Harry Sunderland Trophy: Rob Burrow

2008 Leeds Rhinos 24-16 St Helens
Old Trafford, Manchester. Att: 68,810. 4 October 2008.
Leeds: Lee Smith (1t), Ryan Hall (1t), Carl Ablett, Keith Senior, Scott Donald; Danny McGuire (2t), Rob Burrow; Kylie Leuluai, Matt Diskin, Jamie Peacock, Jamie Jones-Buchanan, Gareth Ellis, Kevin Sinfield (c) (4g). Subs: Nick Scruton, Ali Lauitiiti, Ian Kirke, Ryan Bailey.
St Helens: Paul Wellens; Ade Gardner (1t), Matt Gidley (1t), Willie Talau, Francis Meli; Leon Pryce, Sean Long (2g); Bryn Hargreaves, Keiron Cunningham (c), James Graham (1t), Lee Gilmour, Jon Wilkin, Chris Flannery. S: Nick Fozzard, Paul Clough, James Roby, Maurie Fa'asavalu.
Harry Sunderland Trophy: Lee Smith

2009 Leeds Rhinos 18-10 St Helens
Old Trafford, Manchester. Att: 63,259. 10 October 2009.
Leeds: Brent Webb; Scott Donald, Lee Smith (2t), Keith Senior, Ryan Hall; Danny McGuire, Rob Burrow (1dg); Kylie Leuluai, Matt Diskin (1t), Jamie Peacock, Jamie Jones-Buchanan, Carl Ablett, Kevin Sinfield (c) (2g, 1dg). S: Ryan Bailey, Luke Burgess, Ian Kirke, Ali Lauitiiti.
St Helens: Paul Wellens; Ade Gardner, Matt Gidley, Kyle Eastmond (1t, 3g), Francis Meli; Leon Pryce, Sean Long; James Graham, Keiron Cunningham (c), Tony Puletua, Jon Wilkin, Lee Gilmour, Chris Flannery. S: James Roby, Bryn Hargreaves, Paul Clough, Maurie Fa'asavalu.
Harry Sunderland Trophy: Kevin Sinfield

2010 Wigan Warriors 22-10 St Helens
Old Trafford, Manchester. Att:71,526. 2 October 2010.
Wigan: Sam Tomkins (1t); Darrell Goulding (1t), Martin Gleeson (2t), George Carmont, Pat Richards (2g); Paul Deacon, Thomas Leuluai; Stuart Fielden, Michael McIlorum, Andy Coley, Harrison Hansen, Joel Tomkins, Sean O'Loughlin (c). S: Mark Riddell (1g), Iafeta Palea'aesina, Liam Farrell, Paul Prescott.
St Helens: Paul Wellens; Jamie Foster (1g), Matt Gidley, Francis Meli (1t), Jonny Lomax; Jon Wilkin, Matty Smith; James Graham, Keiron Cunningham (c), Bryn Hargreaves, Iosia Soliola, Chris Flannery, Tony Puletua. S: Paul Clough, James Roby, Andrew Dixon (1t), Jacob Emmitt..
Harry Sunderland Trophy: Thomas Leuluai

2011 Leeds Rhinos 32-16 St Helens
Old Trafford, Manchester. Att: 69,107. 8 October 2011.
Leeds: Brent Webb (1t); Ben Jones-Bishop, Zak Hardaker (1t), Carl Ablett (1t), Ryan Hall (1t); Kevin Sinfield (c) (6g), Danny McGuire; Kylie Leuluai, Danny Buderus, Jamie Peacock, Jamie Jones-Buchanan, Brett Delaney, Chris Clarkson. S: Rob Burrow (1t), Ryan Bailey, Ian Kirke, Ali Lauitiiti.
St Helens: Paul Wellens (c); Tom Makinson (1t), Michael Shenton (1t), Francis Meli, Jamie Foster (4g); Lee Gaskell, Jonny Lomax; James Graham (c), James Roby, Tony Puletua, Jon Wilkin, Iosia Soliola, Paul Clough. S: Andrew Dixon, Scott Moore, Louie McCarthy-Scarsbrook, Gary Wheeler.
Harry Sunderland Trophy: Rob Burrow

2012 Leeds Rhinos 26-18 Warrington Wolves
Old Trafford, Manchester. Att: 70,676. 6 October 2012.
Leeds: Zak Hardaker; Ben Jones-Bishop (1t), Kallum Watkins, Carl Ablett (1t), Ryan Hall (1t); Kevin Sinfield (c) (1t, 5g), Danny McGuire; Kylie Leuluai, Rob Burrow, Jamie Peacock, Jamie Jones-Buchanan, Brett Delaney, Ryan Bailey. S: Ian Kirke, Darrell Griffin, Stevie Ward, Shaun Lunt.
Warrington: Brett Hodgson (3g); Joel Monaghan, Stefan Ratchford, Ryan Atkins (1t), Chris Riley; Lee Briers, Richard Myler (1t); Chris Hill, Mick Higham, Ben Harrison, Ben Westwood, Trent Waterhouse, Simon Grix. S: Adrian Morley (c), Michael Monaghan (1t), Paul Wood, Michael Cooper.
Harry Sunderland Trophy: Kevin Sinfield

2.3 REGAL TROPHY FINALS 1980 - 1996

This tournament started out as the Players No.6 Trophy in 1971 before being renamed the John Player Trophy in 1977. In 1983, it became the John Player Special Trophy and finally the Regal Trophy in 1989. It was scrapped after the 1996 final as a result of the sport's move to summer. Finals were played at a variety of venues.

1979-80 Bradford Northern 6-0 Widnes
Headingley, Leeds. Att: 9,909. 5 January 1980.
Bradford: Keith Mumby (1g); David Barends, David Redfearn, Derek Parker (1t), Les Gant; Nigel Stephenson (1dg), Alan Redfearn; Jimmy Thompson (c), Keith Bridges, Colin Forsyth, Jeff Grayshon, Gary van Bellen, Len Casey. S: Steve Ferres, Ian van Bellen.
Widnes: David Eckersley, Stuart Wright, Mal Aspey, Wilf George, Mick Burke; Eric Hughes, Reg Bowden (c); Brian Hogan, Keith Elwell, Glyn Shaw, Les Gorley, David Hull, Mick Adams. S: Alan Dearden (dnp), Jim Mills.
Man of the Match: Len Casey

1980-81 Warrington 12-5 Barrow
Central Park, Wigan. Att: 12,820. 24 January 1981.
Warrington: Steve Hesford (2g, 2dg); Rick Thackray, Ian Duane, John Bevan (2t), Mike Kelly; Ken Kelly (c), Alan Gwilliam; Neil Courtney, Tony Waller, Brian Case, Tommy Martyn, Ian Potter, Eddie Hunter. S: Jimmy Fairhurst (dnp), Bob Eccles.
Barrow: David Elliott; Ralph McConnell, Nigel French, Ian Ball (c) (1g), Tony Wainwright; Mel Mason (1t), David Cairns; Dave Chisnall, Howard Allen, Malcolm Flynn, Kevin James, Steve Kirkby, Derek Hadley. S: Mel James (dnp), Eddie Syzmala.
Man of the Match: Tommy Martyn

1981-82 Hull 12-4 Hull Kingston Rovers
Headingley, Leeds. Att: 24,245. 23 January 1982.
Hull: Barry Banks; Dane O'Hara, Chris Harrison, James Leuluai, Paul Prendiville; Terry Day, Tony Dean (1dg); Trevor Skerrett, Ron Wileman (1t), Charlie Stone (c), Mick Crane, Lee Crooks (4g), Steve Norton. S: Kevin Harkin, Sammy Lloyd (dnp).
Hull KR: George Fairbairn (2g); Steve Hubbard, Mike Smith, Phil Hogan, Peter Muscroft; Steve Hartley, Paul Harkin; Roy Holdstock, David Watkinson, Steve Crooks, Phil Lowe, Len Casey (c), David Hall. S: Chris Burton, John Millington.
Man of the Match: Trevor Skerrett

1982-83 Wigan 15-4 Leeds
Elland Road, Leeds. Att: 19,553. 22 January 1983.
Wigan: Barry Williams; Dennis Ramsdale, David Stephenson, Colin Whitfield (c) (4g, 1dg), Henderson Gill (1t); Martin Foy, Jimmy Fairhurst; Glyn Shaw, Nicky Kiss, Danny Campbell, Graeme West, Mick Scott, John Pendlebury. S: Brian Juliff (1t), Brian Case.
Leeds: Neil Hague; Mark Campbell, Ian Wilkinson, Les Dyl, Andy Smith; John Holmes, Kevin Dick (2g); Roy Dickinson, David Ward (c), Tony Burke, Andy Sykes, Wayne Heron, David Heron. S: Mark Conway (dnp), David Heselwood (dnp).
Man of the Match: Martin Foy

1983-84 Leeds 18-10 Widnes
Central Park, Wigan. Att: 9,510. 14 January 1984.
Leeds: Ian Wilkinson, Paul Prendiville, David Creasser (5g), Dean Bell, Andy Smith; John Holmes (1t), Kevin Dick (1t); Keith Rayne, David Ward (c), Kevin Rayne, Gary Moorby, Mark Laurie, Terry Webb. S: Neil Hague (dnp), Kevin Squire.
Widnes: Mick Burke (1g); Stuart Wright, Keiron O'Loughlin, Joe Lydon (1t), Ralph Linton (1t); Eric Hughes (c), Andy Gregory; Steve O'Neill, Keith Elwell, Kevin Tamati, Les Gorley, Fred Whitfield, Mick Adams. S: John Myler (dnp), Eric Prescott (dnp).
Man of the Match: Mark Laurie

1984-85 Hull Kingston Rovers 12-0 Hull
Boothferry Park, Hull. Att: 25,326. 26 January 1985.
Hull KR: George Fairbairn; Garry Clark (1t), Ian Robinson, Gary Prohm (1t), David Laws; Gordon Smith, Paul Harkin; Mark Broadhurst, David Watkinson (c), Asuquo Ema, Chris Burton, Phil Hogan (1t), Gavin Miller. S: John Lydiat (dnp), Len Casey (dnp).
Hull: Gary Kemble; Steve Evans, Fred Ah Kuoi, James Leuluai, Dane O'Hara; David Topliss (c), Peter Sterling; Phil Edmonds, Shaun Patrick, Paul Rose, Lee Crooks, Wayne Proctor, Gary Divorty. S: Garry Schofield, Andy Dannatt.
Man of the Match: Paul Harkin

1985-86 Wigan 11-8 Hull Kingston Rovers
Elland Road, Leeds. Att: 17,573. 11 January 1986.
Wigan: Steve Hampson; Ray Mordt, David Stephenson (1g), Ellery Hanley, Henderson Gill; Steve Ella, Mike Ford (1t); Greg Dowling (1dg), Nicky Kiss, Shaun Wane (1t), Graeme West (c), Andy Goodway, Ian Potter. S: Shaun Edwards, Nick du Toit.

Hull KR: John Lydiat (1t); Garry Clark, Mike Smith, John Dorahy, David Laws (1t); Gordon Smith, Paul Harkin; Peter Johnston, David Watkinson (c), Asuquo Ema, Chris Burton, Andy Kelly, Gavin Miller. S: Ian Robinson, Chris Rudd (dnp).
Man of the Match: Paul Harkin

1986-87 Wigan 18-4 Warrington
Burnden Park, Bolton. Att: 21,144. 10 January 1987.
Wigan: Steve Hampson; David Stephenson, Joe Lydon, Dean Bell (1t), Henderson Gill (2t, 1g); Ellery Hanley, Shaun Edwards; Graeme West (c), Martin Dermott, Brian Case, Ian Roberts, Ian Potter, Andy Goodway (1t). S: Mike Ford (dnp), Rob Louw (dnp).
Warrington: Brian Johnson; Kevin Meadows, Paul Cullen, Joe Ropati, Mark Forster (1t); Ken Kelly, Steve Peters; Les Boyd (c), Kevin Tamati, Bob Jackson, Gary Sanderson, Mark Roberts, Mike Gregory. S: Ronnie Duane, Alan Rathbone.
Man of the Match: Andy Goodway

1987-88 St Helens 15-14 Leeds
Central Park, Wigan. Att: 16,669. 9 January 1988.
St Helens: Phil Veivers; David Tanner, Paul Loughlin (2t, 3g), Mark Elia, Les Quirk; Shane Cooper, Neil Holding (1dg); Tony Burke, Paul Groves, Peter Souto, Paul Forber, Roy Haggerty, Andy Platt. S: David Large (dnp), Stuart Evans.
Leeds: Marty Gurr, Steve Morris, Garry Schofield, Peter Jackson (1t), John Basnett; David Creasser (1t, 3g), Ray Ashton; Peter Tunks, Colin Maskill, Kevin Rayne, Roy Powell, Paul Medley, David Heron. S: Carl Gibson, John Fairbank.
Man of the Match: Paul Loughlin

1988-89 Wigan 12-6 Widnes
Burnden Park, Bolton. Att: 20,709. 7 January 1989.
Wigan: Steve Hampson; Dean Bell, Kevin Iro (1t), Joe Lydon (2g), Tony Iro; Ged Byrne, Shaun Edwards; Adrian Shelford, Martin Dermott, Shaun Wane, Denis Betts, Ian Potter, Ellery Hanley (c) (1t). S: Andy Gregory, Andy Goodway.
Widnes: Alan Tait; Rick Thackray, Andy Currier (1g), Darren Wright (1t), Martin Offiah; Tony Myler, David Hulme; Kurt Sorensen (c), Phil McKenzie, Joe Grima, Mike O'Neill, Emosi Koloti, Richie Eyres. S: Barry Dowd (dnp), Paul Hulme.
Man of the Match: Ellery Hanley

1989-90 Wigan 24-12 Halifax
Headingley, Leeds. Att: 17,810. 13 January 1990.
Wigan: Joe Lydon (2g); David Marshall, Kevin Iro, Dean Bell, Mark Preston; Shaun Edwards (1t), Andy Gregory; Ian Lucas, Martin Dermott, Andy Platt, Denis Betts, Ian Gildart, Ellery Hanley (c) (3t). S: Andy Goodway (1t), Shaun Wane.
Halifax: Colin Whitfield; Eddie Riddlesden, Tony Anderson, Brian Hetherington, Wilf George; John Dorahy (c), John Lyons; Brendan Hill (1t), Seamus McCallion, Lindsay Johnston, Peter Bell, Richard Milner, Les Holliday (4g). S: Steve Smith, Mick Scott.
Man of the Match: Ellery Hanley

1990-91 Warrington 12-2 Bradford Northern
Headingley, Leeds. Att: 11,154. 12 January 1991.
Warrington: David Lyon (4g); Des Drummond (c), Allan Bateman, Tony Thorniley, Mark Forster; Chris O'Sullivan, Kevin Ellis; Neil Harmon, Duane Mann, Gary Chambers, Gary Mercer, Billy McGinty, Paul Cullen. S: Mark Thomas (1t), Rowland Phillips.
Bradford: Ian Wilkinson; Gerald Cordle, Darrall Shelford, Roger Simpson, Tony Marchant; Neil Summers, Brett Iti; David Hobbs (1g), Brian Noble, Jon Hamer, Paul Medley, David Croft, John Pendlebury (c). S: Phil Hellewell, Craig Richards (dnp).
Man of the Match: Billy McGinty

1991-92 Widnes 24-0 Leeds

Central Park, Wigan. Att: 15,070. 11 January 1992.

Widnes: Alan Tait (1t); John Devereux, Andy Currier, Darren Wright, Mark Sarsfield; Jonathan Davies (c) (1t, 3g, 1dg), Barry Dowd; Kurt Sorensen (1t), Paul Hulme, David Smith, Harvey Howard, Richie Eyres, Les Holliday (1t, 1dg). S: Paul Atcheson, Joe Grima.

Leeds: Morvin Edwards; Phil Ford, David Creasser, Simon Irving, John Bentley; Garry Schofield (c), Bobbie Goulding; Shaun Wane, Richard Gunn, Mike O'Neill, Roy Powell, Paul Dixon, Gary Divorty. S: Carl Gibson, Steve Molloy.

Man of the Match: Les Holliday

1992-93 Wigan 15-8 Bradford Northern

Elland Road, Leeds. Att: 13,221. 23 January 1993.

Wigan: Steve Hampson (1dg); Jason Robinson (1t), Dean Bell (c), Andrew Farrar, Martin Offiah; Frano Botica (3g), Shaun Edwards (1t); Neil Cowie, Martin Dermott, Andy Platt, Denis Betts, Billy McGinty, Phil Clarke. S: Joe Lydon, Sam Panapa.

Bradford: Dave Watson; Tony Marchant, Steve McGowan (1t), Tony Anderson, Roger Simpson; Neil Summers, Deryck Fox; David Hobbs (c) (1g), Brian Noble, Roy Powell, Paul Medley, Karl Fairbank, David Heron. S: Keith Mumby (1g), Trevor Clark.

Man of the Match: Shaun Edwards

1993-94 Castleford 33-2 Wigan

Headingley, Leeds. Att: 15,626. 22 January 1994.

Castleford: Graham Steadman; St John Ellis, Richie Blackmore, Grant Anderson (1t), Simon Middleton; Tony Kemp (1dg), Mike Ford; Lee Crooks (c) (1t, 6g), Richard Russell, Martin Ketteridge (2t), Tony Morrison, Ian Smales, Tawera Nikau (1t). S: Andy Hay, Dean Sampson.

Wigan: Joe Lydon; Jason Robinson, Barrie-Jon Mather, Gary Connolly, Martin Offiah; Frano Botica (1g), Shaun Edwards; Kelvin Skerrett, Martin Dermott, Andy Platt (c), Neil Cowie, Andy Farrell, Phil Clarke. S: Sam Panapa, Mick Cassidy.

Man of the Match: Martin Ketteridge

1994-95 Wigan 40-10 Warrington

McAlpine Stadium, Huddersfield. Att: 19,636. 28 January 1995.

Wigan: Henry Paul; Jason Robinson, Va'aiga Tuigamala (2t), Gary Connolly (1t), Martin Offiah (1t); Frano Botica (1t, 8g), Shaun Edwards (c); Kelvin Skerrett, Martin Hall, Neil Cowie, Denis Betts, Mick Cassidy, Phil Clarke. S: Paul Atcheson, Barrie McDermott (1t).

Warrington: Jonathan Davies (1g); Mark Forster (2t), Allan Bateman, Iestyn Harris, Robert Myler; Francis Maloney, Greg Mackey (c); Gary Tees, Tukere Barlow, Bruce McGuire, Paul Cullen, Paul Darbyshire, Kelly Shelford. S: Andy Bennett, Gary Sanderson.

Man of the Match: Phil Clarke

1995-96 Wigan 25-16 St Helens

McAlpine Stadium, Huddersfield. Att: 17,590. 13 January 1996.

Wigan: Gary Connolly; Jason Robinson, Va'aiga Tuigamala (1t), Kris Radlinski (1t), Martin Offiah; Henry Paul (2t, 4g), Shaun Edwards (c) (1dg); Neil Cowie, Martin Hall, Terry O'Connor, Scott Quinnell, Mick Cassidy, Simon Haughton. S: Rob Smyth, Martin Dermott.

St Helens: Steve Prescott; Joey Hayes (1t), Scott Gibbs, Paul Newlove (1t), Anthony Sullivan; Karle Hammond, Bobbie Goulding (c) (2g); Apollo Perelini, Keiron Cunningham (1t), Ian Pickavance, Chris Joynt, Simon Booth, Dean Busby. S: Andy Northey, Vila Matautia.

Man of the Match: Keiron Cunningham

2.4 PREMIERSHIP FINALS 1980 - 1997

When the Rugby Football League scrapped its Championship play-offs in 1973, and used the first-past-the-post system to decide its champions, they introduced the Premiership tournament, an end-of-season knockout tournament. Finals were played at a variety of stadia until the 1987 final was played at Old Trafford, where it stayed thereafter. The competition was stopped after the 1997 season when the Super League play-offs were introduced. The man of the match was presented with the Harry Sunderland Trophy, a tradition which lives on in the Super League Grand Final.

1979-80 Widnes 19-5 Bradford Northern
Station Road, Swinton. Att: 10,215. 17 May 1980.
Widnes: Mick Burke (1g); Stuart Wright (1t), Wilf George, Mal Aspey (1t), Keith Bentley (1t); David Eckersley (1dg), Reg Bowden (c); Glyn Shaw, Keith Elwell (1t, 1dg), Mike O'Neill, Les Gorley (1t), David Hull, Mick Adams. S: David Moran (dnp), Brian Hogan.
Bradford: Keith Mumby (1g); Ian MacLean, David Redfearn (1t), Derek Parker, Les Gant; Nigel Stephenson, Alan Redfearn; Jimmy Thompson (c), Keith Bridges, Colin Forsyth, Geoff Clarkson, Jeff Grayshon, Gary Hale. S: Steve Ferres, Gary van Bellen.
Harry Sunderland Trophy: Mal Aspey

1980-81 Hull Kingston Rovers 11-7 Hull
Headingley, Leeds. Att: 29,448. 16 May 1981.
Hull KR: Paul Proctor; Steve Hubbard (1g), Mike Smith (1t), Phil Hogan (1t), Peter Muscroft; Steve Hartley (1t), Paul Harkin; Roy Holdstock, David Watkinson, John Millington, Phil Lowe, Len Casey (c), David Hall. S: Chris Burton, Kevin Watson (dnp).
Hull: Paul Woods (2g); Gary Peacham, Graham Walters, David Elliott, Tim Wilby, Paul Prendiville; Barry Banks, Tony Dean; Keith Tindall, Ron Wileman, Charlie Stone (c), Trevor Skerrett, Mick Crane (1t), Steve Norton. S: Robin Chester (dnp), Ian Madley.
Harry Sunderland Trophy: Len Casey

1981-82 Widnes 23-8 Hull
Headingley, Leeds. Att: 12,100. 15 May 1982.
Widnes: Mick Burke (1t, 4g); Stuart Wright (1t), Keiron O'Loughlin, Eddie Cunningham, John Basnett (1t); Eric Hughes (1t), Andy Gregory; Mike O'Neill, Keith Elwell, Brian Lockwood, Les Gorley, Eric Prescott, Mick Adams (c) (1t). S: Tony Myler, Fred Whitfield.
Hull: Gary Kemble; Dane O'Hara, James Leuluai, Steve Evans, Paul Prendiville; David Topliss (c), Kevin Harkin; Keith Tindall, Ron Wileman, Charlie Stone, Trevor Skerrett, Lee Crooks (1t, 2g, 1dg), Steve Norton. S: Terry Day, Sammy Lloyd.
Harry Sunderland Trophy: Mick Burke

1982-83 Widnes 22-10 Hull
Headingley, Leeds. Att: 17,813. 14 May 1983.
Widnes: Mick Burke; Ralph Linton, Eric Hughes (c), Joe Lydon (5g), John Basnett (2t); Tony Myler (1t), Andy Gregory (1t); Mike O'Neill, Keith Elwell, Les Gorley, Fred Whitfield, Eric Prescott, Mick Adams. S: David Hulme, Steve O'Neill.
Hull: Gary Kemble; Dane O'Hara (1t), Terry Day, James Leuluai, Steve Evans; David Topliss (c) (1t), Tony Dean; Trevor Skerrett, Keith Bridges, Charlie Stone, Paul Rose, Lee Crooks (2g), Steve Norton. S: Patrick Solal, Mick Crane.
Harry Sunderland Trophy: Tony Myler

1983-84 Hull Kingston Rovers 18-10 Castleford
Headingley, Leeds. Att: 12,515. 12 May 1984.
Hull KR: George Fairbairn; Garry Clark, Mike Smith (1t), Gary Prohm (1t), David Laws (1t, 1g); John Dorahy (1t), Paul Harkin; Roy Holdstock, Chris Rudd, John Millington, Chris Burton, Mark Broadhurst, David Hall (c). S: John Lydiat, Ian Robinson.
Castleford: David Roockley; Darren Coen, Tony Marchant, Gary Hyde, John Kear (1t); Steve Robinson, Bob Beardmore (c) (3g); Kevin Ward, Stuart Horton, Gary Connell, Jimmy Crampton, Brett Atkins, John Joyner. S: Ian Orum (dnp), Dean Mountain (dnp).
Harry Sunderland Trophy: John Dorahy

1984-85 St Helens 36-16 Hull Kingston Rovers
Elland Road, Leeds. Att: 15,518. 11 May 1985.
St Helens: Phil Veivers (1t); Barrie Ledger (2t), Steve Peters, Mal Meninga (2t), Sean Day (4g); Chris Arkwright, Neil Holding; Tony Burke, Gary Ainsworth (1t), Peter Gorley, Andy Platt, Roy Haggerty, Harry Pinner (c) (1t). S: Shaun Allen, Paul Forber.
Hull KR: George Fairbairn (1t, 2g); Garry Clark, Ian Robinson (1t), Gary Prohm, David Laws (1t); Mike Smith, Gordon Smith; Mark Broadhurst, David Watkinson (c), Asuquo Ema, Andy Kelly, Phil Hogan, David Hall. S: Paul Harkin, John Lydiat.
Harry Sunderland Trophy: Harry Pinner

1985-86 Warrington 38-10 Halifax
Elland Road, Leeds. Att: 13,683. 18 May 1986.
Warrington: Paul Ford; Mark Forster (1t), Paul Cullen, Ronnie Duane, Brian Carbert; Paul Bishop (1t, 5g), Andy Gregory; Les Boyd (c) (2t), Kevin Tamati (1t), Bob Jackson (1t), Gary Sanderson, Mark Roberts, Mike Gregory. S: Brian Johnson (1t), Billy McGinty.
Halifax: Colin Whitfield (3g); Eddie Riddlesden, Tony Anderson, Chris Anderson (c) (1t), Scott Wilson; John Crossley, Gary Stephens; Mick Scott, Seamus McCallion, Geoff Robinson, Brian Juliff, Neil James, Paul Dixon. S: Steve Smith, Steve Bond.
Harry Sunderland Trophy: Les Boyd

1986-87 Wigan 8-0 Warrington
Old Trafford, Manchester. Att: 38,756. 17 May 1987.
Wigan: Steve Hampson; Henderson Gill (1g), David Stephenson (1g), Dean Bell, Joe Lydon (1t); Shaun Edwards, Andy Gregory; Brian Case, Nicky Kiss, Shaun Wane, Ian Potter, Andy Goodway, Ellery Hanley (c). S: Richard Russell, Graeme West.
Warrington: Brian Johnson; Des Drummond, Joe Ropati, Barry Peters, Mark Forster; Paul Cullen, Paul Bishop; Kevin Tamati, Mark Roberts, Bob Jackson (c), Tony Humphries, Gary Sanderson, Ronnie Duane. S: Mike Gregory, Bob Eccles.
Harry Sunderland Trophy: Joe Lydon

1987-88 Widnes 38-14 St Helens
Old Trafford, Manchester. Att: 35,252. 15 May 1988.
Widnes: Duncan Platt (1g); Rick Thackray, Andy Currier (4g), Darren Wright (2t), Martin Offiah; Barry Dowd, David Hulme (2t); Kurt Sorensen (c) (1t), Phil McKenzie (1t), Joe Grima, Mike O'Neill, Paul Hulme, Richard Eyres. S: Alan Tait (1t), Steve O'Neill.
St Helens: Paul Loughlin (3g); Barrie Ledger (1t), David Tanner, Mark Elia, Les Quirk; Mark Bailey, Neil Holding; Tony Burke, Paul Groves (c), Stuart Evans, Paul Forber, John Fieldhouse, Roy Haggerty (1t). S: Shaun Allen, Bernard Dwyer.
Harry Sunderland Trophy: David Hulme

1988-89 Widnes 18-10 Hull
Old Trafford, Manchester. Att: 40,194. 14 May 1989.
Widnes: Alan Tait; Jonathan Davies (3g), Andy Currier (1t), Darren Wright (1t), Martin Offiah (1t); David Hulme, Paul Hulme; Kurt Sorensen (c), Phil McKenzie, Joe Grima, Mike O'Neill, Emosi Koloto, Richard Eyres. S: Tony Myler, Derek Pyke.
Hull: Paul Fletcher, Paul Eastwood, Brian Blacker, Richard Price, Dane O'Hara (c); Gary Pearce (3g), Phil Windley; Andy Dannatt, Lee Jackson, Lee Crooks, Paul Welham (1t), Jon Sharp, Gary Divorty. S: Rob Nolan, Tim Wilby.
Harry Sunderland Trophy: Alan Tait

1989-90 Widnes 28-6 Bradford Northern
Old Trafford, Manchester. Att: 40,796. 13 May 1990.
Widnes: Alan Tait (2t); Jonathan Davies (4g), Andy Currier (2t), Darren Wright, Martin Offiah; David Hulme, Paul Hulme; Kurt Sorensen (c), Phil McKenzie, Mike O'Neill, Emosi Koloto, Richard Eyres, Les Holliday (1t). S: Tony Myler, Joe Grima.
Bradford: Ian Wilkinson; Gerald Cordle, Steve McGowan, Tony Marchant (1t), Richard Francis;

Roger Simpson, Paul Harkin; Kelvin Skerrett, Brian Noble, David Hobbs (c), Paul Medley, Karl Fairbank, Keith Mumby (1g). S: David Cooper, Craig Richards.
Harry Sunderland Trophy: Alan Tait

1990-91 Hull 14-4 Widnes
Old Trafford, Manchester. Att: 42,043. 12 May 1991.
Hull: Richard Gay (1t); Paul Eastwood (1g), Damien McGarry, Brad Webb, Neil Turner; Greg Mackey (c), Patrick Entat; Karl Harrison, Lee Jackson, Andy Dannatt, Ian Marlow, Russ Walker (1t), Jon Sharp. S: Gary Nolan (1t), Dean Busby.
Widnes: Alan Tait; John Devereux, Andy Currier, Jonathan Davies (c), Martin Offiah (1t); Barry Dowd, David Hulme; Kurt Sorensen, Phil McKenzie, Joe Grima, Paul Hulme, Emosi Koloto, Steve McCurrie. S: Darren Wright, Harvey Howard.
Harry Sunderland Trophy: Greg Mackey

1991-92 Wigan 48-16 St Helens
Old Trafford, Manchester. Att: 33,157. 17 May 1992.
Wigan: Steve Hampson; Joe Lydon; Dean Bell (c), Gene Miles (1t), Martin Offiah (2t); Frano Botica (10g), Shaun Edwards; Neil Cowie, Martin Dermott, Andy Platt (1t), Denis Betts (2t), Billy McGinty, Phil Clarke. S: David Myers (1t), Sam Panapa.
St Helens: Phil Veivers; Alan Hunte, Gary Connolly, Paul Loughlin (1t, 2g), Anthony Sullivan (2t); Tea Ropati, Paul Bishop; Jonathan Neill, Bernard Dwyer, Kevin Ward, Sonny Nickle, George Mann, Shane Cooper (c). S: Jonathan Griffiths, Paul Groves.
Harry Sunderland Trophy: Andy Platt

1992-93 St Helens 10-4 Wigan
Old Trafford, Manchester. Att: 36,598. 16 May 1993.
St Helens: David Lyon; Mike Riley, Gary Connolly (1t), Paul Loughlin (1t), Alan Hunte; Tea Ropati, Gus O'Donnell (2dg); Jonathan Neill, Bernard Dwyer, George Mann, Chris Joynt, Sonny Nickle, Shane Cooper (c). S: Jonathan Griffiths, Phil Veivers.
Wigan: Paul Atcheson; Jason Robinson, Sam Panapa, Andrew Farrar, Martin Offiah; Frano Botica, Shaun Edwards (c); Neil Cowie, Martin Dermott, Kelvin Skerrett, Mick Cassidy, Andy Farrell, Phil Clarke. S: Mike Forshaw (1t), Ian Gildart.
Harry Sunderland Trophy: Chris Joynt

1993-94 Wigan 24-20 Castleford
Old Trafford, Manchester. Att: 35,644. 22 May 1994.
Wigan: Paul Atcheson; Jason Robinson, Sam Panapa (1t), Gary Connolly, Martin Offiah; Frano Botica (1t, 4g), Shaun Edwards (c); Kelvin Skerrett, Martin Hall, Neil Cowie, Denis Betts (1t), Andy Farrell (1t), Phil Clarke. S: Joe Lydon, Mick Cassidy.
Castleford: St John Ellis; Chris Smith, Richie Blackmore, Tony Smith, Simon Middleton; Graham Steadman (1t, 2g), Mike Ford; Lee Crooks (c) (2g), Richard Russell, Dean Sampson (1t), Martin Ketteridge, Andy Hay, Tawera Nikau. S: Ian Smales, Nathan Sykes (1t).
Harry Sunderland Trophy: Sam Panapa

1994-95 Wigan 69-12 Leeds
Old Trafford, Manchester. Att: 30,160. 21 May 1995.
Wigan: Henry Paul (1t); Jason Robinson, Kris Radlinski (3t), Gary Connolly (3t), Martin Offiah; Frano Botica (10g), Shaun Edwards (c) (1t); Kelvin Skerrett (1t), Martin Hall (1t), Neil Cowie, Denis Betts (1t), Andy Farrell (1dg), Phil Clarke. S: Simon Haughton (1t), Mick Cassidy.
Leeds: Alan Tait; Jim Fallon, Kevin Iro (c), Phil Hassan, Francis Cummins; Craig Innes (1t), Graham Holroyd (2g); Harvey Howard, James Lowes, Esene Faimalo, George Mann, Richie Eyres (1t), Gary Mercer. S: Marcus Vassilakopolous, Neil Harmon.
Harry Sunderland Trophy: Kris Radlinski

1996 Wigan 44-14 St Helens
Old Trafford, Manchester. Att: 35,013. 8 September 1996.
Wigan: Kris Radlinski; Danny Ellison (3t), Gary Connolly (1t), Va'aiga Tuigamala, Jason Robinson (1t); Henry Paul (1t), Shaun Edwards (1t); Kelvin Skerrett, Martin Hall, Terry O'Connor, Simon Haughton (1t), Mick Cassidy, Andy Farrell (c) (4g). S: Neil Cowie, Steve Barrow, Andy Johnson, Craig Murdock (1t).
St Helens: Steve Prescott; Joey Hayes, Alan Hunte, Paul Newlove (1t), Anthony Sullivan; Tommy Martyn (1t), Bobbie Goulding (c) (3g); Apollo Perelini, Keiron Cunningham, Adam Fogerty, Derek McVey, Chris Morley, Karle Hammond. S: Ian Pickavance, Danny Arnold, Andy Haigh, Simon Booth.
Harry Sunderland Trophy: Andy Farrell

1997 Wigan Warriors 33-20 St Helens
Old Trafford, Manchester. Att: 33,389. 28 September 1997.
Wigan: Jason Robinson (1t); Andy Johnson (1t), Kris Radlinski (1t), Gary Connolly, Danny Ellison; Henry Paul, Tony Smith; Neil Cowie, Jon Clarke, Lee Hansen, Simon Haughton (1t), Mick Cassidy, Andy Farrell (c) (1t, 6g). S: Nigel Wright (1dg), Terry O'Connor, Stephen Holgate, Gael Tallec.
St Helens: Danny Arnold; Anthony Stewart, Alan Hunte, Paul Newlove (1t), Anthony Sullivan; Karle Hammond (1t), Sean Long (2g); Andy Leatham, Keiron Cunningham, Julian O'Neill, Apollo Perelini, Derek McVey (1t), Chris Joynt (c). S: Simon Booth, Ian Pickavance, Chris Morley, Paul Anderson (1t).
Harry Sunderland Trophy: Andy Farrell

2.5 LANCASHIRE CUP FINALS 1980 - 1992

The County Cups were first introduced in 1905. They were scrapped when the game reverted to two divisions at the start of the 1993-94 season.

1980-81 Warrington 26-10 Wigan
Knowsley Road, St Helens. Att: 6,279. 4 October 1980.
Warrington: Derek Finnegan; Rick Thackray (1t), Ian Duane, John Bevan (1t), Steve Hesford (1t, 7g); Ken Kelly (c), Alan Gwilliam; Neil Courtney, Tony Waller, Brian Case, Tommy Martyn (1t), Bob Eccles, Eddie Hunter. S: Tony Worrall (dnp), Ian Potter.
Wigan: George Fairbairn (c) (1t, 2g); Dennis Ramsdale (1t), David Willicombe, Steve Davies, Jim Hornby; Martin Foy, Les Bolton; Steve Breheny, John Pendlebury, Steve O'Neill, Billy Melling, John Clough, Terry Hollingsworth. S: Bernard Coyle, Malcolm Smith.
Man of the Match: Tony Waller

1981-82 Leigh 8-3 Widnes
Central Park, Wigan. Att: 9,011. 26 September 1981.
Leigh: Mick Hogan; Des Drummond, Terry Bilsbury (1t), Steve Donlan (1dg), Graham Worgan; John Woods (c) (2g), Ken Green; Alf Wilkinson, Ray Tabern, Tony Cooke, Tommy Martyn, Geoff Clarkson, Mick McTigue. S: Phil Fox (dnp), Billy Platt.
Widnes: Mick Burke; Mick George, Eric Hughes, Eddie Cunningham, Keith Bentley (1t); David Moran, Andy Gregory; Mike O'Neill, Keith Elwell, Brian Lockwood, Les Gorley, Eric Prescott, Mick Adams (c). S: John Myler (dnp), Glyn Shaw (dnp).
Man of the Match: Ray Tabern

1982-83 Warrington 16-0 St Helens
Central Park, Wigan. Att: 6,462. 23 October 1982.
Warrington: Steve Hesford (2g); Paul Fellows (1t), Ronnie Duane, John Bevan, Mike Kelly (1t); Paul Cullen, Ken Kelly (c) (1t); Neil Courtney, Carl Webb, Tony Cooke, Bob Eccles (1t), John Fieldhouse, Mike Gregory. S: Derek Finnegan (dnp), Dave Chisnall.
St Helens: Brian Parkes; Barrie Ledger, Chris Arkwright, Roy Haggerty, Denis Litherland; Steve

Peters, Neil Holding; Mel James, Graham Liptrot, Gary Bottell, Gary Moorby, Peter Gorley, Harry Pinner (c). S: John Smith, Roy Mathias.
Man of the Match: Steve Hesford

1983-84 Barrow 12-8 Widnes
Central Park, Wigan. Att: 7,007. 1 October 1983.
Barrow: Steve Tickle (1dg); Terry Moore, Andy Whittle, Ian Ball (3g, 1dg), David Milby; Ralph McConnell (1t), David Cairns; Alan Hodkinson (c), Les Wall, Mark McJennett, Steve Herbert, Eddie Syzmala, Steve Mossop. S: David Elliott (dnp), Dave Tyson (dnp).
Widnes: Mick Burke; Joe Lydon (1t, 2g), Eric Hughes (c), Keiron O'Loughlin, John Basnett; Tony Myler, Andy Gregory; Steve O'Neill, Keith Elwell, Kevin Tamati, Fred Whitfield, Eric Prescott, Mick Adams. S: Tony Garritty (dnp), Paul Houghton (dnp).
Man of the Match: David Cairns

1984-85 St Helens 26-18 Wigan
Central Park, Wigan. Att: 26,074. 28 October 1984.
St Helens: Phil Veivers; Barrie Ledger, Shaun Allen, Mal Meninga (2t), Sean Day (1t, 5g); Chris Arkwright, Neil Holding; Tony Burke, Graham Liptrot, Peter Gorley, Andy Platt, Paul Round, Harry Pinner. S: John Smith, Roy Haggerty (1t).
Wigan: Shaun Edwards; John Ferguson, David Stephenson, Colin Whitfield (3g), Henderson Gill (1t); Mark Cannon, Jimmy Fairhurst; Neil Courteney, Nicky Kiss (1t), Brian Case, Graeme West (c) (1t), Shaun Wane, Ian Potter. S: John Pendlebury, Mick Scott.
Man of the Match: Mal Meninga

1985-86 Wigan 34-8 Warrington
Knowsley Road, St Helens. Att: 19,202. 13 October 1985.
Wigan: Shaun Edwards (1t); Gary Henley-Smith, David Stephenson (7g), Ellery Hanley (1t), Colin Whitfield; Steve Ella (2t), Mike Ford; Greg Dowling, Nicky Kiss (1t), Shaun Wane, Nick du Toit, Andy Goodway (c), Ian Potter. S: Steve Hampson, Brian Case.
Warrington: Brian Johnson (1t); Brian Carbert (2g), Paul Cullen, Phil Blake, Rick Thackray; Ken Kelly (c), Andy Gregory; Bob Eccles, Carl Webb, Bob Jackson, Les Boyd, Mike Gregory, Alan Rathbone. S: Mark Forster, Kevin Tamati.
Man of the Match: Steve Ella

1986-87 Wigan 27-6 Oldham
Knowsley Road, St Helens. Att: 20,180. 19 October 1986.
Wigan: Shaun Edwards (2t); Joe Lydon (1t, 1dg), David Stephenson, Dean Bell, Henderson Gill (5g); Ellery Hanley, Mike Ford (1t); Graeme West (c), Martin Dermott, Brian Case, Ian Roberts, Ian Potter, Andy Goodway. S: Steve Hampson, Rob Louw.
Oldham: Hussein M'Barki; Paul Sherman, Gary Bridge (1t), Gary Warnecke, Mike Taylor; David Topliss (c), Paddy Kirwan; Bruce Clark, Terry Flanagan, David Hobbs (1g), Tom Naidole, Mick Worrall, Stuart Raper. S: Neil Clawson, Colin Hawkyard.
Man of the Match: Mike Ford

1987-88 Wigan 28-16 Warrington
Knowsley Road, St Helens. Att: 20,237. 11 October 1987.
Wigan: Steve Hampson; Richard Russell, David Stephenson (1g), Joe Lydon (5g), Henderson Gill (1t); Shaun Edwards, Andy Gregory; Brian Case, Nicky Kiss, Shaun Wane, Andy Goodway, Ian Potter, Ellery Hanley (c) (2t). S: Dean Bell, Graeme West (1t).
Warrington: Brian Johnson; Des Drummond, Mark Forster (2t), Barry Peters, Brian Carbert; John Woods (2g), Keith Holden; Kevin Tamati (c), Carl Webb, Tony Humphries, Gary Sanderson, Mark Roberts, Mike Gregory (1t). S: David Lyon, Neil Harmon.
Man of the Match: Shaun Edwards

1988-89 Wigan 22-17 Salford
Knowsley Road, St Helens. Att: 19,154. 23 October 1988.
Wigan: Steve Hampson; Tony Iro, Kevin Iro (2t, 3g), Dean Bell (1t), Joe Lydon; Shaun Edwards, Andy Gregory; Ian Lucas, Martin Dermott, Adrian Shelford (1t), Andy Platt, Andy Goodway, Ellery Hanley (c). S: Ged Byrne, Denis Betts.
Salford: Peter Williams (c); Tex Evans (1t), Keith Bentley (1t), Ken Jones, Adrian Hadley; Paul Shaw, David Cairns; Steve Herbert (1t), Mark Moran, Peter Brown (2g), Ian Gormley, Mick Worrall (1dg), Mark Horo. S: Ian Blease, Mick McTigue.
Man of the Match: Paul Shaw

1989-90 Warrington 24-16 Oldham
Knowsley Road, St Helens. Att: 9,990. 14 October 1989.
Warrington: David Lyon; Des Drummond, Joe Ropati (1t), Tony Thorniley, Mark Forster (1t); Robert Turner (4g), Greg Mackey; Tony Burke, Mark Roskell, Steve Molloy, Bob Jackson (2t), Gary Sanderson, Mike Gregory (c). S: Paul Darbyshire, Ronnie Duane.
Oldham: Duncan Platt (1g); Steve Robinson (1t), Gary Hyde (1g), Richard Irving (1t), Paul Lord (1t); Brett Clark, Mike Ford; Leo Casey, Andy Ruane, John Fieldhouse, Shaun Allen, Keith Newton, John Cogger (c). S: Richard Russell, John Fairbank.
Man of the Match: Bob Jackson

1990-91 Widnes 24-18 Salford
Central Park, Wigan. Att: 7,485. 29 September 1990.
Widnes: Alan Tait; Darren Wright, Andy Currier (1t), Jonathan Davies (4g) (c), Martin Offiah (1t); Tony Myler (1t) (c), David Hulme; Kurt Sorensen, Phil McKenzie, Chris Ashurst, Richard Eyres, Emosi Koloto, Les Holliday. S: John Devereux, David Smith (1t).
Salford: Steve Gibson; Tex Evans, Martin Birkett, Peter Williams (1t), Adrian Hadley; David Fell (1t), Steve Kerry (3g); Ian Sherratt, Mark Lee, Chris Whiteley, Arthur Bradshaw, Ian Blease (c) (1t), Andy Burgess. S: Frank Cassidy, Shane Hansen.
Man of the Match: David Fell

1991-92 St Helens 24-14 Rochdale Hornets
Wilderspool, Warrington. Att: 9,269. 20 October 1991.
St Helens: David Tanner; Mike Riley, Gary Connolly, Tea Ropati, Anthony Sullivan; Phil Veivers (2t), Paul Bishop (1t, 2g); Jonathan Neill, Paul Groves, Kevin Ward, John Harrison, George Mann (2t), Shane Cooper (c). S: Mark Bailey, Paul Forber.
Rochdale: Colin Whitfield (c) (1g); Phil Fox, Darren Abram (1t), Ronnie Duane (1t), Tony Garrity; Brett Clark, Steve Gartland; Tony Humphries, Martin Hall, Bob Marsden, Cliff Eccles, Paul Okesene, Mike Kuiti (1t). S: Matt Calland, Simon Bamber.
Man of the Match: Bob Marsden

1992-93 Wigan 5-4 St Helens
Knowsley Road, St Helens. Att: 20,534. 18 October 1992.
Wigan: Steve Hampson; Jason Robinson, Joe Lydon, Andrew Farrar, Martin Offiah; Frano Botica (2g, 1dg), Shaun Edwards (c); Kelvin Skerrett, Martin Dermott, Andy Platt, Denis Betts, Billy McGinty, Dean Bell (c). S: Martin Crompton, Neil Cowie.
St Helens: Phil Veivers; Alan Hunte, Gary Connolly, Jarrod McCracken, Anthony Sullivan; Tea Ropati, Jonathan Griffiths; John Harrison, Bernard Dwyer (2g), Kevin Ward, Chris Joynt, Sonny Nickle, Shane Cooper (c). S: Gus O'Donnell, Paul Forber.
Man of the Match: Bernard Dwyer

2.6 YORKSHIRE CUP FINALS 1980 - 1992

The man of the Match in Yorkshire Cup Finals was awarded the White Rose Trophy. In the 1987-88 final, this was awarded to Paul Harkin after a drawn game between Bradford Northern and Castleford, and not to Brendan Hill, the man of the match in the replay.

1980-81 Leeds 8-7 Hull Kingston Rovers

Fartown, Huddersfield. Att: 9,751. 8 November 1980.
Leeds: Willie Oulton; Alan Smith (1t), David Smith, Neil Hague, John Atkinson; John Holmes, Kevin Dick (2g, 1dg); Mick Harrison, David Ward (c), Steve Pitchford, Graham Eccles, Phil Cookson, David Heron. S: John Sanderson (dnp), John Carroll.
Hull KR: Ian Robinson; Gary McHugh (1t), Mike Smith, Phil Hogan (2g), Wally Youngman; David Hall, Paul Harkin; Roy Holdstock, Ray Price, Steve Crooks, Phil Lowe, Len Casey (c), Mick Crane. S: Ged Dunn (dnp), Paul Rose.
White Rose Trophy: Kevin Dick

1981-82 Castleford 10-5 Bradford Northern

Headingley, Leeds. Att: 5,852. 3 October 1981.
Castleford: George Claughton; Terry Richardson, Steve Fenton, Gary Hyde (1t), Geoff Morris; John Joyner (c) (1t), Bob Beardmore; Alan Hardy, Bob Spurr, Barry Johnson, David Finch (2g), Kevin Ward, Andrew Timson. S: Paul Norton, Ian Birkby (dnp).
Bradford: Keith Mumby; David Barends, Gary Hale, Alan Parker (1t), Les Gant; Ellery Hanley (1g), Alan Redfearn (c); Jeff Grayshon, Brian Noble, Phil Sanderson, Gary van Bellen, Graham Idle, Alan Rathbone. S: David Redfearn, Dick Jasiewicz.
White Rose Trophy: Barry Johnson

1982-83 Hull 18-7 Bradford Northern

Headingley Stadium, Leeds. Att: 11,755. 2 October 1982.
Hull: Gary Kemble; Steve Evans (1t), Terry Day, James Leuluai, Paul Prendiville (1t); David Topliss (c), Kevin Harkin; Trevor Skerrett, Keith Bridges, Charlie Stone, Paul Rose (2t), Lee Crooks (2g, 2dg), Mick Crane. S: Barry Banks (dnp), Steve Norton.
Bradford: Keith Mumby; David Barends, Les Gant, Alan Parker, Steve Pullen; Keith Whiteman (1t), Dean Carroll (1g, 2dg); Jeff Grayshon (c), Brian Noble, Gary van Bellen, Graham Idle, Dick Jasiewicz, Gary Hale. S: David Smith, Phil Sanderson.
White Rose Trophy: Keith Mumby

1983-84 Hull 13-2 Castleford

Elland Road, Leeds. Att: 14,049. 15 October 1983.
Hull: Gary Kemble; Patrick Solal, Garry Schofield, James Leuluai, Dane O'Hara (1t); David Topliss (c), Tony Dean; Phil Edmonds, Ron Wileman, Trevor Skerrett, Wayne Proctor (1t), Lee Crooks, Mick Crane (1t, 1dg). S: Barry Banks, Paul Rose.
Castleford: Darren Coen; Steve Fenton, Tony Marchant, Gary Hyde, John Kear; John Joyner, Bob Beardmore (c) (1g); Gary Connell, Stuart Horton, Malcolm Reilly, Andrew Timson, Neil James, Keith England. S: Ian Orum, Alan Hardy.
White Rose Trophy: Mick Crane

1984-85 Hull 29-12 Hull Kingston Rovers

Boothferry Park, Hull. Att: 25,237. 27 October 1984.
Hull: Gary Kemble (2t); James Leuluai, Garry Schofield (4g, 1dg), Steve Evans (1t), Dane O'Hara; Fred Ah Kuoi, Peter Sterling; Phil Edmonds, Shaun Patrick, Lee Crooks (c) (1t), Steve Norton (1t), Wayne Proctor, Gary Divorty. S: David Topliss, Paul Rose.
Hull KR: George Fairbairn (1t); Garry Clark, Ian Robinson (1t), Gary Prohm, David Laws; Mike Smith, Mike Harkin; Mark Broadhurst, David Watkinson (c), Asuquo Ema, Chris Burton, Andy Kelly, David Hall (1t). S: Steve Hartley, Chris Rudd.
White Rose Trophy: Peter Sterling

1985-86 Hull Kingston Rovers 22-18 Castleford

Headingley, Leeds. Att: 12,686. 27 October 1985.
Hull KR: George Fairbairn; Garry Clark (1t), John Dorahy (5g), Gary Prohm, David Laws; Gordon Smith, Paul Harkin; Des Harrison, David Watkinson (c), Asuquo Ema, Chris Burton, Phil Hogan, Gavin Miller (2t). S: John Lydiat, Andy Kelly.
Castleford: Gary Lord; David Plange, Tony Marchant (2t), Gary Hyde, Chris Spears; Steve

Diamond (1g), Bob Beardmore (1t, 2g); Kevin Ward, Kevin Beardmore, Barry Johnson, Keith England, Martin Ketteridge, John Joyner (c). S: David Roockley, Stuart Horton.
White Rose Trophy: Gavin Miller

1986-87 Castleford 31-24 Hull
Headingley, Leeds. Att: 11,132. 11 October 1986.
Castleford: Gary Lord; David Plange, Tony Marchant, Chris Johns, Gary Hyde; John Joyner (c), Bob Beardmore (1dg); Kevin Ward (1t), Kevin Beardmore (2t), Barry Johnson, Martin Ketteridge (1t, 5g), Brett Atkins (1t), Keith England. S: Gary Lord, Alan Shillito.
Hull: Gary Kemble; Michael Brand (2t), Garry Schofield, Dane O'Hara (2t), Paul Eastwood; Fred Ah Kuoi, Phil Windley; Dave Brown, Shaun Patrick, Andy Dannatt, Steve Norton, Lee Crooks (c) (4g) Jon Sharp. S: Neil Puckering, Gary Divorty.
White Rose Trophy: Kevin Beardmore

1987-88 Bradford Northern 12-12 Castleford
Headingley, Leeds. Att: 10,947. 17 October 1987.
Bradford: Gary Mercer; Phil Ford, Steve McGowan, Roger Simpson, Richard Francis; Keith Mumby (2g), Paul Harkin (c); Jeff Grayshon, Brian Noble, Brendan Hill, Kelvin Skerrett, Karl Fairbank (1t), Terry Holmes. S: Neil Roebuck, David Hobbs (2g).
Castleford: David Roockley; David Plange (1t), Tony Marchant, Michael Beattie, Gary Hyde; John Joyner (c), Roy Southernwood; Alan Shillito, Kevin Beardmore, Kevin Ward, Martin Ketteridge (2g), John Fifita, Bob Lindner (1t). S: Bob Beardmore, Dean Sampson.
White Rose Trophy: Paul Harkin

Replay: Bradford Northern 11-2 Castleford
Elland Road, Leeds. Att: 8,175. 31 October 1987.
Bradford: Keith Mumby; Phil Ford, Steve McGowan, Gary Mercer, Roger Simpson; Russell Stewart, Paul Harkin (c); David Hobbs (1g, 1dg), Brian Noble, Brendan Hill (1t), Kelvin Skerrett, Karl Fairbank, Wayne Heron (1t). S: Neil Roebuck, David Redfearn.
Castleford: David Roockley; David Plange, Tony Marchant, Michael Beattie, Gary Hyde; Roy Southernwood, Bob Beardmore; Kevin Ward, Kenny Hill, John Fifita, Martin Ketteridge (1g), Keith England, John Joyner (c). S: Giles Boothroyd, Dean Sampson.
Man of the Match: Brendan Hill

1988-89 Leeds 33-12 Castleford
Elland Road, Leeds. Att: 22,968. 16 October 1988.
Leeds: Gary Spencer; Andrew Ettingshausen, Garry Schofield (2t, 1dg), David Stephenson (6g), Carl Gibson (2t); Cliff Lyons, Ray Ashton; Lee Crooks (c), Colin Maskill, Hugh Waddell, Roy Powell, Mark Brooke-Cowden, David Heron. S: Paul Medley (1t), Sam Backo.
Castleford: Gary Belcher; David Plange, Tony Marchant, Giles Boothroyd (1t), Chris Chapman; Grant Anderson, Bob Beardmore; Kevin Ward, Kevin Beardmore, Keith England, Martin Ketteridge (2g), Ron Gibbs, John Joyner (c) (1t). S: David Roockley, Dean Sampson.
White Rose Trophy: Cliff Lyons

1989-90 Bradford Northern 20-14 Featherstone Rovers
Headingley, Leeds. Att: 12,607. 5 November 1989.
Bradford: Ian Wilkinson; Gerald Cordle (2t), Steve McGowan, Roger Simpson, Richard Francis; Ivan Henjak, Paul Harkin (2t); Kelvin Skerrett, Glenn Barraclough, Jon Hamer, David Hobbs (c) (2g), Karl Fairbank, John Pendlebury. S: Keith Mumby, Paul Medley.
Featherstone: Chris Bibb; Barry Drummond, Iva Ropati (1t), Paul Newlove, Alan Banks; Ian Smales, Deryck Fox (c) (3g); Jeff Grayshon, Trevor Clark, Glen Bell, Gary Price, Glen Booth, Peter Smith (1t). S: Alan Dakin, Andy Fisher.
White Rose Trophy: Paul Harkin

1990-91 Castleford 11-8 Wakefield Trinity
Elland Road, Leeds. Att: 12,420, 23 September 1990.
Castleford: Steve Larder; St John Ellis, Shaun Irwin, Grant Anderson, David Plange (1t); Graham

Steadman, Gary Atkins (1t); Lee Crooks (c) (1g), Graham Southernwood, Dean Sampson, Neil Battye, Jeff Hardy, Neil Roebuck (1dg). S: Keith England, Martin Ketteridge.
Wakefield: Kevin Harcombe (2g); David Jones, Andy Mason (1t), Phil Eden, Andy Wilson; Tracy Lazenby, Mark Conway; Adrian Shelford, Billy Conway, John Thompson, Andy Kelly (c), Gary Price, Nigel Bell. S: Chris Perry, Richard Slater.
White Rose Trophy: Tracy Lazenby

1991-92 Castleford 28-6 Bradford Northern
Elland Road, Leeds. Att: 8,916, 20 October 1991.
Castleford: Graham Steadman (2t, 4g); St John Ellis, Graeme Bradley, Richie Blackmore, David Nelson; Tony Smith (1t), Mike Ford (1t); Dean Sampson, Graham Southernwood, Keith England, Neil Battye (1t), Shaun Irwin, Tawera Nikau (c). S: Grant Anderson, Martin Ketteridge.
Bradford: Roger Simpson; Daio Powell (1t), Darrall Shelford, Steve McGowan, Tony Marchant; Tony Anderson, Brett Iti; David Hobbs (1g), Brian Noble, Jon Hamer, Paul Medley, Karl Fairbank (c), Steve Barnett. S: David Croft, Craig Richards.
White Rose Trophy: Graham Steadman

1992-93 Wakefield 29-16 Sheffield Eagles
Elland Road, Leeds. Att: 7,918. 18 October 1992.
Wakefield: Gary Spencer (1t); David Jones, Andy Mason (1t), Peter Benson (3g), Andy Wilson; Nigel Wright (1g, 1dg), Geoff Bagnall (c) (1t); Mark Webster, Nigel Bell, John Glancy, Gary Price (1t), Darren Fritz, Richard Slater (1t). S: Richard Goddard, Billy Conway.
Sheffield: Garry Jack; Mark Gamson (1t), Richard Price, David Mycoe (2g), David Plange; Mark Aston, Tim Lumb; Paul Broadbent, Mick Cook, Dale Laughton, Bruce McGuire (c) (2t), Paul Carr, Anthony Farrell. S: Andy Young, Hugh Waddell.
White Rose Trophy: Nigel Wright

2.7 THE CHARITY SHIELD 1985 - 1995

Originally sponsored by Okells, an Isle of Man brewer, the Charity Shield, competed for by the league champions and the Challenge Cup winners, was first played in August 1985 and when they won both trophies in 1990 and 1991, they played the Premiership winners. When Wigan won all three in 1992 and 1995, they played the Division One runners-up. From 1987 the man of the match was awarded the Jack Bentley Trophy, named after the Daily Express rugby league correspondant.

1985-86 Wigan 34-6 Hull Kingston Rovers
Douglas Bowl, Isle of Man. Att: 4,066. 25 August 1985.
Wigan: Steve Hampson; Phil Ford, David Stephenson (7g), Steve Donlan (2t), Henderson Gill (2t); Shaun Edwards, Mike Ford (1t); Neil Courtney, Nicky Kiss, Danny Campbell, Graeme West (c), Nick du Toit, Shaun Wane. S: Ian Lucas, John Mayo.
Hull KR: George Fairbairn; Garry Clark (1t), Ian Robinson, Gary Prohm, David Laws; Mike Smith, Gordon Smith; Des Harrison, David Watkinson (c), Asuquo Ema, Andy Kelly, Chris Burton, Phil Hogan. S: John Lydiat (1g), Chris Rudd.
Man of the Match: Shaun Edwards

1986-87 Halifax 9-8 Castleford
Douglas Bowl, Isle of Man. Att: 3,276. 24 August 1986.
Halifax: Steve Smith; Eddie Riddlesden, Colin Whitfield (1t), Neil Hague (1dg), Wilf George (1t); Chris Anderson (c), Gary Stephens; Roy Dickinson, Seamus McCallion, Brian Juliff, Mick Scott, Peter Bell, Paul Dixon. S: Scott Wilson, Neil James.
Castleford: David Roockley; David Plange, Gary Lord (1t), Shaun Irwin, Tony Spears; John Joyner (c), Bob Beardmore; Kevin Ward, Kevin Beardmore, Barry Johnson, Martin Ketteridge (2g), Dean Mountain, Keith England. S: Roy Southernwood, Ian Fletcher.
Man of the Match: Chris Anderson

1987-88 Wigan 44-12 Halifax

Douglas Bowl, Isle of Man. Att: 4,804. 23 August 1987.

Wigan: Steve Hampson (2t); David Stephenson (8g), Ged Byrne, Dean Bell (2t), Henderson Gill (1t); Shaun Edwards (2t), Andy Gregory; Graeme West (c), Nicky Kiss, Brian Case, Ian Gildart, Ian Potter, Andy Goodway. S: Richard Russell, Shaun Wane.

Halifax: Graham Eadie; Mike Taylor, Scott Wilson, Tony Anderson (1t), Wilf George; Andy Simpson, Gary Stephens (c); Roy Dickinson, John Pendlebury, Graham Beevers, Neil James, Mick Scott, Paul Dixon (1t). S: Brian Juliff (1t), Peter Bell.

Jack Bentley Trophy: Shaun Edwards

1988-89 Widnes 20-14 Wigan

Douglas Bowl, Isle of Man. Att: 5,044. 21 August 1988.

Widnes: Alan Tait; Rick Thackray, Andy Currier (4g), Darren Wright (1t), Martin Offiah (1t); Barry Dowd, David Hulme; Kurt Sorensen (c), Phil McKenzie (1t), Joe Grima, Mike O'Neill, Paul Hulme, Richard Eyres. S: Steve O'Neill (dnp), Derek Pyke.

Wigan: Steve Hampson; Henderson Gill, Joe Lydon (1t, 1g), Dean Bell, Mark Preston; Ged Byrne, Andy Gregory (c); Adrian Shelford, Nicky Kiss, Brian Case, Tony Iro (2t), Shaun Wane, Andy Goodway. S: Denis Betts, Ian Lucas

Jack Bentley Trophy: Phil McKenzie

1989-90 Widnes 27-22 Wigan

Anfield, Liverpool. Att: 17,263. 27 August 1989.

Widnes: Alan Tait (1dg); Brimah Kebbie (1t), Jonathan Davies (1t, 5g), Darren Wright, Martin Offiah (1t); Tony Myler, David Hulme (1t); Kurt Sorensen (c), Paul Hulme, Joe Grima, Mike O'Neill, Emosi Koloto, Richard Eyres. S: David Marsh (dnp), Derek Pyke.

Wigan: Steve Hampson; Dean Bell (c), Kevin Iro (1t), Joe Lydon (1t, 5g), Mark Preston; Ged Byrne, Andy Gregory; Ian Lucas, Nicky Kiss, Andy Platt (1t), Denis Betts, Ian Gildart, Andy Goodway. S: John Gilfillan, Ged Stazicker.

Jack Bentley Trophy: Denis Betts

1990-91 Widnes 24-8 Wigan

Vetch Field, Swansea. Att: 11,178. 19 August 1990.

Widnes: Alan Tait; John Devereux (1t), Andy Currier, Jonathan Davies (3t, 2g), Martin Offiah (1t); Tony Myler (c), David Hulme; Chris Ashurst, Phil McKenzie, Joe Grima, Paul Hulme, Emosi Koloto, Les Holliday. S: Darren Wright, Kurt Sorensen.

Wigan: John Gilfillan; David Myers, Dean Bell (c), Ged Byrne, Mark Preston; Frano Botica (1t, 2g), Bobbie Goulding; Kelvin Skerrett, Russell Bridge, Shaun Wane, Ian Gildart, Andy Platt, Denis Betts. S: Shaun Edwards, Mike Forshaw.

Jack Bentley Trophy: Jonathan Davies

1991-92 Wigan 22-8 Hull

Gateshead International Stadium. Att: 10,248. 25 August 1991.

Wigan: Steve Hampson; David Myers (1t), Dean Bell (c) (2t), Joe Lydon, Frano Botica (3g); Shaun Edwards (1t), Andy Gregory; Ian Lucas, Martin Dermott, Kelvin Skerrett, Denis Betts, Andy Platt, Andy Goodway. S: Mike Forshaw, Ian Gildart.

Hull: Steve Feather; Paul Eastwood (2g), Brian Blacker, Gary Nolan (1t), Neil Turner; Lee Hanlan, Greg Mackey (c); Steve Durham, Lee Jackson, Ian Marlow, Steve McNamara, Russ Walker, Dean Busby. S: Mike Dixon, Mark Jones.

Jack Bentley Trophy: Dean Bell

1992-93 St Helens 17-0 Wigan

Gateshead International Stadium. Att: 7,364. 23 August 1992.

St Helens: Alan Hunte; Mark Riley, Gary Connolly, Tea Ropati (1t, 2g), Anthony Sullivan (1t); Jonathan Griffiths, Gus O'Donnell (1dg); Jonathan Neill, Bernard Dwyer, Kevin Ward, John Harrison, George Mann, Shane Cooper (c) (1t). S: Les Quirk, Paul Forber.

Wigan: Steve Hampson; Sam Panapa, Dean Bell (c), Joe Lydon, Martin Offiah; Frano Botica,

Martin Crompton; Ian Lucas, Mick Cassidy, Kelvin Skerrett, Denis Betts, Billy McGinty, Phil Clarke. S: David Myers, Andy Goodway.
Jack Bentley Trophy: Alan Hunte

1995-96 Wigan 45-20 Leeds
Royal Showground, Dublin. Att: 5,716. 13 August 1995.
Wigan: Henry Paul; Jason Robinson, Va'aiga Tuigamala, Gary Connolly (1t), Kris Radlinski; Nigel Wright (2t, 1dg), Craig Murdock; Kelvin Skerrett, Martin Hall, Neil Cowie, Simon Haughton (1t), Mick Cassidy (1t), Andy Farrell (c) (1t, 8g). S: Rob Smyth, Matthew Knowles, Andy Johnson, Terry O'Connor (1t).
Leeds: Alan Tait; Jim Fallon, Kevin Iro, Francis Cummins, Paul Cook (4g); Tony Kemp (1t), Marcus Vassilakopolous; Neil Harmon, James Lowes (c), Esene Faimalo (1t), Gary Mercer, George Mann, Mike Forshaw (1t). S: Marvin Golden, David Gibbons, Adrian Morley, Nick Fozzard.
Jack Bentley Trophy: Andy Farrell

3 DOMESTIC RUGBY LEAGUE - AUSTRALIAN
3.1 AUSTRALIAN GRAND FINAL RESULTS

Grand Final man of the matches (apart from the Super League Final of 1997) have been awarded the Clive Churchill Medal since 1986, in memory of the Australian international fullback from the 1950s. In 2008, retrospective awards were made going back to 1954, and those from 1980 are recognised here with an asterisk. The forwards are listed in the traditional manner from prop to loose forward, not how the Australian game listed them for many years. Melbourne Storm were stripped of the 2007 and 2009 titles for salary cap breaches, although the Clive Churchill Medals are still acknowledged.

1980 Canterbury Bankstown 18-4 Eastern Suburbs
Sydney Cricket Ground, Sydney. Att: 52,881. 27 September 1980.
Canterbury: Greg Brentnall; Chris Anderson (1t), Chris Mortimer, Peter Mortimer, Steve Gearin (1t, 6g); Garry Hughes, Steve Mortimer; John Coveney, George Peponis (c), Geoff Robinson, Graeme Hughes, Steve Folkes, Mark Hughes.
Easts: Marty Gurr; David Michael, Kerry Boustead, Noel Cleal, Steve McFarlane; Ken Wright (2g), Kevin Hastings; John Harvey, John Lang, Royce Ayliffe (c), John Tobin, Des O'Reilly, Gary Warnecke.
*****Clive Churchill Medal**: Steve Gearin

1981 Parramatta Eels 20-11 Newtown Jets
Sydney Cricket Ground, Sydney. Att: 57,333. 27 September 1981.
Parramatta: Steve McKenzie; Graeme Atkins (1t), Mick Cronin (4g), Steve Ella (1t), Eric Grothe; Brett Kenny (2t), Peter Sterling; Ron Hilditch, Steve Edge (c), Bob O'Reilly, John Muggleton, Kevin Stevens, Ray Price. S: Steve Sharp, Paul Taylor.
Newtown: Phil Sigsworth; John Ferguson, Mick Ryan, Brian Hetherington (1t), Ray Blacklock; Paul Morris (1g), Tommy Raudonikis (c) (1t); Steve Blythe, Barry Jensen, Craig Ellis, Michael Pitman, Phil Gould, Graeme O'Grady (1t). S: Geoff Bugden, Jim Walters, Ken Wilson, Shane McKellar.
*****Clive Churchill Medal**: Bob O'Reilly

1982 Parramatta Eels 21-8 Manly Warringah
Sydney Cricket Ground, Sydney. Att: 52,186. 26 September 1982.
Parramatta: Paul Taylor; Neil Hunt (1t), Mick Cronin (3g), Steve Ella (1t), Eric Grothe (1t); Brett Kenny (2t), Peter Sterling; Geoff Bugden, Steve Edge (c), Chris Phelan, John Muggleton, Steve Sharp, Ray Price. S: Peter Wynn, Mark Laurie.
Manly: Graham Eadie (1g); John Ribot, Chris Close, Michael Blake, Phil Carey; Alan Thompson (c), Phil Blake (1t); Geoff Gerard, Ray Brown, Terry Randall, Paul Vautin, Les Boyd (1t), Paul McCabe. S: Max Krilich, Bruce Walker, Ian Thomson.
*****Clive Churchill Medal**: Brett Kenny

1983 Parramatta Eels 18-6 Manly Warringah

Sydney Cricket Ground, Sydney. Att: 40,285. 25 September 1983.
Parramatta: Paul Taylor; David Liddiard, Mick Cronin (3g), Steve Ella, Eric Grothe (1t); Brett Kenny (2t), Peter Sterling; Stan Jurd, Steve Edge (c), Paul Mares, Peter Wynn, Steve Sharp, Ray Price. S: Chris Phelan, Don Duffy, Mark Laurie, Gary Martine.
Manly: Graham Eadie (1g); John Ribot, Chris Close, Phil Sigsworth (1t), Kerry Boustead; Alan Thompson (c), Phil Blake; Geoff Gerard, Ray Brown, Paul McCabe, Paul Vautin, Noel Cleal, Ian Schubert. S: Glenn Ryan, Rick Chisholm, Michael Blake.
***Clive Churchill Medal**: Brett Kenny

1984 Canterbury Bankstown 6-4 Parramatta Eels

Sydney Cricket Ground, Sydney. Att: 47,076. 23 September 1984.
Canterbury: Mick Potter; Steve O'Brien, Andrew Farrar, Chris Mortimer (1g), Peter Mortimer; Terry Lamb, Steve Mortimer (c); Peter Tunks, Mark Bugden (1t), Peter Kelly, Brian Battese, Steve Folkes, Paul Langmack. S: Geoff Robinson, Darryl Brohman, Greg Mullane.
Parramatta: Paul Taylor; Neil Hunt, Mick Cronin (1t), Steve Ella, Eric Grothe; Brett Kenny, Peter Sterling; Stan Jurd, Steve Edge (c), Paul Mares, Chris Phelan, John Muggleton, Ray Price. S: David Liddiard, Steve Sharp, Ron Quinn, Glen Mansfield.
***Clive Churchill Medal**: Peter Kelly

1985 Canterbury Bankstown 7-6 St George

Sydney Cricket Ground, Sydney. Att: 44,569. 29 September 1985.
Canterbury: Mick Potter; Matthew Callinan, Chris Mortimer, Andrew Farrar (1g, 1dg), Peter Mortimer (1t); Michael Hagan, Steve Mortimer (c); Peter Kelly, Billy Johnstone, Peter Tunks, Brian Battese, Steve Folkes, Paul Langmack. S: David Gillespie, Greg Mullane, Mark Bugden.
St George: Glen Burgess; Steve Morris (1t), Michael O'Connor (1g), Michael Beattie, Denis Kinchela; Steve Linnane, Perry Haddock; Pat Jarvis, Phil Ritchie, Craig Young (c), Graeme Wynn, Billy Noke, Graeme O'Grady. S: Chris Johns, Chris Guider, Stephen Funnell, Alan Neil.
***Clive Churchill Medal**: Steve Mortimer

1986 Parramatta Eels 4-2 Canterbury Bankstown

Sydney Cricket Ground, Sydney. Att: 45,843. 28 September 1986.
Parramatta: Paul Taylor; Mick Delroy, Mick Cronin (2g), Steve Ella, Eric Grothe; Brett Kenny, Peter Sterling; Geoff Bugden, Michael Moseley, Terry Leadbetter, Mark Laurie, John Muggleton, Ray Price (c). S: Peter Eynn, Tony Chalmers.
Canterbury: Phil Sigsworth; Andrew Farrar, Michael Hagan, Chris Mortimer, Steve O'Brien; Terry Lamb (1g), Steve Mortimer (c); Peter Tunks, Mark Bugden, Peter Kelly, Paul Dunn, Steve Folkes, Paul Langmack. S: Geoff Robinson, David Boyd.
Clive Churchill Medal: Peter Sterling

1987 Manly Warringah 18-8 Canberra Raiders

Sydney Cricket Ground, Sydney. Att: 50,201. 27 September 1987.
Manly: Dale Shearer; David Ronson, Darrell Williams, Michael O'Connor (1t, 5g), Stuart Davis; Cliff Lyons (1t), Des Hasler; Phil Daley, Mal Cochrane, Kevin Ward, Noel Cleal, Ron Gibbs, Paul Vautin (c). S: Mark Pocock, Paul Shaw.
Canberra: Gary Belcher (1g); Chris Kinna, Mal Meninga (1g), Peter Jackson, Matthew Corkery; Chris O'Sullivan (1t), Ivan Henjak; Brent Todd, Steve Walters, Sam Backo, Gary Coyne, Ashley Gilbert, Dean Lance (c). S: Kevin Walters, Terry Regan.
Clive Churchill Medal: Cliff Lyons

1988 Canterbury Bankstown 24-12 Balmain Tigers

Sydney Football Stadium, Sydney. Att: 40,000. 11 September 1988.
Canterbury: Jason Alchin; Glen Nissen (1t), Tony Currie, Andrew Farrar, Robin Thorne; Terry Lamb (1t, 4g), Michael Hagan (1t); Paul Dunn, Joe Thomas, Peter Tunks (c), David Gillespie (1t), Steve Folkes, Paul Langmack. S: Steve Mortimer, Brandon Lee, Darren McCarthy, Mark Budgen.

Balmain: Garry Jack; Russell Gartner, Ellery Hanley, Michael Pobjie, Ross Conlon (2g); Michael Neil, Gary Freeman; Bruce McGuire (1t), Benny Elias (1t), Kerry Helmsley, Paul Sironen, David Brooks, Wayne Pearce (c). S: Kevin Hardwick, Steve Edmed, Scott Gale.
Clive Churchill Medal: Paul Dunn

1989 Canberra Raiders 19-14 Balmain Tigers (aet)
Sydney Football Stadium, Sydney. Att: 40,500. 24 September 1989.
Canberra: Gary Belcher (1t); Matthew Wood, Mal Meninga (c) (3g), Laurie Daley, John Ferguson (1t); Chris O'Sullivan (1dg), Ricky Stuart; Brent Todd, Steve Walters, Glenn Lazarus, Dean Lance, Gary Coyne, Bradley Clyde. S: Kevin Walters, Steve Jackson (1t), Paul Martin.
Balmain: Garry Jack; Steve O'Brien, Tim Brasher, Andy Currier (3g), James Grant (1t); Michael Neil, Gary Freeman; Steve Roach, Benny Elias, Steve Edmed, Paul Sironen (1t), Bruce McGuire, Wayne Pearce (c). S: Kevin Hardwick, Shaun Edwards, Michael Pobjie.
Clive Churchill Medal: Bradley Clyde

1990 Canberra Raiders 18-14 Penrith Panthers
Sydney Football Stadium, Sydney. Att: 41,535. 23 September 1990.
Canberra: Gary Belcher; Paul Martin, Mal Meninga (c) (3g), Laurie Daley (1t), John Ferguson (1t); Chris O'Sullivan, Ricky Stuart; Brent Todd, Steve Walters, Glenn Lazarus, Nigel Gaffey, Gary Coyne, Dean Lance. S: Matthew Wood (1t), Phil Carey, Craig Bellamy, David Barnhill.
Penrith: David Greene; Alan McIndoe, Brad Fittler (1t), Col Bentley, Paul Smith (1t); Brad Izzard, Greg Alexander (1t, 1g); Paul Clarke, Royce Simmons, Barry Walker, Mark Geyer, John Cartwright, Chris Mortimer. S: Steve Carter, Joe Vitanza.
Clive Churchill Medal: Ricky Stuart

1991 Penrith Panthers 19-12 Canberra Raiders
Sydney Football Stadium, Sydney. Att: 41,815. 22 September 1991.
Penrith: Greg Barwick; Graham Mackay, Brad Fittler, Col Bentley, Paul Smith; Steve Carter, Greg Alexander (c) (3g, 1dg); Paul Clarke, Royce Simmons (2t), Paul Dunn, Mark Geyer, Barry Walker, Col van der Voort. S: Brad Izzard (1t), John Cartwright.
Canberra: Gary Belcher; Paul Martin, Mal Meninga (c) (1g), Mark Bell, Matthew Wood (2t, 1g); Laurie Daley, Ricky Stuart; Brent Todd, Steve Walters, Glenn Lazarus, David Barnhill, Gary Coyne, Bradley Clyde. S: Scott Gale, Darren Fritz.
Clive Churchill Medal: Bradley Clyde

1992 Brisbane Broncos 28-8 St George
Sydney Football Stadium, Sydney. Att: 41,560. 27 September 1992.
Brisbane: Julian O'Neill; Michael Hancock, Steve Renouf (1t), Chris Johns, Willie Carne; Kevin Walters, Allan Langer (c) (2t); Glenn Lazarus, Kerrod Walters, Gavin Allen, Trevor Gillmeister, Alan Cann (2t), Terry Matterson (4g). S: Mark Hohn, Andrew Gee, John Plath, Tony Currie.
St George: Mick Potter; Ricky Walford (1t), Mark Coyne, Michael Beattie (c), Ian Herron; Peter Coyne, Noel Goldthorpe; Tony Priddle, Wayne Collins, Neil Tierney, David Barnhill, Scott Gourley (1t), Jeff Hardy. S: Brad Mackay, Matthew Elliott, Tony Smith, Rex Terp.
Clive Churchill Medal: Allan Langer

1993 Brisbane Broncos 14-6 St George
Sydney Football Stadium, Sydney. Att: 42,329. 26 September 1993.
Brisbane: Julian O'Neill (1g); Michael Hancock, Steve Renouf, Chris Johns (1t), Willie Carne (1t); Kevin Walters, Allan Langer (c); Glenn Lazarus, Kerrod Walters, Mark Hohn, Trevor Gillmeister, Alan Cann, Terry Matterson (1t). S: Gavin Allen, Andrew Gee, John Plath, Peter Ryan.
St George: Mick Potter (c); Ricky Walford, Mark Coyne, Graeme Bradley, Ian Herron (3g); Tony Smith, Noel Goldthorpe; Tony Priddle, Wayne Collins, Jason Stevens, David Barnhill, Scott Gourley, Brad Mackay. S: Nathan Brown, Phil Blake, Gorden Tallis, Jeff Hardy.
Clive Churchill Medal: Brad Mackay

1994 Canberra Raiders 36-12 Canterbury Bankstown

Sydney Football Stadium, Sydney. Att: 42,234. 25 September 1994.
Canberra: Brett Mullins; Ken Nagas (2t), Mal Meninga (c) (1t), Ruben Wiki, Noa Nadruku (1t); Laurie Daley (1t), Ricky Stuart; Quentin Pongia, Steve Walters, Paul Osborne, David Furner (1t, 4g), Jason Croker (1t), Bradley Clyde. S: Brett Hetherington, David Westley.
Canterbury: Scott Wilson; Jason Williams (1t), Steven Hughes, Jarrod McCracken, Daryl Halligan (2g); Terry Lamb (c), Craig Polla-Mounter; Darren Britt, Jason Hetherington (1t), Martin Bella, Dean Pay, Jason Smith, Jim Dymock. S: Matthew Ryan, Steve Price, Simon Gillies, Mark Brokenshire.
Clive Churchill Medal: David Furner

1995 Sydney Bulldogs 17-4 Manly Sea Eagles

Sydney Football Stadium, Sydney. Att: 41,127. 24 September 1995.
Bulldogs: Rod Silva (1t); Jason Williams, John Timu, Matthew Ryan, Daryl Halligan (2g); Terry Lamb (c) (1dg), Craig Polla-Mounter; Darren Britt, Jason Hetherington, Dean Pay, Steve Price (1t), Simon Gillies, Jim Dymock. S: Jason Smith, Glen Hughes (1t), Mitch Newton.
Manly: Matthew Ridge (2g); Craig Hancock, Danny Moore, Terry Hill, John Hopoate; Cliff Lyons, Geoff Toovey (c); David Gillespie, Des Hasler, Mark Carroll, Steve Menzies, Ian Roberts, Nik Kosef. S: Owen Cunningham, Daniel Gartner, Solomon Haumono.
Clive Churchill Medal: Jim Dymock

1996 Manly Sea Eagles 20-8 St George

Sydney Football Stadium, Sydney. Att: 40,985. 29 September 1996.
Manly: Matthew Ridge (3g); Danny Moore (1t), Craig Innes (1t, 1g), Terry Hill, John Hopoate; Nik Kosef, Geoff Toovey (c); David Gillespie, Jim Serdaris, Mark Carroll, Steve Menzies (1t), Daniel Gartner, Owen Cunningham. S: Craig Hancock, Des Hasler, Cliff Lyons, Neil Tierney.
St George: Dean Raper; Nick Zisti (1t), Mark Coyne (c), Mark Bell, Adrian Brunker; Anthony Mundine, Noel Goldthorpe; Troy Stone, Jeff Hardy, Luke Felsch, Scott Gourley, Kevin Campion, Wayne Bartrim (2g). S: Nathan Brown, Lance Thompson, David Barnhill, Colin Ward.
Clive Churchill Medal: Geoff Toovey

1997 Newcastle Knights 22-16 Manly Sea Eagles (ARL)

Sydney Football Stadium, Sydney. Att: 42,482. 28 September 1997.
Newcastle: Robbie O'Davis (2t); Darren Albert (1t), Adam MacDougall, Owen Craigie, Mark Hughes; Matthew Johns, Andrew Johns (5g); Tony Butterfield, Billy Peden, Paul Harragon (c), Wayne Richards, Adam Muir, Marc Glanville. S: Troy Fletcher, Scott Conley, Lee Jackson, Steve Crowe.
Manly: Shannon Nevin (1t, 2g); Danny Moore, Craig Innes (1t), Terry Hill, John Hopoate (1t); Geoff Toovey (c), Craig Field; David Gillespie, Anthony Colella, Mark Carroll, Steve Menzies, Daniel Gartner, Nik Kosef. S: Cliff Lyons, Neil Tierney, Scott Fulton, Andrew Hunter.
Clive Churchill Medal: Robbie O'Davis

1997 Brisbane Broncos 26-8 Cronulla Sharks (Super League)

ANZ Stadium, Brisbane. Att: 58,912. 20 September 1997.
Brisbane: Darren Lockyer (5g); Michael de Vere, Steve Renouf (3t), Anthony Mundine, Wendell Sailor; Kevin Walters, Allan Langer (c); Brad Thorn, Andrew Gee, Shane Webcke, Gorden Tallis, Peter Ryan, Darren Smith. S: Tonie Carroll, John Plath, Michael Hancock (1t), Ben Walker.
Cronulla: David Peachey; Mat Rogers (2g), Andrew Ettingshausen (c), Russell Richardson (1t), Geoff Bell; Mitch Healey, Paul Green; Danny Lee, Dean Treister, Jason Stevens, Craig Greenhill, Chris McKenna, Tawera Nikau. S: Adam Dykes, Sean Ryan, Les Davidson, Nathan Long.
Man of the Match: Steve Renouf

1998 Brisbane Broncos 38-12 Canterbury Bulldogs

Sydney Football Stadium, Sydney. Att: 40,857. 27 September 1998.
Brisbane: Darren Lockyer (5g); Michael de Vere (1t), Steve Renouf, Darren Smith (1t), Wendell Sailor (1t); Kevin Walters, Allan Langer (c); Shane Webcke, Phillip Lee (1t), Andrew Gee, Gorden

Tallis (1t), Brad Thorn, Tonie Carroll (1t). S: Michael Hancock, John Plath, Kevin Campion (1t), Petero Civoniceva.

Canterbury: Rod Silva; Gavin Lester, Shane Marteene, Willie Talau (1t), Daryl Halligan (2g); Corey Hughes, Craig Polla-Mounter; Darren Britt (c), Jason Hetherington, Steve Price, Tony Grimaldi (1t), Robert Relf, Travis Norton. S: Steve Reardon, Glen Hughes, Troy Stone, David Thompson.

Clive Churchill Medal: Gorden Tallis

1999 Melbourne Storm 20-18 St George-Illawarra Dragons
Stadium Australia, Sydney. Att: 107,999. 26 September 1999.
Melbourne: Robbie Ross; Craig Smith (1t, 3g), Aaron Moule, Tony Martin (1t), Marcus Bai; Matt Geyer (1g), Brett Kimmorley; Glenn Lazarus (c), Richard Swain, Rodney Howe, Stephen Kearney, Paul Marquet, Tawera Nikau. S: Matt Rua, Russell Bawden, Ben Roarty (1t), Danny Williams.
St George: Luke Patten; Jamie Ainscough, Paul McGregor (c) (1t), Shaun Timmins, Nathan Blacklock (1t); Anthony Mundine, Trent Barrett; Craig Smith, Nathan Brown, Chris Leikvoll, Lance Thompson, Darren Treacy, Wayne Bartrim (2g). S: Craig Fitzgibbon (1t, 1g), Rod Wishart, Brad Mackay, Colin Ward.
Clive Churchill Medal: Brett Kimmorley

2000 Brisbane Broncos 14-6 Sydney Roosters
Stadium Australia, Sydney. Att: 94,277. 27 August 2000.
Brisbane: Darren Lockyer; Lote Tuqiri (1t), Tonie Carroll, Michael de Vere (3g), Wendell Sailor (1t); Ben Ikin, Kevin Walters (c); Shane Webcke, Luke Priddis, Dane Carlaw, Gorden Tallis, Brad Thorn, Kevin Campion. S: Shaun Berrigan, Ashley Harrison, Michael Hancock, Harvey Howard.
Roosters: Luke Phillips (1g); Matt Sing, Shannon Hegarty, Ryan Cross, Anthony Minichiello; Brad Fittler (c), Adrian Lam; Ian Rubin, Simon Bonetti, Peter Cusack, Bryan Fletcher, Craig Fitzgibbon (1t), Luke Ricketson. S: Craig Wing, Shane Rigon, Dallas Hood, David Solomona.
Clive Churchill Medal: Darren Lockyer

2001 Newcastle Knights 30-24 Parramatta Eels
Stadium Australia, Sydney. Att: 90,414. 30 September 2001.
Newcastle: Robbie O'Davis; Timana Tahu (1t), Matt Gidley, Mark Hughes, Adam MacDougall; Sean Rudder, Andrew Johns (c) (5g); Josh Perry, Danny Buderus, Matt Parsons, Steve Simpson (1t), Ben Kennedy (1t), Bill Peden (2t). S: Paul Marquet, Clinton O'Brien, Glenn Grief, Daniel Abraham.
Parramatta: Brett Hodgson (2t); Luke Burt (4g), Jamie Lyon (2t), David Vaealiki, Jason Moodie; Michael Buettner, Jason Taylor; Nathan Cayless (c), Brad Drew, Michael Vella, Nathan Hindmarsh, Ian Hindmarsh, Daniel Wagon. S: PJ Marsh, Andrew Ryan, Alex Chan, David Solomona.
Clive Churchill Medal: Andrew Johns

2002 Sydney Roosters 30-8 New Zealand Warriors
Telstra Stadium, Sydney. Att: 80,130. 6 October 2002.
Roosters: Luke Phillips; Brett Mullins, Shannon Hegarty (1t), Justin Hodges, Anthony Minichiello; Brad Fittler (c), Craig Wing (1t); Jason Cayless, Simon Bonetti, Peter Cusack, Adrian Morley, Craig Fitzgibbon (1t, 5g), Luke Ricketson. S: Bryan Fletcher (1t), Andrew Lomu, Chris Flannery (1t), Michael Crocker.
NZW: Ivan Cleary (2g); Justin Murphy, John Carlaw, Clinton Toopi, Francis Meli; Motu Tony, Stacey Jones (c) (1t); Jerry Seuseu, PJ Marsh, Mark Tookey, Ali Lauitiiti, Awen Guttenbeil, Kevin Campion. S: Lance Hohaia, Richard Villasanti, Wairangi Koopu, Logan Swann.
Clive Churchill Medal: Craig Fitzgibbon

2003 Penrith Panthers 18-6 Sydney Roosters

Telstra Stadium, Sydney. Att: 81,166. 5 October 2003.
Penrith: Rhys Wesser; Luke Lewis, Ryan Girdler (1g), Paul Whatuira, Luke Rooney (2t); Preston Campbell (2g), Craig Gower (c); Joel Clinton, Luke Priddis (1t), Martin Lang, Joe Galuvao, Tony Puletua, Scott Sattler. S: Ben Ross, Trent Waterhouse, Shane Rodney, Luke Swain.
Roosters: Anthony Minichiello; Todd Byrne, Ryan Cross, Shannon Hegarty (1t), Chris Walker; Brad Fittler (c), Craig Wing; Jason Cayless, Michael Crocker, Ned Catic, Adrian Morley, Craig Fitzgibbon (1g), Luke Ricketson. S: Brett Finch, Andrew Lomu, Chad Robinson, Chris Flannery.
Clive Churchill Medal: Luke Priddis

2004 Canterbury Bulldogs 16-13 Sydney Roosters

Telstra Stadium, Sydney. Att: 82,127. 3 October 2004.
Canterbury: Luke Patten; Hazem El Masri (1t, 2g), Ben Harris, Willie Tonga, Matt Utai (2t); Braith Anasta, Brent Sherwin; Mark O'Meley, Adam Perry, Willie Mason, Reni Maitua, Andrew Ryan (c), Tony Grimaldi. S: Corey Hughes, Roy Asotasi, Sonny Bill Williams, Johnathan Thurston.
Roosters: Anthony Minichiello (1t); Shannon Hegarty, Ryan Cross, Justin Hodges, Chris Walker (1t); Brad Fittler (c), Brett Finch (1dg); Jason Cayless, Craig Wing, Peter Cusack, Adrian Morley, Michael Crocker, Craig Fitzgibbon (2g). S: Chad Robinson, Chris Flannery, Ned Catic, Anthony Tupou.
Clive Churchill Medal: Willie Mason

2005 Wests Tigers 30-16 North Queensland Cowboys

Telstra Stadium, Sydney. Att: 82,453. 2 October 2005.
Wests: Brett Hodgson (5g); Daniel Fitzhenry (1t), Shane Elford, Paul Whatuira, Pat Richards (1t); Benji Marshall, Scott Prince (c); Anthony Laffranchi (1t), Robbie Farah, John Skandalis, Ben Galea, Mark O'Neill, Dene Halatau. S: Liam Fulton, Chris Heighington, Bryce Gibbs (1t), Todd Payten (1t).
NQ: Matt Bowen (1t); Ty Williams, Josh Hannay (2g), Paul Bowman, Matt Sing (1t); Justin Smith, Jonathan Thurston; Paul Rauhihi, Aaron Payne, Shane Tronc, Steve Southern, Luke O'Donnell, Travis Norton (c) (1t). S: Brett Firman, Rod Jensen, David Faiumu, Mitchell Sargent.
Clive Churchill Medal: Scott Prince

2006 Brisbane Broncos 15-8 Melbourne Storm

Telstra Stadium, Sydney. Att: 79,609. 1 October 2006.
Brisbane: Justin Hodges (1t); Darius Boyd, Brent Tate (1t), David Stagg, Karmichael Hunt; Darren Lockyer (c) (2g, 1dg), Shane Perry; Shane Webcke, Shaun Berrigan, Petero Civoniceva, Sam Thaiday, Brad Thorn, Tonie Carroll. S: Corey Parker (1g), Dane Carlaw, Ben Hannant, Casey McGuire.
Melbourne: Billy Slater; Matt Geyer, Matt King (1t), Greg Inglis, Steve Turner (1t); Scott Hill, Cooper Cronk; Antonio Kaufusi, Cameron Smith (c), Brett White, David Kidwell, Ryan Hoffman, Dallas Johnson. S: Adam Blair, Jeremy Smith, Ben Cross, Nathan Friend.
Clive Churchill Medal: Shaun Berrigan

2007 Melbourne Storm 34-8 Manly-Warringah Sea Eagles

Telstra Stadium, Sydney. Att: 81,392. 30 September 2007.
Melbourne: Billy Slater; Steve Turner, Matt King (1t), Israel Folau, Anthony Quinn (2t); Greg Inglis (2t), Cooper Cronk; Ben Cross, Cameron Smith (c) (3g), Brett White, Clint Newton (1t), Ryan Hoffman, Dallas Johnson. S: Jeremy Smith, Matt Geyer, Michael Crocker (1t), Jeff Lima.
Manly: Brett Stewart; Michael Robertson, Steve Bell, Steve Matai (1t), Chris Hicks (1t); Jamie Lyon, Matt Orford (c); Jason King, Michael Monaghan, Brent Kite, Anthony Watmough, Glenn Stewart, Luke Williamson. S: Adam Cuthbertson, Jack Afamasaga, Mark Bryant, Steve Menzies.
Clive Churchill Medal: Greg Inglis

2008 Manly-Warringah Sea Eagles 40-0 Melbourne Storm

ANZ Stadium, Sydney. Att: 80,388. 5 October 2008.
Manly: Brett Stewart; Michael Robertson (3t), Steve Bell (1t), Steve Matai (2t), David Williams (1t); Jamie Lyon (2g), Matt Orford (c); Brent Kite (1t), Matt Ballin (1t), Josh Perry, Anthony Watmough, Glenn Hall, Glenn Stewart. S: Heath L'Estrange, Mark Bryant, Jason King, Steve Menzies (1t).

Melbourne: Billy Slater; Steve Turner, Matt Geyer, Israel Folau, Anthony Quinn; Greg Inglis, Cooper Cronk (c); Jeff Lima, Russell Aitken, Brett White, Jeremy Smith, Michael Crocker, Dallas Johnson. S: Antonio Kaufusi, Scott Anderson, Adam Blair, Sika Manu.
Clive Churchill Medal: Brent Kite

2009 Melbourne Storm 23-16 Parramatta Eels

ANZ Stadium, Sydney. Att: 82,538. 4 October 2009.
Melbourne: Billy Slater (1t); Steve Turner, Will Chambers, Greg Inglis (1t, 1dg), Dane Nielsen; Brett Finch, Cooper Cronk; Aiden Tolman, Cameron Smith (c) (3g), Brett White, Adam Blair (1t), Ryan Hoffman (1t), Dallas Johnson. S :Ryan Hinchcliffe, Jeff Lima, Ryan Tandy, Brett Anderson.
St George: Jarryd Hayne; Luke Burt (2g), Krisnan Inu, Joel Reddy (1t), Eric Grothe (1t); Daniel Mortimer, Jeff Robson; Nathan Cayless (c), Kris Keating, Fuifui Moimoi (1t), Nathan Hindmarsh, Ben Smith, Todd Lowrie. S: Kevin Kingston, Feleti Mateo, Joe Galuvao, Tim Mannah.
Clive Churchill Medal: Billy Slater

2010 St George-Illawarra Dragons 32-8 Sydney Roosters

ANZ Stadium, Sydney. Att: 82,334. 3 October 2010.
St George: Darius Boyd; Brett Morris, Mark Gasnier (1t), Matt Cooper, Jason Nightingale (2t); Jamie Soward (6g), Ben Hornby (c); Neville Costigan, Dean Young (1t), Michael Weyman, Beau Scott, Ben Creagh, Jeremy Smith. S: Nathan Fien (1t), Trent Merrin, Matt Prior, Jarrod Saffy.
Roosters: Anthony Minichiello; Joseph Leilua, Kane Linnett, Shaun Kenny-Dowall, Sam Perrett; Todd Carney, Mitchell Pearce; Jason Ryles, Jake Friend, Lopini Paea, Nate Myles, Mitchell Aubusson (1t), Braith Anasta (c) (1t). S: Frank-Paul Nuuausala, Martin Kennedy, Jared Waerea-Hargreaves, Daniel Conn.
Clive Churchill Medal: Darius Boyd

2011 Manly-Warringah Sea Eagles 24-10 New Zealand Warriors

ANZ Stadium, Sydney. Att: 81,988. 2 October 2011.
Manly: Brett Stewart (1t); Michael Robertson (1g), Jamie Lyon (c) (1t, 3g), Steve Matai, William Hopoate; Kieran Foran, Daly Cherry-Evans (1t); Joe Galuvao, Matt Ballin, Brent Kite, Anthony Watmough, Tony Williams, Glenn Stewart (1t). S: Shane Rodney, Jamie Buhrer, Vic Mauro, George Rose.
NZ: Kevin Locke; Bill Tupou, Lewis Brown, Krisnan Inu, Manu Vatuvei (1t); James Maloney (1g), Shaun Johnson; Russell Packer, Lance Hohaia, Jacob Lillyman, Simon Mannering (c), Elijah Taylor (1t), Micheal Luck. S: Sam Rapira, Aaron Heremaia, Feleti Mateo, Ben Matulino.
Clive Churchill Medal: Glenn Stewart

2012 Melbourne Storm 14-4 Canterbury Bulldogs

ANZ Stadium, Sydney. Att: 82,976. 30 September 2012.
Melbourne: Billy Slater (1t); Sisi Waqa, Dane Nielsen, Will Chambers, Justin O'Neill (1t); Gareth Widdop, Cooper Cronk: Jesse Bromwich, Cameron Smith (c) (1g), Bryan Norrie, Sika Manu, Ryan Hoffman (1t), Todd Lowrie. S: Ryan Hinchcliffe, Kevin Proctor, Jaiman Lowe, Richie Fa'aoso.
Canterbury: Ben Barba, Sam Perrett (1t), Josh Morris, Krisnan Inu, Jonathan Wright; Josh Reynolds, Kris Keating; Aiden Tolman, Michael Ennis (c), Sam Kasiano, Frank Pritchard, Josh Jackson, Greg Eastwood. S: James Graham, Dale Finucane, Corey Payne, David Stagg.
Clive Churchill Medal: Cooper Cronk

3.2 STATE OF ORIGIN SERIES
The series winner's score is recorded first for each match. In 1999 and 2002, the series was drawn but Queensland were awarded the Shield on the basis that they were the holders going into the series. After 2002, it was decided that golden-point extra-time would be played after drawn matches. In 1987, a fourth match was played in the United States of America for promotional purposes. The result was not included in official records, but the individual performances were.

1980 Queensland   20-10
1981 Queensland   22-15

1982 Queensland	16-20, 11-7, 10-5
1983 Queensland	24-12, 6-10, 43-22
1984 Queensland	29-12, 14-2, 12-22
1985 New South Wales	18-2, 21-14, 6-20
1986 New South Wales	22-16, 24-20, 18-16
1987 Queensland	16-20, 12-6, 10-8
1988 Queensland	26-18, 16-6, 38-22
1989 Queensland	36-6, 16-12, 36-16
1990 New South Wales	8-0, 12-6, 10-14
1991 Queensland	6-4, 12-14, 14-12
1992 New South Wales	14-6, 5-4, 16-4
1993 New South Wales	14-10, 16-12, 12-24
1994 New South Wales	12-16, 14-0, 27-12
1995 Queensland	2-0, 20-12, 24-16
1996 New South Wales	14-6, 18-6, 15-14
1997 New South Wales	8-6, 15-14, 12-18
1998 Queensland	24-23, 10-26, 19-4
1999 Queensland	9-8, 8-12, 10-10
2000 New South Wales	20-16, 28-10, 56-16
2001 Queensland	34-16, 8-26, 40-14
2002 Queensland	4-32, 26-18, 18-18
2003 New South Wales	25-12, 27-4, 6-36
2004 New South Wales	9-8 (aet), 18-22, 36-14
2005 New South Wales	20-24 (aet), 32-22, 32-10
2006 Queensland	16-17, 30-6, 16-14
2007 Queensland	25-18, 10-6, 18-14
2008 Queensland	10-18, 30-0, 16-10
2009 Queensland	28-18, 24-14, 16-28
2010 Queensland	28-24, 34-6, 23-18
2011 Queensland	16-12, 8-18, 34-24
2012 Queensland	18-10, 12-16, 21-20

3.2.1 STATE OF ORIGIN MAN OF THE MATCHES

8 Wally Lewis
4 Peter Sterling, Allan Langer, Andrew Johns, Johnathan Thurston
3 Benny Elias, Ricky Stuart, Darren Lockyer, Cameron Smith, Greg Bird
2 Chris Close, Sam Backo, Martin Bella, Bob Lindner, Tim Brasher, Gary Larson, Geoff Toovey, Billy Slater
1 Mal Meninga, Rod Morris, Steve Mortimer, Peter Wynn, Wally Fullerton-Smith, Royce Simmons, Brett Kenny, Les Davidson, Kerrod Walters, Steve Walters, Dale Shearer, Willie Carne, Paul Harrogan, Jason Smith, Adrian Lam, Steve Menzies, Paul McGregor, Rodney Howe, Shane Webcke, Jason Hetherington, Laurie Daley, Wendell Sailor, Adam MacDougall, Ryan Girdler, Gorden Tallis, Trent Barrett, Chris McKenna, Luke Bailey, Matt Sing, Shaun Timmins, Craig Fitzgibbon, Steve Price, Anthony Minichiello, Willie Mason, Brent Tate, Greg Inglis, Israel Folau, Sam Thaiday, Anthony Watmough, Paul Gallen, Nate Myles

4 INDIVIDUAL HONOURS
4.1 THE GOLDEN BOOT

The Golden Boot is given to the player adjudged to be the best in the world. It was first awarded by Open Rugby magazine in 1985, and was presented to Wally Lewis on account of his performances a year earlier. Open Rugby stopped the award in 1990 and it was resumed in 1999 when League Publications Ltd bought the magazine. In 2011, Garry Schofield was retrospectively given the award for his 1990 achievements after Harry Edgar, the Open Rugby publisher, revealed that Schofield had been in line to receive it that year, had the award still been in existence.

1984 Wally Lewis (Australia)
1985 Brett Kenny (Australia)
1986 Garry Jack (Australia)
1987 Hugh McGahan (New Zealand) & Peter Sterling (Australia)
1988 Ellery Hanley (Great Britain)
1989 Mal Meninga (Australia)
1990 Garry Schofield (Great Britain)
1999 Andrew Johns (Australia)
2000 Brad Fittler (Australia)
2001 Andrew Johns (Australia)
2002 Stacey Jones (New Zealand)
2003 Darren Lockyer (Australia)
2004 Andrew Farrell (Great Britain)
2005 Anthony Minichiello (Australia)
2006 Darren Lockyer (Australia)
2007 Cameron Smith (Australia)
2008 Billy Slater (Australia)
2009 Greg Inglis (Australia)
2010 Benji Marshall (New Zealand)
2011 Johnathan Thurston (Australia)
2012 Kevin Sinfield (England)

4.2 THE ERNEST WARD MEMORIAL TROPHY

This was awarded by Open Rugby magazine to the best British international over a calendar year.

1987 Kevin Ward
1988 Hugh Waddell
1989 Shaun Edwards
1990 Garry Schofield
1991 Andy Platt
1992 Deryck Fox
1993 Phil Clarke
1994 Lee Jackson

4.3 THE MAN OF STEEL

The Man of Steel is currently awarded at the end of every season to the best player in Super League and is voted for by all Super League players. Previously it was judged by a small panel made up of members of the rugby league media and in its early years it wasn't necessarily awarded to the game's best player, but to the personality judged to have contributed most to the season. It was won in 1982 by a lower-division player and in 1983 by a non-playing coach, although Allan Agar did play one match for Carlisle.

1980 George Fairbairn (Wigan)
1981 Ken Kelly (Warrington)
1982 Mick Morgan (Carlisle)
1983 Allan Agar (Featherstone Rovers)

1984 Joe Lydon (Widnes)
1985 Ellery Hanley (Bradford Northern)
1986 Gavin Miller (Hull Kingston Rovers)
1987 Ellery Hanley (Wigan)
1988 Martin Offiah (Widnes)
1989 Ellery Hanley (Wigan)
1990 Shaun Edwards (Wigan)
1991 Garry Schofield (Leeds)
1992 Dean Bell (Wigan)
1993 Andy Platt (Wigan)
1994 Jonathan Davies (Warrington)
1995 Denis Betts (Wigan)
1996 Andy Farrell (Wigan)
1997 James Lowes (Bradford Bulls)
1998 Iestyn Harris (Leeds Rhinos)
1999 Adrian Vowles (Castleford Tigers)
2000 Sean Long (St Helens)
2001 Paul Sculthorpe (St Helens)
2002 Paul Sculthorpe (St Helens)
2003 Jamie Peacock (Bradford Bulls)
2004 Andy Farrell (Wigan Warriors)
2005 Jamie Lyon (St Helens)
2006 Paul Wellens (St Helens)
2007 James Roby (St Helens)
2008 James Graham (St Helens)
2009 Brett Hodgson (Huddersfield Giants)
2010 Pat Richards (Wigan Warriors)
2011 Rangi Chase (Castleford Tigers)
2012 Sam Tomkins (Wigan Warriors)

4.4 THE ALBERT GOLDTHORPE MEDAL

The Albert Goldthorpe Medal is awarded annually by League Express. After each Super League match (but not the play-offs), the newspaper's match reporters award the game's best player three points, the second best two points and the third best one point. At the end of the regular rounds of Super League, the player with the highest tally is awarded the medal.

2008 Danny Brough (Wakefield Trinity Wildcats)
2009 Michael Dobson (Hull Kingston Rovers)
2010 Pat Richards & Sam Tomkins (both Wigan Warriors)
2011 Rangi Chase (Castleford Tigers)
2012 Scott Dureau (Catalans Dragons)

4.5 AUSTRALASIAN PLAYER OF THE YEAR

Between 1968 and 1996, the winner of the Rothmans Medal was judged to be the player of the year in the NSWRL, which was known as the Winfield Cup from 1982. Although the Dally M Medal ran alongside it it was a secondary medal until the beginning of the

NRL in 1998 when it replaced the Rothmans Medal. Neither was awarded in 1997, the year of two competitions. The ARL player of the year was awarded the Provan-Summons Medal and the Super League player of the year was given the Telstra Medal. The Dally M Medal was not awarded in 2003 because of a dispute between the NRL and the players' association. It is believed that Craig Gower of the Penrith Panthers was to be the winner.

1980 Geoff Bugden (Newtown)
1981 Kevin Hastings (Eastern Suburbs)
1982 Greg Brentnall (Canterbury Bankstown)
1983 Mike Eden (Eastern Suburbs)
1984 Terry Lamb (Canterbury Bankstown)
1985 Wayne Pearce (Balmain Tigers)
1986 Mal Cochrane (Manly Warringah)
1987 Peter Sterling (Parramatta Eels)
1988 Barry Russell (Cronulla Sharks)
1989 Gavin Miller (Cronulla Sharks) & Mark Sargent (Newcastle Knights)
1990 Peter Sterling (Parramatta Eels)
1991 Ewan McGrady (Canterbury Bankstown)
1992 Allan Langer (Brisbane Broncos)
1993 Ricky Stuart (Canberra Raiders)
1994 David Fairleigh (North Sydney Bears)
1995 Paul Green (Cronulla Sharks)
1996 Jason Taylor (North Sydney Bears)
1997 ARL: Brad Fittler (Sydney City Roosters) & SL: Laurie Daley (Canberra Raiders)
1998 Andrew Johns (Newcastle Knights)
1999 Andrew Johns (Newcastle Knights)
2000 Trent Barrett (St George Illawarra Dragons)
2001 Preston Campbell (Cronulla Sharks)
2002 Andrew Johns (Newcastle Knights)
2003 Not Awarded
2004 Danny Buderus (Newcastle Knights)
2005 Johnathan Thurston (North Queensland Cowboys)
2006 Cameron Smith (Melbourne Storm)
2007 Johnathan Thurston (North Queensland Cowboys)
2008 Matt Orford (Manly Sea Eagles)
2009 Jarryd Hayne (Parramatta Eels)
2010 Todd Carney (Sydney Roosters)
2011 Billy Slater (Melbourne Storm)
2012 Ben Barba (Canterbury Bulldogs)

4.6 WORLD XIIIS 1980-2012
The World XIII was inaugurated in 1978 by Open Rugby magazine. Occasionally two teams per year were picked. From 1994 onwards, with the exception of 1996, the team was voted upon at the end of the year, and took into account autumn internationals.

The World XIII has always been selected by a panel of worldwide rugby league media. At the end, I have compiled an overall XIII (for the purposes of this, in years when there were two World XIIIs, each player inclusion counts as half), and also a XIII for each of the three major Test-playing nations.

September 1980
1 George Fairbairn (Great Britain)
2 Kerry Boustead (Australia)
3 Jean-Marc Bourret (France)
4 Steve Rogers (Australia)
5 Mitch Brennan (Australia)
6 Alan Thompson (Australia)
7 Tommy Raudonikis (Australia)
8 Craig Young (Australia)
9 John Lang (Australia)
10 Brian Lockwood (Great Britain)
11 Rod Reddy (Australia)
12 Kurt Sorensen (New Zealand)
13 Ray Price (Australia)

January 1981
1 George Fairbairn (Great Britain)
2 Kerry Boustead (Australia)
3 Mick Cronin (Australia)
4 Jean-Marc Bourret (France)
5 Dane O'Hara (New Zealand)
6 Fred Ah Kuoi (New Zealand)
7 Steve Mortimer (Australia)
8 Craig Young (Australia)
9 John Lang (Australia)
10 Mark Broadhurst (New Zealand)
11 Kurt Sorensen (New Zealand)
12 Graeme Wynn (Australia)
13 Mark Graham (Australia)

September 1981
1 Marcel Pillon (France)
2 Des Drummond (Great Britain)
3 John Joyner (Great Britain)
4 Mick Cronin (Australia)
5 Terry Fahey (Australia)
6 Fred Ah Kuoi (New Zealand)
7 Steve Mortimer (Australia)
8 Craig Young (Australia)
9 David Ward (Great Britain)
10 Mark Broadhurst (New Zealand)
11 Kurt Sorensen (New Zealand)
12 Les Boyd (Australia)
13 Mark Graham (New Zealand)

February 1982
1 Phil Sigsworth (Australia)
2 Des Drummond (Great Britain)
3 Steve Rogers (Australia)
4 Mick Cronin (Australia)
5 Gary Prohm (New Zealand)
6 Fred Ah Kuoi (New Zealand)
7 Peter Sterling (Australia)
8 Mark Broadhurst (New Zealand)

9 Christian Macalli (France)
10 Royce Ayliffe (Australia)
11 Kurt Sorensen (New Zealand)
12 Bruce Walker (Australia)
13 Steve Norton (Great Britain)

October 1982
1 Greg Brentnall (Australia)
2 Des Drummond (Great Britain)
3 Steve Rogers (Australia)
4 Mick Cronin (Australia)
5 Kerry Boustead (Australia)
6 Wally Lewis (Australia)
7 Steve Mortimer (Australia)
8 Mark Broadhurst (New Zealand)
9 Christian Macalli (France)
10 Trevor Skerrett (Great Britain)
11 Les Boyd (Australia)
12 Bruce Walker (Australia)
13 Ray Price (Australia)

February 1983
1 Greg Brentnall (Australia)
2 Eric Grothe (Australia)
3 Mal Meninga (Australia)
4 Steve Rogers (Australia)
5 Kerry Boustead (Australia)
6 Brett Kenny (Australia)
7 Peter Sterling (Australia)
8 Craig Young (Australia)
9 Max Krilich (Australia) & Christian Macalli (France)
10 Les Boyd (Australia)
11 Mark Graham (New Zealand)
12 Rod Reddy (Australia)
13 Wayne Pearce (Australia)

October 1983
1 Greg Brentnall (Australia)
2 Eric Grothe (Australia)
3 Steve Rogers (Australia)
4 James Leuluai (New Zealand)
5 Kerry Boustead (Australia)
6 Wally Lewis (Australia)
7 Peter Sterling (Australia)
8 Geoff Gerard (Australia)
9 Howie Tamati (New Zealand)
10 Dane Sorensen (New Zealand)
11 Mark Graham (New Zealand)
12 Kurt Sorensen (New Zealand)
13 Wayne Pearce (Australia)

March 1984
1 Joe Kilroy (Australia)
2 Eric Grothe (Australia)
3 Mick Cronin (Australia)
4 Steve Ella (Australia)
5 Kerry Boustead (Australia)
6 Wally Lewis (Australia)
7 Peter Sterling (Australia)
8 Dane Sorensen (New Zealand)
9 Thierry Bernabé (France)
10 Mark Broadhurst (New Zealand)

11 Paul McCabe (Australia)
12 Mark Graham (New Zealand)
13 Ray Price (Australia)

October 1984
1 Gary Kemble (New Zealand)
2 Eric Grothe (Australia)
3 James Leuluai (New Zealand)
4 Ellery Hanley (Great Britain)
5 Kerry Boustead (Australia)
6 Wally Lewis (Australia)
7 Peter Sterling (Australia)
8 Kevin Tamati (New Zealand)
9 Howie Tamati (New Zealand)
10 Greg Dowling (Australia)
11 Noel Cleal (Australia)
12 Kurt Sorensen (New Zealand)
13 Wayne Pearce (Australia)

April 1985
1 Gary Kemble (New Zealand)
2 John Ferguson (Australia)
3 Ellery Hanley (Great Britain)
4 Brett Kenny (Australia)
5 Eric Grothe (Australia)
6 Wally Lewis (Australia)
7 Peter Sterling (Australia)
8 Kevin Tamati (New Zealand)
9 Mario Fenech (Australia)
10 Greg Dowling (Australia)
11 Noel Cleal (Australia)
12 Andy Goodway (Great Britain)
13 Wayne Pearce (Australia)

April 1986
1 Garry Jack (Australia)
2 Eric Grothe (Australia)
3 Steve Ella (Australia)
4 Ellery Hanley (Great Britain)
5 Dean Bell (New Zealand)
6 Brett Kenny (Australia)
7 Clayton Friend (New Zealand)
8 Kurt Sorensen (New Zealand)
9 David Watkinson (Great Britain)
10 Peter Kelly (Australia)
11 Mark Graham (New Zealand)
12 Paul Vautin (Australia)
13 Hugh McGahan (New Zealand)

April 1987
1 Garry Jack (Australia)
2 Michael O'Connor (Australia)
3 Gene Miles (Australia)
4 Brett Kenny (Australia)
5 Henderson Gill (Great Britain)
6 Wally Lewis (Australia)
7 Peter Sterling (Australia)
8 Greg Dowling (Australia)
9 Benny Elias (Australia)
10 Kurt Sorensen (New Zealand)
11 Mark Graham (New Zealand)
12 Noel Cleal (Australia)
13 Wayne Pearce (Australia)

April 1988
1 Garry Jack (Australia)
2 Dale Shearer (Australia)
3 Gene Miles (Australia)
4 Garry Schofield (Great Britain)
5 Michael O'Connor (Australia)
6 Wally Lewis (Australia)
7 Peter Sterling (Australia)
8 Peter Tunks (Australia)
9 Royce Simmons (Australia)
10 Kurt Sorensen (New Zealand)
11 Les Davidson (Australia)
12 Trevor Gillmeister (Australia)
13 Hugh McGahan (New Zealand)

April 1989
1 Garry Jack (Australia)
2 John Ferguson (Australia)
3 Andrew Farrar (Australia)
4 Michael O'Connor (Australia)
5 Martin Offiah (Great Britain)
6 Wally Lewis (Australia)
7 Allan Langer (Australia)
8 Kevin Ward (Great Britain)
9 Benny Elias (Australia)
10 Paul Dunn (Australia)
11 Gavin Miller (Australia)
12 Mike Gregory (Great Britain)
13 Ellery Hanley (Great Britain)

June 1990
1 Gary Belcher (Australia)
2 Martin Offiah (Great Britain)
3 Mal Meninga (Australia)
4 Kevin Iro (New Zealand)
5 Michael Hancock (Australia)
6 Wally Lewis (Australia)
7 Gary Freeman (New Zealand)
8 Steve Roach (Australia)
9 Ben Elias (Australia)
10 Martin Bella (Australia)
11 Gavin Miller (Australia)
12 Gene Miles (Australia)
13 Bradley Clyde (Australia)

December 1990
1 Gary Belcher (Australia)
2 Andrew Ettingshausen (Australia)
3 Mal Meninga (Australia)
4 Mark McGaw (Australia)
5 Martin Offiah (Great Britain)
6 Garry Schofield (Great Britain)
7 Peter Sterling (Australia)
8 Glenn Lazarus (Australia)
9 Benny Elias (Australia)
10 Andy Platt (Great Britain)
11 Bob Lindner (Australia)
12 Tawera Nikau (New Zealand)
13 Ellery Hanley (Great Britain)

June 1991
1 Gary Belcher (Australia)
2 Andrew Ettingshausen (Australia)

3 Mal Meninga (Australia)
4 Kevin Iro (New Zealand)
5 Martin Offiah (Great Britain)
6 Garry Schofield (Great Britain)
7 Andy Gregory (Great Britain)
8 Glenn Lazarus (Australia)
9 Benny Elias (Australia)
10 Andy Platt (Great Britain)
11 Denis Betts (Great Britain)
12 Paul Sironen (Australia)
13 Ellery Hanley (Great Britain)

December 1991
1 Andrew Ettingshausen (Australia)
2 Willie Carne (Australia)
3 Mal Meninga (Australia)
4 Jarrod McCracken (New Zealand)
5 Rod Wishart (Australia)
6 Laurie Daley (Australia)
7 Allan Langer (Australia)
8 Martin Bella (Australia)
9 Steve Walters (Australia)
10 Andy Platt (Great Britain)
11 Denis Betts (Great Britain)
12 Mark Geyer (Australia)
13 Bradley Clyde (Australia)

June 1992
1 Andrew Ettingshausen (Australia)
2 Willie Carne (Australia)
3 Mal Meninga (Australia)
4 Dean Bell (New Zealand)
5 Martin Offiah (Great Britain)
6 Laurie Daley (Australia)
7 Allan Langer (Australia)
8 Glenn Lazarus (Australia)
9 Benny Elias (Australia)
10 Andy Platt (Great Britain)
11 Denis Betts (Great Britain)
12 Mark Geyer (Australia)
13 Bradley Clyde (Australia)

December 1992
1 Garry Jack (Australia)
2 Michael Hancock (Australia)
3 Mal Meninga (Australia)
4 Dean Bell (New Zealand)
5 Martin Offiah (Great Britain)
6 Garry Schofield (Great Britain)
7 Allan Langer (Australia)
8 Glenn Lazarus (Australia)
9 Steve Walters (Australia)
10 Andy Platt (Great Britain)
11 Bob Lindner (Australia)
12 Paul Sironen (Australia)
13 Bradley Clyde (Australia)

June 1993
1 Tim Brasher (Australia)
2 Willie Carne (Australia)
3 Brad Fittler (Australia)
4 Steve Renouf (Australia)
5 Martin Offiah (Great Britain)

6 Laurie Daley (Australia)
7 Allan Langer (Australia)
8 Andy Platt (Great Britain)
9 Steve Walters (Australia)
10 Glenn Lazarus (Australia)
11 Bob Lindner (Australia)
12 Paul Sironen (Australia)
13 Brad Mackay (Australia)

December 1993
1 Dale Shearer (Australia)
2 Willie Carne (Australia)
3 Brad Fittler (Australia)
4 Mal Meninga (Australia)
5 Martin Offiah (Great Britain)
6 Laurie Daley (Australia)
7 Allan Langer (Australia)
8 Glenn Lazarus (Australia)
9 Steve Walters (Australia)
10 Paul Harragon (Australia)
11 Paul Sironen (Australia)
12 Denis Betts (Great Britain)
13 Phil Clarke (Great Britain)

1994
1 Brett Mullins (Australia)
2 Andrew Ettingshausen (Australia)
3 Mal Meninga (Australia)
4 Steve Renouf (Australia)
5 Rod Wishart (Australia)
6 Laurie Daley (Australia)
7 Ricky Stuart (Australia)
8 Glenn Lazarus (Australia)
9 Steve Walters (Australia)
10 John Lomax (New Zealand)
11 Bradley Clyde (Australia)
12 Dean Pay (Australia)
13 Brad Fittler (Australia)

1995
1 Tim Brasher (Australia)
2 Jason Robinson (England)
3 Steve Renouf (Australia)
4 Mark Coyne (Australia)
5 Rod Wishart (Australia)
6 Brad Fittler (Australia)
7 Adrian Lam (Papua New Guinea)
8 Dean Pay (Australia)
9 Lee Jackson (England)
10 Mark Carroll (Australia)
11 Steve Menzies (Australia)
12 Gary Larson (Australia)
13 Andy Farrell (England)

September 1996
1 Tim Brasher (Australia)
2 Jason Robinson (England)
3 Andrew Ettingshausen (Australia)
4 Gary Connolly (England)
5 Brett Dallas (Australia)
6 Brad Fittler (Australia)
7 Bobbie Goulding (England)
8 Glenn Lazarus (Australia)

9 Keiron Cunningham (Wales)
10 Jason Lowrie (New Zealand)
11 David Fairleigh (Australia)
12 Stephen Kearney (New Zealand)
13 Andy Farrell (England)

1997
1 Robbie O'Davis (Australia)
2 Jason Robinson (Great Britain)
3 Steve Renouf (Australia)
4 Andrew Ettingshausen (Australia)
5 Wendell Sailor (Australia)
6 Laurie Daley (Australia)
7 Andrew Johns (Australia)
8 Paul Harragon (Australia)
9 Geoff Toovey (Australia)
10 Mark Carroll (Australia)
11 Stephen Kearney (New Zealand)
12 Adam Muir (Australia)
13 Andy Farrell (Great Britain)

1998
1 Darren Lockyer (Australia)
2 Jason Robinson (Great Britain)
3 Darren Smith (Australia)
4 Steve Renouf (Australia)
5 Wendell Sailor (Australia)
6 Laurie Daley & Kevin Walters (Australia)
7 Allan Langer (Australia)
8 Quentin Pongia (New Zealand)
9 Jason Hetherington (Australia)
10 Shane Webcke (Australia)
11 Gorden Tallis (Australia)
12 Stephen Kearney (New Zealand)
13 Andy Farrell (Great Britain)

1999
1 Darren Lockyer (Australia)
2 Wendell Sailor (Australia)
3 Ryan Girdler (Australia)
4 Terry Hill (Australia)
5 Mat Rogers (Australia)
6 Brad Fittler (Australia)
7 Andrew Johns (Australia)
8 Shane Webcke (Australia)
9 Keiron Cunningham (Great Britain)
10 Jason Stevens (Australia)
11 Gorden Tallis (Australia)
12 Stephen Kearney (New Zealand)
13 Tawera Nikau (New Zealand)

2000
1 Darren Lockyer (Australia)
2 Mat Rogers (Australia)
3 Ryan Girdler (Australia)
4 Matt Gidley (Australia)
5 Wendell Sailor (Australia)
6 Brad Fittler (Australia)
7 Andrew Johns (Australia)
8 Shane Webcke (Australia)
9 Keiron Cunningham (Wales)
10 Craig Smith (New Zealand)
11 Gorden Tallis (Australia)

12 Bryan Fletcher (Australia)
13 Scott Hill (Australia)

2001

1 Darren Lockyer (Australia)
2 Adam MacDougall (Australia)
3 Matthew Gidley (Australia)
4 Jamie Lyon (Australia)
5 Lote Tuqiri (Australia)
6 Trent Barrett (Australia)
7 Andrew Johns (Australia)
8 Shane Webcke (Australia)
9 Keiron Cunningham (Wales)
10 Nathan Cayless (New Zealand)
11 Ben Kennedy (Australia)
12 Nathan Hindmarsh (Australia)
13 Brad Fittler (Australia)

2002

1 Darren Lockyer (Australia)
2 Timana Tahu (Australia)
3 Nigel Vagana (New Zealand)
4 Keith Senior (Great Britain)
5 Hazem El Masri (Australia)
6 Brad Fittler (Australia)
7 Stacey Jones (New Zealand)
8 Shane Webcke (Australia)
9 Richard Swain (New Zealand)
10 Stuart Fielden (Great Britain)
11 Gorden Tallis (Australia)
12 Andy Farrell (Great Britain)
13 Paul Sculthorpe (Great Britain)

2003

1 Darren Lockyer (Australia)
2 Francis Meli (New Zealand)
3 Keith Senior (Great Britain)
4 Clinton Toopi (New Zealand)
5 Brian Carney (Great Britain)
6 Brad Fittler (Australia)
7 Andrew Johns (Australia)
8 Shane Webcke (Australia)
9 Danny Buderus (Australia)
10 Stuart Fielden (Great Britain)
11 Craig Fitzgibbon (Australia)
12 Adrian Morley (Great Britain)
13 Luke Ricketson (Australia)

2004

1 Anthony Minichiello (Australia)
2 Brian Carney (Great Britain)
3 Keith Senior (Great Britain)
4 Willie Tonga (Australia)
5 Luke Rooney (Australia)
6 Darren Lockyer (Australia)
7 Brett Kimmorley (Australia)
8 Shane Webcke (Australia)
9 Danny Buderus (Australia)
10 Stuart Fielden (Great Britain)
11 Andy Farrell (Great Britain)
12 Nathan Hindmarsh (Australia)
13 Sonny Bill Williams (New Zealand)

2005

1 Anthony Minichiello (Australia)
2 Brent Tate (Australia)
3 Mark Gasnier (Australia)
4 Matt Cooper (Australia)
5 Lesley Vainikolo (New Zealand)
6 Darren Lockyer (Australia)
7 Andrew Johns (Australia)
8 Stuart Fielden (Great Britain)
9 Keiron Cunningham (Great Britain)
10 Ruben Wiki (New Zealand)
11 Craig Fitzgibbon (Australia)
12 Jamie Peacock (Great Britain)
13 Ben Kennedy (Australia)

2006

1 Brent Webb (New Zealand)
2 Greg Inglis (Australia)
3 Mark Gasnier (Australia)
4 Justin Hodges (Australia)
5 Matt King (Australia)
6 Darren Lockyer (Australia)
7 Johnathan Thurston (Australia)
8 Ruben Wiki (New Zealand)
9 Cameron Smith (Australia)
10 Roy Asotasi (New Zealand)
11 Jamie Peacock (Great Britain)
12 Nathan Hindmarsh (Australia)
13 Ben Kennedy (Australia)

2007

1 Matt Bowen (Australia)
2 Jarryd Hayne (Australia)
3 Justin Hodges (Australia)
4 Mark Gasnier (Australia)
5 Israel Folau (Australia)
6 Trent Barrett (Australia)
7 Johnathan Thurston (Australia)
8 Steve Price (Australia)
9 Cameron Smith (Australia)
10 Jamie Peacock (Great Britain)
11 Gareth Ellis (Great Britain)
12 Nathan Hindmarsh (Australia)
13 Dallas Johnson (Australia)

2008

1 Billy Slater (Australia)
2 Manu Vatuvei (New Zealand)
3 Israel Folau (Australia)
4 Greg Inglis (Australia)
5 David Williams (Australia)
6 Darren Lockyer (Australia)
7 Johnathan Thurston (Australia)
8 Steve Price (Australia)
9 Cameron Smith (Australia)
10 James Graham (England)
11 Anthony Laffranchi (Australia)
12 Simon Mannering (New Zealand)
13 Jeremy Smith (New Zealand)

2009
1 Billy Slater (Australia)
2 Brett Morris (Australia)
3 Greg Inglis (Australia)
4 Michael Jennings (Australia)
5 Taniela Tuiaki (New Zealand)
6 Darren Lockyer (Australia)
7 Johnathan Thurston (Australia)
8 Fuifui Moimoi (New Zealand)
9 Cameron Smith (Australia)
10 James Graham (England)
11 Gareth Ellis (England)
12 Anthony Watmough (Australia)
13 Sam Burgess (England)

2010
1 Billy Slater (Australia)
2 Jason Nightingale (New Zealand)
3 Shaun Kenny-Dowall (New Zealand)
4 Brent Tate (Australia)
5 Manu Vatuvei (New Zealand)
6 Benji Marshall (New Zealand)
7 Nathan Fien (New Zealand)
8 James Graham (England)
9 Cameron Smith (Australia)
10 David Shillington (Australia)
11 Sam Thaiday (Australia)
12 Sam Burgess (England)
13 Paul Gallen (Australia)

2011
1 Billy Slater (Australia)
2 Akuila Uate (Australia)
3 Greg Inglis (Australia)
4 Jamie Lyon (Australia)
5 Ryan Hall (England)
6 Darren Lockyer (Australia)
7 Johnathan Thurston (Australia)
8 James Graham (England)
9 Cameron Smith (Australia)
10 Paul Gallen (Australia)
11 Sam Thaiday (Australia)
12 Gareth Ellis (England)
13 Anthony Watmough (Australia)

2012
1 Billy Slater (Australia)
2 Brett Morris (Australia)
3 Greg Inglis (Australia)
4 Josh Morris (Australia)
5 Ryan Hall (England)
6 Johnathan Thurston (Australia)
7 Cooper Cronk (Australia)
8 James Graham (England)
9 Cameron Smith (Australia)
10 Sam Kasiano (New Zealand)
11 Nate Miles (Australia)
12 Sam Burgess (England)
13 Paul Gallen (Australia)

World XIII (1980-2012)
1 Darren Lockyer (Australia)
2 Andrew Ettingshausen (Australia)
3 Mal Meninga (Australia)
4 Greg Inglis (Australia)
5 Martin Offiah (Great Britain)
6 Wally Lewis (Australia)
7 Peter Sterling (Australia)
8 Shane Webcke (Australia)
9 Cameron Smith (Australia)
10 Glenn Lazarus (Australia)
11 Andy Farrell (Great Britain)
12 Kurt Sorensen (New Zealand)
13 Brad Fittler (Australia)

Great Britain (1980-2012)
1 George Fairbairn
2 Jason Robinson
3 Ellery Hanley
4 Keith Senior
5 Martin Offiah
6 Garry Schofield
7 Bobbie Goulding
8 James Graham
9 Keiron Cunningham
10 Stuart Fielden
11 Gareth Ellis
12 Sam Burgess
13 Andy Farrell

Australia (1980-2012)
1 Darren Lockyer
2 Andrew Ettingshausen
3 Mal Meninga
4 Greg Inglis
5 Kerry Boustead
6 Wally Lewis
7 Peter Sterling
8 Shane Webcke
9 Cameron Smith
10 Glenn Lazarus
11 Gorden Tallis
12 Nathan Hindmarsh
13 Brad Fittler

New Zealand (1980-2012)
1 Gary Kemble
2 Manu Vatuvei
3 Dean Bell
4 James Leuluai
5 Lesley Vainikolo
6 Fred Ah Kuoi
7 Stacey Jones
8 Mark Broadhurst
9 Howie Tamati
10 Ruben Wiki
11 Kurt Sorensen
12 Stephen Kearney
13 Mark Graham

BIBLIOGRAPHY

NEWSPAPERS & MAGAZINES
Rugby League Express
Rugby League World
Rugby Leaguer
Rugby League Journal
Thirteen
Big League
The Guardian
The Independent
Sydney Morning Herald

BOOKS
Rothmans Rugby League Yearbooks from 1981 to 1999 (Ray Fletcher & David Howes)
Gillette Rugby League Yearbooks from 1996 to 2012 (Tim Butcher & Daniel Spencer)
Rugby League Lions - 100 Years of Test Matches (Robert Gate)
The Kangaroos - The Saga of Rugby League's Great Tours (Ian Heads)
The Encyclopedia of Rugby League Players (Alan Whitaker & Glen Hudson)
The Best Years of our Lives (Paul Wilson)
100 Years of Rugby League (Sydney Daily Telegraph)
Seasons in the Sun - A Rugby Revolution (Edited by Tony Hannan)
Sterlo - The Story of a Champion (Peter Sterling with Ian Heads)
The Bald Truth (Keith Senior with Peter Smith)
Offiah - A Blaze of Glory (Martin Offiah with David Lawrenson)
Touch & Go (A History of Professional Rugby in London. Dave Farrar & Peter Lush)
Freddy - The Brad Fittler Story (Brad Fittler with Richard Sleeman)
Coming Clean (Terry Nwton with Phil Wilkinson)

DVD
Pride of the Lions (PDI Media)